Designing, Building, and Installing Custom Cabinets for the Home

Designing, Building, and Installing Custom Cabinets for the Home

G. WILLIAM SCHERER

Director of Vocational Education
Martin County Cooperative Center
Fairmont, Minnesota

PRENTICE-HALL, INC., Englewood Cliffs, NJ 07632

Library of Congress Cataloging in Publication Data

SCHERER, G. WILLIAM. (date)
    Designing, building, and installing custom cabinets for the home.

    Includes index.
    1. Cabinet-work. I. Title.
TT197.S34 1986   694.6   85-9354
ISBN 0-13-200627-8

Editorial/production supervision
    and interior design: *Theresa A. Soler*
Cover design: *Joe Curcio*
Manufacturing buyer: *Gordon Osbourne*

Printed in the United States of America

10 9 8 7 6 5

ISBN 0-13-200627-8 01

PRENTICE-HALL INTERNATIONAL, INC., *London*
PRENTICE-HALL OF AUSTRALIA PTY. LIMITED, *Sydney*
PRENTICE-HALL DO BRASIL, LTDA., *Rio de Janeiro*
PRENTICE-HALL CANADA INC., *Toronto*
PRENTICE-HALL HISPANOAMERICANA, S.A., *Mexico*
PRENTICE-HALL OF INDIA PRIVATE LIMITED, *New Delhi*
PRENTICE-HALL OF JAPAN, INC., *Tokyo*
PRENTICE-HALL OF SOUTHEAST ASIA PTE. LTD., *Singapore*
WHITEHALL BOOKS LIMITED, *Wellington, New Zealand*

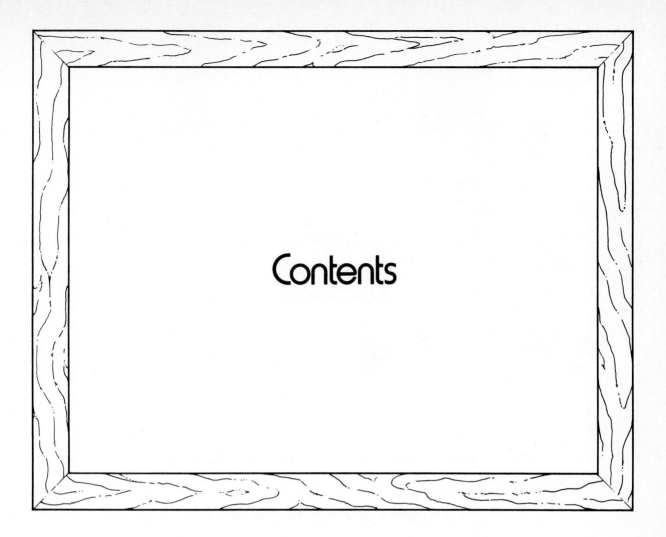

Contents

3 THE CABINETMAKER'S TOOLS AND EQUIPMENT 56

4 GETTING THE MOST—SAFELY—FROM BASIC SHOP MACHINERY 82

5 CONSTRUCTING THE BASE CABINET 114

6 CONSTRUCTING LIPPED DRAWERS 162

7 INSTALLING DRAWERS IN THE BASE CABINET 178

Preface

Designing, Building, and Installing Custom Cabinets for the Home has been written to fill a need for a comprehensive textbook on commercial custom cabinetmaking for use by high school, vocational school, and college woodworking, carpentry, and building courses. The thrust of the text is on the skills and knowledge required to build those cabinets that are normally installed in the home.

This book is intended for persons who have mastered the basic skills of woodworking and who desire to learn to design, build, and install home cabinets either as a beginning professional or a "do-it-yourselfer." The reader is made familiar with the basic tools and equipment with which cabinets can be built. For a beginning professional, however, those additional production machines are described that would be purchased as business and profits warrant.

The sequence of chapters in the text follow the pattern that many cabinetmakers follow in producing home cabinets. The base cabinets are built first, then the drawers and shelves are added. The upper units follow. The doors are then made for both the upper and the lower units. Finally, the countertop is fabricated and the cabinets installed in the home. Special chapters present the skills and knowledge required to build corner cabinets for both base and upper cupboards, as well as details on bathroom vanities, china cabinets, bookcases, and linen closets.

A pioneer vocational educator, Verne Fryklund, defined learning as, "Knowing HOW to do, and being ABLE to do." This text places considerable emphasis on being ABLE to do. Any seemingly difficult job becomes easier if the tricks of the trade or "moves" are revealed. This book is filled with professional methods and know-how designed to make cabinetmaking easier for both the amateur and the budding professional.

The text thoroughly covers two systems of home cabinet building: the traditional box-and-frame method and the more unique "casework" system. Each is presented in step-by-step detail from designing and planning through actual building to the installation. Hundreds of clear, precise perspective drawings and actual photos taken in many professional cabinet shops help to make the instructions clear and simple. Included also is a complete chapter on the fabrication and installation of plastic-laminate countertops and backsplashes. There are chapters on the materials used in cabinetmaking as well as on estimating the amounts required and making out correct orders for these materials.

Throughout the text special attention is paid to jigs and fixtures that enable the builder to make accurate multiple operations. Special "tips" are highlighted that the author has garnered from cabinet builders that provide ease and know-how in cabinet-building operations.

There are as many ways to build cabinets as there are cabinetmakers. Each builder has methods and a cabinet system that is preferred. Although this text highlights two cabinet-building systems, the author recognizes that there is no "pure" system, no right or wrong way, and that cabinetmakers borrow freely from each other and are quick to adapt to new materials, methods, and equipment that will allow speedier construction and greater profits. Hopefully, this text will provide the basic knowledge needed to get the fledgling professional under way or the ambitious amateur woodworker acquainted with professional cabinetmaking methods.

Many cabinetmakers contributed both time and knowledge to the skills and techniques contained on these pages. They allowed the author to make photographs in their establishments, which occasionally upset production, and they permitted many photos to be taken while installing cabinets and countertops. For this assistance they are given a hearty thanks. Special acknowledgment is given to Irwin "Bud" Prieve, owner of Prieve Cabinets, Hutchinson, Minnesota, and to O&M Cabinets of the same city. For advice and assistance with the many problems of photography, William Seaman and David Skaar are singled out for special thanks. Delta International Machinery Corporation has been especially cooperative.

G. William Scherer

1

Designing and Planning
the Kitchen Area and Its Cabinets

A home, it is often said, is just walls, roof, plaster, and rooms until the owner selects the millwork and cabinetry that is to be installed in the house. Nothing puts the stamp of the owner's taste and personality on the house as much as the style, choice of wood, and type of finish for the cabinetry. The warmth of wood, the beauty of the grain, and the admirable qualities of excellent craftsmanship combine to change the bare construction into a charming and appealing home. The kitchen, perhaps more than any other area, is the room that catches the eye of the visitor and sets the decor for the rest of the house. "Cupboards are not just places to store dishes," is a remark often attributed to interior decorators and designers of fine homes. Kitchen cabinets today are representative of fine furniture that is both functional and beautiful and although still a place to store, prepare, and serve food, a modern kitchen is also a space center for family living. Certainly, the kitchen should be a pleasant, happy place that meets one's personal needs (Fig. 1-1). To meet this goal, careful planning together with an understanding of kitchen layout for maximum efficiency is a necessity. Although we are concerned primarily with the cabinetry, some space will be devoted to overall design of the kitchen and the principles of work spacing. Surprisingly, the professional cabinetmaker is not too often involved in the design of the kitchen itself. This is most often dictated by the floor plan of the house which the homeowner or the architect has already laid out. The cabinetmaker draws up working drawings of the cabinets themselves which fulfill the layout designated on the

Figure 1-1 A kitchen should be the focal point of the home.
(Courtesy Merillat Industries, Inc., Adrian, Mich.)

floor plan or reflect the ideas of the homeowner. However, the "do-it-yourselfer" might well be involved in the basic kitchen layout and the plan of the cabinets, as well as building the finished product.

SPACE NEEDS IN THE MODERN KITCHEN

Modern living and kitchens of today generally require a generous work area with plenty of space for culinary pursuits. This space, while generous, should also be compact enough for efficiency—where everything is close and convenient. The homemakers of today also seem to demand a space for eating either in the kitchen or in very close proximity to the kitchen. Other considerations might well be planning a kitchen area that is close to an outdoor dining area, a preschooler's play area, and in creating a kitchen that is an attractive place—one that is pleasant and cheerful as well as efficient.

How much space should be devoted to all of this? Two important studies done at two of our leading universities have influenced tremendously the design and size of modern kitchens. The Cornell Kitchen Study tells us that a kitchen's minimum size should be 80 sq. ft., but recommends 95 sq. ft. for greater efficiency and 112 sq. ft. if a wall oven and a dishwasher are built in. To have an eating area in the kitchen, you need a room at least 11 ft. by 12 ft. Thus it would seem that the average family will want at least 100 sq. ft., arranged for a central location that is convenient to all parts of the house and to outdoor living areas, yet remains out of indoor traffic patterns.

The "Rule of Twenty-Two"

The efficient kitchen has what we call a *work triangle,* composed of the cooking, mixing, and sink centers. The sum of the distances between these three should not exceed 22 ft. The Small Homes Council of the University of Illinois recommends that this triangle have from 4 to 6 ft. between range and sink (measured from the center fronts of the appliances), 4 to 7 ft. between refrigerator and sink, and 4 to

9 ft. between range and refrigerator. They maintain that a work triangle with a total distance of from 15 to 22 ft. is considered satisfactory (Figs. 1–2 to 1–4). Efficiency will be improved if there are no more than 4 ft. between cabinets and appliances on opposite walls, 3 ft. between cabinets placed at right angles, 4 ft. between appliances placed at right angles, 3 ft. in front of an oven door, and 16 in. between the counter-top and the cabinets above it. Where there are cabinets over the range, there should be 24 in. of clearance between the range top and the cabinets. It would be well to double check the local building code, especially for the clearance dimensions over the stove.

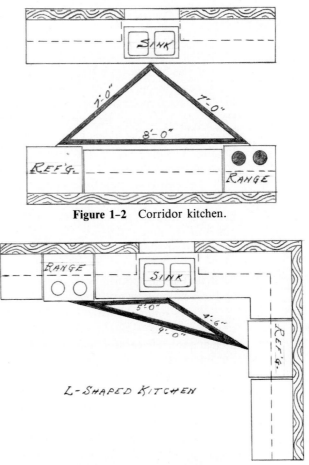

Figure 1–2   Corridor kitchen.

Figure 1–3   L-shaped kitchen.

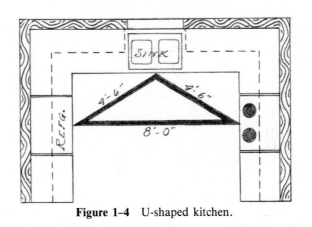

Figure 1–4   U-shaped kitchen.

Kitchen Storage Space

The Small Homes Council recommends 20 linear feet of wall space (base cabinets plus wall cabinets) as a liberal amount of kitchen storage space, 17½ ft. for average use, and 15 ft. as the minimum for any kitchen. Four feet must be added to compensate for each corner used for storage cupboards (although use of a lazy Susan or any other well-designed method of corner cupboard usage might negate this requirement). Desirable counter space should include 15 in. beside the refrigerator on the side the door opens, 36 in. on the right side of sink for stacking dishes, 30 in. on the left of the sink, and 36 in. of unbroken counter space for mixing near the sink.

BASIC KITCHEN LAYOUTS

Although changes do take place in the theory of kitchen layouts and seemingly the kitchen has become an increasingly more important space in today's smaller homes, the general layouts are still basic: the one-wall, corridor, L-shaped, and U-shaped kitchens. Each is planned around three major appliances: refrigerator, sink, and range. Peninsula and island kitchens are variations of the basic layouts. Ideally, the refrigerator should be located near the service door with an adjoining counter for unloading. Ordinarily, the sink comes between the refrigerator and the range. Work space between the sink and range requires an absolute minimum of 36 in.

The *two-wall* or *corridor* kitchen requires an 8-ft. minimum room width to provide 4 ft. between counters. In the corridor kitchen, counter space is broken and traffic must pass through the work area—always an undesirable feature in any kitchen layout. For working efficiency, the sink and range should be on the same wall with a minimum of 30 in. at the end of the sink nearest the wall and a minimum of 24 in. on the side of the range nearest the opposite wall. The length of space between should be 36 in. On the opposite wall, the refrigerator and the wall oven may be at the ends, with an eating or work area between (Fig. 1-5).

The *U-shaped* kitchen is probably the most popular because it is compact and step-saving. The sink is placed inside the U, with the range center near the dining area and the refrigerator near the outside door. In the U-shaped kitchen, traffic does not interfere. The little space left for a breakfast table makes counter service more feasible. The main disadvantage of the U-shaped kitchen is the difficulty of making good use of the two corner areas (Fig. 1-6). However, as mentioned previously, a skilled cabinetmaker has several means of making the space usable (Fig. 1-7).

The *one-wall* kitchen is acceptable when space is limited. The sink should be in the center, with the longest counter space between the sink and the range for food preparation. The refrigerator may be on one end, with the door opening toward the work area, and a wall oven may be on the other end (Fig. 1-8).

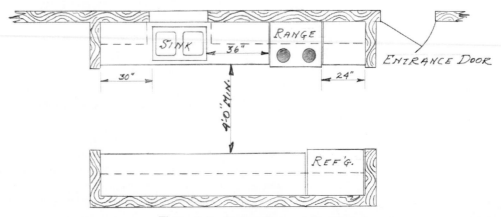

Figure 1-5   Two-wall or corridor layout.

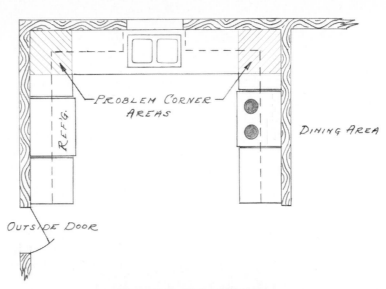

Figure 1-6 U-shaped kitchen.

Figure 1-7 Excellent example of a U-shaped kitchen. (Courtesy Merillat Industries, Inc., Adrian, Mich.)

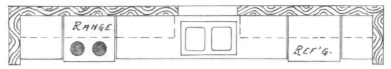

Figure 1-8 One-wall kitchen.

The *L-shaped* kitchen was found to be the most efficient in the Cornell Kitchen Study. This arrangement provides an uninterrupted work area and leaves two walls free for doors, a cleaning closet, table, and chairs. Ample counter space is desirable near the dining area for quick meals and occasional snacks (Figs. 1-9, 1-10A, and 1-10B).

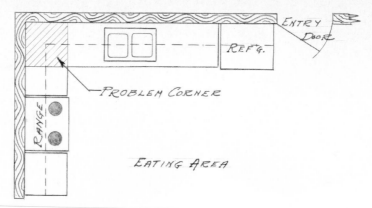

Figure 1–9 L-shaped kitchen.

Figure 1–10A Period-styled L-shaped kitchen.

Figure 1–10B Opposite wall of the kitchen in Fig. 1–10A.

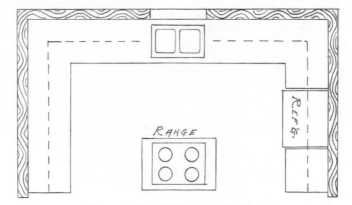

Figure 1-11   U-kitchen with island.

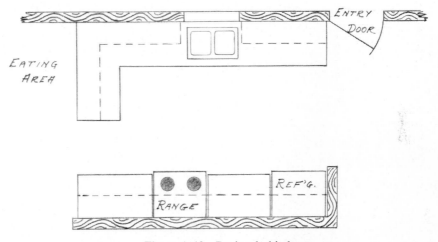

Figure 1-12   Peninsula kitchen.

The *island* kitchen may be within an "L" or a "U." In some plans the island contains the surface cooking units and a snack bar. In other plans the island contains a trash receptacle, a second sink, and a dishwasher. It actually combines an L-shape and corridor or a U-shape and corridor. An island is inefficient when one has to cross the floor between range and sink, and hazardous when the range is too near the table (Fig. 1-11).

The *peninsula* makes use of one arm of the U- or L-shaped kitchen by backing up an eating or laundry area. The peninsula may be a divider between kitchen and dining room with a double-width counter. Cabinets may be suspended from the ceiling back to back (or doors on both sides of a single-width cabinet) to provide cabinet access for both areas. The space between the wall cabinets and lower cabinets is usually open for a pass-through effect (Fig. 1-12).

STANDARDS FOR CABINET CONSTRUCTION

Because the appliance industry has standardized its products as to height and depth, cabinetmakers have followed suit and maintain standard dimensions in their products. Base cabinet height, for example, is almost universally manufactured at 36 in. from the floor to the top of the counter, and a depth—front to rear—of 24 in. These standards conform to the 36 in. height of kitchen stoves and the height of under-the-counter dishwashers. Only in the rare instance of an exceptionally tall homemaker (or a very short one) does the custom cabinet builder vary from these two dimensions.

Upper cabinets are universally 12 in. deep and 32 in. high. These standards maintain the recommended distance of 16 in. between the base cabinets and the upper units. The soffit or dropped ceiling is usually 12 in. high, giving an overall height of 96 in.—the usual floor-to-ceiling height in most homes today. The 16 in. between the base and upper cabinets is maintained even in the event that the homeowner desires the upper cabinets built all the way to the ceiling (Figs. 1-13 and 1-14). This is not unusual, especially in older homes undertaking a kitchen remodeling and when a drop ceiling is not desired. After all, there still is a substantial amount of good storage space for seasonal and rarely used items in that space above the kitchen window. The homeowner often seeks out the custom cabinetmaker for that very reason—to have the individual's own design features incorporated into cabinetry.

In many modern homes the soffit is omitted altogether and the space simply left open between the upper cabinets and the ceiling. Often a decorative railing is built around the top of the cabinets, which adds a nice touch. This space, although a dust catcher, can be used for displaying decorative plates, silver pieces, or other bric-a-brac.

The standards of the cabinetmaking industry have been arrived at through years of development, cooperation with kitchen appliance manufacturers, and the desir-

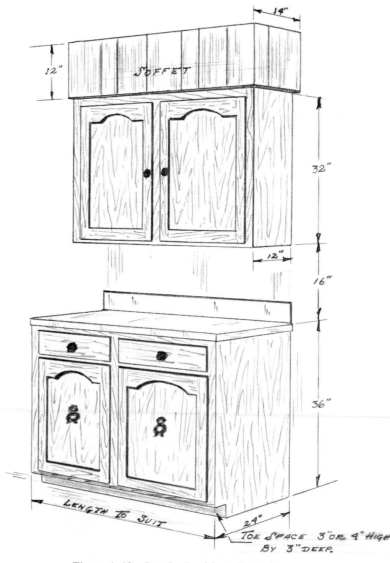

Figure 1-13 Standard cabinet dimensions.

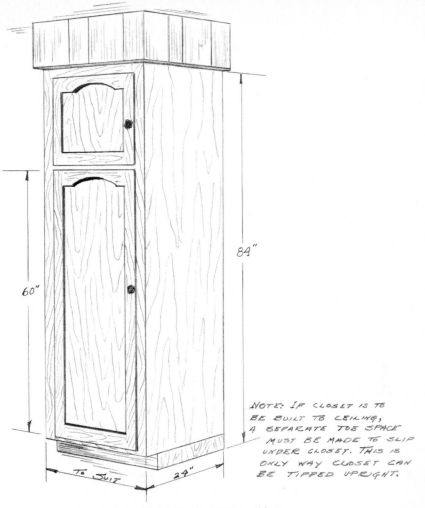

NOTE: IF CLOSET IS TO BE BUILT TO CEILING, A SEPARATE TOE SPACE MUST BE MADE TO SLIP UNDER CLOSET. THIS IS ONLY WAY CLOSET CAN BE TIPPED UPRIGHT.

84"

60"

24"

TO SUIT

Figure 1–14 Utility cabinet.

ability of making the most economical use of the lumber, plywood, plastic laminates, and hardware available for the building of cabinets. Variation from these standards should be undertaken with caution, as strange variations can often have unexpected consequences. A home with unusually high kitchen countertops ordered especially for a 6-ft.-tall housewife might find resale a few years later quite difficult in a home-buying market populated by homemakers who average closer to 5 ft. 2 in. in height.

Another advantage of conforming to the standards is that the cabinetmaker can quickly learn the height and depth measurements of the cabinet parts, as these stay the same from job to job—only the length dimensions change. This is one of the reasons kitchen cabinets lend themselves to mass production. Many of the internal pieces that are concerned only with the height and depth of the cabinet can be turned out in quantity and stockpiled to be used later on the assembly line of the manufacturing plant.

PREPARING DETAILED CABINET PLANS FOR SHOP USE

Once the general kitchen layout has been decided on, the next—and extremely important job—is to prepare a detailed and dimensioned working plan for the cabinets themselves. Some experience with a T-square, triangle, and drawing board will be of great help in this department. A scale of 1″ = 1′-0″ is quite convenient for cabinet details.

Figure 1-15   Model kitchen on which the lessons are based.

For purposes of learning the cabinet system presented in this book, a fairly simple straight wall of cabinets is presented as an example. Figures 1-15 and 1-16 describe the kitchen in which the model set of cabinets will theoretically be placed. The model cabinet presented in the text will be concerned only with the cabinets to be installed on the window wall, as illustrated in Fig. 1-17. By studying the text and the drawings it should be possible for a competent craftsperson to adapt these lessons to an actual cabinet project.

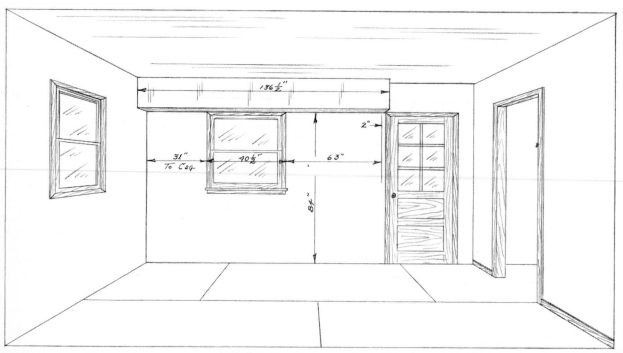

Figure 1-16   Kitchen ready to be measured for the cabinets.

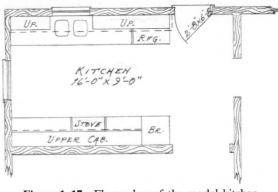

Figure 1-17 Floor plan of the model kitchen.

Measuring the Space for Cabinets

Probably nothing is more important or basic to an accurate cabinet detail than the on-site measurements. On new construction these measurements are commonly taken on completion of the drywall application. The measuring is somewhat simplified, too, if the trim molding has been applied to the windows and doors. If the trim has not been applied, allowance will have to be made for the width of the trim being used and the application technique of the installer. If the carpenter doing the work has not applied the trim prior to measuring for the cabinets, have him indicate by pencil marking the wall where the trim will be positioned when applied. This will vary somewhat between carpenters, so by having him mark exactly where the trim will be applied makes it possible to obtain an accurate measurement for the abutting cabinets.

Make a rough pencil sketch of the wall where the cabinets will be located, sketching in windows, doors, dropped ceiling (soffit), and any other room features that might affect the cabinetry (Fig. 1-18). The kitchen being used for instructional pur-

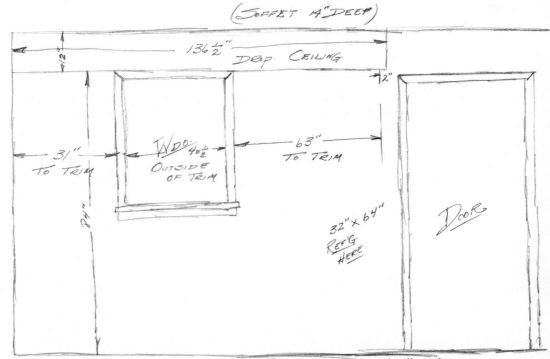

Figure 1-18 Typical rough sketch of on-site dimensions.

poses in this text has a dropped ceiling 14 in. deep by 136½ in. long. Upper cabinets are 12 in. deep or 2 in. less than the depth of the soffit. This 2 in. should be maintained as the amount the soffit should extend beyond the end of the right-hand upper cabinet. Make a mark on the wall 2 in. to the left of the end of the soffit. This mark represents the overall length of the cabinets together with the refrigerator featured on this wall. Measure from the left wall to this mark. It is 134½ in. Measure next from this right end mark to the trim on the right side of the window. This distance represents the overall length of the right-hand upper cabinet. Note that the width allowance for the refrigerator must be determined and incorporated into the design of this section of wall cabinet as well as allowed for in the length of the base cabinet.

Problems Concerning Refrigerators

How much must be allowed for the width of the refrigerator? This will depend on where the refrigerator will be placed and the style and age of the unit. Older refrigerators must be given a "door-opening allowance" if they are located between cabinets or between a cabinet and a wall. Usually, 3 in. is sufficient. Check the refrigerator itself to determine if this allowance is necessary (Fig 1–19). If the refrigerator is one of the newer designs, this door-opening allowance is not necessary, as the refrigerator door when opened does not extend beyond the edge of the main part of the unit. If this is the case, ½ to 1 in. allowance on each side of the refrigerator is sufficient for pushing the unit in place and for proper air circulation. Thus if the refrigerator measures 32 in. at its widest, 33 to 34 in. is sufficient allowance even if the unit is flanked by cabinets or a wall.

Back to Measuring the Cabinets

Carefully measure the distance from the left-hand wall to the left window trim. Jot down the *actual measurements* in all cases. How much allowance to calculate into the plans of the cabinets will be addressed later. It is a good idea to take this measurement in a couple of places—near the top of the window and again near the bottom. If the window opening is slightly out of plumb, this would be revealed and compensated for by using the smaller distance. Now mark on the windowsill (or window stool if installed) the exact center of the window unit. Measure the distance in inches from the left wall to the mark indicating the window center. This is important if the sink is to be installed under the window, to be certain that the center of the sink exactly lines up with the center of the window.

Measure the height from the floor to the underside of the dropped ceiling—or to the ceiling if there is no soffit. Also measure from the top of the window trim to the ceiling if the cabinets are to be built and installed above the window. The thickness of the floor underlayment should also be taken into consideration if not already installed.

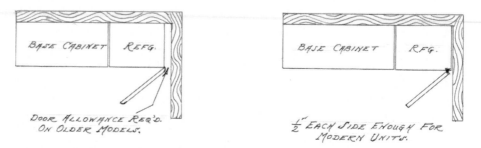

Figure 1–19   Modern refrigerators need approximately ½ in. on each side.

If the cabinet is to fit between two walls, check the overall measurements carefully from wall to wall. Make one measurement along the floor next to the wall. Take another measurement about 2 ft. out from the wall. Buildup of plaster in the corners or tape and cement in the corners could result in considerable variation. Use the shorter measurement if the variation is over ⅛ in. or so. If the variation is only ⅛ in. or a bit more, the tolerances built into the cabinet will be enough to allow the cabinet to slip into place. This allowance will be discussed in the section that follows on the cabinet detailed plan.

Finally, be certain to check the room layout so as to be certain that the finished cabinet can be moved into position through the doors, hallways, and so on, making whatever turns might be necessary. Real embarrassment might result if the cabinets, after being built in the shop, could not be carried into the area for which they were intended.

Other Appliances and Built-ins

Freestanding kitchen range

Some consideration is required in calculating the proper allowance for the kitchen range. A very common width for this unit is 30 in. (Fig. 1–20). If cabinets are to be placed on either or both sides of the stove, a certain amount must be planned to allow the unit to slide into place; ⅛ to ¼ in. is usually enough for this.

Tip: Remember—whether it is an appliance or a cabinet, some allowance or "play" must be planned for so that the unit will slide or fit into place. A 30-in. cabinet or stove will *not* slide into a 30-in. opening!

Dishwashers, range hoods, drop-in ranges, countertop cooking units, and wall ovens

The procedure on most of these units that are of the built-in type is to obtain the installation specification sheet from the appliance dealer and follow the instructions as described.

For general plan and layout purposes these sizes will suffice:

Dishwasher: 23⅞-in. unit width. 24-in. cabinet opening required. Unit adjusts in height from 34 to 34½-in.

Wall oven: 24-in. door. 22-in. cabinet opening required.

Figure 1–20 Details for built-in appliances.

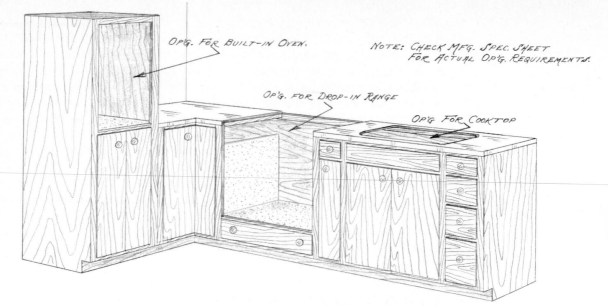

Figure 1–21   Typical cabinet openings for built-in appliances.

Figure 1–22   Typical range hood installation.

Countertop stove unit: Requires a 30- or 36-in. base cabinet below, depending on the size of the unit. Countertop cutout to manufacturer's specifications (Fig. 1–21).

Range hoods: Varies with the size of range. 30 and 36 in. are most common. If ducts are required, they must be planned for in the cabinet. Only a $\frac{1}{16}$- to $\frac{1}{8}$-in. allowance required (Fig. 1–22).

Drop-in range: Varies with the range size. 30 and 36 in. are most common. Follow manufacturer's specifications carefully.

Sinks

Ninety-nine percent of kitchen sinks are of two types:

1.   Cast-iron porcelain-enameled in size 32 in. × 21 in., double bowl (Fig. 1–23). These are installed with a special rim. The countertop cutout required is $32\frac{3}{8}$ in. × $21\frac{3}{8}$ in. The rim can be used as a template for the rounded corners of the cutout, or the box in which the rim is packed usually has

Figure 1–23 A 21 in. × 32 in. cast-iron sink using a separate sink rim. (Courtesy The Kohler Company)

a template and installation directions printed on it. Special clips installed from below hold the sink and rim in the countertop. Plumber's putty or caulking compound seals the rim.

2. 33 in. × 22 in. self-rimmed stainless steel two-bowl sink. This sink also requires 32⅜ × 21⅜ countertop cutout (Fig. 1–24). The manufacturer furnishes installation instructions and cutout template on the shipping box. In most instances the installation of the sink is done by the plumber. The cutout is the job of the cabinetmaker. More detailed instructions are given in Chapter 10.

Figure 1–24 Sinks are available in unique and varied styles. (Courtesy Elkay Mfg. Co., Oak Brook, Ill.)

Figure 1-25 Unique corner sink with self-rim. (Courtesy Elkay Mfg. Co., Oak Brook, Ill.)

Figure 1-26 Sinks are beautiful as well as functional. (Courtesy The Kohler Company)

In both instances the cabinet opening designed into the base cabinet is 32 in. wide. There are a wide variety of sink styles on the market (Figs. 1-25 and 1-26). The cabinetmaker should again work from the manufacturer's installation instructions. In practically every case, the width of the cabinet opening is designed to be the same size as the width of the sink.

SOME DESIGN CONSIDERATIONS

After the cabinet standards, measuring techniques, and appliance installation and information are all studied, attention must be paid to some general considerations regarding cabinet layout and practical usage.

Base Cabinets

As a general principle, shelving is generally more useful and more accommodating to a variety of storage problems than are drawers. The point is—do not overdo the number of drawers designed into the cabinet. They are limited in storage capacity and are more expensive and time consuming to build than shelving. Some drawers can be designed to be selective in their usage, such as:

Divided for silverware (Fig. 1–27)
A wide upper-row drawer for kitchen linens
A laminate-lined drawer with sliding top for bread storage (Fig. 1–28)

Although cabinet standards call for a row of drawers to be smaller on the top and get progressively larger toward the bottom, this arrangement can be altered. Custom cabinets, happily, can be designed to incorporate the builder's or owner's special ideas.

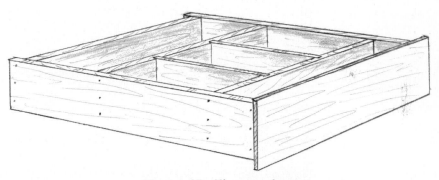

Figure 1–27 Silverware drawer.

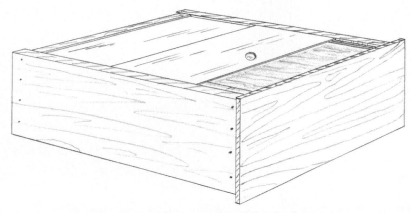

Figure 1–28 Bread drawer with sliding laminate cover.

Alternative Shelf Treatments in Base Cabinets

Three basic treatments are available for base cabinet shelving:

1. Shelves that are permanently nailed in position or rest on a supportive cleat (Fig. 1–29)
2. Adjustable shelves that make use of one of the various types of adjustable tracks and clips that are on the market (Fig. 1–30)
3. Sliding shelves that are specially designed and built to slide in and out of the cupboard in grooved runners (Figs. 1–31 and 1–32)

Each treatment has its unique advantages and disadvantages. Of the three, choice 1 is probably the least popular, in that the shelf has no capability of being adjusted to accommodate storing items of varying height. Although this is also a disadvantage of the sliding shelf, it is offset by the easy pull-out access to the stored items. The adjustable shelf is convenient for height adjustment but does not possess the convenience of pull-out access. In the end the owner/builder must ponder and decide which method will best meet the needs and the budget of the purchaser.

Figure 1–29 Shelf supported by permanent cleats.

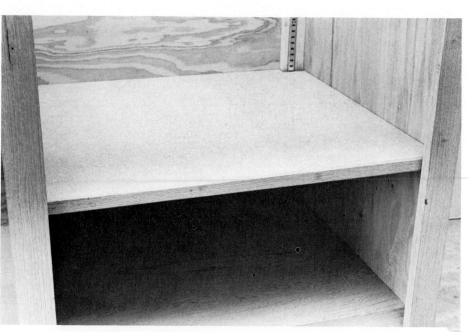

Figure 1–30 Base cabinet adjustable shelf.

Figure 1–31 Hardwood grooved runners for sliding shelves.

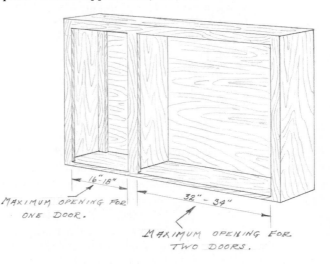

Figure 1–32 Typical sliding shelf.

Width of Drawers and Cupboard Openings

Some thought should be given to the width allotted to both drawers and cupboard openings. In the case of drawers a general rule to follow is to build drawers no narrower than 12 in. and no wider than 16 in. Although again this rule does not need to be followed, practical usage would seem to dictate dimensions very close to the 12- and 16-in. extremes. The dimension refers to the opening in the face frame of the cabinet. Thus a 12-in. opening in the frame means that a drawer with ½-in. sides has a usable space of about 10⅞ in. Little can be stored in a drawer much narrower than this. Conversely, building drawers much wider than 16 in. creates a drawer that is bulky and does not lend itself to good storage. The one exception is a drawer for the storage of kitchen linens. One 20- to 24-in.-wide drawer works well for these items and is usually all that is required for the average household. Again bear in mind that if the owner wants drawers of *any size,* the custom cabinetmaker can be accommodating.

Cupboard openings can be of almost any size. One practical problem of kitchen design is concerned with using one cabinet door or two doors on the opening designed into the cabinets. A good general rule in this regard is to use one door for openings up to 16 to 18 in. wide and go to two doors for wider openings. The maximum width of a cupboard opening should be about 32 to 34 in. (Fig. 1–33). Openings wider than this would require a pair of doors wider than 16 or 17 in. each and these doors would be very susceptible to warping. Structurally, too, an upper cabinet would require vertical support every 32 to 34 in.

Figure 1–33 Maximum openings for upper cabinets.

Figure 1-34   Side-mounted towel bar. (Courtesy Knape and Vogt)

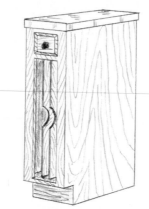

Figure 1-35   Divide a narrow space for cookie sheets, large covers, etc.

What to do with a narrow base cabinet opening

Occasionally, no matter how carefully planned a cabinet is, the designer ends up with an odd 5 to 7 in. that just cannot be designed away. A couple of things can be done with a space of this size:

1. *Towel bar:*   If the space is near the kitchen sink, a commercial sliding towel rack can be planned in a space 6 to 8 in. wide (Fig. 1-34). A narrow drawer would probably also be built above this cupboard space, and this narrow drawer is handy storage for some kitchen tools: pliers, screwdriver, small hammer, and so on.

2. *Cover, lid, cookie sheet storage* (Fig. 1-35): Installing a vertical divider or two in this narrow space leaving division openings of about 2 in. makes fine storage for large pan covers and large flat objects such as cookie sheets.

The problem of base cabinet "dead" corners

The kitchen designer quickly comes head-on with the problem of what to do with "dead" corners when working with U-shaped and L-shaped kitchens. Over the years many clever and unique ideas have been designed into kitchens of this type to overcome the dead space resulting from butting base cabinets together in kitchen corners. Years ago the cabinetmaker simply butted the two sections of cabinet together in the corner, placed a door adjacent to the corner, extended his shelf back into the dead space and made the homeowner grope back into this dark, dead area. Needless to say, housewives soon were clamoring for more efficient use of this valuable storage space. Over the years several treatments have been developed that deserve attention:

1. The 45-degree cabinet front across the corner was possibly the first innovative approach developed by cabinetmakers to make better use of the corner space (Fig. 1-36). Although it did provide direct access into the corner area, it also increased the depth of the cabinet and necessitated the construction of an extra framed section involving angles. Inefficient use of countertop materials was also a result of this construction method. The angled front was soon coupled with a lazy Susan installed in the corner, which increased the accessibility to the area.

Figure 1-36 Angled front corner cabinet.

2. The next design improvement was to incorporate ''corner doors'' into the corner area. This eliminated the need for the extra 45-degree frame construction and still provided direct access to the corner space. Lazy Susans were used together with the corner doors simply by notching the turntable to fit the corner itself (Fig. 1-37). Corner doors were simple to design by allowing 8 to 10 in. on either side of the corner and fitting a door on each side (Fig. 1-38). The doors could be unequal as well. The door on one side of the corner can be, say, 6 in. and the door on the other side may be 8 or 10 in. or so. If the doors are to be the same size, 8 to 10 in. is a nice size to design them. Notice also that these corner doors have a vertical opening that is full size in the base cabinet and no drawer is planned above. This creates a larger opening into the corner, providing better access (Figs. 1-39 and 1-40).

3. Another method of gaining access to the dead corner is to build and install swinging shelf units: one quarter-round unit that swings out of the cabinet itself, and another that is attached to the door. These are both quarter-round in shape. Although attention grabbing and cute, these units are not very efficient in that a lot of wasted space still remains in the cabinet (Figs. 1-41 and 1-42).

Figure 1-37 Corner base cabinet with lazy Susan (doors removed).

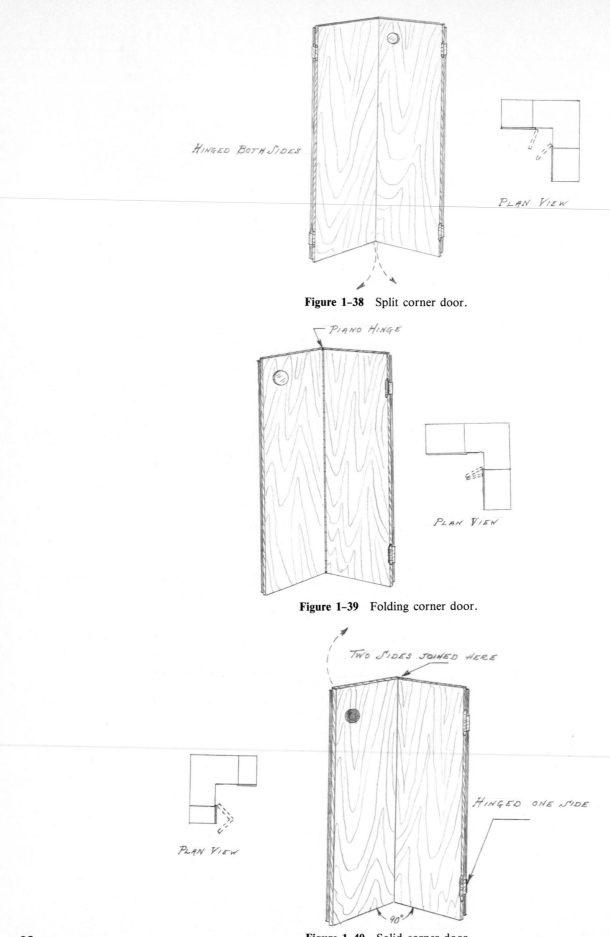

HINGED BOTH SIDES

PLAN VIEW

Figure 1–38 Split corner door.

PIANO HINGE

PLAN VIEW

Figure 1–39 Folding corner door.

TWO SIDES JOINED HERE

PLAN VIEW

HINGED ONE SIDE

90°

Figure 1–40 Solid corner door.

Figure 1-41 Quarter-round swinging shelf units.

Figure 1-42 Corner cabinet swing-out shelf.

4. Another means of access to the "dead" corner is unique to the L-shaped kitchen that has an open return—that is, the peninsula cabinet does not butt to a wall and thus is accessible from both sides of the peninsula cabinet. Drawers and cupboard space may be designed into the "dead" corner that is accessible from the dining room side of the peninsula cabinet (Fig. 1-43).

Figure 1-43 Dining side access to a peninsula cabinet.

DRAWING THE DETAILED AND DIMENSIONED CABINET PLAN

The Importance of Careful, Detailed Plans

Too much importance cannot be placed on the need for a carefully drawn, accurately scaled working plan of the proposed cabinet.

The scale drawing is proportionately accurate

When drawn to scale, the finished drawing accurately represents the finished cabinet. It is in correct proportion and thus gives the prospective purchaser, housewife, or even the builder a true picture of the way the cabinet will look when completed. Many people have great difficulty visualizing from a plan view. The more picturelike the drawing is, the easier it is for them to comprehend the finished product. This is important to the cabinetmaker, as it saves difficulty with the customer who says: "But I didn't think it would look like this!" Changes are easy to make on paper but very expensive to make in a completed cabinet.

An accurate scale drawing is a good sales tool

Many cabinetmakers rely on their drawings to help make the sale. Some even go so far as to prepare "rendered perspective" drawings that truly picture the cabinets the way they would appear to the eye. Many of the drawings in this text are drawn in this true perspective. A neat, accurate, well-turned-out scale drawing creates an impression of craftsmanship and care that may well mean the difference in obtaining a sale.

An accurate scale drawing is used for estimating

The drawing is nearly always used to estimate the amount of material that needs to be ordered for the job. Such things as plywood, plastic laminate, hardware, particle board, and so on, can be accurately determined if the drawing is drawn carefully to scale.

Too, the cabinetmaker often will estimate the cost to the customer by using an estimating method based on a price per lineal foot of base and upper cabinet or on a price per square foot of cabinet surface. An accurate drawing would be vital to determining final price to the consumer.

The drawing is often the only contract

Many small cabinet shops do not use a formal contract form when they complete a sale. The final price is usually agreed upon and possibly given in writing to the customer, but what the customer is to receive for that amount of money is represented only by the drawing the cabinetmaker has prepared. Thus in the case of questions or possible misunderstandings the plan itself becomes the contract and the basis of agreement between the buyer and the seller. "As per plan" is a phrase used commonly in the cabinet business.

The only conclusion that can be drawn from the above is that some good, basic training in fundamental drafting is all-important to anyone considering a career in the cabinetmaking field.

Floor, Ceiling, and Soffit

To make an accurate, scaled drawing of the kitchen, the rough sketch and the dimensions taken at the job site will be referred to often. It is extremely important that those measurements be made as accurately as possible, and if the cabinet is to be built for a customer, details and preferences should be discussed with the owners.

This preliminary discussion should include such things as the type of wood to be used, the style of the cabinets, the type of hardware, the type of countertop, and specific interior cabinet features. All of these items will have some impact on the working drawings prepared by the cabinetmaker.

The working plans for our model cabinet were prepared using the following procedure:

1. Start with a horizontal line drawn across the lower portion of the drawing paper to represent the floor of the kitchen. Near the left side of the paper, draw a vertical line to indicate the left wall of the kitchen.
2. Measure 96 in. up from the floor line and draw in another horizontal line to represent the ceiling.
3. Measure 12 in. down from the ceiling and draw another horizontal line to designate the lower edge of the soffit.
4. Measure along this lower soffit line exactly 136½ in., which is the measured length of the soffit taken at the site.
   a. At this end point draw a vertical line establishing the right end of the soffit.
   b. Measure 2 in. *to the left* of this end point of the soffit. This point establishes the right end of the cabinet above the refrigerator.

Locating the Outer Window Trim Lines

Remember, the measurements taken at the site determined the location of the trim or window casing the carpenter has installed (or will install) around the window. From the rough sketch and its measurements, next draw in the outer lines of the window casings.

1. From the left wall line, measure 31 in. to the right and draw a vertical line representing the outside edge of the left window casing.
   a. From this casing line, measure 40½ in. farther right and draw another vertical line, indicating the outside edge of the right-hand casing.
   b. These two lines will also indicate the left and right ends of the upper cabinets that butt to the window casings.
2. The lower edge of the soffit and the top window casing are indicated by the same line.
3. Other window details are not required unless so desired.

With the major components of the kitchen wall thus blocked in, the cabinets themselves are ready for detailing (Fig. 1–44).

Drawing the Base Cabinet

Figuring the length of the base cabinet

Mathematically, the length of the base cabinet can be figured out by doing some simple subtraction:

Overall soffit length	136½ in.
Upper cabinet setback	− 2 in.
Overall cabinet length	134½ in.
Refrigerator allowance	− 32 in.
Base cabinet length	102½ in.

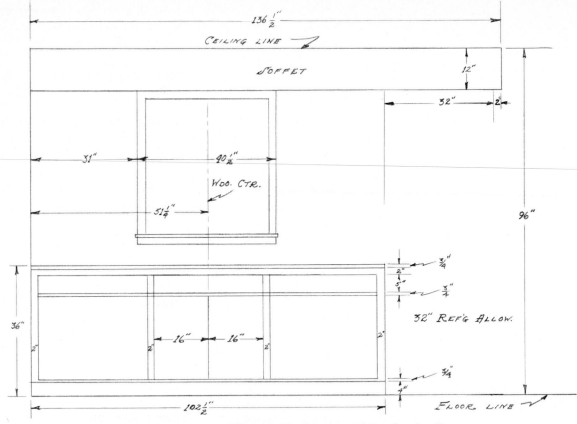

Figure 1-44   Step 1: working plan details.

The base cabinet length may be blocked out quickly on the drawing by measuring 32 in. to the left of the mark at the end of the soffit, indicating the right end of the upper cabinet over the refrigerator. (*Remember:* The upper cabinets are set back 2 in. from the soffit both at the front and at the end.) Drop a line from this point down to the floor line. This line will represent both the end of the base cabinet and the end of the upper cabinet just to the left of the refrigerator.

Detailing the base cabinet

The overall dimensions of the base cabinet are 102½ in. long by 36 in. high by 24 in. deep. The height and depth measurements are, as noted previously, standard for base cabinets. Block out the base cabinet to these length and height dimensions (Fig. 1-45).

1. Measure up from the floor line 4 in. for the height of the toe space and then another ¾ in. above that for the cabinet bottom.
2. Measure down from the top line ¾ in. for the thickness of the countertop, another 2 in. for the top rail of the base cabinet, and then another 5 in. down for the full-length cross-rail, which is ¾ in. thick.
3. Measure in from each end 2 in. for each vertical stile.
4. Next, locate the exact middle of the window and drop a light line down through the base cabinet from this midpoint. This will represent the middle of the kitchen sink and the meeting line of the double doors under the sink. Measure 16 in. from each side of this midline to lay out the width of the under-sink cabinet doors and then measure off another 2 in. on each side for the vertical stiles.

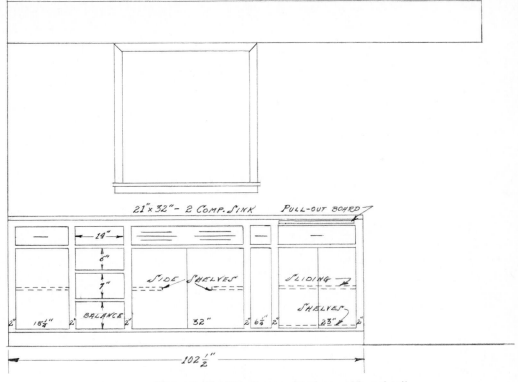

Figure 1–45 Step 2: complete base cabinet details.

5. The major base cabinet areas are now blocked out. The balance of this cabinet is a matter of judgment, personal preference, and good design.

6. A 14-in. row of drawers and a single-door cabinet would seem to fit nicely to the left of the sink. Measure 14 in. to the left of the sink opening and draw another 2-in. vertical stile. The remaining space to the left of 15½ in. will be just about right for a single-door cupboard opening.

   Design the vertical row of drawers as follows:
   a. The top drawer is already laid out and is 5 in. high. These vertical measurements will vary from cabinetmaker to cabinetmaker, but the dimensions used here have been used for years with no complaints from the purchasing public.
   b. Measure down 6 in. for the opening for the second drawer and draw in another ¾-in. cross-rail.
   c. Measure 7 in. for the third drawer opening and draw the final cross-rail, leaving what space remains for the bottom drawer, which is the largest opening.

7. The right side of the base cabinet will need a larger cupboard and a drawer for kitchen linens. An opening of 23 in. or so is a fine size for this. Measure 23 in. to the left of the vertical end stile and draw another 2-in. vertical stile.

8. The remaining space is just 6¼ in., which will be about right for a sliding towel bar—always a nice feature in the modern kitchen.

9. Add details with notes or drawings indicating:
   a. Pull-out board. (*Note:* Do not locate this above a busy drawer such as the silver drawer!)
   b. Drawer divided for silverware.
   c. Sliding shelves if desired.
   d. Side shelves under the sink.
   e. Location of the drawer pulls and door handles. Location of the door handles will indicate which way the door is to swing.

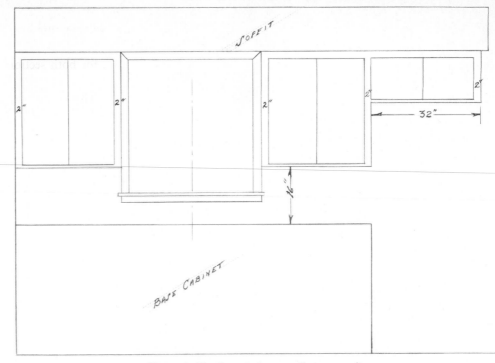

Figure 1–46   Step 3: layout of upper units.

Drawing the Upper Cabinets

Left upper cupboard

The left upper cabinet can be designed and blocked out with little effort (Fig. 1–46). Measure up from the top of the base cabinet exactly 16 in.—this is the recommended space between the upper and base cabinets. Draw a horizontal line at this point on both sides of the window space. This line represents the bottom of the upper units.

1. The left upper cabinet is now outlined—the left wall to the window casing and from the soffit to the line indicating the bottom of the upper units.
2. Lay out the left and right stiles and the upper rail by measuring 2 in. for each of these pieces.
3. The bottom of the cabinet is ¾ in. thick, so measure up this amount to indicate the cabinet bottom.
4. Draw a vertical line through the middle of the upper cabinet to indicate that a pair of doors will be placed on this unit.
5. Indicate with drawing details and notes where the door pulls are located and the type of shelves the cabinet will have.

Right-side upper cabinet

An experienced drafter will project with a T-square many of the vertical measurements required for the right cabinet across the drawing from the left cabinet.

The major dimensions for this right-side cabinet have already been plotted. The length was determined by the point located 2 in. to the left of the end of the soffit. The length of the cabinet over the refrigerator has also been noted by the 32-in. measurement made to the left of the end of the unit. The upper and lower limits have been determined by the soffit and the bottom line projected across from the left cabinet.

1. Measure 2 in. each for the end stiles and the top rail of this cabinet.
2. The cabinet over the refrigerator will measure just 14 in. high, so measure down from the soffit to establish this height.
3. Add the cabinet bottom of ¾ in. for both sections of this cabinet.
4. The right side of the cabinet next to the window has already been located by measuring for the refrigerator. This side of the upper unit should line up with the end of the base cabinet. Mark the right-hand stile of this cabinet in 2 in. from the right.
5. Locate the midpoints of each of these two divisions of this cabinet and draw vertical lines indicating that a pair of doors will be placed in each opening. Note the location of the door pulls and indicate type of shelving.

Dimensioning the Working Drawings

Be particularly careful and exact in dimensioning the working drawing, as any errors here will show up in the cabinets themselves and errors can be *costly*. Slight variations from exact scale in the drawing may be overlooked, but the dimensions must be *correct*. To avoid any confusion, always dimension the working plans in *inches only!* It is possible that 10′8″ might be misread as 108″. To avoid this happening, all dimensions are placed on the working drawing in inches.

Dimensioning the base cabinets

For experienced cabinetmakers only the length measurements are required, as they know that the base section is 36 in. high and 24 in. deep. What is needed are the exact opening dimensions and an *exact* overall length dimension (Fig. 1–47).

1. Each vertical stile is 2 in. wide, so start dimensioning by placing that figure on each stile.

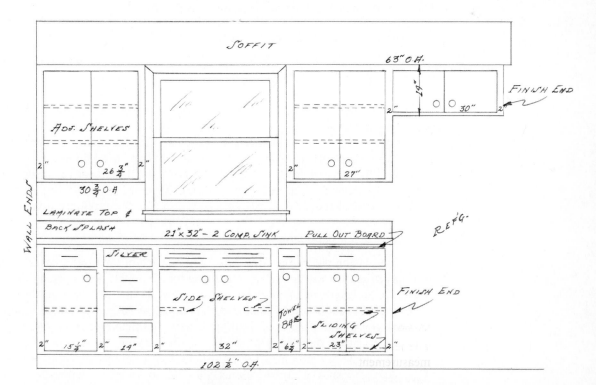

Figure 1–47 Completed detail drawing of model cabinet.

2. Next, place the dimensions on the drawing that are known standard measurements:
    a. The cabinet under the sink is exactly 32 in.
    b. The opening for the row of drawers is 14 in. wide.
    c. The opening for the sliding towel bar is 6 in. wide.

3. At this point, check the measurement taken on site from the left wall to the center of the window. This was 51¼ in. This is also the length of the cabinet from the left wall to the center of the sink section. To determine the width of the single door opening on the left side of the cabinet, add all of the left side *known* dimensions together. These would be 16 in. (representing one-half of the sink opening), plus 6 in. (for the three 2-in. stiles on this left side), plus 14 in. for the opening for the row of drawers. This totals up to be 36 in. By subtracting the 36 in. total from the 51¼ in. leaves exactly 15¼ in. for the last remaining opening to the left of the sink.

4. To determine exactly the dimensions for the spaces to the right side of the sink opening, reference must be made once again to the on-site measurements. The total space allotted for cabinets was established as 134½ in. (just 2 in. less than the overall length of the soffit). Subtracting the 32 in. used for the refrigerator space leaves exactly 102½ in. for the overall length of the base cabinet. The left side of the base cabinet used 51¼ in., so exactly 51¼ in. remains for use on the right side.

    NOTE: In this case the sink is exactly in the center of the base cabinet, but very often this does not happen. The cabinetmaker should be exceedingly careful to check the dimensions to be certain that the sink is centered on the window. Carefully total all dimensions both to the left and right of the window centerline and to the left and right of the centerline of the base cabinet sink section.

5. As a final check on the accuracy of the dimensions, total the entire series of dimensions to see that they total 102½ in.

Dimensioning the upper cabinets

Again the experienced cabinetmaker needs no height or depth dimensions for the upper cabinets, as the 12-in. depth and the 32-in. height is standard. Any change from these standards should, of course, be indicated on the working drawings. Only sections that are not standard need to be dimensioned, such as the height of the section over the refrigerator.

Begin by again dimensioning 2 in. for each stile. The space for the left upper cabinet was exactly 31 in. from wall to window casing. A minimum of ¼ in. must be allowed for this cabinet to be positioned (the "play" that was discussed earlier), so the overall length of this left section cannot be longer than 30¾ in. Subtracting the 4-in. width of the stiles leaves exactly 26¾ in. for the cupboard door opening.

Right upper cupboard

After having placed the 2-in. dimension on each of the three stiles, the section over the refrigerator will have 30 in. remaining for the double door opening. Inasmuch as the overall length of this right-hand cabinet is 63 in., we arrive at the opening size of the other cupboard by adding 6 in. (stiles) plus 30 in. (refrigerator cupboard opening), for a total of 36 in. This 36 in. is now subtracted from our overall length of 63 in., leaving a dimension of 27 in. for this section.

The overall dimension of the right-hand upper cabinet of 63 in. was arrived at by adding 30¾ in. (left upper cabinet) plus 40½ in. (window dimension from outside of window casings) for a total of 71¼ in. The 71¼ in. is then subtracted from the total space allotted for the cabinets of 134½ in., leaving 63¼ in. Remember, however, that ¼ in. was used as "play" to allow the left upper cabinet to be positioned. Thus exactly 63 in. remains as the exact length of the right-side upper cabinet.

A nice size for the height of the section over the refrigerator is 14 in. The top rail of all the upper sections is 2 in. wide, and as mentioned previously, the bottom of these upper sections is ¾ in. thick.

REVIEW QUESTIONS

1.1. How many square feet should the average modern kitchen contain?

1.2. If the kitchen is to include an eating area, what should the minimum kitchen dimensions be?

1.3. In the "Rule of Twenty-Two," what is the importance of the number 22?

1.4. How many lineal feet of cabinets is considered adequate for the average kitchen?

1.5. Which kitchen layout is considered to be the most efficient?

1.6. Standard base cabinet measurements are _____ in. high and _____ in. deep (front to back). Upper cabinet standard measurements are _____ in. high and _____ in. deep. The space between the upper and base cabinets should be a minimum of _____ in.

1.7. What is a soffit, and where is it located in the kitchen?

1.8. An excellent scale to use for kitchen drawing is _____.

1.9. What is the most common width of the opening for the cabinet doors under the kitchen sink?

1.10. List three types of shelf treatments for shelves used in base cabinets.

1.11. What is the recommended maximum width for openings for upper cabinet doors?

1.12. List three good reasons for a cabinetmaker to prepare accurate drawings of a proposed cabinet job.

SUGGESTED CLASS ACTIVITIES AND STUDENT ASSIGNMENTS

1.1. Have the students visit building supply dealers and request cabinet literature that can be studied in regard to kitchen layout and design of the cabinets.

1.2. Have the students collect pictures from the leading home magazines of kitchens that represent the various kitchen layouts.

1.3. Have each member of the class prepare a 1″ = 1′ −0″ scale drawing with all the necessary shop dimensions of a 10-ft. wall of cabinets that has these features: a 32 in. × 21 in. sink with a window above it and a built-in dishwasher.

1.4. Arrange a field trip to a small one- or two-worker cabinet shop and visit with the proprietor as to background or training, shop equipment and layout, successful business requirements, and so on. Have the class examine the work in progress noting what type of treatment is being used in "dead" corners, base cabinet shelves, upper cabinet shelves, and general drawer layout.

1.5. Invite a person from a local building supply dealership to speak to the class on cabinetry. Suggested topics for the speaker could include (a) custom versus manufactured cabinets, (b) differences in quality, (c) most popular styles and types of wood, and (d) most desirable interior features.

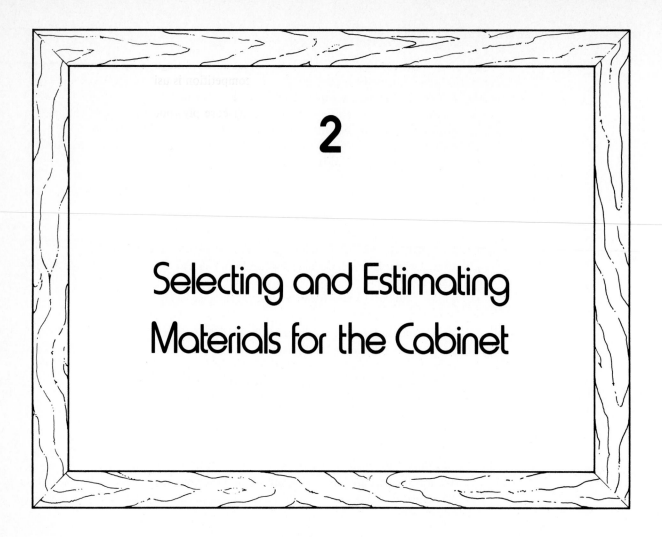

2

Selecting and Estimating Materials for the Cabinet

The two principal cost items to the cabinetmaker are labor and materials—labor, of course, being the item of greatest expense to the professional. To the home crafts-person or "weekend woodworker," the cost of materials is of the greatest concern, for labor is not an item of expense for such a person. To be competitive, however, the professional cabinetmaker must make every effort to purchase materials as economically as possible and to make use of the least expensive products that can be purchased. Expense of materials must be balanced with quality of product, however. If a shoddy cabinet is the outcome of using cheap material, the competitiveness of the marketplace will soon drive out the shoddy product.

The cabinetmaker soon realizes that labor and material are intertwined. This question must always be uppermost in mind: If this particular material is used, will time be saved? For example, a less expensive thickness of plywood can be used, let's say, for the bottoms and ends of a base cabinet. However, if it requires more time to turn out reinforcing strips for the thinner material and glue these pieces into position, the end result could easily be a higher total cost for using the less expensive material. By constantly being alert to new products entering the market and by always looking for a faster and easier means of accomplishing the varied tasks involved in turning out a high-quality cabinet, professional cabinetmakers soon become quite expert at being able to turn out the greatest amount of work in the least amount of time, thus making the most profit in their businesses.

The choice of materials can also be used to advantage in selling the cabinets to potential customers. For example, if the competition is using hardwood plywood with a particle-board core for cabinet doors, a real sales point might be that a higher-quality product is being used, such as lumber-core plywood.

SELECTING HARDWOOD LUMBER AND PLYWOOD FOR THE CABINET

Where Hardwood Lumber Is Used in the Cabinet

The generally accepted rule for the use of hardwood lumber and/or plywood is: Those areas of the cabinet that are exposed to normal sight lines should be of the selected wood. The rule holds true, of course, for cabinets that are to be finished with a clear or transparent finish and are not to be painted. Normally, these portions of the cabinet would be expected to be of the selected hardwood: all face frames, toe space boards, fronts of all drawers (although plywood is often used here), frames and raised panels of cabinet doors, valance boards, and the trim or casing applied around the cabinet.

Matching hardwood veneered plywood of either ¾ or ¼ in. thickness is used for most cabinet doors, plain paneled doors, cabinet finished ends, and usually for exposed bottoms such as the bottom of a cabinet over the refrigerator or range.

Purchasing Lumber and Plywood

Where to purchase hardwood lumber and plywood

Not too surprisingly, most neighborhood lumberyards do not carry a large and complete stock of hardwoods. Although they may carry a few pieces of oak and birch, their stock would be quite limited and also quite expensive. The professional cabinet-maker locates wholesale suppliers who cater to cabinet shops in their area and can supply them with a well-rounded inventory of practically all their needs. Weekend woodworkers, because they purchase in such limited quantities, cannot take advantage of the selection and prices of these wholesalers, but they often can do quite well by purchasing from cabinetmakers in their area.

How lumber and plywood is sold

Generally speaking, hardwood lumber is priced by the species, grade, and thickness, with the basic unit of measure being the board foot. The cost is based on the price per board foot times the number of board feet. Plywood, on the other hand, is sold by the square foot, with these other factors affecting price: species, thickness, and core material. Thus plywood is purchased by calculating the number of square feet of a selected variety and multiplying times the price per square foot.

Figuring board feet

Board feet is often abbreviated bd ft. A board foot is a piece of lumber 1 in. thick by 12 in. long and 12 in. wide or 1 in. $\times$ 12 in. $\times$ 1$'$ $-$ 0$''$ (or other combinations of dimensions that total 144 cubic inches). Lumber thinner than 1 in. is still calculated at the 1-in. thickness, while lumber over 1 in. thick is calculated in multiples of ¼ in. up to 2 in. thick (Fig. 2–1). Another common abbreviation used is RW&L (or simply RWL) meaning "random width and length," which applies to selection of the pieces in a lumber order. Ordering specific lengths will mean a slight additional charge for selecting the specified lengths, and one always pays for a full foot of length. Calculating a problem in board feet is a rather simple arithmetic process

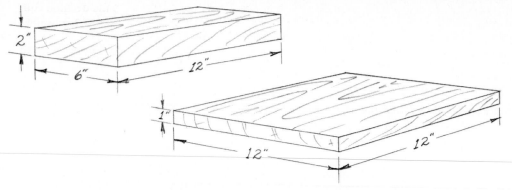

Figure 2-1   Illustration of 1 board foot.

and should not be too mysterious with a bit of practice. The basic formula for calculating the number of board feet is

$$\frac{\text{no. pieces} \times \text{width (in.)} \times \text{thickness (in.)} \times \text{length (ft.)}}{12}$$

Example: $\dfrac{10 \text{ pcs.}-2 \times 4-10 \text{ ft. long}}{12}$

Calculation: $10 \times 2 \times 4 \times 10 = 800$
$800 \div 12 = 66 \frac{2}{3}$ bd. ft.

Cost = number of bd. ft. × price per board foot

Example: Three pieces of oak are ordered 1 × 8—12 ft. long.
  Calculation: $\dfrac{3-1 \times 8-\cancel{12}}{\cancel{12}} = 24$ bd. ft.

(*Note:* Where 12 appears both above and below the formula line, they can be canceled out and the remaining numbers multiplied.)

Practical retail usage rounds off the fractional portion of a board foot to the nearest whole foot using the standard round-off rule: less than half a foot, drop it; half or over go up to the next foot.

  Lumber thicker than 1 in. (four quarter) is designated by adding quarters to the standard 1 in. Thus lumber measuring 1¼ in. thick is called ⁵⁄₄ (five-quarter), 1½ in. thick is known as ⁶⁄₄ (six-quarter), 1 ¾ in. is ⁷⁄₄ (seven-quarter), and 2 in. is ⁸⁄₄ (eight-quarter). To calculate the cost of lumber measuring ⁵⁄₄ in thickness, simply calculate the number of board feet using the formula for the 1 in. thickness and then add ¼, ½, or ¾ more. Thus 6 pieces ⁵⁄₄ × 8—12 ft. long is figured

$$\frac{6 \text{ pcs.}-1 \times 8-\cancel{12} \text{ ft.} = 48}{\cancel{12}}$$

$$48 \times \tfrac{1}{4} = 12$$

$$48 + 12 + 60 \text{ bd. ft.}$$

Or very simply with a small hand electronic calculator, the problem can easily be entered and figured thus:

Enter 6 × 1.25 × 8 × 12 ÷ 12 = 60 bd. ft.

In each case of the extra thickness, substitute the decimal equivalent in the formula: ⁵⁄₄ = 1.25, ⁶⁄₄ = 1.50, and ⁷⁄₄ = 1.75. Of course, a 2-in. thickness is entered directly as 2.

Example: What is the price of 6 pieces of oak measuring ⁶⁄₄ × 10 in. × 10 ft. long if the price per board foot is $1.95?

Solution (using the electronic calculator):

$$\text{Enter: } 6 \times 1.5 \times 10 \times 10 \div 12 = 75 \text{ bd. ft.}$$
$$75 \text{ bd. ft.} \times \$1.95 = \$146.25$$

Using just a pencil, the calculation would be

$$\frac{6 \times 1 \times 10 \times 10}{12} = \frac{600}{12} = 50$$

$$50 \times \tfrac{1}{2} = 25$$

$$50 + 25 = 75 \text{ bd. ft.}$$

Understanding lumber thickness measurements

Another of the minor mysteries in purchasing lumber is in understanding the *actual* measurements of a board as opposed to its described or *nominal* size. When a standard size 2 × 4 is bought, for example, one actually receives a piece of lumber 1½ in. × 3½ in. in size. Why is this? Lumber is sized at the sawmill where it is first sawed to rough size from the still-green log. Because of shrinkage in the kiln-drying process and the amount removed in the planing mill, the actual size of the finished piece ready for retailing is considerably less (Fig. 2–2).

It is important for the cabinetmaker to be aware of the S2S (surfaced two sides) dimensions of the hardwoods that are commonly put to use in the cabinet shop. If an order for oak, for example, specifies 1 in. oak S2S, the lumber received will measure 13/16 in. in thickness. If the order specifies 1 in. oak ¾ in. thick, a milling charge will have to be paid for planing the boards to the ordered dimension. Whatever the case, it is equally important for the cabinetmaker to be consistent in purchasing so that lumber of varied thicknesses is not on inventory. It is a real source of aggravation to mix thicknesses of lumber in a cabinet face frame. The end result could be a lot of extra belt sanding to even off the assembled frame. Softwood lumber when sold at retail in the finished state or surfaced on four sides (S4S) has the measurements shown in Fig. 2–3.

Nominal (rough)	Surfaced 2 sides (S2S)
1″	¹³⁄₁₆″
1¼″	1 ¹⁄₁₆″
1½″	1 ⁵⁄₁₆″
2″	1 ¾″
3″	2 ¾″
4″	3 ¾″

Figure 2–2 Standard hardwood lumber dimensions. (National Hardwood Lumber Association)

Nominal		Actual	Nominal		Actual
1 × 2	=	¾″ × 1½″	2 × 10	=	1½″ × 9¼″
1 × 3	=	¾″ × 2½″	2 × 12	=	1½″ × 11¼″
1 × 4	=	¾″ × 3½″	3 × 3	=	2½″ × 2½″
1 × 5	=	¾″ × 4½″	3 × 4	=	2½″ × 3½″
1 × 6	=	¾″ × 5½″	3 × 6	=	2½″ × 5½″
1 × 8	=	¾″ × 7¼″	3 × 8	=	2½″ × 7¼″
1 × 10	=	¾″ × 9¼″	3 × 10	=	2½″ × 9¼″
1 × 12	=	¾″ × 11¼″	3 × 12	=	2½″ × 11¼″
2 × 2	=	1½″ × 1½″	4 × 4	=	3½″ × 3½″
2 × 3	=	1½″ × 2½″	4 × 6	=	3½″ × 5½″
2 × 4	=	1½″ × 3½″	4 × 8	=	3½″ × 7¼″
2 × 6	=	1½″ × 5½″	4 × 10	=	3½″ × 9¼″
2 × 8	=	1½″ × 7¼″	4 × 12	=	3½″ × 11¼″

Figure 2-3 Softwood lumber actual dimensions when surfaced four sides (S4S).

Grading of hardwood lumber

The National Hardwood Lumber Association has had grading rules for many years. They were the result of a need expressed by the furniture industry to obtain some uniformity among lumber manufacturers as to the grading of their product. Grading is done according to the number of defects present in any given board, or of special interest to the cabinetmaker—the amount of defect-free lumber that can be obtained from a board. Grading is a difficult and complicated subject, and it is not necessary for either the professional cabinetmaker or the home craftsperson to understand it fully. However, it is a good idea to have at least a "conversational" acquaintance with the lumber grades so that an intelligent order may be made out for the lumber dealer. Also, by having at least a working knowledge of the rules, the customer will have a reasonable knowledge of what to expect when ordering a specified grade.

FAS (first and seconds): Requires clear rippings on the poorest face of at least 4 in. wide × 5 ft. long or 3 in. wide by 7 ft. long. FAS is graded from the poorer side so that the opposite side is going to be even better. This is the top grade of lumber found in the hardwoods. Walnut, cherry, red gum, and poplar must have at least two-thirds heartwood on one face. Clear rippings must be $^{10}\!/_{12}$ of the surface with a minimum board width of 6 in. and a minimum length of 8 ft.

Selects: A select board is FAS on its best face. Where only one good side is commonly seen, this grade is good enough for most cabinetwork. There must be no holes or decay in the board and the opposite side is grade No. 1 Common. Minimum width is 4 in. and minimum length is 6 ft.

No. 1 common: This grade is considered the best and most economical grade to purchase for home cabinetry, as it produces about 66% clear rippings with the grading done from the poorer side. Clear rippings that must be obtainable are 4 in. wide and 2 ft. long or 3 in. wide and 3 ft. long. In practical cabinet usage, experience shows that No. 1 common can produce clear cuttings 1½ to 2 in. wide by 8 to 10 ft. long, which makes it ideal for face frames.

No. 2 common: Again this grade is graded on the poorer side and must produce clear rippings 3 in. wide by 2 ft. long over $^{6}\!/_{12}$ of the surface. This grade may be useful in the production of frames for raised panel cabinet doors, where shorter clear rippings are usable.

There are lower grades as well, but unless one is building a product that requires only very short, clear pieces, these lower grades are not a practical purchase for the cabinetmaker.

Popular Varieties of Hardwoods Used in Cabinetry

The most popular cabinet wood is without question red oak used in a wide variety of stains, finishes, and cabinet styles. It has a beautiful grain that becomes even more attractive when stained. Oak is a very durable wood that will stand up well under hard usage, yet is reasonably easy to work with ordinary machines and tools that are kept well sharpened.

Next in popularity by a distant second is birch. Where a light-grained, durable cabinet material is desired, birch nicely fills the bill. Its color can vary from select white to a mixture of white and reddish brown. Most cabinetmakers do not care to mix the colors of birch and will order birch lumber and birch plywood either select white or select dark.

Many other species are occasionally used where the customer requests it and is willing to pay what in many cases could be a premium price. Mahogany, black walnut, cherry, and even knotty pine and fir are just a few of the many woods that are sometimes demanded.

One other item of note should be mentioned. Home decorators tell us that decorating the home is cyclical both as to style and colors. So over a period of several years one wood with a particular finish is quite popular and then, a few years later, is replaced by something quite different. This explains the periodic return to popularity of painted millwork and cabinetry in the home. The many home magazines published in this country report these trends and changes and perhaps even lead them. The cabinetmaker should always try to be abreast of what is happening in home decorating trends.

SELECTING SOFTWOODS FOR THE CABINET

Where Softwoods Are Used in Cabinet Construction

Whereas hardwoods are used where they can be seen in the cabinets, softwoods are used in cabinetry where they are not ordinarily visible. Practically all interior support pieces or reinforcing pieces in the cabinet are built of softwood as well as drawer runners and on occasion even drawer sides. Often a cabinet that is to be painted will have the face frame constructed of softwood and the cabinet doors made of the less expensive varieties of plywood.

The varieties of softwoods used in cabinetmaking will vary from region to region as the cabinetmaker will make use of those species which are the least expensive. Various species of pine, fir, basswood, native poplar, and even aspen are varieties available in the author's locale.

Grading of Softwood Lumber

The Department of Commerce's National Bureau of Standards has supplied the industry with grading rules for softwood lumber under the title *American Lumber Standards*. If possible, the softwood grading system is even more confusing than that for hardwoods. Familiarity with these grades of softwood lumber should be adequate for the average cabinetmaker:

No. 1 common: Seldom will one find lumber of this grade in the average retail lumberyard. It is practically a clear, fine-appearing, defect-free grade.

No. 2 common: Excellent for painted surfaces, shelves, and paneling.

No. 3 common: Much the same uses as No. 2 Common, with just a few more allowable defects. It should be used where strength and appearance are required.

No. 4 common: This grade is commonly used in construction for concrete forms, subfloors, and other uses where it will not ordinarily be seen.

Shop grade factory select: The two top "shop" grades are of the most interest to the cabinetmaker, as these grades will yield the most in long, clear rippings that will need to be used in the construction of the interior portions of the cabinets. Factory Select must produce clear cuttings of 70% of 9½ in. or wider by 18 in. or longer; or 5 in. or wider × 36 in. or longer; or 9½ in. or wider, less than 36 in. long if good on both sides; or 4 in. or wider × 36 in. or longer C Select or better.

No. 1 shop: Much the same as Factory Select except that the yield percent drops to 50 to 70% clear rippings.

No. 2 shop: Is graded in relationship to No. 1 Shop Grade in that this grade need yield only 33 to 50% of the No. 1 size in clear cuttings.

A final word on grading of lumber

If most of the material that will be used in a cabinet is purchased from a local lumberyard, try to find one that will allow the customer to "hand-pick" the pieces desired. Once a good customer relationship has been established with the lumber dealer, many will allow this and even assist in picking out the better boards. Thus while the picking may be done in a stock of No. 2 or 3 Common, by being allowed to be selective, the stock purchased is really of a much higher grade but priced at the lower!

USE OF HARDWOOD PLYWOOD IN THE CABINET

Where Hardwood Plywood Is Used in the Cabinet

Hardwood plywood that is ¾ in. thick is by far the most widely used. Cabinet doors, end panels, and drawer fronts are normally made of this type of plywood. Hardwood plywood in the ¼-in. thickness is used mainly for paneling in certain styles of cabinet doors and for overlays. An example of an overlay would be where the cabinetmaker constructs the bottom of an upper cabinet over the refrigerator of particle board and then covers or "overlays" the particle board with ¼-in. hardwood plywood to match the face of the cabinet.

The exception to this use of ¼-in. plywood is in the "casework system" presented as one of the cabinet-building systems in this text. Here a wider use of ¼-in. plywood is called for. Finish end panels of both base cabinets and upper cabinets are made of ¼ in., replacing the more expensive ¾-in. thickness. Of course, these thinner panels must be supported with softwood reinforcing strips, as explained in later chapters.

Grades of Hardwood Plywood

Cabinet-grade plywood in the ¾-in. thickness is distinguished and priced based on several factors: species, quality of the veneer surfaces, type of grain, the color of the veneer with some species, and the type of core to which the veneered surface is applied.

The cabinetmaker will most often be interested in veneer quality of three grades: A-2, A-3, and Shop. These grades are described thus:

A-2   good two sides: Both veneer faces of the 4 × 8 sheet are of the species ordered such as oak. The veneered face must be of smoothly cut, high-quality veneers which are carefully matched both as to color and grain. No defects should appear on either side. This grade is used extensively for cabinet doors and drawer fronts, where both sides of the piece will be seen by the homeowner.

A-3   good one side: Only one side of the panel fits the description of the A-2 grade. The opposite or back side will contain a variety of types of defects. This grade is used for end panels of cabinets where only the one good side is visible. Drawer fronts, too, are sometimes made of this grade.

Shop   shop grade: Slight defects are allowable in this grade. Used where the sheet will be cut into smaller pieces and the defects can be eliminated. Also used for backs of cabinets with glass doors, such as china cabinets, gun cabinets, and so on.

The core material of plywood also ranges in quality, with three distinct types used in the plywood industry:

Lumber core: The interior material used is solid lumber strips. This plywood often is used in high-quality cabinet doors. Aspen and basswood are often used for core material.

Veneer core: Made in "sandwiches" of three, five, seven, or nine plies. The five- and seven-ply types are those most often used for cabinet doors in the ¾-in. thickness.

Fiber core: This variety has gained rapid acceptance in the cabinet industry, as it is less expensive than the other two types. It is a very stable panel that is seldom subject to warping. The weight is sometimes a problem and the screw-holding power is somewhat less than with the other cores.

Finally, the thickness of the plywood ordered, the type of grain specified, and the species determine the cost of hardwood plywood. Some dealers give the customers a price break, too, on quantity orders. Typical catalog descriptions are illustrated in Fig. 2–4.

	Less than 6 pieces	*6 pieces or more*
Red oak (Rotary cut) — Veneer core		
⅛" 4 × 8 A-3		
¼" 4 × 8 A-3		
4 × 8 A-2		
⅜" 4 × 8 A-2		
½" 4 × 8 A-2		
¾" 4 × 6 A-2		
4 × 7 A-2		
4 × 8 A-2		
4 × 8 Shop grade		
Red oak (Plain sliced) — Veneer core		
¾" 4 × 8 A-2		

Figure 2–4   Typical hardwood plywood catalog listing.

Red oak (Rotary cut) — Solid lbr. core

¾" 4 × 6 A-2 (Aspen core)
    4 × 8 A-2 (Aspen core)
   72 × 24″ A-2 Door stock (Bass. core).
   72 × 30″
   72 × 36″
   72 × 42″
   72 × 48″

Red oak (Rotary cut) — Fiber core

½" 4 × 8 A-2
¾" 4 × 8 A-2
   60 × 24″ A-2 Door stock
   60 × 30″
   60 × 36″
   60 × 42″
   60 × 48″

Figure 2–4 Continued

Note that in material description the width is always listed first and the length second. In plywood this is extremely important, as this dimension description determines the direction of the grain. Thus in the catalog listing a 4 ft. × 8 ft. sheet of plywood will have the grain running the 8-ft. length. However, in the listing of the cabinet door stock above in size 72 in. × 24 in., the grain runs the 24-in. length. Many cabinetmakers purchase the cabinet door stock, as it cuts very economically into doors with a minimum of waste.

USE OF SOFTWOOD PLYWOOD IN THE CABINET

Where Softwood Plywood Is Used in Cabinetry

Softwood plywood in the ¼-in. thickness is widely used for such applications as cabinet backs and drawer bottoms. Douglas fir plywood has been over the years the standard species used for these functions, although some 70 species of wood is used in the manufacture of softwood plywood. However, in recent years more and more use is being made of some of the less expensive hardwood plywoods and particle board. Mahogany plywood or luan plywood in the ¼-in. thickness is one of these. The appearance of luan is excellent and the price is only a few cents per square foot higher than fir. Particle board in various thicknesses is being used more and more for interior partitions, drawer sides and backs, bottoms, countertops, shelving, and, in some cases, for cabinet backs. Typically, the ½-in. thickness is being used for partitions and drawer sides and backs. Depending on the system of cabinetmaking used, other typical applications of less expensive plywood in the ¼-in. thickness are base cabinet bottoms, backs, wall ends, upper cabinet tops, and drawer bottoms.

Grades of Softwood Plywood

Softwood plywood is divided into two basic types: exterior and interior. The exterior grade is bonded with waterproof glue, while the interior is bonded with just a water-resistant glue. For practical cabinet purposes the grade designations range from A to D, with A being the best quality. Only the interior grade is ordinarily used for cabinets in the home.

Grade A: Smooth and paintable. Patches permitted usually in the form of round "plugs" or small, football-shaped repairs. Widely used for backs in grade A-D.

Fir

¼	4 × 8	AA	Int
¼	4 × 8	AD	Int
¼	4 × 8	AC	Ext
¼	4 × 8	Sanded Shop	
⅜	4 × 8	AD	Int
⅜	4 × 8	AC	Ext
⅜	4 × 8	Sanded shop	
⅜	4 × 8	CDX sheathing	Ext
½	4 × 8	BB	Int
½	4 × 8	AD	Int
½	4 × 8	AC	Ext
½	4 × 8	Sanded shop	
½	4 × 8	CDX sheathing	Ext
⅝	4 × 8	BB	Int
⅝	4 × 8	AD	Int
⅝	4 × 8	AC	Ext
⅝	4 × 8	Sanded shop	
⅝	4 × 8	CDX sheathing	Ext
¾	4 × 8	AA	Int
¾	4 × 8	BB	Int
¾	4 × 8	AD	Int
¾	4 × 8	AC	Ext
¾	4 × 8	Sanded shop	
¾	4 × 8	CDX sheathing	Ext

Figure 2–5 Softwood plywood catalog listing.

Grade B: Solid surface veneer. Plugs permitted as well as tight knots. Good grade to use for partitions and drawer sides and backs in grade B-B, where both sides can be seen.

Grade C and C plugged: Knotholes up to 1½ in. and splits to ½ in. are permitted under certain conditions. No use made of this and lower grades in cabinetry. Will appear only as a backing for the A face, such as grade A-C.

Grade D: Used for interior plies and backs. Grade A-D, for example.

Sizes of Softwood Plywood Available

Although the most commonly sold size of softwood plywood is 4 ft. × 8 ft. sheets, it is obtainable in widths of 36, 48, and 60 in. Thicknesses on the market range from ¼ to 1¼ in., while lengths available are 60 to 144 in. in 1-ft. increments. A typical catalog listing of a wholesale dealer's stock of softwood plywood is illustrated in Fig. 2–5.

USE OF PARTICLE BOARD IN HOME CABINETRY

Particle board is one of the newer human-made materials being widely used in the cabinet industry. Made of what the industry once considered a waste product only to be burned—sawdust, shavings, chips, and so on—particle board, especially in the heavier densities, has many practical applications and has largely replaced softwood plywood in the cabinet manufacturing industry. When this product was first marketed,

41

only the underlayment grade was available. Some cabinetmakers, eager to avail themselves of the rather substantial cost savings, used this underlayment grade for cabinet shelves only to find that these shelves soon sagged under even a medium load. Particle board received rather a bad name for a short while insofar as cabinet usage was concerned. Soon, however, higher-density panels began to be manufactured that enjoyed complete success in cabinet manufacturing. Particle board in the 45-lb. density in the ¾-in. thickness is widely used for shelving and countertops. (The density figure is based on the weight per cubic foot of the board.)

Typical Uses of Particle Board in Cabinets

The most widely used thicknesses of particle board are the ½- and ¾-in. varieties. The ½-in. thickness is used for cabinet partitions and in the construction of drawers for the sides and backs. The ¾-in. thickness enjoys wide popularity for shelving, upper cabinet bottoms, and countertops when plastic laminate is to be applied. Where the shelf span is less than about 36 in., even thinner material can be used, such as ⅝ in. thickness.

Also available is particle board in ½- and ¼-in. thicknesses that has a direct-print oak grain imposed on the board and it is used for drawer sides, bottoms, and cabinet backs. This is also available in the ¾-in. thickness and is used for shelving. Both of these items are manufactured in the common widths needed for their application in the cabinet. The ½-in. variety is available in strips 4⅝, 7½, 9½, and 24 in. wide by 97 in. long and is sold by the lineal foot. The ¾-in. oak-grained particle board used for shelving is sold in pieces 11½-in. wide by 97 in. long and is sold by the lineal foot. The average one-person cabinet shop has not made wide use of the oak-grained particle board because of its cost. The manufacturers of ready-made units, however, have made wide application of this product.

Where the typical ½- and ¾-in. particle board is used for drawer sides and shelving, the raw edge of the board needs to be covered with a facing strip—especially on shelving. Typically, this strip might be of a variety to match the wood used in the face frame. Many cabinetmakers leave the raw edge of the particle board exposed when used for drawer sides, but a cap strip of matching hardwood makes a neat and more-expensive-looking drawer. As mentioned previously, the extra labor and material involved in applying cap strips to the drawer sides might be a real sales point over your competitors.

Available Sizes of Particle Board

One advantage that particle-board manufacturers have over the plywood industry is that their standard sheet sizes are an inch wider and longer than plywood. Thus 49 in. × 97 in. is a standard sheet. This extra inch is a real blessing when the particle-board sheet is ripped into countertops and shelving. Two full 24-in. pieces can be cut from the 49-in. width or four full 12-in. pieces. Particle-board sheets are manufactured in lengths of up to 16-ft. long and 5-ft. wide, which means less splicing. The real advantage of these oversized pieces is that they are billed at the standard sheet size. Thus a 49 in. × 97 in. sheet is billed at the 48 in. × 96 in. price. Thicknesses available vary from ³⁄₁₆ to 1⅛ in. A catalog listing of available sizes from a wholesale outlet is shown in Fig. 2–6.

Hardwood-Veneered Flake-Core Panels

Enjoying wide acceptance among today's cabinetmakers is hardwood veneer applied to flake board basically in the ½- and ¾-in. thicknesses. This product in the ¾-in.

Particleboard		Fiberboard	
Duraflake & Korpine (45 lb. density)		**Glacier edge—Medium density Fiberboard (MDF)**	
⅜	49 × 97 ......(4 × 8 billing)	³⁄₁₆	61 × 97 ......(5 × 8 billing)
⅜	49 × 121 ....(4 × 10 billing)	¼	49 × 97 ......(4 × 8 billing)
⅜	49 × 145 ....(4 × 12 billing)	⅜	49 × 97 ......(4 × 8 billing)
		⁷⁄₁₆	49 × 97 ......(4 × 8 billing)
½	49 × 97 ......(4 × 8 billing)	½	49 × 97 ......(4 × 8 billing)
½	49 × 121 ....(4 × 10 Billing)	⅝	49 × 97 ......(4 × 8 billing)
		¾	49 × 97 ......(4 × 8 billing)
⅝	49 × 97 ......(4 × 8 billing)	1	49 × 97 ......(4 × 8 billing)
¹¹⁄₁₆	49 × 97 ......(4 × 8 billing)	**Drawer sides & bottoms—(MDF) Direct print—Oak woodgrain**	
¾	23¼ × 145 .(24 × 144 billing)	½	4⅝ × 97 ....
	25 × 97	½	7½ × 97 ....
	25 × 121	½	9½ × 97 ....
	25 × 145	¼	24 × 97 ....
	30 × 97		
	30 × 121	**Shelving—(MDF) Direct print—Oak woodgrain**	
	30 × 145		
	36 × 97	34	11½ × 97 ....
	36 × 121	¾	11½ × 121 ....
	36 × 145		
	49 × 97 ......(4 × 8 billing)	**Korpine—Shelving (Bull-nosed)**	
	49 × 121 ....(4 × 10 billing)		
	49 × 145 ....(4 × 12 billing)	¾	11½ × 97 ....
	49 × 193 ....(4 × 16 billing)		11½ × 121 ....
			11½ × 145 ....
	60½ × 97 .....(5 × 8 billing)		
	60½ × 121 ...(5 × 10 billing)		
	60½ × 145 ...(5 × 12 billing)		
1″	49 × 97 ......(4 × 8 billing)		
	49 × 121 ....(4 × 10 billing)		
1⅛″	49 × 97 ......(4 × 8 billing)		
	49 × 121 ....(4 × 10 billing)		

Figure 2–6 Catalog listing of particle board and fiberboard.

thickness is widely used for cabinet doors by cost-conscious artisans. These panels are practically free from warpage and the flake-core edge when sanded smooth and stained is no more unattractive than either plywood or lumber core.

The main disadvantages seem to be the weight of flake-core panels and the inability of the product to take a knock or two without chipping and exposing a ragged, sawdust-interior-core material. Many discriminating cabinetmakers and their customers still insist on the use of either veneer-core or lumber-core plywood for their cabinet doors and drawer fronts.

Working with this product in any amount almost necessitates the use of carbide-tipped saw blades and router/shaper blades. The glue used in bonding the core materials has a rapid, dulling effect on ordinary woodworking blades.

ORDERING LUMBER, PLYWOOD, AND PARTICLE BOARD

The cabinetmaker should have a working knowledge of the "language" of the lumber and plywood supplier, so a common understanding will exist in doing business in these products.

Making Out a Hardwood Lumber Order

How is an order for lumber put together so the dealer understands the cabinetmaker's needs and misunderstanding is held to an absolute minimum? First, the cabinetmaker must decide what lumber specifications will be most economical. Can RW&Ls (random width and length) be used? Does the shop have a surfacer? If not, will the lumber be ordered surfaced to a specified thickness? Mill charges and "picking" charges will have to be paid if surfacing is required and specified widths and lengths are called for on the order. What grade of hardwood lumber has been determined to be adequate for the cabinets in mind? Finally, must the lumber be KD (kiln dried)? The answer to this question is yes, of course, as green lumber is *never* used in fine cabinetry. All of the above must be put together in an intelligible order conforming to the custom of the industry.

When the cabinetmaker's needs are best met by specified widths and lengths and the stock needs to be received surfaced, an order will look like this:

6 pcs. ¾ × 6 × 10 ft. No. 1 Comm. Red Oak—KD—S2S ¾ in.

The dealer is being told in logical sequence (1) the number of pieces and the thickness, width, and length of those pieces desired; (2) the grade of hardwood acceptable; (3) the species of hardwood being ordered; (4) that the lumber should be kiln dried; and (5) that the lumber should be surfaced to a thickness of ¾ in. If in the order above the description had read: 6 pcs. ¾ × 6 × 10 ft. No. 1 Comm. Red Oak—KD—S2S, the cabinetmaker would receive lumber planed to a thickness of $^{13}/_{16}$ in. rather than ¾ in., as $^{13}/_{16}$ in. is the standard actual dimension for 1 in.-thick hardwood S2S.

If, however, the job requires no particular widths and lengths, a typical order for about the same amount of lumber would look like this:

30 bd. ft. ¾ No. 1 Comm. Red Oak—RWL—S2S ¾ in.

The dealer is now being told that the cabinetmaker wants to purchase a number of red oak boards in various widths and lengths that total 30 bd. ft., wants the grade to be No. 1 Common, and that the boards should be planed to a thickness of ¾ in.

Ordering Softwood Lumber

The specifications in ordering softwood lumber are possibly not quite as demanding as for hardwood lumber. Usually, the cabinetmaker will simply go to a local lumber dealer to pick up what he or she requires in softwood—pine, for example. The dealer has these stocked in piles that are sorted by width, length, and grade. Let's say the cabinetmaker requires 8 pieces 1 × 8—12 ft. of No. 2 pine. The clerk at the yard is given this order, and the customer is directed to that portion of the yard where the pine 1 × 8—12 ft. long in No. 2 grade is piled. If it is permissible, some selecting can be done and the better boards picked as the lumber clerk fills the order for the eight pieces. In the local yard these boards are already S4S and accurately cut to length.

If the ordering must be done from a supplier out of town, the same type of information must be given the dealer as was done for the hardwood varieties. A typical order might look like this:

100 bd. ft. ¾ No. 2 Shop Ponderosa Pine—RWL—KD—S2S

Ordering Plywood and Particle Board

Ordering plywood calls for a complete and accurate description. A typical order for Douglas fir plywood might look like this:

12 pcs. ¼ in. 4 × 8 AD Int. Doug. Fir Ply

The sequence of descriptive items in the order is standard and should be followed closely. In this order the customer is (1) ordering 12 pieces, (2) of ¼-in. thickness, (3) in size 4 ft. × 8 ft. sheets, (4) of grade AD, (5) of interior-type glue, and (6) of Douglas fir plywood.

An order for hardwood plywood might look like this:

4 pcs. ¾ in. 4 × 8 A-2 Red Oak Ply (Rotary Cut)

An order for particle board would be of the same sequence:

8 pcs. ½ in. 49 × 121 Duraflake 45 lb.

How Plywood and Particle Board Are Priced

Rather than basing the price of plywood on so much per board foot as is done in the lumber industry, the plywood manufacturers simply charge by the *square foot*. Each species in its various thicknesses will have a different per square foot price. As an example, a 4 ft. × 8 ft. piece of plywood ¾ in. thick, grade A-2, in red oak in veneer core might be priced at $1.50 per square foot. A 4 ft. × 8 in. sheet of plywood contains 32 sq. ft. (length multiplied times width) and 32 sq. ft. × $1.50 = $48.00 plus any sales tax or delivery charge.

OTHER MATERIALS NEEDED FOR THE CABINET

Cabinet Hardware

An entire separate chapter is devoted to the hardware commonly used in the construction of cabinets for the home. However, at this point all that will be mentioned is the various hardware items that must be considered and ordered from a supplier for a cabinet job. Just as there are wholesalers in lumber and plywood that cater to cabinet shops of all sizes, there are, too, cabinet hardware wholesalers. The home craftsperson or weekend woodworker will probably buy most cabinet hardware from the local building supply outlet. But if the person's requirements are of any appreciable amount, some difficulty might be encountered. Say, for example, that 40 or 50 pairs of cabinet door hinges are required for the job at hand. This might be difficult for the local dealer to fill from stock on hand, but the dealer will probably be most happy to special order the quantities needed.

Drawer handles, pulls, knobs, door hinges, and so on, are seldom stocked in any quantity even by the professional shop because of the wide range of styles available from hardware manufacturers. These items are on display boards in the shop from which the customer can select the hardware of choice. This choice is then ordered in quite exact quantities from the wholesaler. This way costly, unused inventory is prevented from being built up that might take years to dispose of.

Hardware items included in the cabinet estimate

These items are typically those that would be included in the ordinary cabinet job:

Door hinges
Door pulls
Drawer pulls
Door catches (if self-closing hinges are not selected)
Adjustable shelf standard and clips (or other shelf support items)
Drawer runners (if metal manufactured runners are used)

Of these items only the shelf standard, clips, door catches, and a supply of drawer runners would ordinarily be stocked in any amount in the shop.

Other items of hardware that might or might not be found in stock in the professional's shop would be:

Speciality catches (bullet catch, elbow catch, magnetic catches, various "saber" catches)
Sliding towel bar
Glass (or panel) retainers
Supply of metal trim molding and cove for plastic laminate

Exact hardware needs should be determined from the scale drawing of the current cabinet job and the order placed early enough so that no delay is encountered when the job is ready to be installed. Inevitably, back orders and out-of-stock notices will be encountered and the customer might be required to select another choice of hardware.

Plastic-Laminate Countertop Material

Like the hardware a customer may choose, the countertop material, too, is very personal in nature and hence the cabinetshop does not attempt to stock plastic laminate. There are literally hundreds of patterns and colors available from several manufacturers in a variety of finishes. Samples of these patterns are furnished the cabinetshops assembled on a chain. Some common trade names are Formica, Wilson Art, and Consoweld (Fig. 2-7).

Standard sizes available

Much more will be said about plastic laminates in Chapter 11, but for estimating purposes the cabinetmaker must know the stock sizes available in the pattern selected and must carefully plan the cutting of the sheets of laminate to be certain enough is on hand to complete the entire countertop and backsplash. As with many of the other materials ordered for a cabinet job, if not used, the material just piles up in the shop as inventory that might be a long time in stock before a use is found for it. Figure 2-8 shows one manufacturer's list of available sizes.

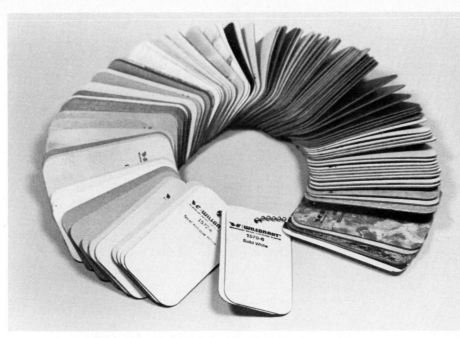

Figure 2-7 Sample chain of plastic-laminate patterns and finishes.

Grade 10—Standard material
(includes –949 white and –909 black)

24 × 48	30 × 48	36 × 48	48 × 48	
24 × 60	30 × 60	36 × 60	48 × 60	60 × 60
24 × 72	30 × 72	36 × 72	48 × 72	60 × 72
24 × 96	30 × 96	36 × 96	48 × 96	60 × 96
24 × 120	30 × 120	36 × 120	48 × 120	60 × 120
24 × 144	30 × 144	36 × 144	48 × 144	60 × 144

Figure 2-8 Range of available sizes of plastic-laminate sheets.

Contact cement for plastic laminate

Several gallons of contact cement will usually be stocked in the cabinet shop. Two types are available—nonflammable and flammable— and both are available in two grades—spray grade and brush grade—with solvents for each type. The average cabinetshop does not get into enough production to warrant spraying contact cement but usually brushes it or uses inexpensive throwaway rollers to apply this adhesive. Contact cement is usually available at the local builder's supply store and is available from wholesalers in containers of various sizes, from pints to 55-gallon drums.

Miscellaneous Supplies to Keep on Hand

Glue

Most cabinetmakers use the two familiar types of glue on the market for gluing wood—white or yellow wood glue. Both are excellent products and are available in sizes from the small squeeze bottle to a 5-gallon pail. Franklin's Titebond and Elmer's Professional Carpenter's Wood Glue are examples of the yellow aliphatic resin glue. These glues "grab" fast yet allow sufficient open time for positioning material. If the temperature in the work area is 60 degrees or warmer, usually one-half hour to an hour of clamp time is all that is required if no strain is to be placed on the glue joint for a time.

The white glues, such as Elmer's Glue-All or Franklin's Evertite, are still widely used and are somewhat less expensive than the yellow glues. Both varieties have excellent strength-of-joint qualities, are nonstaining, and clean up with water. Every effort should be made to clean the excess glue that is squeezed out of the joint. Even a thin film of glue allowed to remain and dry will present problems. If the glue spot is not completely removed, stain and finish when applied later will not penetrate the wood and a lighter spot will be noticeable that is very objectionable. Both types of glue should be kept from freezing.

There are several other types of glue that may be found in the cabinet shop. Some cabinetmakers still prefer to use plastic resin glue. This is a urea resin that is available in powder form and must be mixed with water just prior to its being used. This glue is highly water resistant but is not considered waterproof. The inconvenience of having to mix it, the rather long setting time, and the short pot life are reasons why this glue is not as popular as it once was.

If a waterproof glue is required, the resorcinal type is used. This comes in two parts—a liquid and a powder—that must be mixed prior to its being used. This glue is widely used for boat building and outdoor furniture but does not have much application in ordinary cabinet building.

Wood fillers

There are various products on the market that are used for filling dents, defects, and set nails. One of the most common is Plastic Wood, which is available in colors to match the most common cabinet woods. Other well-known fillers are Durotite and Famowood. Two or three small cans of this wood filler should be on hand in various colors: natural for filling pine, birch, beech, and other near-white woods; oak filler for fir, cherry, and oak; walnut and mahogany fillers for matching with those varieties. Techniques of applying and working with these fillers are discussed in detail in Chapter 5.

Sandpaper and sander belts

Sandpaper and sander belts have become increasingly expensive over the past few years and should be purchased carefully. If at all possible, both should be purchased from a wholesaler in standard packaged amounts to obtain the best buy.

For general sanding purposes, both hand sanding and for use in the finishing sander, aluminum oxide sandpaper in the stock size 9 in. × 11 in. in the "open coat" type fills the bill nicely. "Open coat" refers to the spread of the abrasive particles on the paper backing. Open coat (as opposed to "closed coat") has these particles spread rather thinly and hence is less inclined to fill up with resins from the wood being sanded. The 9 in. × 11 in. size can quickly be cut into the required size to fit the finishing sander.

Figure 2–9 illustrates the grits available. A supply of sandpaper in the 80A, 120A, 220A, and 320A grits will accomplish practically all sanding jobs. *A word of caution*—using the coarser grits, such as those coarser than 120A, in the finishing sander can result in "swirl" marks on the surface of the wood. These are a real aggravation and can require a lot of effort scraping and resanding to remove. Use of the finer grits will prevent this from happening.

Other sandpapers available are garnet and silicon carbide abrasives. Garnet is a reddish-brown mineral of medium hardness and is widely used for reconditioning surfaces before finishing. It is recommended for the removal of varnish, paper, or lacquer. Silicon carbide is a shiny, black mineral and is used widely on rubbing paper for producing fine finishes. Silicon carbide is bonded to its backing with a waterproof adhesive and can be used with water as a lubricant in rubbing out a finish. Figure 2–10 lists the grits available for silicon carbide rubbing paper.

For wood and metal sanding. It is our very best all-purpose abrasive for shop use. Open-coated with tough, hard aluminum oxide mineral.

Production paper "C and D" wt. All prices per sheet			Production paper "A" wt. All prices per sheet		
	Minimum package	Unit		Minimum Package	Unit
9 × 11	100	1000	9 × 11	100	1000
150C			320A		
120C			280A		
100C			240A		
			220A		
9 × 11	50	500	180A		
			150A		
80D			120A		
60D			100A		
50D					
40D			9 × 11	50	500
			80A		

Figure 2–9 Available grits for production paper.

	Minimum Package	Unit
9 × 11	50	500
600A		
500A		
400A		
320A		
280A		
220A		

Figure 2–10 Standard silicon carbide grits.

Production cloth belts (sander belts) are available in sizes to fit all standard portable belt sanders as well as in a variety of grits. The basic abrasive used on sander belts intended for wood is aluminum oxide. If available, open coat should be purchased. Figure 2–11 shows the grits and belt sizes available from a wholesale outlet as well as the standard packaging.

Because sander belts are becoming increasingly expensive, many cabinet shops make use of abrasive cleaner sticks to remove the resin and gums that plug a belt and slow its sanding action. Sometimes the life of a belt can be extended three and four times by using a belt cleaner.

Nails and brads

A good supply of various sizes and types of nails should be kept on hand. In finish nails sizes 4d and 6d will usually satisfy most requirements. A box or two of wire brads ¾ in. and 1 in. in length in 16 gauge should be stocked, as they will be used quite often. Box nails should be purchased with a resin coating (simply called "coated") in 4d, 6d, and 8d. A nail used in quite large amounts is the 1-in. wire

While the tough Aluminum Oxide mineral can penetrate metals, these belts are primarily intended for wood-working operations.

	Production cloth belts, closed coat All prices per belt					
	Minimum package	Unit		Minimum package	Unit
3 × 21	**10**	**50**	**4 × 27**	**10**	**50**
120×			120×		
100×			100×		
80×			80×		
60×			60×		
50×					
40×					
3 × 24	**10**	**50**	**4 × 37¹³⁄₁₆**	**10**	**50**
120×			120×		
100×			100×		
80×			80×		
60×			60×		
50×					
40×					
4 × 21¾	**10**	**50**	**6 × 48**	**10**	**20**
120×			120×		
100×			100×		
80×			80×		
60×			60×		
4 × 24	**10**	**50**			
120×					
100×					
80×					
60×					
50×					

Figure 2–11   Available belt sizes and grits for sander belts.

nail. This nail used to be available as a 2d coated box nail but is very difficult to purchase today. The cabinetmaker will probably have to be contented with buying the small boxes of 1-in. wire nails available at the local hardware store. The 1-in. size is especially handy when nailing plywood to a ¾-in. softwood reinforcing piece, as it does not extend beyond the combined thickness of the two woods.

Air staplers and nailers

Many cabinet shops, even the small one-person establishments, use air-powered staplers and nailers. A small compressor is all that is required to operate this tool and the staples can be purchased in a wide variety of lengths. The air stapler is fast, efficient, and economical and has many applications in cabinet construction.

Screws

Flathead wood screws are used extensively, especially in the casework system of cabinet building. Sizes to purchase are the 1¼-, 1½-, 2½-, and 3-in. lengths in the No. 8 size. For greatest economy these screws should be purchased by the box of 100 rather than in the small packets available in most stores.

DETERMINING THE AMOUNT OF MATERIAL FOR A CABINET JOB

Large cabinet concerns have specialty people who prepare plans and bills of materials, and estimate costs. In the small shop, however, all of these jobs fall on the proprietor, who often must do them in the evening after a full day of working in the shop. An accurate estimate of the material that a job requires is important for two reasons. First, if the material is ordered by the job, it is necessary to determine quite closely the amount to order from the supplier. If the material is ordered from a supplier out of town, enough must be ordered to satisfy the job requirements. Reordering is to be avoided because of the duplication of freight charges (or travel time if trucking one's own orders) and the delay caused by material shortages. Second, the material list provides an accurate record of the amount of material that is to be charged to a particular job. This record becomes more and more valuable as a basis for easily estimating future jobs and determining a margin of profit.

The goal in material estimating is to order enough to cover waste and possible errors but not enough over to have a lot of unused material on inventory. If the business is of a size that an inventory is carried of stock material—plywood, particle board, hardwood lumber, and so on—then overages in ordering are not as crucial, but accurate stock billing should still be done to ensure that proper job charges are made.

Developing and Using a Material Estimating Form

Rather than attempting to rely on memory, it is good business practice to develop a stock billing form that covers all the items that go into the custom cabinet job. It is extremely easy to forget items that can throw an estimate or bid off by many dollars. Use of some kind of a form developed by the cabinetmaker will at least hold this type of error to a minimum.

One acceptable and accurate means of stock billing is by type of material. The estimator using this system determines all the pieces that are required of a particular material throughout the entire cabinet job. If it is ¾-in. plywood, for example, that is being estimated for cabinet doors, the required number of square feet are estimated. The square feet are then converted to full 4 ft. × 8 ft. sheets of plywood and the total cost of that item is determined. The same is done for each and every separate item throughout the job. Figures 2–12 and 2–13 are an example of an estimate form developed for the casework system. Naturally, a different system of cabinet construction would call for different items that would be unique to the system being used.

Using the form to estimate plywood and particle board

Again the importance of the accurately scale drawn plan of the cabinets comes into play. To estimate the quantities of ¾-in. A-2 plywood in the species of the customer's choice, use the architect's scale (ruler) to measure the approximate sizes of the doors. In the case of the base cabinet which has both doors and drawers, simply figure plywood over the entire front surface. If, for example, the base cabinet is 8′–6″ long, multiply this length times 3′–0″ (the height of the cabinet) for a total of 25½ sq. ft. This method allows for some waste and cutting problems. Do the same for

CABINET MATERIAL ESTIMATE

Customer _____ Price _____   Delivery date _____

¾" Hardwood Plywood A-2, (Species _____)

	Sq. feet.	
Cabinet doors	_____	
Drawer fronts	_____	(4′ × 8′ sheets _____)
_____	_____	
Total	_____	× $ _____ per sq. ft. = $ _____

¼" Hardwood Plywood, A–3

	Sq. feet.	
Finish end panels	_____	
Cab't/ door panels	_____	(4′ × 8′ sheets _____)
Overlays	_____	
_____	_____	
Total	_____	× $ _____ per sq. ft. = $ _____

¼" Softwood Plywood

Base cab't. backs	_____	
Upper cab't. backs	_____	
Wall ends	_____	
Upper cab't. tops	_____	
Drawer bottoms	_____	
Base cab't. bottom	_____	(4′ × 8′ sheets _____)
_____	_____	
Total	_____	× $ _____ per sq. ft. = $ _____

½" Softwood Plywood (or particle board)

Drawer sides and backs	_____	
Interior partitions	_____	
Sliding shelves & sides	_____	(4′ × 8′ sheets _____)
_____	_____	
Total	_____	× $ _____ per sq. ft. = $ _____

¾" Particle Board

Counter tops	_____	
Adjustable shelves	_____	
Upper cab't/ bottoms	_____	
Sink comp. side shelves	_____	(4′ × 8′ sheets _____)
_____	_____	
Total	_____	× $ _____ per sq. ft. = $ _____

Plastic Laminate

Counter tops	_____	
Back splash	_____	
Drawer liner	_____	(size to order _____)
_____	_____	
Total	_____	× $ _____ per sq. ft. = $ _____

¾" Hardwood Lumber (Species _____)

Face frames _____	_____	
Toe space boards	_____	
Paneled door frames	_____	
Raised door panels	_____	
Valance boards	_____	
Shelf facing strips	_____	
Drawer cap strips	_____	
Sliding shelf runners	_____	
Total	_____	× $ _____ per bd. ft. = $ _____

Figure 2–12 Cabinet material estimate forms.

Sq. feet.

1" Softwood Lumber
  Base cabinets:
    Bottom supports   _____
    Drawer runners   _____
    Cross-braces   _____
    Panel reinforcing   _____
      (ends and backs)
    Shelf cleats   _____
_____   _____

  Upper cab't.
    Back reinforcing   _____
    Panel reinforcing   _____
_____

Total   _____   × $ _____ per bd. ft. = $ _____

Hardware
  Hinges   _____ Pairs @ $ _____ per pair = $ _____
  Door pulls   _____ @ $ _____ each = $ _____
  Drawer pulls   _____ @ $ _____ each = $ _____
  Door catches   _____ @ $ _____ each = $ _____
  Adjustable shelf track   _____ feet @ $ _____ per ft. = $ _____
  Shelf support clips   _____ @ $ _____ each = $ _____
  Metal drawer runners   _____ pairs @ $ _____ per pair = $ _____
  Towel bar   _____ @ $ _____ each = $ _____
_____   _____ @ $ _____ = $ _____
_____   _____ @ $ _____ = $ _____
                          Hardware total $ _____

Miscellaneous Supply Allowance
  Glue
  Sandpaper
  Sander belts
  Nails
  Screws
  Contact Cement
_____
_____

                             Total supply allowance $ _____
                             Est. freight & handling $ _____
                                    GRAND TOTAL $ _____

Figure 2-13   Page 2 of the cabinet estimate form.

the upper cabinet door openings using the dimensions to the closest half-foot. For example, if an upper cabinet opening measures 26 in. × 29½ in. figure the plywood at 2½ ft. × 2½ ft. When the total number of square feet of A-2 plywood has been calculated, enter this figure on the estimate forms and calculate the cost. Convert the square feet to standard sheets of plywood for the actual order that will go to the supplier. Interior partitions, end panels, backs, and so on, are all quite standard in size and can be estimated quickly and easily.

Estimating hardwood and softwood lumber quantities

Here the cabinetmaker must bear in mind the lesson learned about nominal and actual lumber sizes. Remember, a piece of face framing that must be ¾ in. × 2 in. × 96 in. *must be calculated as a 1 in. × 3"-8'.* Carefully take from the scale drawing the actual sizes of the pieces that are used in the face frames. Some of these will be quite small such as ¾ in. × 1½ in. × 14 in. If a number of these small pieces are the same, lump them together and calculate as one longer piece. As an example, if the face frame contains 4 pieces ¾ in. × 1¼ × 12 in., figure this as one piece 1 in. × 2 in. × 4′–0″ or ⅔ bd. ft.

After calculating the approximate number of board feet of hardwood lumber, a percentage must be added for waste depending on the grade being ordered. In the case of No. 1 Common about 25 to 30% should be added.

If just a small quantity of hardwood is to be ordered (less than 100 bd. ft.), probably the best strategy is to order specified widths and lengths. This way the cabinetmaker will be certain the necessary lengths can be ripped from the material ordered. If the cabinet job requires a couple of fairly large pieces of clear lumber—toe space boards and a valance board—the order should contain a couple of boards in the Select grade.

Pricing the material estimate

Prices on lumber, plywood, and other cabinet material can fluctuate tremendously and it is necessary for the cabinetmaker always to keep an up-to-date price list. Many wholesalers of plywood do not list current prices of softwood plywood but instruct the customer to call for the latest price. One other item of extreme importance that must be figured in the total cost is the freight charge. Freight charges can often amount to more than 10% of the cost of the merchandise, so it is a cost of doing business that must be reckoned with. Even if the cabinetmaker is doing his or her own hauling, time and cost of gasoline should be figured into the price of the material.

REVIEW QUESTIONS

2.1. What are the two main cost items that the cabinetmaker must try to estimate in determining the cost of a cabinet?

2.2. Describe a board foot of lumber.

2.3. What is the cost of 6 pieces of 1 in. × 8 in. × 10 ft. of No. 1 Common red oak at $1.65 per board foot?

2.4. What is the cost of three 4 ft. × 8 ft. sheets of Douglas fir plywood in the ¼-in. thickness at 47 cents per square foot?

2.5. What are the actual dimensions of a piece of walnut lumber 1 in. × 8 in. S4S?

2.6. What are the actual dimensions of a standard softwood 2 × 4?

2.7. What grade of hardwood is usually the most economical for the cabinetmaker to purchase for face-frame construction?

2.8. List these items for a lumber order in their proper sequence: RWL—S2S; walnut; 100 bd. ft.; No. 1 Common; KD.

2.9. In the order in Review Question 2.8, what will be the thickness of the lumber received?

2.10. Particle board used for cabinetry should be of what density?

2.11. What is the danger in using a coarse grit in the finishing sander?

2.12. In estimating the amount of material that goes into a cabinet job, what is the cabinetmaker's goal insofar as quantities are concerned?

SUGGESTED CLASS ACTIVITIES AND STUDENT ASSIGNMENTS

2.1. Using the scale drawing prepared as an exercise for Chapter 1, estimate the number of board feet of hardwood lumber that should be ordered for all face framing, toe space boards, valance boards, and edge banding for the shelves.

2.2. After determining the system of building cabinets that will be used, develop a material estimating form similar to that illustrated in Figs. 2–12 and 2–13.

2.3. Arrange a class visit to the nearest wholesale lumber dealer that sells to cabinet shops in the area. Ask the dealer to discuss and illustrate grades of hardwood and softwood lumber, and arrange to see their plywood, particle board, and specialty cabinet items. Tour their planing mill if they have one.

2.4. Have the members of the class determine and list the wholesale cabinet hardware dealers, plastic-laminate dealers, and wholesale lumber and specialty dealers that serve the immediate area.

2.5. Have the class gather current prices on all the items listed on their cabinet estimate form as prepared in Activity 2.2. Have each student prepare a well-organized price book that is to be kept current and up to date.

3

The Cabinetmaker's Tools and Equipment

Whether the woodworker is a beginner or an aspiring professional, the cabinet shop must have some very basic tools and equipment. The purchase of these items should be made carefully and quality should be an uppermost consideration for they will be expected to serve for possibly a lifetime. The old adage "A workman is no better than his tools" is as true today as it was several generations ago. Good craftspeople purchase their tools with care and take excellent care of their tools.

THE BASIC SET OF HAND TOOLS AND SMALL EQUIPMENT

A good and complete set of hand tools is a basic necessity for anyone even considering the building of a set of cabinets. Although the period we live in is considered the machine age, the cabinetmaker must still rely on hand tools for many of the everyday woodworking chores. The craftsperson seems to be constantly adding to his or her collection of tools as new and better products come on the market. The question often asked, however, is: "What do I really need to get started?" The list of tools that follows is classified by function and will provide a good basis on which to build.

Smoothing and Scraping Tools (Fig. 3-1)

Planes

Although the power jointer is thought of as the basic wood-smoothing machine, there are many times that the only tool that will do the job is the hand plane. Every shop should have at least two planes:

9-in. smoothing plane (either smooth or corrugated bottom) or 14-in. jack plane (either smooth or corrugated bottom)
6-in. block plane with adjustable cutter

Files and rasps

Several wood files and rasps should be in the cabinetmaker's toolbox. Several metal files as well come in for considerable use in sharpening saw blades, scraper blades, and so on. Some consideration might also be given to purchasing the new Surform tools, which are quite popular

Wood files: 1 each flat and half-round
1 round (or rat-tail) wood file

Note: Some manufacturers have discontinued making "wood" files because they are too closely related to the regular half-round, round, and flat metal files. They recommend the metal file for use on wood as well as metal.

Wood rasps: used for more rapid removal of material and have a coarser cutting action.
1 each half-round, flat, and round cabinet rasp in the 10-in. length

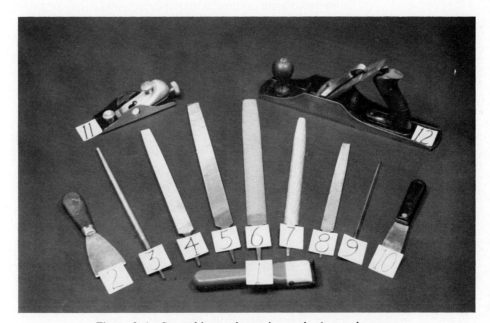

Figure 3-1 Smoothing and scraping tools: 1, wood scraper; 2, 2-in. blade scraper; 3, rat-tail or round file; 4, wood file; 5, 10-in. mill file; 6, half-round wood rasp; 7, half-round wood file; 8, 8-in. bastard mill file; 9, 7-in. slim taper file; 10, 1¼-in. putty knife; 11, 6-in. block plane; 12, 14-in. jack plane.

Saw Files, mill and tapor (triangular): The mill file is used for sharpening circular saws, drawfiling, and finishing metal. The triangular file is used to sharpen all types of saws with 60-degree-angle teeth.

    1 bastard mill file, 8-in.
    1 extra-slim-taper saw file, 7-in.
    1 extra-slim-taper saw file, 5-in.

Wood scrapers

One of the handiest tools in the toolbox when it comes to scraping off dried glue or wood filler, and for the removal of scratches and minor blemishes on the wood surface. They are easily sharpened with a file and replacement blades may be purchased for most makes. The Red Devil flip-over wood scraper works fine for either coarse or fine work.

    1 wood scraper, 1½-in. blade

Putty knives

This versatile little tool can be used to apply wood fillers, glaze a window, as a scraper, and for other chores around the shop.

    1 1⅛-in. common putty knife

    1 1¼-in. stiff-blade putty knife

Drilling Tools and Accessories (Fig. 3–2)

Although the portable electric drill with its wide array of accessories has practically replaced hand drilling tools, the cabinetmaker might still want to consider purchasing some of the tools listed in this section. The possibility still exists that work might have to be done where no electricity is available. A brace and set of bits could be indispensible in such a situation. However, the brace-and-bit often languishes on the tool rack for months and months without ever being put into action. For this reason, the purchase of these items might well be postponed for some time.

    1 ratchet brace with 10-in. sweep
    1 set auger bits, ¼ through 1 in. in 1/16-in. increments
    1 expansive bit, 7/8 to 3 in.
    1 screwdriver, bit size No. 5 5/16-in. tip

Clamping and Holding Tools (Fig. 3–3)

A few clamps are never enough! It is a good idea to purchase a few to begin with and then add clamps as the pressure of the jobs demands.

    6 C-clamps, 6 in. size
    6 C-clamps, 4 in. size
    2 bar clamps, 2 ft. long
    2 bar clamps, 4 ft. long
    2 pairs Pony pipe clamp fixtures (these are used with ordinary ¾-in. pipe as the bar; pipe can be screwed together to provide clamps of almost unlimited length)

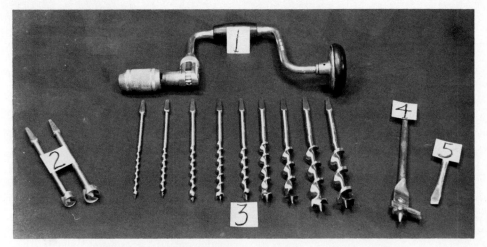

Figure 3–2 Drilling tools and accessories: 1, 10-in. ratchet brace; 2, forstner bits; 3, auger bits ¼ to 1-in; 4, expansive bit ⅞ to 3-in.; 5, screwdriver bit.

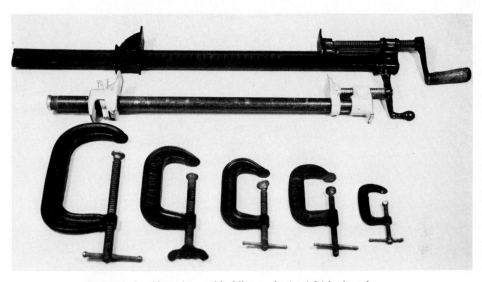

Figure 3–3 Clamping and holding tools: (top) 24-in. bar clamp; (center) pipe clamp; (bottom) assorted C-clamps.

Measuring, Squaring, and Leveling Tools (Fig. 3–4)

These tools are among the most used in the cabinetmaker's shop:

1 power return measuring tape, ¾-in.-wide blade, 10 or 12 ft. long

1 steel square, 24-in. body, 16-in tongue (purchase the less expensive type that does not have the carpenter's framing scales)

1 combination square with 12-in. removable blade

1 try square with 8-in. blade

1 sliding T-bevel with 8-in. blade

1 24- or 48-in. level with two levels and two plumbs

1 torpedo level, 9 in.

1 wing divider, 8 in.

1 pencil compass

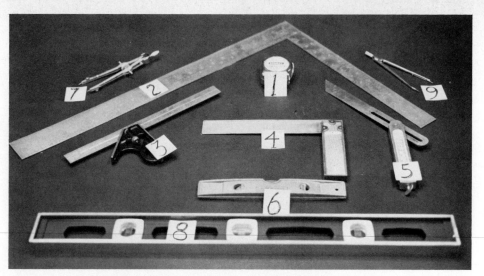

Figure 3-4 Measuring, leveling, and squaring tools: 1, 10-in. or 12-in. steel tape; 2, 24-in. × 16-in. carpenter's square; 3, combination square; 4, try square; 5, sliding T-bevel; 6, torpedo level; 7, compass; 8, 24-in. level; 9, dividers.

Hammers and Screwdrivers (Fig. 3-5)

As with most tools on the market today, there are high-quality ones and ones of much less quality. At least a couple of hammers should be in the toolbox as well as a wide assortment of screwdrivers. Spend just a bit more on these, use them correctly, and they will give a lifetime of service.

1 claw hammer, 13 or 16 oz.

1 claw hammer, 7 or 8 oz.

(the 7 or 8 oz. hammer is especially handy for cabinetwork for pounding small finish nails, brads, and so on, where hitting one's fingers is a problem)

1 rubber mallet, 13 oz.

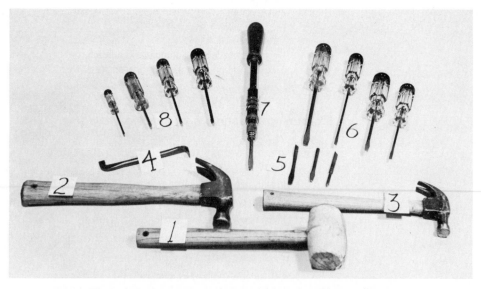

Figure 3-5 Hammers and screwdrivers: 1, rubber mallet; 2, 13-oz claw hammer; 3, 7-oz claw hammer; 4, offset screwdriver; 5, ratchet screwdriver bits; 6, assorted regular screwdrivers; 7, auto-return ratchet screwdriver; 8, assorted Phillips head screwdrivers.

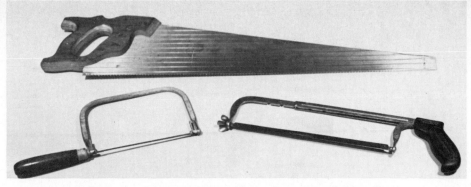

Figure 3–6 Hand saws: (top) 10-pt crosscut saw; (left) coping saw; (right) hacksaw.

Figure 3–7 Miter boxes: 1 and 2, commercial miter boxes; 3, shop-made miter box.

1 spiral spring-return ratchet screwdriver, large size about 25 in. or so extended (purchase with assorted driver bits with both standard and Phillips heads; Yankee makes one about this size)

Assorted hand screwdrivers in both standard and Phillips head from the 2-in. "stubby" to the 10-in. size

1 offset screwdriver in standard and Phillips heads

Sawing, Cutting, and Ripping Tools (Fig. 3–6)

The list of tools in this category is quite lengthy and covers several types of hand tools.

Saws

The hand saw is still used considerably in the day-to-day work of a cabinet-maker. The purchase of one good wood-cutting handsaw is usually sufficient. This should be the crosscut type, as a hand ripsaw is so seldom used that its purchase is not called for.

1 crosscut saw, 10 point (10 teeth per inch)

1 hacksaw (adjustable for 8- to 12-in. blade)

1 coping saw with about a 6-in. throat

1 miter box (this can be as simple as a hardwood box type on up to the more expensive automatic metal type) (Fig. 3–7)

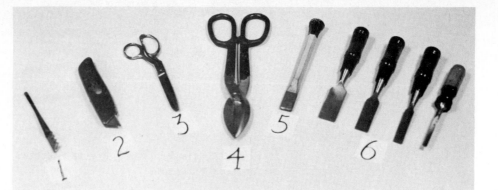

Figure 3–8 Cutting tools: 1, glass cutter; 2, utility knife; 3, scissors; 4, tin snips; 5, cold chisel; 6, assorted wood chisels ¼ to 1-in.

Cutting tools (Fig. 3–8)

1 set wood chisels, ¼, ½, ¾, 1, and 1¼ in.
1 utility knife
1 cold chisel, ½ in.
1 tin snips 10 in.
1 pair straight shears, 8 in.
1 glass cutter

Ripping tools (Fig. 3–9)

1 ripping bar, ½ in. × 12 in.
1 pry bar, Wonder Bar

Safety Equipment for the Shop (Fig. 3–10)

Perhaps nothing is more important but more overlooked than some of the more common safety items for the shop. These need not be elaborate but should be on hand and *used* as safe practice demands.

1 first-aid kit
1 pair Safety glasses and/or goggles
1 face shield, 8 in., clear type
1 fire extinguisher, foam and/or CO_2 type

Miscellaneous Tools and Equipment

Miscellaneous tools

Pliers, nippers, and wrenches

These should be availabe in assorted sizes and types.

1 combination plier, slip joint, 8 in.
1 long-nose plier, side cutting, 6 in.
1 cutting nipper, 7 in.
1 pair utility pliers, 10 in. Rib Joint
1 adjustable wrench, 8 in.
1 Vise-Grip wrench, 7 in.
   (Fig. 3–11)

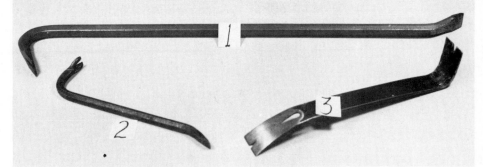

Figure 3–9 Ripping tools: 1, ripping bar ¾-in. × 24-in.; 2, ripping bar ½-in. × 12-in.; 3, pry bar (wonder bar).

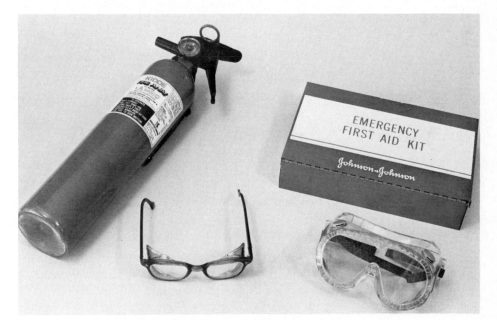

Figure 3–10 Safety equipment: *(left to right)* fire extinguisher; safety glasses; first-aid kit; safety goggles.

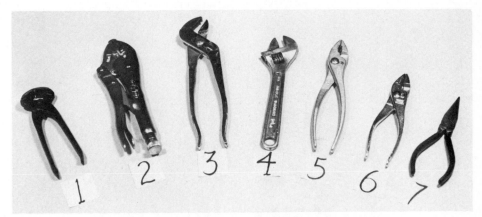

Figure 3–11 Pliers, nippers, and wrenches: 1, end cutting nipper; 2, vise Grip wrench; 3, slip-joint pliers; 4, 8-in. adjustable wrench; 5, 8-in. combination pliers; 6, 6-in. combination pliers; 7, long-nose side cutting pliers.

Figure 3–12 Miscellaneous tools: 1, set Allen wrenches; 2, $\frac{2}{32}$-in. and $\frac{3}{32}$-in. nail sets; 3, wire brush; 4, combination bench sharpening stone; 5, oil can.

Other tools

1 combination bench sharpening stone with oil and oil can

1 set Allen wrenches, $\frac{5}{64}$ to $\frac{1}{4}$ in.

2 nail sets, $\frac{2}{32}$ in. and $\frac{3}{32}$ in.

1 nail puller

1 wire brush

   (Fig. 3–12)

Miscellaneous Equipment

Sawhorses

At least two sawhorses 30 in. high should be available in the shop and prefer-ably four. Two horses 23¼ in. high are also very handy at certain stages of cabinet construction. Although these need not be elaborate in construction, they should be sturdy and stable. Figure 3–13 presents a working drawing of a simple but very service-able sawhorse.

Sawhorses are used to support work at a convenient working height and when used with either several 2 × 4's or 2 × 6's about 8 ft. long makes a very handy work-ing and support surface upon which upper cabinets can be built.

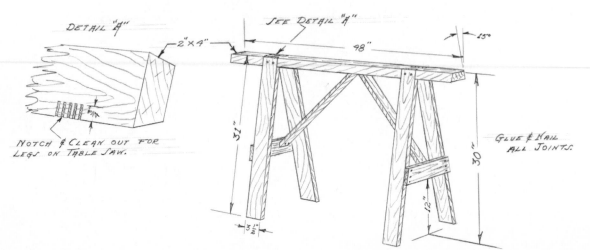

Figure 3–13 Sawhorse for cabinet shop.

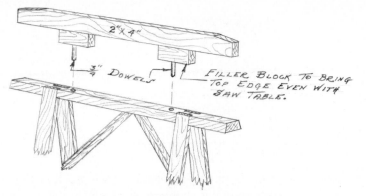

Figure 3-14 Table saw work support.

Another convenient use for sawhorses is to support boards and plywood sheets that are being ripped on the table saw. A simple height-extension devise is illustrated in Fig. 3–14. This should be carefully built so that the combined height of the sawhorse and the extension exactly matches the height of the table saw.

Other equipment

At least a couple of serviceable extension cords are needed in the shop and certainly will be used extensively when the cabinetmaker installs the cabinets in the home. Another item that will be needed is a 6-ft. step ladder. This, too, will come into use during the cabinet installation work.

Plastic-laminate tools

There are a number of specialty tools available for working with plastic laminate. These are discussed in Chapter 11, which is devoted exclusively to installing this material.

Workbench and vise

A good, sturdily built workbench is an asset to any shop. It should be of solid construction and be equipped with a high-quality woodworking vise with at least 4 in. × 7 in. jaws. The rapid-action device is a handy feature for this vise to have and the jaws should be cushioned with pieces of hardwood. Besides the storage that can be built into a workbench, the surface area of the top is one of the handiest work areas available in the cabinet shop (Fig. 3–15).

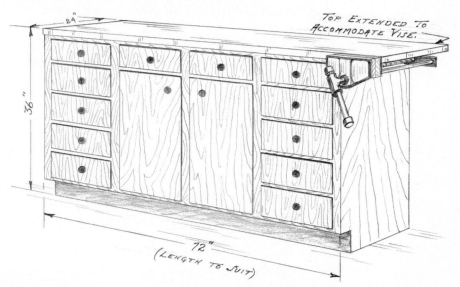

Figure 3-15 Work/storage bench.

Lighting for the shop

The cabinet shop should have plenty of light available at all times. Besides being a real safety feature, good lighting contributes to high-quality workmanship as well as providing a pleasant working atmosphere. With inexpensive two-bulb fluorescent shop lights available at very reasonable prices, there is really no reason why a shop should be anything but well lighted.

PORTABLE ELECTRIC TOOLS FOR THE CABINET SHOP

The beginning cabinetmaker will no doubt have to rely on a number of less expensive portable electric power tools. Initial outlay for equipment will be much less and as business improves, more sophisticated production machinery can be added to the shop. These electric tools range from the least expensive "do-it-yourself" quality available at discount stores to the higher-quality "industrial" grade designed for years of hard use by professionals. Purchasers will have to decide what price range and type will best meet their needs.

Electric Drill

This tool is probably the most used in the cabinet shop and comes in what seems to be a bewildering array of selections. First, the electric drill is categorized by the capacity of the chuck. For example, a ¼-in drill will be able to handle drills up to ¼ in. in diameter, while a ⅜- or ½-in. size can handle drills of those diameters. Second, electric drills are sold in either single-speed or variable-speed types, and many of the variable-speed models have a reversing feature. Third, the electric drill is designated by the speed of the drill and the amperage of the motor. Speed ranges from 0 to 2500 rpm on some variable-speed models and amperage from 2 to 3.2 amperes on the more powerful types. The "do-it-yourselfer" or occasional cabinet builder will be satisfied with a discount-store ¼- or ⅜-in. electric drill in the single speed. High-speed drills are available in larger sizes with ¼-in. shanks, so the ¼-in. chuck is really no handicap. The professional will, no doubt, want to spend a bit more and obtain an electric drill that will last a good long time under constant use.

Electric drill accessories

What makes the electric drill so versatile is that with the many accessories available, the drill seems to be in constant use. These are accessories that should be in the cabinetmaker's tool inventory:

> 1 countersink, ¼-in. shank, 82-degree angle
> 1 set countersink bits (available in various sizes to accommodate different-size wood screws)
> 1 set high-speed drills, ¹⁄₁₆ through ¼ in. by 64ths
> 1 set Spade-type bits, ⅜ through 1 in. by ¹⁄₁₆ths (available up to 1½ in. size)
> 1 or 2 small rubber sanding drums in different sizes
> 1 set assorted-size hole saws (Fig. 3–16)

Some other accessories that the cabinetmaker might want to purchase are:

> Doweling jig
> Screw and nut driver
> Assortment of masonry drills
> Electric drill guide (a unique accessory that assures accurate 90-degree holes)

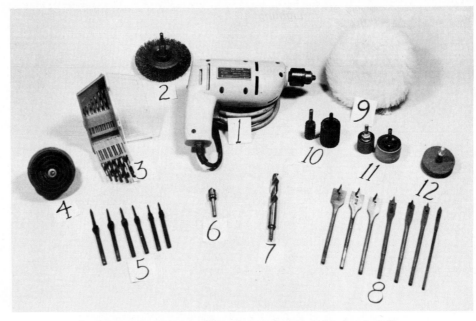

Figure 3–16 Electric drill and accessores: 1, ¼-in. electric drill; 2, wire brush; 3, assorted bits ¹⁄₁₆ to ¼-in.; 4, hole saws; 5, assorted countersink bits; 6, ½-in. rose-type countersink; 7, ½-in. drill with ¼-in. shank; 8, power bit set ¼ to 1-in.; 9, lamb's-wool polisher; 10, assorted wood rasps; 11, assorted sanders; 12, grinding wheel with ¼-in. shank.

Portable Jigsaw (Saber Saw or Bayonet Saw)

Every shop must have a machine for cutting curves in wood. Even if the shop is equipped with a bandsaw, a portable jigsaw is indispensable when cutting curves in large pieces of plywood, for making sink cutouts in countertops, and a thousand and one other jobs around the cabinet shop and out on the job. These, too, are available in a very wide range of quality and price. Because this tool is used so much and in a variety of wood thicknesses, it might be well to spend a bit more money and purchase one of the higher-quality machines. The higher-quality jigsaw will cut much faster through thicker material than will its less expensive counterpart (Fig. 3–17).

Figure 3–17 Portable electric tools: *(left)* portable circle saw; *(center)* router; *(right)* portable jigsaw (saber saw).

Figure 3–18   *(left)* finish sander; *(right)* portable belt sander.

Finishing Sander

Two sanders should be available in the cabinet shop: the finishing sander and the portable belt sander (Fig. 3–18). However, this requires a considerable outlay of money and the "do-it-yourselfer" might have to make a choice. A beginning professional would definitely want both. If a choice must be made, the finishing sander would be the one to purchase first. Although this recommendation might cause some minor debate, these reasons would seem to indicate that the finishing sander be the first choice. First, the belt sander is used primarily to give the cabinet face frames their initial sanding. This job *can* be done with a finishing sander—admittedly much slower and if the joints are poorly made, a hand plane might be required to do some leveling off. Second, much more finish sanding than belt sanding is done on a cabinet job. The belt sander cannot be substituted for this finish sanding; thus the finishing sander will be in use many more hours.

Discount stores carry inexpensive finishing sanders, but these would not stand up to day-by-day production work. Some of the more expensive machines sand at a speed of 10,000 orbits per minute and do an excellent job under heavy use. Most finishing sanders operate with an orbital (circular) sanding action of the pad, although at least one sander on the market switches from orbital to straight-line sanding. The larger production models take sandpaper in the $4\frac{1}{2}$ in. $\times$ 11 in. size (one-half a standard sheet), while the less expensive sanders have a smaller sanding surface and take one-third of a regular sandpaper sheet or $3\frac{5}{8}$ in. $\times$ 9 in. There is also a small sander available that takes only a $4\frac{1}{2}$ in. $\times$ $5\frac{1}{2}$ in. paper size.

Portable Belt Sander

The serious woodworker soon invests in a portable belt sander, as it is the only machine in the small shop that will efficiently remove machining marks or "planer waves" left by the jointer and the surfacer. Available in a variety of sizes, the belt sander does a rapid job of surface and edge sanding. The belt sander's size is determined by the width and length of the belt the machine will accommodate. The more common belt sanders come in sizes from 3 in. × 21 in. up to 4 in. × 24 in. One of the most popular and commonly used sanders in the small cabinet shop is the 3 in. × 24 in. size. A good heavy-duty, portable belt sander is getting to be a good-sized investment. There are sanders on the market in the 3 in. × 24 in. size, however, that are moderately priced, so even the nonprofessional can afford this machine.

Many of the sanders on the market come equipped with a dust-catching bag. Although this feature is desirable insofar as dust control is concerned, the bag often seems to be in the way and is an awkward accessory. Again, the purchaser will have to decide whether the dust-collecting bag is a desirable feature.

The most extensive application of the belt sander in the cabinet shop is for sanding the face frames of the cabinet. The technique for this operation is discussed in detail in Chapter 5. Belt grits and sizes are listed in Chapter 2.

Router

In the beginning cabinetmaker's shop the router will be put to extensive use. Although the professional will continue to use the router, many of its operations will be replaced by the spindle shaper. Until the time arrives, however, that a shaper is a practical purchase for the growing cabinet shop, the router will be depended on to perform a number of operations. Among these are edge shaping of cabinet doors as well as cutting the $\frac{3}{8}$ in. × $\frac{3}{8}$ in. lip, easing (rounding) the edge of drawer sides and shelves, and trimming plastic laminate (although there are special laminate trimmers on the market for this). These are just a few of the many, many jobs that can be accomplished with the router (Fig. 3-17).

A seemingly unlimited variety of router bits is available in both carbide-tipped and high-speed steel. No attempt will be made to list or picture this range of router cutters, as these are available at builder's supply stores, mail-order firms, and even discount stores.

Routers are designated by the horsepower the machine generates. A router listed as a "hobby" type has a horsepower rating of $\frac{1}{2}$ hp. The range in ratings continues upward—$\frac{3}{4}$, 1, $1\frac{1}{2}$, up to $3\frac{1}{2}$ hp. Where production routing is required, overhead stationary routing machines are brought into use. Speed is also an item of importance in selecting a portable router, with most generating no-load speeds of over 20,000 rpm, thus assuring a smooth cut. Routers in the midrange of horsepower—1 to $1\frac{1}{2}$ hp—would seem to meet the needs of most small cabinet shop operators.

Many accessories are available that increase the versatility of the router. Often a table is purchased (or built by the cabinetmaker) that will convert the router into a small shaper. The router is mounted upside down under the table and the work is moved rather than the router. This is very handy when edging cabinet doors and the like. Dovetail fixtures are commonly used with the router to produce the fine-looking drawer joints that appear on high-quality furniture. Complete template sets are available that are used to mortise door edges and jambs for butt hinges. One accessory that is widely used in cabinet shops makes possible the routing of cabinet doors with a decorative veining in a colonial (or other) pattern. These are just a few of the many accessories that make the router a highly used machine in the cabinet shop.

Portable Circular Saw

This is another portable machine whose purchase might be postponed, but chances are that the cabinetmaker will want one, for the circular saw performs any number of jobs in the shop (Fig. 3-17). If the table saw is the only saw in the shop and must be used for cutoff work, the portable circular saw is especially handy for rough-cutting stock to length, and then finish cutting is done on the table saw. It is quite awkward to have to attempt to cut 10- or 12-ft-long boards into specific lengths on the table saw even with the use of "outrigger" supports. This is one reason why many cabinet shops are equipped with a radial arm saw as soon as is economically possible. Cutting large sheets of plywood into specified pieces is often accomplished with the use of the circular saw. Plastic laminate is also cut to rough size using this machine.

Circular saws are classified by the size of the saw blade they will accomodate—usually 5½ to 7¼ in.—as well as their horsepower. Horsepower ratings range from ¾ hp to over 2 hp. A carpenter would pick one of the heavier-duty models because of the everyday use of the circular saw. The cabinetmaker can get by with one of the less expensive models on the market or even the type on sale at a discount store. Like any tool, if the blade is kept well set and sharpened so that the motor is not overworked, it will give many years of satisfactory service.

Bench Grinder

Although not classified as a portable machine, the bench grinder is quite small and certainly is a necessity in the shop (Fig. 3-19). The bench grinder is needed to sharpen plane irons, chisels, drill bits, hook scrapers, and for many other jobs. This machine need not be expensive and can be purchased quite economically from any of the leading mail-order houses or discount stores. Accessories are available for using the grinder for buffing and polishing, and special wheels are now being sold that enable the craftsperson to sharpen carbide-tipped tools.

Figure 3-19 Bench grinder. (Courtesy Delta International Machinery Corp.)

Figure 3-20 Motorized miter box. (Courtesy Delta International Machinery Corp.)

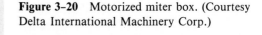

Motorized Miter Box

One of the handiest machines in the shop, and one that can be taken on the job site, is the motorized miter box. This machine is basically a cutoff saw that can handle pieces no wider than 4 to 5 in., but it cuts accurate angles and is widely used by carpenters for trim work. In the cabinet shop it serves as an inexpensive cutoff saw that is ideal for face-frame stock and other narrow material. Cabinetmakers rig this machine with clever outrigger supports so that long stock can be handled with ease. Relatively inexpensive, this machine should be added to the shop as soon as is economically feasible (Fig. 3–20).

WOODWORKING MACHINES FOR THE SMALL CABINET SHOP

There are certain basic woodworking machines without which anyone thinking about building custom cabinets would have a very difficult time. Most cabinetmakers start small and over the years add tools and machines as their need grows. Thus a "do-it-yourselfer," hobbyist, or beginning professional can do quite an adequate job of cabinet work with certain basic machines, whereas a full-time three- or four-person shop would require much more in the way of laborsaving equipment.

What would be the very basic machinery requirements needed to start building cabinets either as an amateur or beginning professional? These machines, used with clever jigs and fixtures, can perform most of the necessary machining operations in building cabinets for the home.

Table Saw

The two machines that are the very heart of the cabinet shop are the table saw and the jointer. Lumber is usually purchased S2S and must be ripped into face-frame material and other cabinet parts. Standard procedure calls for the edge of the board to be squared and straightened on the jointer, then ripped to desired widths plus an allowance for jointing the opposite edge. Plywood and particle board, as well as most other products used in the cabinet, are constantly being cut to size on these machines. These two machines put in hours of service every day in the shop (Fig. 3–21).

As with most of the tools and machines that have been examined, the table saw is available in a variety of sizes and quality from the hobbyist's machine to large

Figure 3–21 Good starting unit for the cabinet shop: a table saw/jointer combination. (Courtesy Delta International Machinery Corp.)

Figure 3–22 Table saw accessories: *(left to right)* miter gauge, table insert for dado head, stop rods, dado set.

Figure 3–23 *(left to right)* crosscut blade, combination blade, all-purpose combination blade; *(bottom)* molding head for table saw.

production equipment. The initial purchase of a table saw should meet these basic requirements.

½- or ¾-hp rating for the motor
Rip fence extends to the right a minimum of 24 in. (exceedingly important as 4 ft. × 8 ft. plywood sheets must be ripped to 24-in. widths very often)
A tilting arbor
At least an 8-in. blade diameter and preferably 10 in.

These accessories would be recommended for purchase with the saw depending on what other machines are available in the cabinet shop (Figs. 3–22 and 3–23).

Miter gauge (usually standard equipment)
Stop rods for miter gauge
Dado insert plate
6- or 8-in. dado set that will cut grooves at least $^{13}\!/_{16}$ in. (also available are "wobble" washer sets—some carbide tipped—that perform this function nicely)

Molding cutter head and assorted knives (only if a spindle shaper is not available)

Saw blades (combination, rip, crosscut)

A table saw meeting these specifications, even when purchased from a mail-order house, is an item of substantial investment. The selection should be made carefully. Even if one of the smaller table saws is purchased at first, as business improves, a larger production model can be added. The smaller saw can always be used as a "second" machine and will be handy to take along to the installation site.

Jointer

Of almost equal importance to the table saw, the jointer is another basic machine that must operate constantly in the shop (Fig. 3–24A). The size of the jointer is designated by the width of the table. A small jointer is classified as a 4-in. model, and models of 6, 8, and 12 in. are also available. Again, anything larger than the 4-in. size is a major equipment investment and the selection should be made with great care. There are several important characteristics to consider when purchasing a jointer. First, both the front and rear tables should be adjustable. If the knives in the cutter head are a bit higher than the rear table, a slight "clip" is produced at the end of a board being jointed. If the blades are lower than the rear table, a tapered board is the result. It is a simple matter to adjust the rear table to correct this, but resetting the knives in the cutterhead is a time-consuming job (Fig. 3–24B). Second, the length of the tables is of primary concern. The longer the tables, the easier it is to joint the edge of long boards straight and true. Some jointers are classified as "long-bed" machines. Third, look for a guard that pivots easily and returns quickly to its position over the knives. Fourth, look for a well-machined jointer with good sealed bearings and "ways" that have positive locks. (Ways are the slanted surfaces

Figure 3–24A Six-inch jointer. (Courtesy of Delta International Machinery Corp.)

Figure 3–24B The rear table should be easily adjusted to match the blade height. (Courtesy Delta International Machinery Corp.)

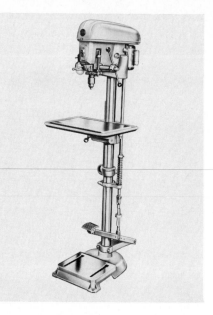

Figure 3-25 Drill press with foot lever. (Courtesy Delta International Machinery Corp.)

on which the tables move up or down for adjusting purposes.) Fifth, the jointer fence should be easily adjustable, tilt right and left, and have positive stops at the vertical and 45-degree positions.

It is safe to say that the 6-in. jointer is the most popular model in small to medium-size cabinet shops. The 4-in. model is somewhat limited by the shortness of its tables. However, as was the case with the smaller model table saw, the 4-in. size may be the first purchase and, after the purchase of a larger machine, kept for a "job-site" machine.

Drill Press

One must consider carefully whether to purchase a drill press. If the cabinetmaker is going to mortise and tenon the face frames of cabinets under production, a drill press with a mortising attachment is a necessity. The only alternative would be to purchase a mortiser, and this would not be practical until quite a production volume is reached. Available with the mortising attachment is a foot-lever accessory that frees the operator from having to pull the drill press hand lever (Fig. 3-25).

Of course, the drill press is a versatile machine that can be used for any number of operations in the shop. For example, besides being available to drill straight and true holes through both wood and metal, sanding drums can be mounted in the chuck for sanding curved areas. Jointer knives can be sharpened in the drill press using a small cup wheel and a holding jig for the knives. Used at its highest speed, even simple routing and shaping can be done, although there are other machines that perform these jobs much more satisfactorily.

EXPANDING AND ENLARGING THE SMALL CABINET SHOP

If the small cabinet shop owner has been attracting a steady volume of business and the orders begin to pile up, expansion ideas soon begin to form. Expansion usually means an increased investment in both space and equipment. Some one-person cabinet shop operators purposely decide to stay small when faced with the alternative of expansion. The prospect of hiring additional employees and the worry of keeping them busy and productive at all times, income tax, Social Security, Workers' Compensation, and so on, are just not worth it, they decide. They are making what they consider a good living in a style with which they are satisfied. Rather than borrow money to enlarge the shop and purchase additional equipment, they decide to stay a one-person shop, maintain their independence, and worry only about keeping one person busy.

Other small cabinet shop operators faced with the same prospects eagerly take the plunge into enlarging and expansion. They attempt to hire qualified help that they can keep over a period of years, locate a source of expansion capital, and increase both the square footage of the shop and the number and quality of the production machines.

Machinery Additions for the Expanding Small Shop

Wood shaper (spindle shaper)

The addition of a wood shaper is possibly one of the first additions that the small professional shop would want to add. If a small table-model shaper has been available (or if only the router has been used), the addition of a table-model heavy-duty shaper should be considered (Figs. 3–26 and 3–27). This is a high-speed industrial machine with a generous table surface that will enable the cabinetmaker to rabbet and lip cabinet doors in one pass, and more important, allow the machining of the raised panel doors so popular with today's cabinet purchasers. Both straight and curved edges can be machined with the wood shaper.

Almost unlimited shapes of knives are available in both regular toolsteel and carbide that enable the manufacturing of fancy-edged coped cabinet joints together

Figure 3-26 Small spindle shape—a good first purchase. (Courtesy Delta International Machinery Corp.)

Figure 3-27 Larger spindle shaper. (Courtesy Delta International Machinery Corp.)

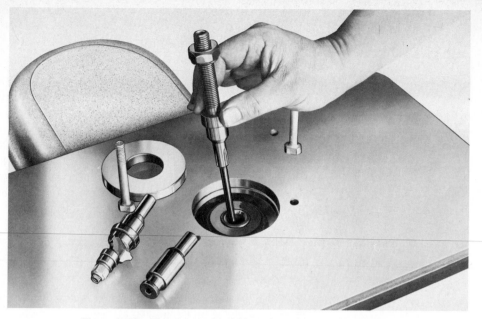

Figure 3–28 The shaper should have interchangeable spindles to accommodate various cutter sizes. (Courtesy Delta International Machinery Corp.)

with the raised panels. A knife holding head is available that will hold the knives that the cabinetmaker has ground to his or her own individual pattern. More information on raised panel doors is given in Chapter 9.

Interchangeable spindles are available for the wood shaper that allow the use of cutters with spindle hole diameters of ½, ¾, and 1 in. (Figs. 3–28 and 3–29). Other accessories usually available are spring hold-downs, ring guard, table extensions, sliding shaper jig, starting pin (for curved work), and tenoning jig. The latter, a larger machine, is usually powered with a 2- or 3-hp motor. The addition of a heavy-duty wood shaper should increase the production and quality of the work in the small to medium-size cabinet shop.

Ten- or 12-in. table saw

Because the professional shop subjects its equipment to many hours of steady production, upgrading the machinery to the industrial type is almost a necessity. Not

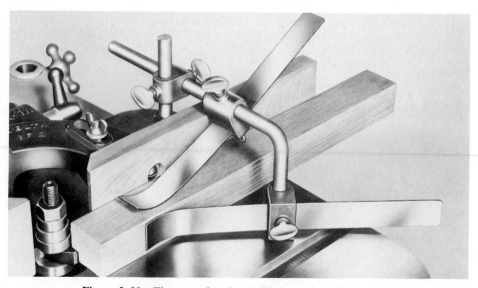

Figure 3–29 The use of spring hold-downs is a fine safety feature. (Courtesy Delta International Machinery Corp.)

Figure 3-30 As the cabinet shop expands, a larger table saw is an early addition. (Courtesy Delta International Machinery Corp.)

only is the capacity of the machine increased by a larger table and a bigger-diameter blade, but the horsepower of the motor is usually increased as well. The size and "wearability" of the main bearings enables this type of machine to operate day after day under production conditions with little worry over costly maintenance. Permanent table extensions as well as out-feed rollers and supports are often made a permanent part of the additions to the central saw. Thus the handling of large, heavy pieces of lumber, plywood, and particle board becomes easier and less time consuming for the operator (Fig. 3-30).

Radial arm saw

For fast, efficient cutoff and accurate length cutting, nothing can beat the radial arm saw (Fig. 3-31). Although it can be used for a number of woodworking opera-

Figure 3-31 The radial arm saw is an excellent machine for cutoff work. (Courtesy Delta International Machinery Corp.)

tions, its basic use in the cabinet shop is for cutting to length and accurate miter cuts. Stop gauges are available that can be set at various length settings that enable the operator to do fast, accurate cutoff work. For one-setting cutoff operations a simple "hook rod" can be clamped to the saw table.

Radial arm saws are designated by the diameter of the blade and by the length of the arm on which the saw travels in making its crosscut. This will vary from small 10- or 12-in. radial arm saws to large industrial machines with a 24-in. arm. The radial arm saw can be used for ripping as well by making some simple adjustments and turning the motor and blade parallel to the back fence. Ripping is seldom performed on this machine in the cabinet shop, however, as the table saw is much handier for this operation. Accessories are available that enable shaping, dadoing, sanding, and even drilling on the radial arm saw. Where production warrants, the addition of the radial arm saw is a fine investment.

Bandsaw

In the higher-production shop, certainly a more efficient method of cutting curves in wood is needed than the portable jigsaw (Fig. 3–32). The professional will soon add a quality bandsaw for this purpose. Depending on the width of the blade, various radii can be cut quickly and smoothly even in wood up to 2-in.-thick and thicker. Occasionally, resawing is done on the bandsaw as well.

Bandsaws are designated by the diameter of the wheels on which the blade runs. Thus bandsaws vary in size from the small 10- and 12-in. sizes available from mail-order houses and discount stores to the more common 14-in. size found in many cabinet shops. Of course, larger production models are found with up to 36-in.-diameter wheels.

Some models are available with sander belts that replace the blade so that the bandsaw is converted to a small belt sander. Other common accessories are the miter gauge, resawing attachments, and a rip fence.

Jointer 6 inch or larger

The discussion on the jointer in the small shop covered quite well the rationale for purchasing a larger machine. The jointer with the wider knives and the longer body simply will do a better job under production conditions of straightening and squaring long pieces of lumber.

Figure 3–32   The 14-in. bandsaw is a standard in the cabinet shop. (Courtesy Delta International Machinery Corp.)

Drill press

If a drill press is not available in the small shop, its purchase should be given serious consideration. As mentioned previously, if the cabinet face frames are to be mortised, a drill press with a mortising attachment probably has already been purchased. Now some thought, if production warrants it, needs to be given to purchasing a mortiser. This, however, is a purchase of considerable capital outlay and would be made only if steady production is anticipated.

Surfacer

The addition of a surfacer is a decision that the small, professional shop finds difficult to make. On the plus side, the addition of this machine makes it possible to purchase lumber in the rough and enjoy the subsequent saving of not having to pay milling charges. In addition, boards can be sized to any desired thickness quickly and efficiently. On the minus side is the need for a sawdust-handling system, for a surfacer produces shavings and dust in huge quantities and these need to be removed from the surfacer as produced. A properly engineered and installed vacuum system is the only efficient means of accomplishing this. Together, these two items make the purchase of even a small surfacer a matter of considerable cash outlay. Also, the surfacer is a machine that requires periodic and consistent maintenance. The knives must be kept properly sharpened and the feed rolls and pressure bar require knowledgeable adjustment for this machine to perform well (Fig. 3–33). Many small shops postpone the purchase of a surfacer and rely on their supplier to mill their orders to the desired specifications.

Wood lathe

If the criterion for adding a machine to the shop is the number of productive hours the machine is operating and thus paying for itself, the wood lathe will probably not be added to the small professional shop. Yet in many cabinet establishments

Figure 3–33 An 18-in. surfacer is an excellent machine for the cabinet shop if an exhaust system is installed to carry off the shavings.

Figure 3-34   The lathe is occasionally required.

one will see a small lathe usually gathering dust along the wall. The reason for this is that occasionally a specialty job requires some turning and there is just no other machine that can be substituted for the lathe to get this job accomplished. The only alternative would be for the cabinetmaker to subcontract the job to a competitor or a hobbyist. Rather than do this, the shop will have a small lathe on hand (Fig. 3–34).

REVIEW QUESTIONS

3.1. What hand tool is used most often to remove glue and plastic wood from the surface of wood?

3.2. List three common squares found in the cabinet shop.

3.3. What is the name of the tool the cabinetmaker uses to mark and transfer angles?

3.4. What size of claw hammer does the cabinetmaker find especially useful?

3.5. List four safety items that should be in every cabinet shop.

3.6. What is the most used portable electric tool found in the cabinet shop?

3.7. What is meant by the classification of an electric drill as a ''¼-in. electric drill''?

3.8. Name two machines that are used to cut curves in wood.

3.9. How are portable belt sanders described as to size? What is the most common size found in small cabinet shops?

3.10. Which two machines are considered to be the ''heart of the cabinet shop''?

3.11. Which machine used with an accessory is used to cut mortises in the small shop?

3.12. How are jointers described as to size? What size is most popular in small and medium-size cabinet shops?

SUGGESTED CLASS ACTIVITIES AND STUDENT ASSIGNMENTS

3.1. Using catalogs from the leading mail-order firms and by visiting hardware and discount stores, complete a price list of the recommended hand tools named in this chapter.

3.2. Obtain prices from various sources on ¼-in. electric drills, finishing sanders, circular saws, routers, portable belt sanders, and saber saws.

3.3. Have the class visit retail establishments that sell power tools for the woodworking trade. Have the proprietor or salesperson explain differences in quality and desirable features of table saws, jointers, drill presses, and so on.

3.4. Using the information gathered from machinery dealers, mail-order catalogs, and hardware dealers, as a class project have the students prepare a list with prices of the basic machines for the small cabinet shop: table saw, jointer, and drill press, with the basic accessories for each.

3.5. Total the costs found for hand tools, portable equipment, and basic machines to determine a minimum capital expenditure for setting up a small shop. Discuss with the class other requirements needed to start a small cabinet business.

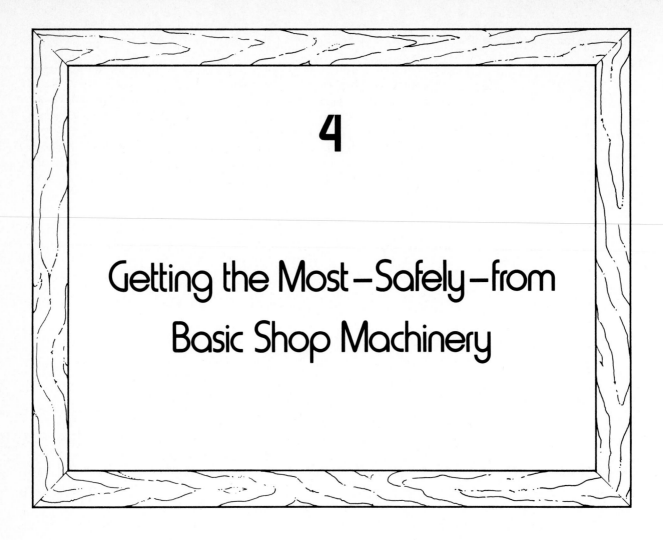

4

Getting the Most –Safely – from Basic Shop Machinery

Special Note: Many of the photos contained in this and the following chapters show the table saw, and occasionally other machines, in use unguarded. There are two reasons for this. First, to demonstrate clearly a specific operation to the reader, the guard has purposely been removed. Second, many of the photos were taken in operating cabinet shops and, regretfully, in most cases their table saws were not guarded. Although there are several operations on the table saw for which a guard is a distinct inconvenience, the author urges the use of the guard for most standard operations on all machines.

Because the small cabinet shop is probably limited in the number of machines available, the owner/operator will want to be able to make those machines that are purchased perform a variety of functions. Yet even though the machines are being adapted to perform operations somewhat beyond their ''normal'' uses, safety is a factor of primary importance. For example, a radial arm saw is a much more efficient cutoff saw than is the regular table saw. However, through the use of clever jigs and supports, the table saw can safely be used as a fairly efficient cutoff machine.

Safety in the cabinet shop, as elsewhere, is a combination of many things: an attitude of care, caution, and respect for the machine; a knowledge of the machine and what it can safely be expected to accomplish; an understanding that a well-sharpened and correctly adjusted piece of equipment is the basis for safe operation;

and a consistent use of machine guards as well as other body-protection devices, such as safety glasses and goggles, push sticks, and hold-downs. In almost 50 years of both commercial and educational woodshop experience, the author has seen many accidents. The greatest percentage of these were caused by (1) not using the guard provided for the machine; or (2) the operator doing something admittedly "foolish"—usually in haste—while using the equipment. The lesson is simple: Take the time to do the job safely!

THE TABLE SAW—A VERSATILE MACHINE

Of all the cabinet shop machines, the table saw is the most adaptable to an almost unlimited number of woodworking functions besides those of ripping and crosscutting. With the many accessories that are available from manufacturers and with the use of shop-made jigs, the table saw can be used for many operations in building cabinets.

Ripping on the Table Saw

The first basic rule for ripping on the table saw, and one that many beginners seem to have trouble mastering, is: To produce straight rippings on the table saw, the edge of the board to be held against the rip fence must first be straightened on the jointer. Watch an old-time woodworker getting a piece of lumber ready for ripping. He will sight one edge to determine what he must accomplish with the jointer. If the edge is bowed in (concave), he will start straightening by taking several jointer cuts at the ends of the board. If the board is bellied (convex), he will start his jointer cuts closer to the middle of the board, removing the bellied area with several passes. Finally, he will be able to take one long, full-length pass, producing a straight edge. Occasionally, the board is so badly bellied that the craftsman must snap a chalk line on the board and roughly straighten the edge with the circular saw and then finish straightening on the jointer (Fig. 4–1).

Selecting the proper blade

If a reasonable amount of ripping is to be done (several boards), a rip blade should be selected and placed on the table saw. Every shop will want a variety of blades on hand—rip, crosscut, and combination, in both regular steel and carbide. Selecting the proper blade for the job at hand is safer, easier, and means less wear and tear on the machine itself. The same holds true if a lot of cutting to length is to be done. A crosscut blade will produce smoother end cuts across the grain and should be used for this operation. Two types of combination blades are available that do a fairly respectable job of both operations. However, the hollow-ground blade should be used for ripping only where a very smooth cut is desired (see Fig. 3–23).

All saw blades should be kept well sharpened, free from pitch, and with the proper amount of "set" to the teeth. Many craftspersons like to file their own blades, at least on a "touch-up" basis, thus saving sharpening expense by having to send the blades continually to a professional sharpener. However, many of the blades on the market today are of a hardened steel that cannot be filed. Although this does

Figure 4–1 Straighten badly bowed lumber by snapping a chalk line and sawing with a circular saw.

USE CHALK LINE OR STRAIGHT EDGE.

mean that the blade will stay sharp longer, it also means that it cannot be touched up in the shop. Carbide blades must also be sent out for sharpening, as a special grinding wheel must do this job.

The larger professional shops have their own sharpening rooms, where one or two persons have the responsibility of sharpening saw blades and jointer and planer knives, and also grinding shaper knives to pattern. Of course, they have at their disposal all the necessary grinding machines and grinding wheels. The smaller shops must rely on the skills of the local saw sharpener, who has purchased sharpening equipment and has "hung out his shingle." Many smaller shops keep a good supply of blades on hand at all times so that those being sharpened can always be replaced with blades in excellent shape.

Adjusting the table saw for safe, efficient operation

A table saw should always be carefully checked for several major alignments:

1. Are the table grooves exactly parallel to the saw blade? This should be checked carefully and corrected by loosening the saw table and readjusting in the parallel position.
2. The 90-degree and 45-degree readings on the tilting arbor protractor should be *accurate.*
3. The rip fence should be parallel to the saw blade. (See the discussion under "Proper Adjustment of the Rip Fence.")
4. The 90-degree and 45-degree stops on the miter gauge should be double-checked for accuracy.
5. The saw guard and splitter should be mounted and checked for proper positioning.

A few minutes devoted to these checks and adjustments may save some major disappointments in the performance of the table saw.

Proper sequence for running out stock

Running out stock to dimension should be done in the proper sequence. These are the steps that should be followed:

1. Straighten one edge of the board on the jointer.
2. Rip on the table saw to the desired width plus a $\frac{1}{32}$-in. allowance (or a bit more) for jointing the opposite edge. If several strips are to be ripped from the same board, more will have to be allowed because both edges will require jointing. The alternative would be to joint the sawn edge after each pass on the saw prior to ripping the next strip.
3. Joint the remaining edge (or both edges if required). Carefully adjust the depth of cut on the jointer so that the amount removed will leave the net size desired. If the net width of the board is to be exactly 2 in. and the board has been ripped at approximately 2 $\frac{1}{16}$ in., adjust the jointer for a shallow test cut and run the board just a few inches over the knives—first one edge and then the other—and check the dimension. Gradually lower the table of the jointer and repeat the process until the exact net measurement after jointing both edges is exactly 2 in.
4. Trim one end of the board square and true. Measure the desired length and cut the opposite end square and true.

Note: If the ripped length is awkward and hard to handle and is to be cut into several shorter pieces, it might be more convenient to cut the ripping into the desired lengths and then complete the jointing of the edges.

Curing a kicking saw

One of the most dangerous features of a table saw is its ability to violently kick a piece being ripped out of the saw backward. If the operator is standing directly in the path of this piece of lumber, a very painful abdominal accident can be the result. The cause of such an accident is twofold:

1. A saw blade that is dull, coated with pitch, or has little or no set to the teeth
2. An improperly adjusted rip fence

Of the two, the second cause is of the utmost importance. Even with a blade in perfect condition, if the rip fence is incorrectly adjusted, violent kicking can result.

Maintaining table saw blades

One of the best rules for maintaining table saw blades is: Remove a blade that is getting dull and no longer giving top performance. After all, a dull blade is only going to get worse by continual use. Better to get it off the machine and replaced with a sharp, clean blade. Periodically cleaning the saw blade of pitch and resins is a simple process. Soak the blade for a few minutes in a shallow pan in enough turpentine or lacquer thinner to cover the blade. After soaking, scrub the blade with very fine steel wool, scraping stubborn spots with a razor blade. After drying, a light waxing with good furniture wax will help in preventing reccurrence.

Keeping the blades sharp with the proper set is probably a matter of getting the blades to the sharpener so that a backlog of blades in fine condition is available at all times. Remember, a well-sharpened blade has a nice "whine" to it!

Proper adjustment of the rip fence

As stated previously, most kicking on the table saw is caused by an improperly adjusted rip fence. To be in proper adjustment, the rip fence should be just slightly wider at its far end than in the front. Most instructions state that the rip fence should be *parallel* to the saw blade. Actually, the fence should be about ¹⁄₆₄ in. farther from the blade at the far edge of the blade: in other words, about ¹⁄₆₄ in. out of parallel with the blade. Figure 4-2 describes this adjustment clearly. When the rip fence is adjusted properly and if the saw blade is in good condition, the operator should be able to remove his or her hand from a board being ripped and the board will lay motionless or creep ever so slowly to the rear.

Figure 4-2 Fence adjustment to help prevent kickback.

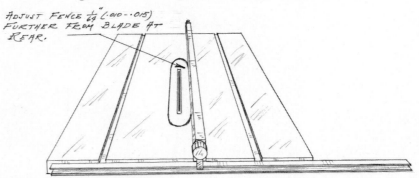

Ripping Safely on the Table Saw

Some general rules for safe ripping of lumber on the table saw are:

1. Set the rip fence to the width desired plus an allowance for jointing.
2. Adjust the height of the saw blade so that it is no more than ¼ in. higher than the thickness of the board being ripped.
3. If the board is a lengthy piece, have a helper ready to assist in supporting the board as it comes through the saw, or have "outriggers" in position to support the work.

Note: If rollers or other outrigger supports are used, they should be lined up carefully with the saw table so that the work is not forced to the right or left as it comes off the saw (Fig 4–3A).

4. Position the saw guard. Check to see that all adjustments are locked in position. Operator should wear safety glasses or goggles.
5. Start the saw and with the jointed, straightened edge against the rip fence, feed the piece into the saw steadily and smoothly and at a rate the motor will handle without slowing down.
6. If the piece is being ripped into narrow strips (3 in. or less), have a push stick ready to finish the ripping so that the operator's fingers do not have to travel between the blade and the fence. Other techniques for handling narrow rippings: (a) If your helper is an experienced woodworker, have the helper pull the board through to complete the last few inches of the rip; or (b) the operator can walk around to the rear of the saw and pull the board through; or (c) the operator can remove the board from the saw, reverse it—keeping the same edge against the fence—and complete the ripping.
7. Immediately turn off the saw on completion of the ripping.

Some helpful techniques

When ripping a long board, take a position near the end of the board. The right hand will grasp the end of the board and the left will grasp the left edge of

Figure 4–3A   A roller support for the table saw is an excellent addition. (Courtesy The Turning Point, West Davenport, N.D.)

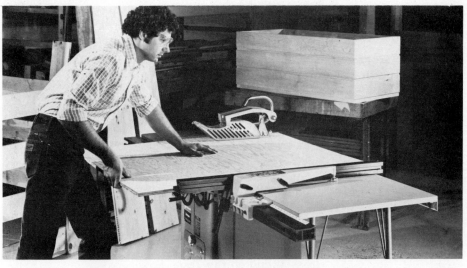

Figure 4-3B Good ripping technique on the table saw. (Courtesy Delta International Machinery Corp.)

the board. In this position the forward thrust is provided by the right hand while the left hand holds the board against the rip fence. The operator moves easily and smoothly forward, feeding the work into the blade at a steady pace, allowing the machine to do its job without forcing. As the end approaches, the right-hand position will change slightly as the right thumb hooks over the end of the board, still providing the forward thrust. The left hand still keeps the board against the fence. Finally, as the board is pushed through its final few inches, the left hand is removed while the right hand pushes through between the blade and the fence—provided that the space is 2 to 3 in. or more. For less space than that a push stick or other technique is used (Fig. 4-3B).

An experienced operator NEVER reaches across the saw blade. Watch an experienced saw operator and notice the person's positions and motions. Contrary to some safety suggestions, the stance taken by most operators when ripping shorter pieces is directly back of the saw table, for any other position is exceedingly awkward. The operator's right-hand thumb hooks the end of the board while the right-hand fingers provide a hold-down pressure to prevent the board from jumping or rising while the left hand keeps the board in contact with the rip fence (Fig. 4-4). Notice how fluid

Figure 4-4 Ripping short pieces on the table saw.

the motions of an experienced operator are, as he or she knows the machine, the blade, and just how fast to feed the work depending on the thickness of the material and species of wood.

A word about horsepower

A general adage around cabinet shops is: "A ¾- or 1-hp motor provides a forgiving table saw." What this means is that a saw powered under, say, 2 hp will forgive an operator's mistake or possible carelessness because the motor will stop if the work should pinch or jam. Larger-horsepower machines will not be as forgiving but will hurl or kick the work with great force. Although the cabinetmaker may become impatient with what seems to be an underpowered machine, the alternatives should be considered carefully before going to a higher horsepower. That is perhaps the reason why the larger machines are often equipped with automatic feeding devices that keep the operator a distance from the machine itself.

Crosscutting on the Table Saw

If the cabinet shop does not possess a radial arm saw, chances are that the table saw will be used for most cutoff work. Using the miter gauge as a support and guide, the cabinetmaker will also be using various jigs to do accurate multiple-length cuttings. Although the newer, motorized miter saws can be used for cutoff jobs, they are limited because of the narrowness of the material they can handle.

Cutoff techniques using the table saw

Always test the miter gauge for an exact square setting with the saw blade. This can be done by making a few test cuts and checking with the try square. If the saw blade is not perfectly sharp, it has a tendency to drift, especially when making a miter cut or cutting close to the end of a board. This can be corrected by keeping the blade very sharp.

Another technique used by many craftspersons is to fasten a piece of wood to the miter gauge and cover the surface of that wood with coarse sandpaper. This enlarges the control area of the miter gauge and the sandpaper prevents drifting.

It is sometimes quite awkward to have to handle long, heavy pieces of lumber on the table saw when cutting to length. Often, it is easier to rough-cut the board to length by using the portable circular saw and then make the final, exact cuts on the table saw. The use of a helper or conveniently placed outrigger supports also makes this job easier (Fig. 4–5).

The basic rule for accurate crosscutting is always to hold the stock firmly against the miter gauge while advancing the material through the saw. Any deviation will result in a cut that is slightly off square.

Techniques for multiple-length cutting

There are several means of making accurate, repeated cuts on the table saw. The objective is to have the pieces cut exactly the same length and to do the job safely and with a minimum of labor expended. Measuring and marking each piece separately is not only time consuming, but the pieces always end up slightly different in length.

Using stop rods and the miter gauge

Stop rods are usually available as an accessory when purchasing a table saw. They are convenient when cutting rather short pieces to length. Many people, however, prefer simply to use the rip fence as a cutoff gauge rather than purchase stop rods (Fig. 4–6).

Figure 4-5 Use an outrigger support when cutting long pieces to length on the table saw.

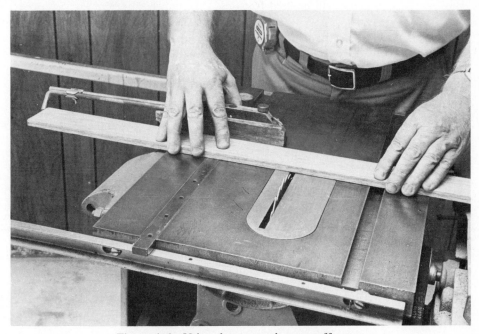

Figure 4-6 Using the stop rods as cutoff gauges.

Using the rip fence as a cutoff jig

The rip fence makes a very convenient cutoff gauge if a few safety rules are observed. Always support the piece that is being cut off with the miter gauge. This means keeping the miter gauge in the right-hand table slot *and between the blade and the fence.* Thus the piece being cut off is pushed through between the blade and the fence (Fig. 4-7). If not done this way, there is a danger that the piece, once the cut has been completed, will jam between the blade and the fence. Once jammed, these pieces can be thrown from the saw with frightening and damaging speed. Although this works well for cutting pieces that are longer than the miter gauge is wide, for shorter pieces another technique may be used. Move the miter gauge back to the left-hand table slot, clamp a short piece of wood to the rip fence, and adjust the fence—plus the block—to the desired length (Fig. 4-8). Now simply butt the work against the block of wood rather than the rip fence and proceed with the cutoff. Now

Figure 4–7   The rip fence makes an excellent cutoff gauge. Be sure to keep the miter gauge between the fence and the blade.

Figure 4–8   When the miter gauge cannot be placed between the blade and the fence, clamp a block of wood to the fence as illustrated.

when the cut is complete, there is plenty of room for the cut piece to lay free with no danger of wedging between the blade and the rip fence.

What about cutting pieces that are longer than the capacity of the rip fence? Here a clever jig comes into use. By clamping this jig to the underside of the guide bars and having available a number of various lengths of hooked strips, practically any length cut can be made quickly and accurately. Figure 4–9 illustrates this jig clearly.

Figure 4-9 For longer pieces a simple shop-made jig is clamped to the fence rails.

Crosscutting safely on the table saw

Many of the safety rules for ripping stock are also applicable for crosscutting. Blade height, proper use of the guard, eye protection, and the use of a helper or outriggers all apply equally to crosscutting operations. Besides these general safety precautions, there are a few specific safety techniques that should be mentioned in reference to crosscutting.

1. Watch the position of the hands at all times. A wayward finger or thumb can easily be nicked if allowed to stray too close to the blade.
2. The nonprofessional has a tendency to keep one hand on the left side of the work and the right hand on the right side. The person then squeezes the work against the saw blade, causing the board to kick or jump. This often happens both in ripping small pieces and in crosscutting. If the right hand is on the right side of the work, it should be used to spread the work slightly as the cut is completed so as not to pinch it against the blade.
3. The amateur also seems to have a "thing" about the piece being cut falling on the floor and will often make a dive for this piece. Let it fall! Severe accidents have happened because a grab was made for the loose piece, forgetting completely about the dangerous saw blade.

Other Operations Performed on the Table Saw

Many other operations can be performed on the table saw with the use of accessories provided by the manufacturer or by using jigs built in the shop. Although many of these operations could be performed better with the special machine designed for that purpose, the nonprofessional and the amateur will want to make do with what is available.

Use of dado blades

There are several devices on the market for dadoing or plowing grooves in wood. The first of these and possibly the best known is the dado set. This is a set of blades made up of two outside cutters and several inside chippers (Fig. 4-10). Used in com-

Figure 4–10 Dado set with table inset and thin cardboard shims or "doughnuts."

bination, these blades can dado and groove as narrow as ⅛ in. to as wide as ¹³⁄₁₆ in. Most cabinetmakers also make themselves a few paper or thin cardboard "dough-nuts" to slightly widen cuts when needed. Using the dado head on the table saw requires a table insert that has a wider slot than that used for an ordinary saw blade. These are usually purchased as an accessory together with the table saw. When using the dado head, the inside chippers should be spread evenly around the saw arbor. The chippers nearest the two outside cutters should be placed so that they line up with the bottom of the gullets of those two blades. This is done because the chipper blades have quite a bit of swag to them and an oversized cut would result if the extra width were not absorbed by placing the blades in line with the gullets.

The blades of the dado head have a tendency to change in size after repeated sharpening. Every effort should be made to keep the blades the same diameter or dados and grooves with rough and uneven bottoms will be the result.

Other mechanisms are available for cutting dados. A set of "wobble" washers is available that is used with an ordinary table saw blade. These are very economical to purchase and give quite satisfactory results. Another device is the adjustable dado, which is similar to the wobble washer in principal. However, this device has its own blade—available carbide-tipped—and is easily set for the correct width of cut by setting a dial (Fig. 4–11).

Figure 4–11 Adjustable dado blade. (Courtesy Delta International Machinery Corp.)

Figure 4-12 Cutting a groove with the dado head.

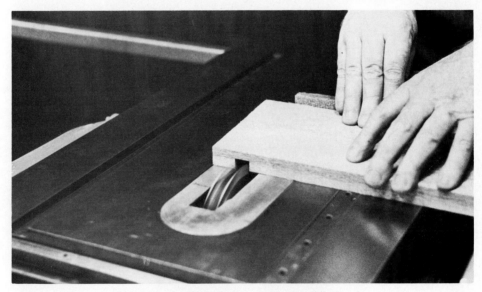

Figure 4-13 A dado is cut with the dado head.

Use of the dado devices is very similar to ordinary ripping and crosscutting. Cutting a groove (a slot cut with the grain of the wood) is done by using the rip fence, while a dado (cutting across the grain) is done with the help of a miter gauge (Figs. 4-12 and 4-13).

In commercial cabinetwork the basic use made of the dado head is to plow grooves in drawer sides, backs, and fronts to accept the plywood bottom. If the face frame of the cabinet is mortised-and-tenoned, the dado head is also used to cut the tenons easily and quickly.

Cutting tenons

To cut tenons with a dado set, place enough blades on the saw arbor (or set the device) to cut a ½-in. dado. This will do well for a tenon about 1 in. long. Use more blades if a longer tenon is to be cut. Next, set the rip fence to act as a stop for the length of tenon being cut. With a piece of scrap wood the same thickness as the finish piece, supported with the miter gauge, raise the dado head to an ap-

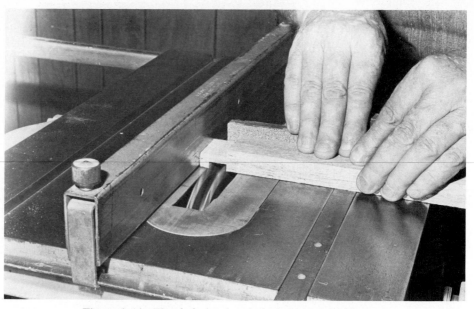

Figure 4-14 The dado head and rip fence are used in combination to cut tenons.

Figure 4-15 Shoulder cuts are made with the saw blade and the rip fence.

proximate height and make a test cut on the scrap piece. Do this first on one side and then on the other. Chances are that the resulting tenon will be a bit too thick or thin when test-fit into the mortise. Raise or lower the dado head as needed and repeat the test cuts. A few seconds of making test cuts soon results in a correct-fitting tenon. Once the setting is correct, proceed to cut all the tenons as required (Fig. 4-14). Shoulder cuts, if required, can just as quickly be cut by placing the regular blade back on the table saw and removing the material for the shoulder cut in two passes on the saw (Figs. 4-15 and 4-16).

Commercial tenoning jigs are available as well as home-made devices. However, the method just described is fast and simple and requires no accessories.

Figure 4-16 Complete the shoulder cut again using the saw blade and the rip fence.

Use of a molding head on the table saw

Simple, straight-line edge molding can be accomplished on the table saw with the various molding heads that are available (Figs. 4–17 and 4–18). Although the quality of the edge shaping is not as good as would be accomplished on a spindle shaper, a satisfactory job can be done. Because the speed of the knives used in the table saw molding head is quite slow in comparison to the shaper, the work must be fed much more slowly when using the table saw. Another drawback to using the

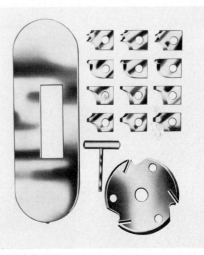

Figure 4-17 One type of molding head for use on the table saw. (Courtesy Delta International Machinery Corp.)

Figure 4-18 Another style of molding head.

Figure 4-19 Shaping the end grain of a drawer front with the molding head. The front is clamped to a sliding piece that travels along the top of the auxiliary fence.

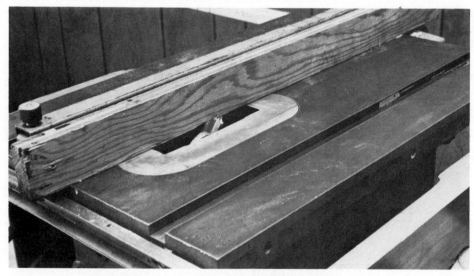

Figure 4-20 An auxiliary wooden fence must be screwed to the rip fence when using the molding head.

table saw for molding the edges of cabinet doors, for example, is that the doors must be stood on end to run over the knives. When running fairly large doors, this makes for an operation that is awkward and sometimes difficult to perform. Short pieces such as the ends of drawer fronts will slip down into the larger table insert area and gouge the work. Thus the piece being run must be supported by a rather clumsy-to-operate support jig (Fig. 4-19).

An auxiliary wood fence must be made and screwed to the regular rip fence for molding operations. This prevents the molding knives from hitting the metal rip fence as it might on some operations (Fig. 4-20).

All in all, judging from the above, running the edges of drawers and doors can be performed much easier and better with either a router or a shaper. But if neither is available, the molding head will have to do.

Rabbeting on the table saw

A rabbet or shoulder cut can be made on the table saw in one of two ways. The single saw blade can be used by making two passes over the blade with the work first in a horizontal position and then held vertically (Fig. 4–21). This is often the way a cabinetmaker will form the lip on the drawer fronts and doors. If the blade is in good shape and smooth-cutting, very little sanding will have to be done to make the cut presentable.

The other means of cutting a rabbet is to use the dado head. The auxiliary wood fence will again have to be used because the blades will have to be partially under the fence itself (Fig. 4–22).

Rabbeting can also be accomplished on the jointer. This operation is discussed in the next section.

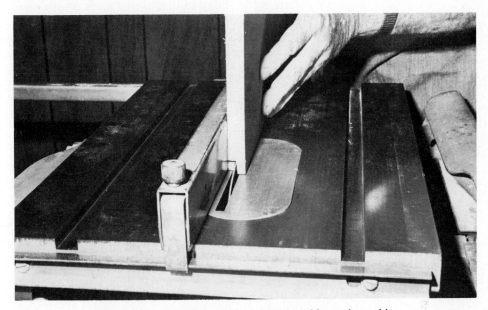

Figure 4–21 A rabbet may be cut on the table saw by making a horizontal cut and then a vertical cut.

Figure 4–22 The dado head may be used also to cut a rabbet.

OPERATING THE JOINTER SAFELY

Although the basic function of the jointer is to smooth, square, and straighten the edge of boards, there are many more jobs that this versatile machine can perform. Edge dressing on the jointer was discussed in Chapter 3. Strangely, many beginning woodworkers have accidents using the jointer. Possibly this is because they do not understand the machine—its functions and limitations.

General Jointer Technique and Operating Tips

"Reading" grain direction

One of the first lessons to be learned in accomplishing high-quality work on the jointer is the ability to "read" the grain on the piece being jointed. If a board is run through the jointer the wrong way, instead of smoothing the edge the result is a torn and roughened surface. This lesson is quickly learned and the cure—reversing the board and rerunning it through the jointer—usually results in a nice, smooth-cutting action (Fig. 4–23). The direction of grain is quite easy to determine on some species and is quite difficult on others. Species such as birch and maple tear up regardless of the direction in which the board is jointed. Others will joint smooth for a few inches, tear for a few inches, and then joint smooth again, alternating in this way for the length of the board. Even experienced professionals shake their heads when confronted with such lumber.

Keeping the jointer knives well sharpened is the first step in preventing grain tear-out. Slowing the rate of feed over the cutter head is another. The fence on one manufacturer's jointer is adjustable so that the work can be fed in a slanted position across the cutter head. This is said to prevent tear-out on curly-grained woods. Perhaps the remark one old-time cabinetmaker made in regard to how he handled grain tear-out is worth mentioning: "Swear or prayer—either one is about as good as the other!"

Rate of feed and knife marks

A problem inherent in any machine that uses knives set in a rotating head is knife marks or "planer waves." These marks are going to be produced by such a machine—the question is how to keep them as inconspicuous as possible. The craftsperson must understand that the number of knife marks per inch of lumber is controlled by the speed of the cutter head, the number of knives in the cutter head, and the rate at which the board is pushed or fed into the machine. Thus a shaper operating at over 10,000 rpm will produce knife marks much closer together than will a jointer operating at 5000 rpm at the same rate of feed. Of course, this assumes that

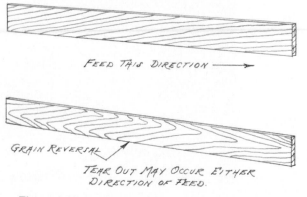

Figure 4–23 Typical problems with wood grain.

the number of knives is the same and that they are set properly in the cutter head and all are cutting equally. Knowing this, the operator can take the time to feed the stock more slowly when desiring a finer-looking result. One of the items that determines quality workmanship in cabinetry is the elimination of knife marks on exposed areas of the finished product. A good craftsperson always sands the knife marks away using belt and finish sanders. A mistake often made by beginners is to believe that stain and varnish will eliminate planer waves, only to discover to their chagrin that, like any blemish, finishing materials only magnify the problem and make them even more noticeable.

Safety tips for the jointer

The jointer should be a relatively safe machine to operate, yet, as mentioned at the start of this section, beginners do seem to have a strange affinity for accidents on this machine. Past observation indicates that the cause of these accidents falls into two categories: (1) attempting to run too short a piece over the cutter head, and (2) the board being kicked out from under the operator's fingers or hands. In the first instance, never attempt to joint a piece less than 10 to 12 in. in length. The larger the machine, the larger is the gap between the front and rear tables. Thus short pieces are even more dangerous to joint, and 12 to 14 in. becomes the rule.

The second cause—the board being kicked out from under the operator's hands or fingers—is corrected by the use of a push block. This type of accident usually occurs when the jointer is being used as a planer and a surface is being machined. If the knives are not in excellent shape, surfacing on the jointer results in a lot of vibration, and if a knot is encountered, the material can be kicked backward, dropping the operator's fingers into the knives. Always make light cuts when surfacing on the jointer. Push boards are easy to make and should always be used when attempting to surface 12- to 16-in. pieces (Fig. 4–24).

The jointer knives should be kept in tip-top condition by frequent honing. This operation can be performed without removing the knives from the cutter head. Dull knives have a pounding effect rather than a shearing action on the wood, which results in a glazed surface. A glazed surface is one cause of poor glue joints, experts tell us. Once the knives become nicked and beyond honing, they must be removed and ground. This operation is discussed later in the chapter.

The jointer guard should be checked often to see that it swings freely and returns quickly after the work has cleared the machine. It should always be in place. There are very, very few operations performed on the jointer where the guard needs to be removed. The maximum depth of cut on the jointer should be about ⅛ in. More commonly, the depth of cut will be around ¹/₁₆ in.

Always check to see that all adjusting features on the machine are locked after making necessary changes. This is especially true of the fence, for if not locked in place, it could slip out of the perpendicular position, throwing the operator's fingers into the cutter head.

While end grain can be jointed safely on the jointer, never attempt to do this on boards narrower than 10 in. or so. Very light cuts should be taken and the stock fed slowly. To prevent tearing the grain at the end of the cut, start with a short cut on one end, reverse the board, and complete the cut (Fig. 4–25).

When jointing a long piece of lumber, it is well to have a helper on hand to

Figure 4–24 Safety push board for jointer.

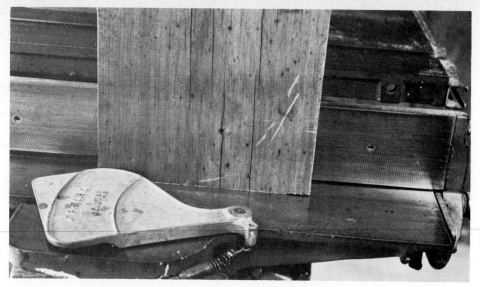

Figure 4–25   Jointing end grain. Note the small clip on the right
end of the piece. This prevents splitting at the end of the cut.

assist in supporting the board as it comes off the rear table. A properly adjusted out-
feed roller that is exactly even with the rear table also works well for supporting long
stock. One distinct advantage of the larger jointers with longer tables is their ability
to support long pieces without the operator having to put undue pressure on the end
of the board.

Other Operations Performed on the Jointer

Rabbeting

A satisfactory rabbet cut can be made on the jointer, but often there is some
tearing of grain on the underside. Making the cut in two passes will help to eliminate
this but will not prevent it entirely. Some people make a saw cut first and then finish
the rabbet on the jointer to prevent the tear-out problem.

To make a rabbet cut, move the fence to the left to the width of rabbet desired.
Lower the rear table to the depth of cut needed (or halfway if two passes are going
to be made) and run the material over the knives (Fig. 4–26)

Figure 4–26   Rabbeting on the jointer. Usually, the guard must
be removed for this operation.

Figure 4–27   Chamfering on the jointer with the fence tilted
to the right.

Figure 4–28   Chamfering on the jointer with the fence tilted
to the left.

Chamfering and stop chamfering

Removal of the sharp corner on a piece of lumber and replacing the corner with
a slight bevel is known as chamfering. This can be done quite efficiently on the jointer.
Chamfering is usually done at a 45-degree angle, so the fence should be tilted to the
right at that setting. Lower the rear table to the depth of cut desired and make the
cut. Try to read the grain for chamfering as for edge jointing. Tilting the fence to
the left allows a chamfer to be made on the other edge of the board with little if
any tear-out, as both cuts will be made with the grain (Figs. 4–27 and 4–28).

Stop chamfering is used frequently in the cabinet shop as an edge treatment
for drawer sides. This gives the top edge of the drawer side a neat appearance, but
leaving the ends square makes a nicer-fitting joint at the drawer front and back (Fig.
4–29). Both the front and rear tables of the jointer must be lowered equally to make
a stop chamfer. If this is not done, a tapered chamfer is the result. Make a pencil

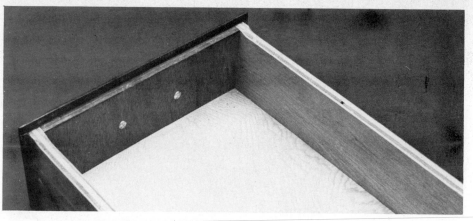

Figure 4-29 Stop chamfering on a drawer side makes a good-looking edge.

(or felt-tip-pen) mark on the fence where the piece will be held to drop onto the cutter head and another mark where the piece will be removed from the jointer. Stop blocks can be clamped to the front and rear tables for this operation; however, if the pieces being chamfered are longer than the tables, blocks will not do (Figs. 4-30 and 4-31).

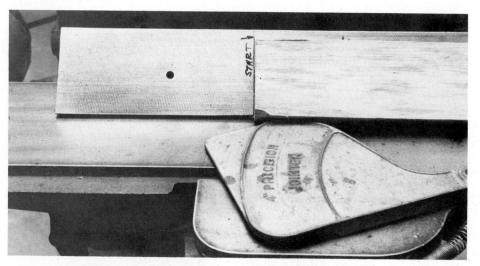

Figure 4-30 Mark the start and stop positions on the jointer fence for stop chamfering. Both tables of the jointer must be lowered the correct amount.

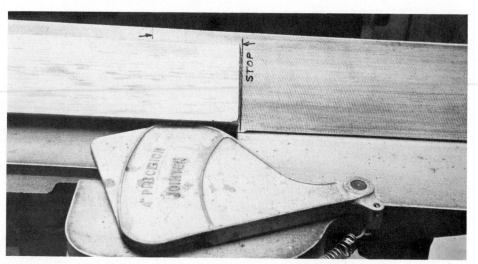

Figure 4-31 Where to stop the chamfer is also marked on the jointer fence.

Figure 4–32 Cutting a short taper on the jointer.

Figure 4–33 Three cuts are taken when making a long taper cut.

Tapering

Tapering is one of the functions the jointer does fast and efficiently. This operation is a simple matter of making multiple cuts on the jointer. When tapering a short piece—shorter than the front table—lower the table to the depth of cut that will make the amount of taper desired. Start the taper by placing the leading edge of the board *on the rear table* so that the knives do not cut as yet. Then feed the stock into the machine. As the piece is fed through the machine, a taper will be cut along its length equal to the depth setting (Fig. 4–32).

For tapering stock longer than the front table, two or more cuts will have to be made. To make a ⅜-in. taper along the edge of a 6-ft. board, mark the board into three 2-ft. sections. Set the machine for a cut ⅛-in. deep. Make the first cut at the 2-ft. mark, the second at the 4-ft. mark, and the final cut the full length of the board (Fig. 4–33).

Sharpening the Jointer Knives

Although many cabinetmakers send their jointer knives out for grinding, it is a rather simple process to perform in the shop. A knife-holding jig must be made to hold the knives at the proper angle, and a small cup wheel must be purchased to be mounted in the drill press to do the grinding. Lacking a drill press, the job can be done on a disc sander with the proper holding jig.

The knife is locked into the jig. The cup wheel is carefully lowered to make contact with the knife and the quill is locked lightly in place. The knife is fed slowly back and forth under the cup wheel, care being exercised not to overheat the metal. As the grinding proceeds, the cup wheel will have to be lowered occasionally to maintain good grinding contact with the knife. All three knives are ground in the same manner (Fig. 4–34). Grinding the same amount on each knife is important, for the knives should be kept the same weight for balance.

Remounting the knives in the cutter head is a touchy job and one that should be done with great care. Replace the knife bar or throat piece in the cutter-head slot, and then place the knife roughly in position. Gently tighten the two end setscrews by reversing the screws until the knife is just held in its position. Place a piece of ¾-in. hardwood about 8 to 10 in. long so that it rests on the rear table but extends across the knife cutting area. Adjust the knife upward until it just touches this piece evenly at both ends of the knife. As the rotated knife touches the wood, the piece will move forward a bit (Fig. 4–35). Next, place each knife in its slot, repeating the adjusting. Carefully adjust each knife until all three hit the hardwood piece in equal amount and move the piece forward the same distance. Keep the left end of all three knives in line so that the rabbeting operation can be done with all knives cutting equally. Carefully check all setscrews to see that they are firmly tightened. Replace the fence and the guard.

Try a few test cuts after the knives are replaced to see that the rear table is adjusted correctly. Raise or lower the rear table as required.

Figure 4-34 A simple holding jig and a small cup grinding wheel will adequately sharpen jointer knives.

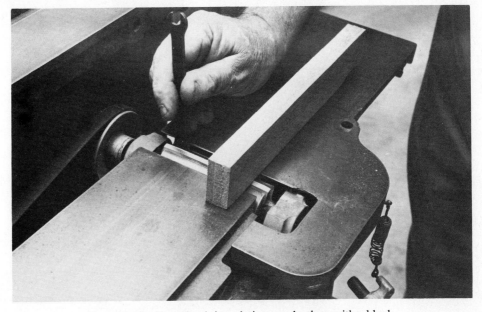

Figure 4–35   Resetting jointer knives can be done with a block
of wood for a gauge.

THE DRILL PRESS

The versatility of the drill press was discussed in Chapter 3. The primary concern
of this section is use of the drill press as a mortising machine for those cabinetmakers
who wish to mortise-and-tenon their face frames. Mortising attachments are available for practically all makes of drill presses. Some drill press manufacturers have
available as an accessory a foot lever that frees the operator from having to pull a
hand lever. If considerable mortising is to be done, it would seem that the foot lever
would be a good investment. Although mortising can be done on the bench-type drill
press, for any sort of production a floor-type drill press with a foot lever would be
a much better machine (Fig. 4–36). The alternative would be to purchase a mortiser,
which would require an investment possibly beyond the means of a small cabinet
shop owner.

Figure 4–36   Drill press used with a mortising
attachment. (Courtesy Prieve Cabinets, Hutchinson, MN)

Figure 4–37 Close-up of the mortising attachment in action. (Courtesy Prieve Cabinets, Hutchinson, MN)

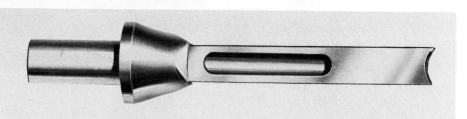

Figure 4–38 Mortising chisel. (Courtesy Delta International Machinery Corp.)

Mortising Attachment

Available as an accessory from most drill press manufacturers, the mortising attachment clamps directly on the quill of the drill press and uses a standard Jacobs chuck to hold the mortise bit. This attachment comes with a guide fence, hooked rods for holding in the work mortised, as well as a vertical hold-down (Fig. 4–37).

The foot feed accessory is made to fit floor-type drill presses with a 64-in. column. The mechanism is clamped to the column in two places and is attached at the drill press head. Maximum quill travel with the foot feed is 6 in. (see Fig. 3–25).

Mortise chisels are available in sizes from ¼ to 1¼ in. in increments of ¹⁄₁₆ in. Most commonly used chisels in the cabinet shop are the ¼-, ⁵⁄₁₆- and ⅜-in. sizes (Fig. 4–38).

Adjusting the Mortising Attachment for Operation

Mounting the mortising attachment to the drill press is a matter of following the manufacturer's directions. One important adjustment that must be made is the relationship between the mortising chisel and the mortising bit. Once the mortising bit has been placed in the drill press chuck, the chisel is slipped over the bit and tightened securely in position with the chisel lock screw. Be certain that the bit extends beyond the end of the chisel just a little so that it does not rub against the chisel. If the bit is allowed to rub against the chisel, friction soon causes enough heat to build to take the temper out of the chisel and render it useless.

The mortise itself must be in the exact center of the face-frame material. The fence must be adjusted and trial cuts made until the mortise is centered. To make this adjustment quickly and easily, make a shallow mortise in a piece of scrap the same thickness as the face-frame material. Reverse this piece, placing the opposite side against the fence and check to see if the chisel is cutting in exactly the same place as the first cut. If not, make the necessary fence adjustments and continue reversing the piece until the chisel cuts in exactly the same spot.

Adjust the hold-down and the hold-ins to the thickness and width of the material being mortised. These should be just loose enough so that the work is held but still slides along the fence smoothly.

Finally, the depth of the mortise cut must be determined. The drill press table should be at the correct height. The table plus the width of the face-frame material should be just short of reaching the end of the mortise chisel. The depth of cut is then determined by adjusting the depth stop control on the drill press. A depth mark on the end of the work being mortised makes for easy depth adjustment of the mortise chisel. Check the squareness of the chisel with the table. For long pieces being mortised, an outrigger support may be required to provide some help in holding up the material.

Marking and Cutting the Mortise

The exact location of all mortises required for the face frame must be determined very accurately. Only lines locating the ends of the mortises need be marked. This is done accurately with the try-square (Fig. 4–39). Where several pieces, such as cabinet stiles, are to be mortised and marked the same, a holding jig that will keep the pieces square and aligned while marking is handy.

If ¾-in. face-frame stock is used, the ¼-in. mortising chisel is the correct size. For ¹³⁄₁₆-in. face framing, many cabinetmakers use the ⁵⁄₁₆-in. chisel. Most tenons are made approximately ⅞ in. long if the stiles are 2-in. in width. That length of tenon will be about right for stiles that have tenons on both sides at the same marking. Set the depth of the mortise cut just a bit deeper than the length of the tenon. That way the joint is sure to shoulder-fit tightly and a chip or a bit of sawdust in the bottom of the hole will not interfere.

The proper technique for making the mortise calls for making the two end cuts first and then cleaning up between the first two cuts. The chisel has a tendency to drift sideways or be forced out of vertical when cutting on only three sides of the chisel. Thus the last cut might be at a slight slant if the cuts were made in exact con-

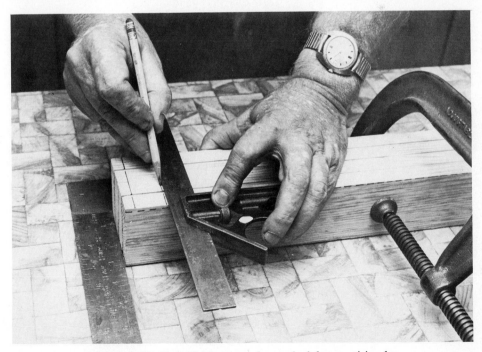

Figure 4–39 Several pieces can be marked for mortising by clamping them square and even.

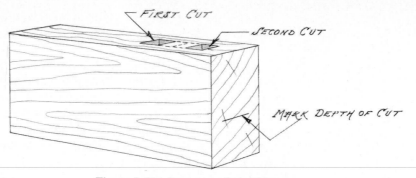

Figure 4-40   Sequence of mortising cuts.

secutive order (Fig. 4-40). Be sure to hold the work firmly against the fence while mortising to assure vertical chisel cuts. Finally, carefully clean the mortises, freeing them of any stray chips or sawdust that might interfere with proper fit of the joint. For mortising, the speed of the drill press should be set at approximately 1000 rpm.

THE SHAPER—THE CABINET SHOP'S FIRST ADDITION

As mentioned in Chapter 3, the spindle shaper is probably not a machine that the beginning professional will have in his or her shop. However, it should be one of the first equipment additions. A good shaper is a relatively expensive machine, but the use made of the shaper in the cabinet shop in extensive. Because it operates at a high speed—usually around 10,000 rpm—the quality of the work turned out on a shaper is excellent. The work can be fed into the knives at a good rate, so the production accomplished is also tops. Basically, the shaper is used for edge shaping of pieces of lumber with decorative moldings. In the cabinet shop the primary use made of the machine is in rabbeting and lipping cabinet doors. If the craftsperson has ambitions of producing the raised paneled doors that are so popular today, the shaper is a necessity (see Fig. 3-17).

Types of Shapers

Although shapers are manufactured in both single-spindle and double-spindle models, the cabinetmaker will probably start by purchasing the smaller, single-spindle machine. The advantage of the larger machines is the increased work table area, which makes handling material being run much easier and safer. The distance the spindle will travel up and down is also greater on the larger models, which means increased capacity. Most spindle shapers are equipped with a reversing switch so that work can be fed from either direction as the spindle and knives change direction. In normal operation the work is fed from right to left as the knives rotate in counterclockwise motion. Some setups, however, require the knives to rotate clockwise and work to be fed from the opposite direction.

Shaper Knives

The small standard shaper uses the ½-in. spindle diameter and three-wing cutters that are available in a wide variety of shapes and patterns. Collars are purchased with the cutters and are used for positioning the cutter on the spindle as well as for depth of cut control when running curved stock using the starting pin (Fig. 4-41).

When an edge shape is required that cannot be met by using a standard three-wing cutter, a special knife-holding clamp-type head is available (Fig. 4-42). These hold straight knives that are ground to the desired pattern by the craftsperson. This

Figure 4–41 Typical shaper cutters and collars for a ½-in. spindle.

Figure 4–42 Clamp-type cutter head for the spindle shaper.

type of cutter head must be set up and operated with great care, as it is possible for the knives to work loose and cause severe damage to the operator. Most cabinet shops producing cabinets for the home rely on the standard three-wing cutters.

Adjustments to Make on the Shaper

The shaper fence must be adjusted properly when running stock on the shaper. The fence is fully adjustable to control depth of cut by moving the fence forward or back. Wing nuts are tightened to lock the fence once it is in position (Fig. 4–43). The fence is also adjustable to compensate for the amount of material being removed by the knives. Being a split fence, one-half of the fence can be adjusted forward an amount equal to the depth of cut being made. If just a pattern is being run on the edge of the board and no actual dimension change is made on the board, the two halves of the fence must be directly in line.

The spindle itself is adjustable vertically by means of a hand lever or hand wheel. The location of the cutter on the spindle is also adjustable by using collars under the cutter to raise its position on the spindle. Once the cutter is located and the spindle raised or lowered to its proper spot, it is important that the spindle be locked in position. If not, vibration will allow the spindle to lower after the machine is started and a spoiled piece of work can be the result.

Figure 4-43   The shaper fence is a split fence with each side adjustable.

Figure 4-44   Shop-made "featherboards" will hold the work safely.

Available as an accessory are spring hold-downs that make an easier and safer job of running fairly thin strips of wood. Shop-made feather boards can be used to accomplish this same purpose (Fig. 4-44).

Operating the Shaper Safely

The actual operating techniques for the shaper are discussed in detail in Chapter 9. That chapter contains a discussion and photographs of shaper operating skills needed to produce all types of cabinet doors.

The general safety procedures for shaper operation are, in many cases, similar to those given for other woodworking machines. The shaper is unique in two respects: (1) It operates at an extremely high rate of speed, and (2) it is a difficult machine to guard adequately.

Two of the most basic safety rules for shaper operation are: (1) Keep the cutters very sharp at all times, and (2) read the grain carefully and always try to feed with the grain. A combination of a dull cutter with the work being fed into the machine against the grain can result in kickbacks and a serious accident. Curved work is run on the shaper by using the "starting pin" against which the work is braced while fed gradually into the cutter and against the depth collar (Fig. 4-45). A firm grip must be kept on the work at this point, for the danger of kickback is great. Once the work has been successfully positioned against the depth collar, it is then kept in contact with the collar while following the contour of the curved work being run. Unless a ball-bearing collar is being used, the edge of the work will be charred slightly by a stationary collar turning with the cutter. This can be minimized to some extent by holding the pressure of the work against the collar to no more than absolutely necessary and by moving the work along at a steady pace. Allowing the work to remain in any one spot will result in a deeper edge burn. However, the craftsperson must be prepared to do some sanding after the run to remove any charring of the edge, however minimal (Fig. 4-46).

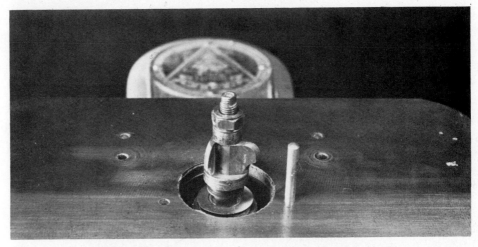

Figure 4-45 For curved work the starting pin and depth collars are used.

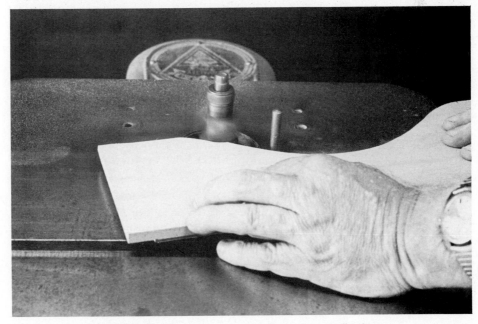

Figure 4-46 Running curved work on the spindle shaper.

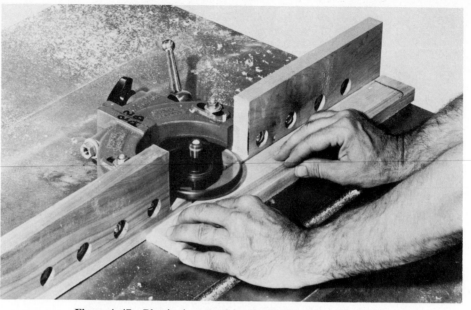

Figure 4-47   Plastic ring guard for the shaper. (Courtesy Delta International Machinery Corp.)

The traditional type of guard used on the shaper has been the ring guard. Although this did give some protection to the operator on straight runs, it had to be put aside when doing curved work. One manufacturer has marketed a plastic, see-through guard that mounts on the spindle together with the collars and cutters but extends somewhat beyond the radius of the cut being made. It can thus be used for both straight runs and curved operations. The safety collar is mounted about ½ in. above the surface of the work being run, so it is a fine position to guard againt accidents involving the fingers (Fig. 4-47).

REVIEW QUESTIONS

4.1. What is a good basic rule for safe operation of woodworking machines?

4.2. What is the first operation that must be performed on a piece of lumber to produce straight rippings on the table saw?

4.3. When ripping lumber on the table saw, what does the phrase "allowance for jointing" mean?

4.4. Give at least two causes for a table saw to "kick" lumber.

4.5. What is a good solvent for removing burned-on pitch or resins on a table saw blade?

4.6. When ripping on the table saw, what is a safe height for the blade to extend above the thickness of the stock being ripped?

4.7. List three different ways of handling long, narrow rippings on the table saw.

4.8. What is meant by the phrase "a forgiving table saw"?

4.9. What are stop rods? What is their purpose?

4.10. If using the rip fence for a cutoff jig, what should be done if the pieces being cut are shorter than the width of the miter gauge?

4.11. Name two devices that are commonly used to groove wood on the table saw.

4.12. In cabinetmaking, what are the most common uses made of the dado set?

4.13. Can edge shaping be done on the table saw? How? What are the difficulties encountered with this method of shaping?

4.14. Name two things that can be done to minimize "grain tearing" when jointing wood.

4.15. What can the operator of a jointer do to minimize the noticeability of knife marks on the wood? What does the craftsperson do to eliminate these?

4.16. What is a chamfer? A stop chamfer? What must be done to produce a stop chamfer on the jointer?

4.17. List at least three operations that are commonly performed on the spindle shaper in the production of custom cabinets.

4.18. What is a three-wing cutter? What other type of cutters are there for the spindle shaper?

4.19. What is the feather board, and what is its use?

4.20. What is a starting pin, and what is its use?

SUGGESTED CLASS ACTIVITIES AND STUDENT ASSIGNMENTS

4.1. Discuss the various types and uses made of table saw guards. When visiting cabinet shops, observe the use made of saw guards.

4.2. Using catalogs, visits to hardware and builders' stores and other sources, have the students gather information on table saw blades—types, price, carbide versus regular steel, and so on.

4.3. Visit a local saw sharpening shop. Ask the proprietor to speak to the class on blade quality, maintenance, and sharpening. Ask the person to demonstrate his or her craft.

4.4. Demonstrate to the class how to adjust the rip fence properly for safe operation and no kicking.

4.5. Demonstrate to the class the proper sequence in running out stock, jointing to dimension, and cutting to length.

4.6. Have the students practice "reading" grain direction. Test by having the students actually run that board on the jointer to see if they are correct. Deliberately pick tough woods to read, grain reverses, curly grain, and so on.

4.7. Have each student make his or her own jointer knife-holding jig for sharpening jointer knives on the drill press. If possible, during the term, have each student remove and reset jointer knives in the cutter head.

4.8. Assign some students to investigate the cost of drill press mortising attachments, foot levers, and mortising chisels, as well as regular mortising machines.

4.9. Assign other students to investigate the costs of spindle shapers in various models. Have them look into cutter costs as well, especially the costs of sets of knives to do panel raising, door coping, and so on. Have them look into the cost of carbide knives in all of these areas.

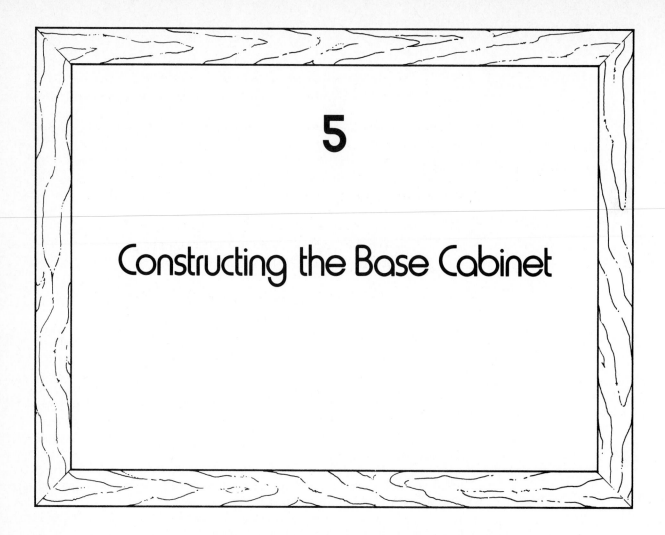

5

Constructing the Base Cabinet

"There are as many ways of building cabinets as there are cabinetmakers." Visit any number of small cabinet shops and the discovery is soon made that all craftspersons have their own particular methods of constructing cabinets. The differences may be based on the machinery the cabinetmaker owns, the type of material that is used, or the cabinetmaker's individual assessment of the amount of labor required for one type of construction over another. In some cases it is simply a matter of the cabinetmaker having been taught one particular system and having become proficient in that method, being comfortable with it and having had success in selling cabinets built that way.

Cabinet-building systems are really not all that different however. The differences that are apparent fall into just a few categories:

1. The method of making the joints in the face frame
2. The type of cabinet base that is built
3. The material used for bottoms, end panels, and interior partitions
4. The type of drawer construction and drawer runners used

Cabinet-building systems are not easy to categorize, for cabinetmakers will combine features from one "system" with those of another if it is found advantageous to do so. This chapter presents the two basic cabinet-building systems as well as ways in which individual cabinetmakers combine these systems by selecting features from each.

THE TWO BASIC CABINET-BUILDING SYSTEMS

Generally speaking, cabinet building can be divided into two basic methods, each of which is presented in this chapter. The choice of which system to use depends on several factors, and these factors are also discussed. In the end it is up to the individual cabinetmaker to make the decision as to which system to use.

Box-and-Frame System

Historically, the oldest kitchen-cabinet-building method is the "build a box and apply a front frame" system. In the days prior to plywood, this was about the only way that cabinets could be made. Panels were glued up from 1 in. × 12 in. lumber for base cabinet ends, partitions, and bottoms. For the most part, cabinets were built without backs—simply fastening the cabinet to the wall and having the wall itself serve as the back (a feature that some cabinetmakers still use).

With the advent of plywood, most cabinetmakers stopped gluing up panels from lumber and started cutting full-size ends, bottoms, and partitions from ¾-in. plywood. The construction system of nailing the frame to the box remained the same. The problems that the old-time cabinetmaker had with these large panels warping by-and-large disappeared with the appearance of plywood.

Traditionally, the front frame of the box-and-frame cabinet was mortised and tenoned or doweled. The mortise and tenon was probably preferred, as a mortising machine or drill press attachment was less expensive than a doweling machine (Fig. 5–1).

With some minor variations the box-and-frame system of building cabinets is still by far the most common method of cabinet construction. Practically all factory-manufactured, unitized cabinets employ this method and dowel the front frame. The small shop cabinetmaker, too, uses the frame-and-box system but more often mortise-and-tenons the front frame. The reason is the same—it is less expensive to purchase a mortising attachment for the drill press than to purchase a sophisticated boring machine for making dowel joints.

Today, rather than use ¾-in. plywood the cabinet builder often substitutes ½-in. plywood or particle board for the end panels and partitions and, of course, uses ¼-in. plywood for cabinet backs and drawer bottoms. The system, however, remains basically the same even with the substitution of thinner material.

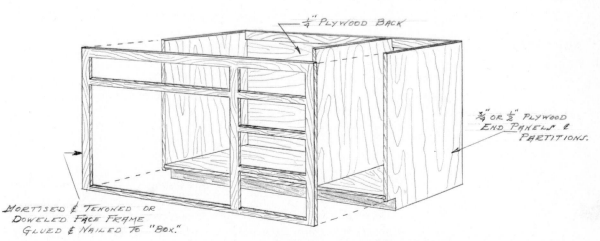

Figure 5–1 Box-and-frame system.

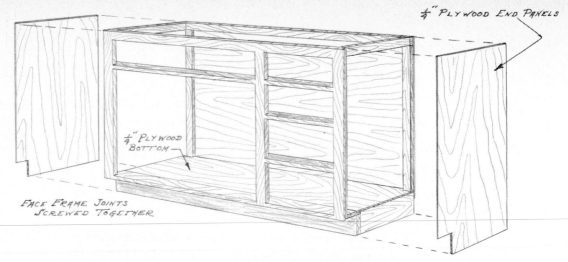

Figure 5–2 Casework system.

Casework System

Adapted from the makers of radio and television cabinets, this system is unique in several ways. First, it substitutes ¼-in. plywood instead of ¾- or ½-in. plywood or particle board for end panels, cabinet bottoms, and tops. Second, although not required, the joints in the framing of the casework system are screwed together rather than mortised-and-tenoned or doweled. Third, the entire technique of construction is different from that system employed in the box-and-frame method. Rather than build a box and then apply the face frame, in the casework system each part of the cabinet is built separately. For example, the face frame is built first, then the toe space and cabinet bottom, followed by the reinforced ¼-in. plywood back. These are then assembled and the plywood end panels and partitions are installed last. This will become clearer as the complete system is presented later in the chapter (Fig. 5–2).

Of course, the ¼-in. plywood panels used in the casework system are reinforced with solid lumber stripping. The subsequent savings in material is substantial over using ¾-in. or even ½-in. hardwood plywood. This is very important to home craftspersons, for the expense of materials is the largest cost item with which they are faced—labor not being a factor to "do-it-yourselfers."

The casework system lends itself very well to the beginning professional, as an absolute minimum of machinery is required to produce high-quality cabinets. No mortising machine or boring machine is required to produce a face frame that is screwed together using the methods described in this chapter. Thus beginners can set up shop and hold their investment in machinery as low as possible. This means that they can be in business and, if successful, after a few years add machinery that will increase their production.

ADVANTAGES AND DISADVANTAGES OF THE TWO SYSTEMS

From the introductory information presented thus far concerning these two cabinet-making systems, it becomes obvious that each has its advantages and disadvantages.

Box-and-Frame System

Advantages

These are the advantages unique to this system:

1. Depending on the type of front-frame construction employed, this system generally requires less labor. Very little machining is required on the plywood and particle-board panels that make up the basic "box."

2. With the proper machinery this system lends itself to high-production factory methods of manufacturing. Sophisticated tenoners, mortisers, boring machines, panel saws, and so on, make high production of face frames and the basic "box" possible.

3. The basic box-and-frame system is quite easily mastered by the beginner or apprentice.

Disadvantages

These are the disadvantages of the box-and-frame system:

1. The cost of materials is higher than those used in the casework system.

2. More machinery is required to produce mortised or doweled face frames than that required to make screwed frames.

3. The average cabinetmaker simply nails the face frame to the basic box, thus having a face frame marred with numerous, filled nail spots.

4. More hours of labor are required to mortise or dowel the face frame than to fasten the face frame with screws. (However, building the "box" requires less labor than is required in the casework system.) A face frame using mortise-and-tenon joints is also a bit more costly than a face frame assembled with screws, as the length of the tenons must be added to the cost.

5. The mortise joints as well as dowel joints must be clamped until the glued joint is set. Although many cabinetmakers will pin their mortises with short brads, thus eliminating long clamping time, this, too, takes additional labor. (In larger shops electronic glue curing speeds this process.)

Casework System

Advantages

The advantages of the casework system are:

1. The cost of materials is less using the casework method.

2. As mortise-and-tenon or dowel joints are not used, there is no investment in this type of machinery. Thus a beginning professional can set up shop with a minimum capital outlay.

3. There is a slight labor advantage in producing face frames that are screwed together over mortised or doweled frames.

4. The face frames are practically free from filled nail holes.

5. The face frame is made up of fewer pieces than a mortised or doweled frame.

Disadvantages

These are the possible disadvantages of the casework system:

1. Overall, it requires slightly more labor to build cabinets using this system.

2. The casework system does not lend itself as well as the box-and-frame method to high-production techniques.

3. It is a slightly more complicated system of cabinet building to learn than the box-and-frame system.

4. Although thoroughly accepted for over 60 years in the cabinetmaking market, the use of ¼-in. panels is sometimes used as a negative feature by competing cabinetmakers.

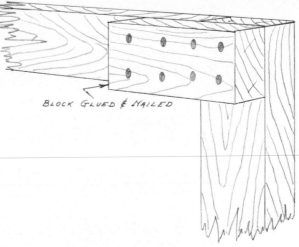

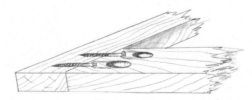

Figure 5-3 Butt-block joint.

Figure 5-4 Screw joint system used by a production frame machine.

As mentioned previously, in the final analysis the would-be cabinetmaker must make the choice of a system (or combination of systems). For the beginning professional the best choice would probably be the casework system with the screwed face frame. For the advanced professional interested in higher production, the box-and-frame system with a mortised or doweled frame would no doubt be the better choice.

Other Face-Frame Joining Methods

Two other face-frame joint procedures are worthy of mention. One fairly common method among small cabinet shop operators is to simply glue and nail joint-reinforcing wood blocks across the butt joints of the face frame (Fig. 5–3). Although this method seems to upset many experienced woodworkers who insist that the *only* joint is a mortise-and-tenon or doweled joint, the butt-block cabinetmakers do seem to carry on quite well in a highly competitive market. This joint system will not be described further in this text, as it is self-explanatory and easy to apply if the cabinetmaker should desire to adopt this technique.

The second method that should be mentioned is a high-production face-frame machine that clamps the entire face together in one assembly and then, using both air and electricity, drills a pilot hole, an angled counterbored hole, and drives screws into the joints (Fig. 5–4). However, this is not a small shop machine, as several thousand dollars are required as the investment, and quantity production would be needed for this machine to pay its way.

BUILDING BASE CABINETS USING THE CASEWORK SYSTEM

Once the working drawing of the cabinets is completed and the plan dimensioned, the actual construction of the cabinets can begin. Building, in the case of the model set of cabinets presented in this text, will begin with the base unit. This is the usual procedure in most shops. In larger cabinet shops where two or three cabinetmakers are employed, the base cabinets and upper units are built simultaneously.

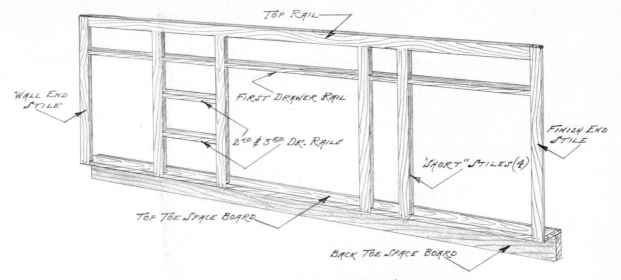

Figure 5-5 Front frame terms.

In custom cabinet work the actual construction always begins with the making of the face frame. The very critical length dimension of the cabinet is accurately built into the face frame. Thus the remaining portions of the cabinet are all constructed in relationship to the measurements of the face frame.

The first job will be to become familiar with the names of the various parts that make up the front frame. Study Fig. 5-5 carefully to become completely familiar with the terminology used. Note that this model cabinet has one *finished* end that will be visible and one *wall* end that will not be seen. Finished ends are built of the same material as the face frame. Wall ends are constructed of much less expensive material, such as softwood plywood or particle board.

All dimensions given in the instructions are based on the type of material listed. The front frame is made of ¾-in. hardwood in this model cabinet. If in the actual building of a base cabinet $^{13}/_{16}$-in. hardwood is used, the front-to-back measurements of the interior pieces of the base cabinets will have to be shortened by $^{1}/_{16}$ in.

Face-Frame Bill of Materials

Once the names of the pieces that make up the face frame have been mastered, the cabinetmaker should prepare a "take-off" list of the exact sizes of these various pieces. This list of pieces is then "run out" by the builder, with extreme care being paid to accuracy of the machining to net size.

The model cabinet face-frame bill of materials will contain these pieces carefully machined to the net size as listed. Standard work procedure is to run out the longest and widest pieces first. The builder continues working his or her way through the stock billing list, cutting the smallest pieces last. This way the sawer is using the culls from the larger pieces as the source for the smaller pieces.

Toe space boards

(Owner's choice of wood for all frame pieces.) Material required:

1 pc. ¾ in. × 4 in. × 101 ¾ in.
1 pc. ¾ in. × 3¾ in. × 101 ¾ in.

(*Note:* All vertical face-frame pieces are dimensioned for a 4-in.-high toe space. If only a 3-in. toe space is wanted, dimensions will have to be adjusted accordingly.)

Some question may arise as to how the 101 ¾-in. length of the toe space boards is arrived at. Three-quarters of an inch is subtracted from the overall cabinet length of 102½ in. because of the ¼-in. rabbet in the finish end stile and the ½-in. rabbet in the wall end stile, leaving a net length of the toe space boards of 101 ¾ in. If both ends, for example, were finished ends, only ½ in. would be subtracted, while a full inch would be subtracted if both ends were wall ends.

Horizontal face-frame members

Material required:

1 pc. ¾ in. × 2 in. × 98½ in.	top rail
1 pc. ¾ in. × 1¾ in. × 100 in.	first drawer rail
2 pcs. ¾ in. × 1¾ in. × 15½ in.	second and third drawer rails

Vertical face-frame members

Material required:

2 pcs. ¾ in. × 2 in. × 31¼ in.	end stiles
4 pcs. ¾ in. × 2 in. × 29¼ in.	short stiles

The dimensions of the horizontal face-frame members are calculated thus:

Top rail: Exactly 4 in. less than the overall length of the cabinet. Subtract the width of the two end stiles.

First drawer rail: 1½ in. longer than the top rail. This rail is notched on the ends to fit behind the end stiles (Fig. 5–6).

Second and third drawer rails: Drawer opening dimension plus 1½ in. These rails are also notched to fit behind the vertical stiles in the same manner as the first drawer rail.

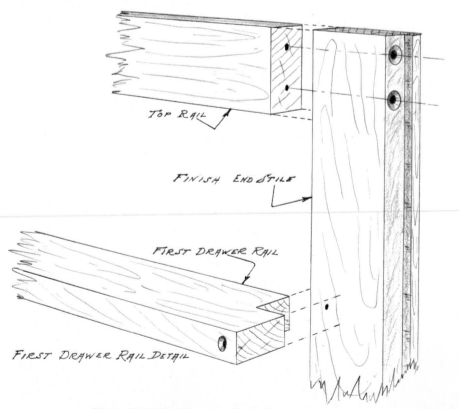

TOP RAIL

FINISH END STILE

FIRST DRAWER RAIL

FIRST DRAWER RAIL DETAIL

Figure 5–6 First drawer rail detail.

The vertical stiles are figured in this manner:

End stiles: The standard cabinet height is 36 in. less ¾ in. for the countertop, less another 4 in. for the toe space, leaving 31¼ in. for the length of the end stiles.

Short stiles: Exactly 2 in. shorter than the end stiles—the width of the top rail.

Machining Required on Face-Frame Members

After the face-frame members have all been machined carefully to the net size required, the next operation is to do the rabbeting, grooving, and dadoing necessary prior to assembling the front frame.

Rabbeting the finish end stile

Rabbet the *finish end stile* with a ¼ in. × ½ in. rabbet (Fig. 5–7).

Tip: Machine the depth of the rabbet just a bit deeper than ¼ in., the thickness of the plywood that will be used for the end panel. After the plywood is later applied, the stile is then sanded or planed *down to the plywood*. If the rabbet should be a bit shallow, it is nearly impossible to sand the plywood down to the stile without sanding through the veneer of the plywood.

Experience has shown that cutting the rabbets by making two passes on the table saw results in less grain tear-out than by using the jointer for this operation.

Rabbeting the wall end stile

The wall end stile is rabbeted with a ½ in. × ½ in. rabbet (Fig. 5–8). This ½ in. × ½ in. rabbet on the wall end stile will recess the end panel by ¼ in. This

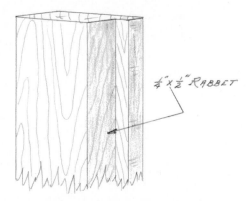

Figure 5–7 Finish end stile detail.

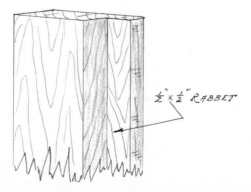

Figure 5–8 Wall end stile detail.

¼ in. extra on the wall end stile can be a real lifesaver at times. If the wall happens to be slightly out of plumb, this extra ¼ in. can be used to scribe a neat fit to the wall. If both ends of a cabinet are wall ends and the cabinet is just a bit too tight to slide into position, the ¼-in. lips can be removed to allow the cabinet to be easily positioned. Often, the plasterer or sheetrock installers build up the material in the room corners and, consequently, the cabinet will be too tight, despite careful original measurements and allowances. Again, the ¼-in. lips on the front frame can be sawed off to provide the cabinet with the necessary freedom to slip into place.

Grooving the four short stiles

To accommodate the ½-in. interior partitions of the cabinet, run a groove ¼ in. deep by ½ in. wide on the back of the four short stiles. Stop this groove about 4 in. from the top end of these stiles. This will forestall any possibility of the groove interfering with the screw joint at that spot (Fig. 5-9).

Tip: Shim the dado head assembly with a thin cardboard "doughnut" to be certain that the ½ in. cabinet partitions will slip nicely into the groove. This might save some laborious sanding or planing if the groove is just a bit too narrow. Occasionally, too, the plywood is a bit oversize, especially if using shop grade. By checking this fit before hand, a lot of wasted labor can be prevented.

Notching the horizontal frame pieces

The position of all the stiles must be carefully laid on the best-looking edge of the top toe space board.

Important: The notch for the wall end stile is marked at 1½ in. because the ½-in. lip on this stile will extend *beyond* the end of the toe space board. The notch for the finish end is marked at exactly 1¾ in. with only ¼ in. extending beyond the toe space board (Fig. 5-10). All other notches for the short stiles are marked at 2 in. Mark these notches carefully by consulting the working drawing.

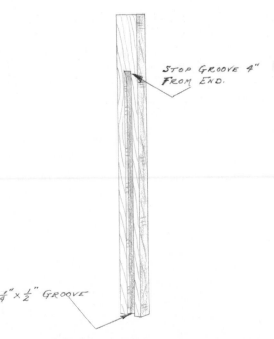

Figure 5-9 Short stile detail.

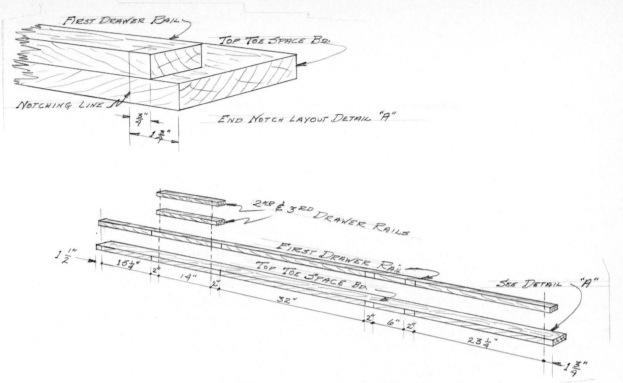

Figure 5–10 Temporary rail assembly for "notching."

Study Fig. 5–10 and 5–11 carefully. These illustrate how the horizontal frame members are assembled in a "bundle" atop the toe space board for notching on the table saw. Each of the cross members is temporarily nailed in position atop the other with 1¼-in. brads or wire nails, taking care not to nail where a notch is to be cut. Keep the front edges of all the assembled pieces perfectly flush. Always select the best-looking edge and place it to the front of the "bundle" as that is the edge that will be visible in the finished cabinet.

Tip: Rubbing the nails with paraffin will make nailing into the hardwood easier and will save a lot of bent nails!

Another crucial layout is the position of the first drawer rail and the two short-drawer rails in this laminated bundle. These rails must be positioned so that when they are notched they will lap *behind* the two end stiles and, in the case of the shorter rails, behind the short stiles exactly ¾ in. When these pieces are nailed in the bundle, be certain their ends extend beyond the stile notch marks exactly ¾ in. on each end.

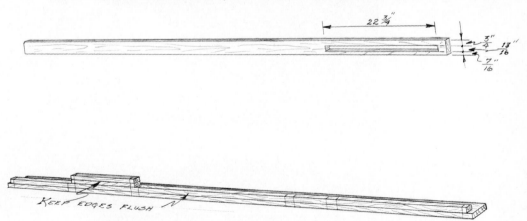

Figure 5–11 (*Top*) hole for the cutting board in the top rail; (*bottom*) rails assembled ready for notching.

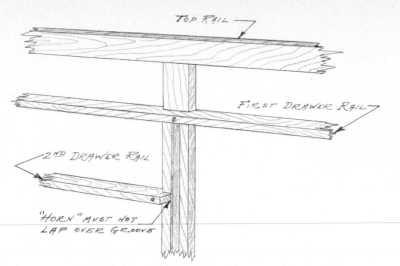

Figure 5-12 Rear view of assembly at short stile.

These "tongues" that will lap behind the short stiles must not interfere with the groove that was plowed in the back of these stiles. If they are just a bit too long or out of position slightly, the ½-in. partition would not be able to be placed in its proper position later (Fig. 5-12).

After the laminated bundle is completed, with your try square carry the marks that were placed on the edge of the top toe space board across the edges of the assembled pieces and onto the surfaces of those pieces as well. The marks will then be visible from any position that the "bundle" might be held while sawing the notches. Figure 5-11 shows this clearly.

All notches are now ready to be cut in all pieces at the same time, ensuring exact lineup with no possible error. *The table saw blade must be exactly as high as the thickness of the wood being used for the front frame.* Ordinarily, this will be ¾ in. However, it could easily vary due to the lumberyard furnishing nominal stock rather than stock surfaced to ¾ in. Make a few test cuts in scrap material before doing the final cuts.

Sawing the notches

If your cabinet frame is of any length beyond 5 to 6 ft., it would be well to have a helper who can hold the end for you—or at least have some sort of outrigger available to support the end of the laminated bundle. A sawhorse built to the exact height of the table saw is perfect for this purpose (Fig. 5-13).

Figure 5-13 Sawing the notches on a table saw.

COMPLETED NOTCH

BREAK AWAY WITH HAMMER, CLEAN BY MOVING ACROSS TOP OF SAW BLADE.

SAW BLADE MUST BE EXACTLY AS HIGH AS FRAME MATERIAL IS THICK.

Figure 5-14   Details of the notching process.

Figure 5-15   Notching operation close-up.

Use a miter gauge to assure squareness of cut. Start the notching by sawing inside of and as close to the lines as possible. Do the two end cuts first. Then make a series of closely spaced cuts about $\frac{1}{16}$ to $\frac{1}{8}$ in. apart through the remaining distance between the first two outside cuts. As you become skilled in the handling of this rather awkward bundle, it is possible to make a cut both on the forward pass over the saw blade and on the reverse pass—just be certain to have a sharp blade in your table saw and a firm grip on the bundle (Figs. 5-14 and 5-15).

Next, with a hammer, break out the material that remains between the closely spaced cuts. Return the bundle to the saw and moving the notched space *slowly forward and at the same time left and right horizontally over the saw blade,* clean up the notched area to the full depth of the saw setting. A few practice tries will make it all seem quite easy and production will quickly improve.

Test-fit one of the vertical stiles in the newly cut notches (Fig 5-16). If the notch is a bit narrow, it can easily be widened a fraction of an inch by a quick pass over the blade. If the cut is just a bit wide, no great difficulty will be encountered, as judicious use of wood filler later will take care of this.

Figure 5-16 Test each notch for proper fit.

After completing all notches, carefully disassemble the bundle, exercising extreme caution that the front edges of the pieces are not marred in any way.

Rabbet in Rear of Top Toe Space Board

Study the toe space illustration carefully (Fig. 5-17). The back edge of the top toe space board must be rabbeted ¼ in. × ½ in. for the ¼-in. plywood cabinet bottom. If material other than ¼-in. thickness is used for the bottom, of course, the rabbet size must be adjusted accordingly. Again be certain that the ¼-in. depth of the rabbet is equal to or just slightly deeper than the thickness of the plywood, to facilitate sanding the toe space board down to the plywood.

Hole for Cutting Board in Top Rail (if desired)

Carefully lay out the hole for the cutting board in the top rail. Follow the dimensions given in Fig. 5-11. This cutout can be done on a table saw, but it is easier to do with a portable circle saw after the cabinet is assembled (Fig. 5-18A). Finish the cutout by using a saber saw to make the end cuts and sand and file the roughness from the opening (Fig. 5-18B).

Assembling the Front Frame

Assemble the toe space pieces

Glue and nail with 4d finish nails the top toe space board to the back toe space piece. By placing the nails in the rabbeted area of the top piece, the nails will later be covered by the cabinet bottom. (Fig. 5-19).

Tip: When the face frame is constructed of hardwood, nailing can be a problem. Snip off the small head of a 4d finish nail and use the nail as a bit in the electric drill. You will have a hole the exact size of the nail and the constant bending of the nails when driven into hardwood will be eliminated. Rubbing a little paraffin on the nail has already been suggested.

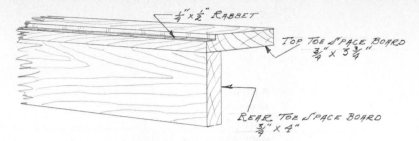

Figure 5–17 Toe space detail.

Figure 5–18A The hole for the cutting board is cut with a circular saw.

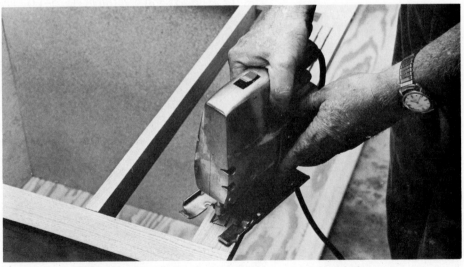

Figure 5–18B Finish the ends of the cutting board hole using a saber saw.

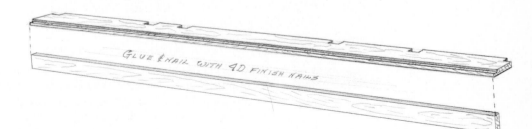

Figure 5–19 Toe space assembly.

Figure 5-20 The finish end stile and the top rail are clamped in a vise.

Assemble the top rail and end stiles

Arrange the top rail and the finish end stile in the bench vise as illustrated in Fig. 5-20. *Be certain that the correct stile is selected for the end of the top rail being assembled.* It is very easy to make an error here and get the wrong end stile in the assembly. Carefully follow these steps in making the screw joints. It might be well to practice a couple of times on some scrap stock. A couple of times through the procedure will help make the assembly of these joints fast and efficient.

1. Drill 3/16 in. shank holes through the stile, making certain not to drill too deeply, if at all, into the end of the top rail. Place glue in the joint prior to assembly.
2. Countersink each hole with a 1/2 in. countersink—exercising care not to mar the edge of the rabbeted area.
3. While still assembled in the vise, drill 3/32 in. pilot holes in the end of top rail.
4. Drive 2½ in. 8FH wood screws into the holes tightly.

Tips on Driving Screws: Lubricate threads of wood screws with mild soap or beeswax. Paraffin does not work well for driving screws. Beeswax, if available, is the best, as it contains no acid to attack the screw threads as does soap.

A large auto-return ratchet screwdriver works well for driving the screws. It is fast and the screwdriver can be used at full extension to obtain good leverage for the final turns. Do not attempt to drive the screws all the way "home" with the ratchet action, as the blade has a tendency to slip out of the screw slot under heavy pressure and damage the work. Open to full length and lock the screwdriver in this position. Turn the final few turns by hand power. Again, a few times through the procedure will make all the moves easier. An alternative that works well for driving the screws is a screwdriver bit used in a brace. It is not as fast or as handy but does give a lot of power (Fig. 5-21).

Now do the opposite end stile. Assemble the pieces in the vise as before, being certain that the *lips on the end stiles are facing in the same direction!* Occasionally, it is difficult to assemble quite long pieces in the vise. A C-clamp and a scrap piece of wood is sufficient to hold the pieces for assembly. Do not be concerned about variations in joint surfaces; face sanding will remove these.

Figure 5-21 Use a ratchet screwdriver to drive the 2½-in. screws that hold the joint.

Position and attach the first drawer rail

Lay the front frame face down on the floor or large working surface. The position of the first drawer rail is exactly 5 in. below the top rail and against the back of the end stiles. Cut a gauge stick from scrap exactly 5 in. long to use as a vertical spacer. It is difficult to hold the piece in position to just a line. Holding the drawer rail firmly against the spacer gauge and tight against the stile, follow these steps:

1. Drill and countersink a ³⁄₁₆ in. shank hole through the "horn" on the end of the drawer rail.
2. Drill a ³⁄₃₂ in. pilot hole in the stile.
3. Apply a drop or two of glue and drive a 1¼ in. 8FH wood screw with the ratchet screwdriver, again lubricating the threads with beeswax (Fig. 5-22). (This lubrication is usually not needed in softwoods—just in the hard varieties) (Fig. 5-22).

Figure 5-22 The first drawer rail is attached to the end stile. Note the use of a 5-in. gauge stick.

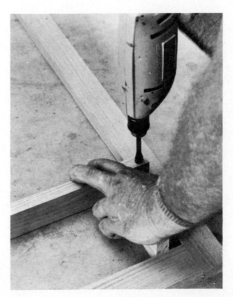

Attach the short stiles to the top rail

1. Transfer the location marks for the short stiles from the top toe space board onto the top rail.

2. Place the short stile in a vise—the top rail will have to be held in position with a C-clamp and a scrap block of wood. Put glue in the joint before attaching the block and clamp.

3. Working carefully between the marks, counterbore two ½ in. holes about ½ in. deep into the top rail.

4. Proceed with the ³⁄₁₆ in. shank hole and the ³⁄₃₂ in. pilot hole and, again, drive two 2½ in. 8FH wood screws with the ratchet screwdriver (Figs. 5-23 and 5-24).

Figure 5-23 Top rail and short stile assembled in a vise for joining.

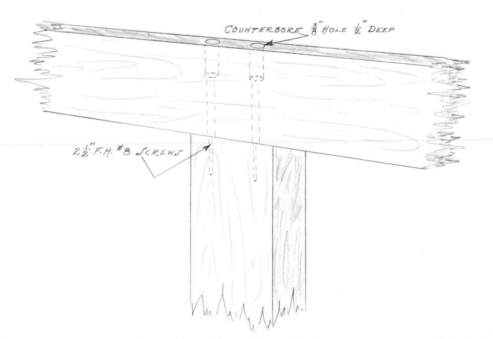

Figure 5-24 Short stile/top rail joint.

Figure 5-25 The first drawer rail and all short drawer rails are fastened with screws.

Attach the remaining short drawer rails

1. Cut two vertical spacer gauges from scrap stock—6 and 7 in. in length.
2. Using the same procedure for installing the first drawer rail, the second drawer rail is installed 6 in. below the first drawer rail and the third drawer rail 7 in. below the second rail (Fig. 5-25).

Constructing the Cabinet Bottom

The assembled face frame is set aside for the moment and the next subassembly is the cabinet bottom. Bill of materials for cabinet bottom:

> 6 pcs. ¾ in. × 4½ in. × 19⁹⁄₁₆ in. (any inexpensive material is suitable)
> 1 pc. ¾ in. × 1½ in. × 101¾ in. (any inexpensive material is suitable)
> 1 pc. ¼ in. fir plywood, 101¾ in. × 20½ in. (wait on cutting this piece to size until exact measurements can be checked on the base assembly)

Run out the above-listed pieces to the net dimensions shown.

Assembly procedure for cabinet bottom

1. Nail the two outside bottom support pieces at the ends of the 1½ in.-long nailer piece with No. 6 box nails (Figs. 5-26A and 5-26B).
2. Space the remaining support pieces about 16 to 18 in. apart in the remaining space. Nail in place through the back strip with No. 6 box nails.

Tip: As an aid to the plumber, mark on the plywood bottom where any braces have been placed so that the drain and water pipes can avoid that spot.

3. Nail the previously assembled toe space to the bottom support pieces with 6d finish nails, squaring each as you nail (Fig. 5-27).

Figure 5–26A The bottom support pieces are nailed to the ends of the stringer.

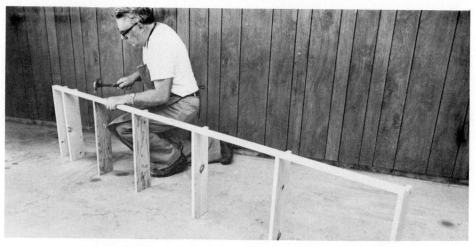

Figure 5–26B The remaining bottom supports are nailed in position.

Figure 5–27 The toe space assembly is nailed to the bottom supports.

Tip: Again use the "nail in the drill" technique to prevent splitting at the ends of the toe space. Be certain that the bottom support pieces are exactly flush with the bottom of the rabbet in the toe space and also flush with the ends of toe space.

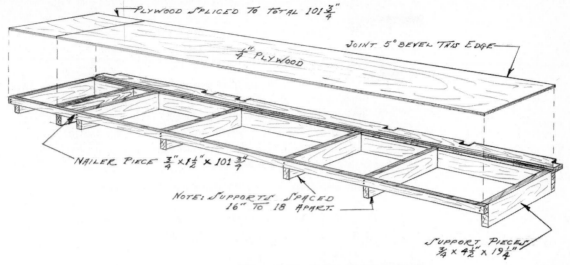

Figure 5–28 Cabinet bottom details.

4. Check the dimensions for the plywood bottom panel and cut to exact size. Joint a 5-degree bevel along one edge of the plywood (Fig. 5–28). Note that the bottom plywood panel will have to be spliced to make up the total length of 101¾ in.

Note: This bevel creates a nice tight joint because it brings the top edge of the plywood tightly up against the solid wood of the rabbet. This will be done later on the end plywood panels as well.

Glue and nail in position pulling the entire bottom assembly into square *to the plywood.* Nail along the toe space rabbet with ¾-in. brads, and throughout the remainder with 4d finish nails.

Constructing the Cabinet Back

Materials required:

1 pc. ¼ in. fir plywood 32¼ in. × 96 in.
1 pc. ¼ in. fir plywood 5¾ in. × 32¼ in.

(The two pieces above will be joined together to make the full cabinet back 101¾ in. long.)

2 pcs. ¾ in. × 2 in. × 30½ in. pine or other inexpensive lumber
1 pc. ¾ in. × 2 in. × 28½ in. pine or other
1 pc. ¾ in. × 2 in. × 97¾ in. pine or other

The pieces above will be visible on the inside of the completed cabinet. Number 2 pine works well for these. High-quality construction would call for nearly knot-free lumber with small, tight knots permissible.

Because the base cabinet is longer than 96 in., the normal length of a sheet of plywood, the 5¾ in. piece will have to be spliced to the 96 in. piece to obtain an overall length for the back of 101¾ in.

Construction steps

1. Glue and nail with 1 in. nails one of the 2 in. × 30½ in. pine pieces along
    one end of the 32¼ in. × 96 in. back. Position the pine piece even with
    the 32¼-in. edge and flush with the top.

    **Tip: Tack the 2 in. piece in position with a couple of 1-in. nails through
    the pine into the plywood—one nail at the top and one at the bottom. Flip
    the assembly over and continue nailing with a full pattern of staggered nail-
    ing through the ¼ in. plywood into the pine strip. The interior of the cabinet
    looks better if the nail heads do not show but are on the back of the cabinet
    (Figs. 5–29A and 5–29B).**

2. Glue and tack into position the top 2 in. × 97¾ in. strip flush with the
    top of the plywood back. The end of this strip will extend past the 96 in.
    length of the longer plywood back piece. Again, flip over and nail with
    a full staggered pattern of 1 in. nails.

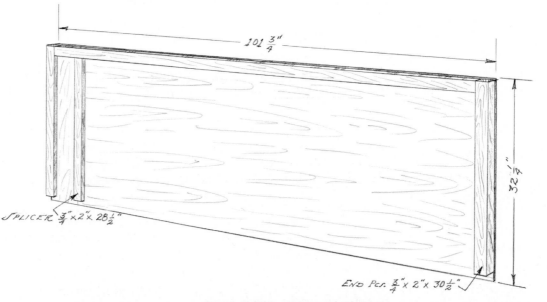

Figure 5–29A Cabinet back details.

Figure 5–29B Nail the plywood back through the plywood
into the pine strips with 1-in. nails.

Figure 5-30 Back splicer piece ready to attach to the main back piece.

Figure 5-31 Back splicing completed.

3. Tack the 2 in. × 28½ in. piece to the opposite end of the 96 in. back. This is the splicing piece, so 1 in. of the piece must extend beyond the end of the ¼ in. plywood back. (Fig. 5-30).

4. Glue and nail the remaining 30½ in. pine piece to the 32¼ in. edge of the ¼ in × 5¾ in. × 32¼ in. plywood piece. The pine piece again must be flush with the top and edge. Be certain to select the correct edge so that it is the opposite of the other end.

5. Glue and nail this splicer piece in its proper position (Fig. 5-31).

Fastening the Front Frame to the Bottom Assembly

The base cabinet subassemblies are now ready to be brought together and assembled into a cabinet. Follow the "moves" as described and this should be a fairly easy process (Fig. 5-32).

Figure 5–32 The face frame is attached to the completed bottom. Note the use of a supporting horse.

1. Stand the bottom assembly upright with the frame notches in the "up" position.
2. Cut two or three strips of ¼ or ½ in. plywood exactly 24 in. long to be used as support pieces for the front frame. Tack these strips to the top rail of the face frame.
3. Carefully place the front frame in position on the bottom assembly and fit all stiles into their respective notches. The scrap strips nailed to the face frame hold the assemblies in a good working position.

   Tip: A sawhorse built exactly 23¼ in. high is excellent to support the face frame while being attached to the bottom assembly. However, for occasional work the strips work well.

4. Drill, glue, and nail with 6d finish nails all stiles in position again using a 6d finish nail in the drill to prevent splitting the stiles.

Making and Installing Interior Cabinet Partitions

Interior cabinet partitions are made from ½ in. fir plywood or ½ in. particle board. If available, grade B-B makes very satisfactory partitions, as it contains no large knots on either side such as are noticeable on grade A-D. If grade A-D must be used, try to install the partitions with the A side visible from the cupboard section. If this is not possible, try to cut the partitions from portions of the plywood sheet with the least amount of visible knots on the D side. Material required:

4 pcs. ½-in. fir plywood (or flakeboard), grade B-B 23¼ in. × 23¾ in. (check the dimensions on the cabinet itself)

Sand both sides with a finish sander before installing.

Installation steps

1. Check the fit of the plywood in the ½-in. groove on the back of the stiles.
2. Check to see that the partitions come out flush with the back edge of the bottom assembly.
3. Glue in position in the groove in back of stiles.
4. Square to a light line drawn on the cabinet bottom (Fig. 5–33).

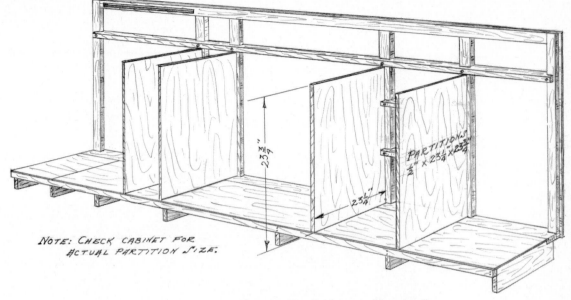

Figure 5-33 Cabinet partition detail.

Installation of Cabinet Back

1. Run a bead of glue along the 1¾-in. plywood lip on the bottom edge of the cabinet back, place carefully in position, and nail along the bottom with 1-in. nails.
2. Nail through the ¼-in. plywood back into the back edges of the ½-in. cabinet dividers (Fig. 5–34).

Making and Installing Cabinet End Panels

The cabinet is now ready to receive the end panels. Machine the panels carefully and accurately to the dimensions noted below. Materials required:

1 pc. 23¾ in. × 35¼ in. − ¼-in. plywood of the same material that has been used on the face frame.

1 pc. 23¾ in. × 35¼ in. − ¼-in. fir plywood (or flakeboard) for the wall end

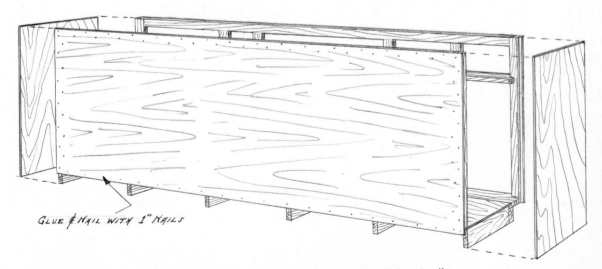

Figure 5-34 Back installation detail.

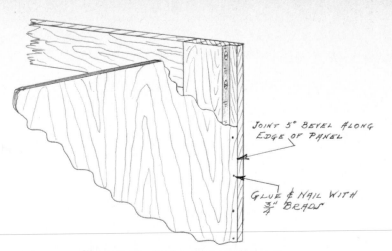

JOINT 5° BEVEL ALONG
EDGE OF PANEL

GLUE & NAIL WITH
3/4" BRADS

Figure 5-35 End panel installation detail.

Figure 5-36 A heavy piece of metal called a "peavey"
supports the stile while the end panel is being nailed.

Installation steps

1. Cut pieces to the net size noted above.
2. On the finish end panel, joint a 5-degree bevel along an edge of the 35¼-in. length (Fig. 5-35).
3. Run a bead of glue down the rabbet on the end stile, along the end of the back, and along the cabinet bottom board.
4. Attach the panel nailing first along the rabbeted edge of the stile. Use ¾-in. brads spaced about 4 in. apart.
5. Continue nailing along the bottom with ¾-in. brads, and along the cabinet back with 4d finish nails. Be sure to pull everything into square to the plywood panel.
6. Set and fill all nail holes with matching plastic wood or other filler.
7. Install the wall end panel using 1-in. nails and glue.

Tip: Some difficulty might be met in nailing the plywood into the rabbeted stile, as it gets rather "bouncy." The use of a small, heavy piece of metal or a small sledge hammer head to back up this nailing surface will make nailing this panel much easier. For lack of a better name, this piece of metal will be called a "peavey" (Fig. 5-36).

Making and Installing Cross-Braces

The cross-braces serve several purposes in the base cabinet. First, they add rigidity and strength to the cabinet; second, they act as top runners for the upper row of drawers so that the drawers will not tip downward when pulled out of the cabinet; and third, two of the cross-braces will be grooved to act as runners for the cutting board. Materials required:

7 pcs. ¾ in. × 2 in. × 22¼ in. knot-free pine or other inexpensive lumber (check the exact length by measuring the cabinet itself at the end where the end panels have just been installed)

6 pcs. ¾ in. × 2 in. × 4 in. pine (or other) to be used to install the cross-braces

Installation steps

1. Glue and clamp with C-clamps one piece along the top edge of the finish end panel and one piece along the top edge of the wall end panel. Be certain to cushion the clamps with scrap so that the clamps do not mar the plywood (Fig. 5–37).

2. Groove two of the cross-braces (Fig. 5–38).

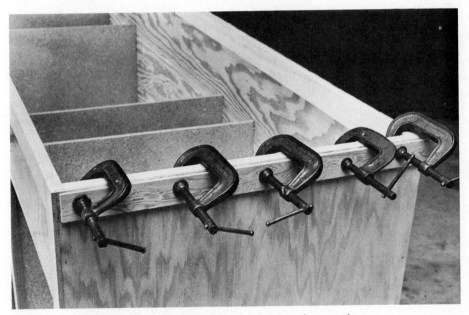

Figure 5–37 Glue and clamp reinforcing pieces at the top of both end panels.

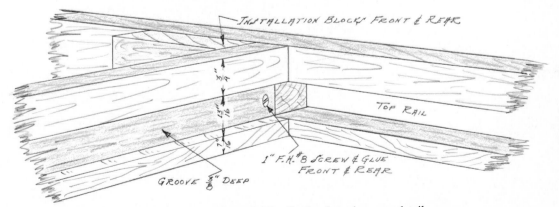

Figure 5–38 Cutting board runner detail.

Figure 5–39 Hold the runner temporarily in position with a bar clamp. Square carefully.

Figure 5–40 Install the runner with 1-in. flathead screws and glue.

3. Carefully install the cutting board runners squarely in position and temporarily hold in place with a bar clamp across the cabinet front to back (Fig. 5–39).

    a. Glue and clamp four short blocks in position back of the runners—cut the blocks to fit the available space.

    b. Drill and countersink $\frac{3}{16}$-in. holes through the groove at the end of the runners and a $\frac{3}{32}$-in. pilot hole into the pine block. Screw and glue permanently in position using 1-in. 8FH screws (Fig. 5–40).

4. Glue two more blocks on the back of the front frame in a position so that the cross-brace, when installed, will come out about in the center of the drawer openings (Fig. 5–41).

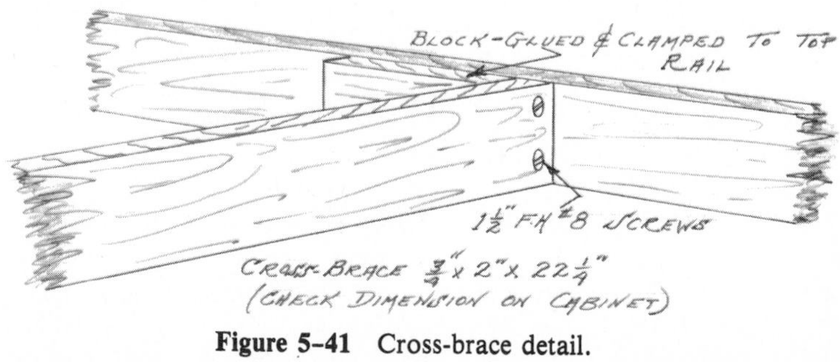

BLOCK - GLUED & CLAMPED TO TOP RAIL

1½" FH #8 SCREWS

CROSS-BRACE ¾" X 2" X 22¼" (CHECK DIMENSION ON CABINET)

140

Figure 5–41 Cross-brace detail.

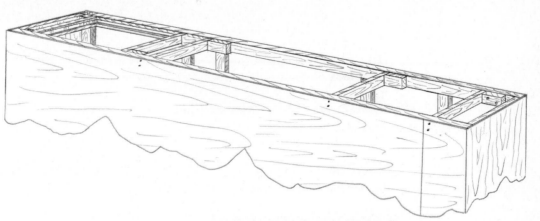

Figure 5–42 Rear view of cross-bracing.

5. Place the cross-brace in position, square, and hold temporarily with a bar clamp.
   a. At the front, glue and screw in position permanently using two 1½-in. 8FH woodscrews in each cross-brace.
   b. At the rear of the cabinet, drive a 2½-in. 8FH woodscrew through the back into the end of the cross-brace (same shank holes and pilot holes as described previously) (Fig. 5–42).
   c. An alternative method that works well in the back is to hammer two 8d ring-shank nails into the ends of the cross-brace. Lay the cabinet face down on the floor to drive these rather large nails into the rear of the cross-braces.

Installing Base Cabinet Shelves

Only the permanent-type shelves for the base cabinet will be discussed here. Special features such as sliding shelves are discussed in Chapter 12.

Common practice is to have the shelves in base cabinets fixed in position, that is, not adjustable. The method used in this system is to have the shelf rest on cleats that are fastened to the cabinet dividers and/or end panels. Simply run out two ¾ in. × 1¼ in. × 22 in. pine cleats for each shelf. Position these in the cabinet so that the shelf, resting on top of the cleat, will be about in the middle of the cabinet opening. Nail and glue the cleat in position by nailing through the side panels into the pine cleat. The shelf itself can be made from ¾-in. plywood or flakeboard with a strip glued and nailed to the front edge that matches the material being used for the front frame. The rear corners of the shelf must be notched to accommodate the vertical pine strips in the cabinet corners, if present (Fig. 5–43).

Shelf Cleat ¾" × 1½" × 23"

Figure 5–43 Detail of shelf support cleat.

If adjustable base cabinet shelves are desired, adjustable shelf standard and clips may be used. Attach the shelf standard to the back of the front stile, to the ½-in. plywood dividers and to the pine reinforcing strip in the back corners as needed. About 12 in. of shelf standard should be adequate for base cabinet shelves. Alternative methods of installing adjustable shelving are discussed in Chapter 8.

Installing the Sliding Towel Bar (Rear Mount)

The towel bar should be fastened with screws to a ¾-in. piece of pine or plywood which is about the size of the metal base of the towel bar. Have a helper hold the towel bar in position in the cabinet and glue and nail through the plywood back into the pine block. A side-mounted towel bar will require a different technique.

Belt-Sanding the Face Frame

(See the section ''Wood Fillers'' that follows.)

The construction of the basic lower cabinet is now complete. The face frame and finish ends are ready to be given a first sanding. This will be done by belt sanding the face frame followed by finish sanding with an oscillating sander. It is a good idea to stay away from the finish plywood with the belt sander, as the danger of sanding through the veneer is extremely great. If the solid wood of the end stile needs cutting down to the plywood of the finished end, do so by using a sharp hook scraper, block plane, and the finish sander.

The technique of handling a portable 3-in. belt sander is one that requires some practice to do a creditable job. Maintaining the sander level while sanding narrow stiles and drawer rails can be difficult. However, a bit of practice will overcome these difficulties and one soon becomes proficient in this technique.

Place a 100-grit belt in the sander. Start by sanding the top rail and the end stiles, letting the sander drift across the face of the adjoining joints. Sand all joints flush and even. Do not worry about going across the grain of the adjoining pieces at this stage. Next, do the short vertical stiles, again allowing the sander to grind the adjoining joints flush and even. Finish up doing the remaining drawer rails. Be especially careful doing the narrow drawer rails so that a dip is not sanded toward the center of these rails. Again, do not be hesitant about crossing the stiles with the sander at this stage (Fig. 5–44).

Switching to a 120-grit belt, again start sanding the top rail, but now try to watch carefully not to drift the sander onto the adjoining joints. Proceed to the vertical stiles the same way. On the short stiles, it will be impossible not to sand onto the cross rails with a 3-in. belt, but you can clean up these sander scratches when the crossrails themselves are sanded. Work carefully up to the joints so as to prevent as much cross-sanding as possible (Fig. 5–45).

After some practice, a ''feel'' for the sander is developed, and it is easier to determine the exact sanding area of the belt and one knows about where to stop when nearing a joint. Keep the sander moving evenly and steadily. Allowing the sander to pause even for a moment in any one place will quickly cause a ''sanding gouge'' in the frame.

Next, with the finish sander containing 100- or 120-grit paper, proceed to sand the entire face frame. As you sand over the joints, examine the area carefully for belt sander scratches. Where these are detected, give the scratched area a few careful strokes with a sharp hook scraper, working with the grain. Knock off any sharp edges along the stiles and rails, especially along the edges of the cupboard openings where doors will later be hung. Do the entire face frame at this time, always checking for sander scratches and working them out as the sanding proceeds. Refill any joints or blemishes that appear during this sanding (Fig. 5–46).

Figure 5-44 Belt-sand the face frame, sanding the rails first.

Figure 5-45 Belt-sand the stiles. Sand all joints even and flush.

Figure 5-46 Give the entire face frame a finish sanding.

Work down the finish end panel at this time also. Carefully scrape the filler from along the stile joint as well as from the nail holes. If the solid wood of the end stile is slightly higher than the plywood, scrape this down carefully to the height of the plywood or use a sharp block plane. Be especially careful as the plywood is approached, as there is the ever-present danger of marring the plywood or going through the veneer.

Give the end panel a quick sanding with the finish sander with 100-grit paper. Again, be careful when sanding on plywood with an orbital-action finish sander with fairly coarse paper in the sander. Tiny circles are likely to appear on the plywood due to the coarse grit or a slight buildup of resin on the surface of the paper. Switch to 220 grit if this is detected. Using 220-grit paper for the end panel sanding will, in most cases, forestall this problem and do the job quite satisfactorily.

Do not forget to sand the vertical toe space board at this time also. The last job is to cut away the plywood corners at the toe space ends. This is carefully done with a fine-toothed handsaw.

Installing Side Shelves in the Under-the-Sink Compartment

A nice touch and a handy accessory is to install 8-in. side shelves under the sink. These can be made from ¾-in. plywood, flakeboard, or lumber. Install these by nailing through the adjoining side panels into the back of the shelves and also nailing through the cabinet back into the rear of the shelves. The center is left open between the shelves for the drain pipes and water supply pipes that the plumber will install later (Fig. 5–47).

Wood Fillers

Another argument that rages among cabinetmakers is whether nail holes should be filled or whether that operation should be left to the wood finisher. Of course, the builder will fill a poor joint or a wood flaw, but often the nail holes are left to the finisher, reasoning that a better matching of color will be done by this professional. However, many other cabinet builders fill all holes and deliver the cabinet "sanded ready for finishing." In many cases to fill or not to fill will depend on what the competition is doing. If they are delivering a fully sanded and filled product, it almost becomes a necessity for others to do the same. If this is not done, a strong sales point for your competitors is not being matched!

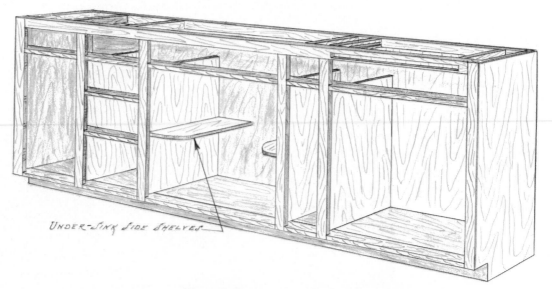

UNDER-SINK SIDE SHELVES

Figure 5–47   Completed basic base cabinet.

If a cabinet is being built by the casework system, filling is a necessity, as the many brads used in attaching the end panels would look poor, indeed, if left unfilled. As these are basically the only nail holes that require filling, it is not much of a labor cost to fill these few holes and have a really fine-looking cabinet to deliver to the customer.

Before starting to sand, all nail holes, poorly fitting joints, and wood flaws, as well as the seam where the finish end panels meet the rabbeted stiles, need to be filled. There are a number of satisfactory fillers on the market, such as Plastic Wood, that are available in colors to match the major cabinet woods. These are available at building supply dealers and hardware stores. These fillers are usually always available in natural wood tints. The colored varieties are more difficult to obtain.

This filler works well, as it has a minimum shrinkage, takes stain well, and certainly will match the surrounding wood if finished natural. One caution: Because the mixture contains lacquer, the area immediately surrounding the hole will be sealed; and if not sanded and scraped carefully, subsequent stains and finishes will not penetrate the wood and the finished product will have light, blotchy areas around the nail holes. However, a quick scrape with a sharp hook scraper and thorough sanding will eliminate this problem. A careful job of filling and sanding will pay dividends in a fine-looking cabinet and the filled areas will be virtually invisible.

BUILDING BASE CABINETS USING THE BOX-AND-FRAME SYSTEM

As with any cabinet-building system, actual construction starts with the building of the face frame. This was done with the casework system and will be the same for the box-and-frame system. Our model cabinet plan will again be used as the instructional method. The material presented should be readily adaptable to an actual cabinet project.

Face Frame: Mortise-and-Tenon Joints

As mentioned earlier in this chapter, the face frame is usually either mortised-and-tenoned or doweled in the box-and-frame system. A screwed face frame could be used, but some extra machining would have to be done on the end panels. A rabbeted edge on the end panels would have to be made to fit into the rabbeted edge of the vertical stile. This is necessary so that the heads of the screws are covered.

Two bills of materials will be presented. One will be for the mortised-and-tenoned face frame and the other for a doweled face frame.

Bill of materials for a mortised face frame

The face frame for the model cabinet would have the following material list:

1. *Vertical Face-Frame Members.* Material required:
     2 pcs. ¾ in. × 2 in. × 31¼ in.   end stiles
     4 pcs. ¾ in. × 2 in. × 30¼ in.   short stiles
2. *Horizontal Face-Frame Members.* Material required:
     1 pc. ¾ in. × 2 in. × 100½ in.   top rail
     2 pcs. ¾ in. × 1 in. × 17¼ in.   left cupboard section rails
     4 pcs. ¾ in. × 1 in. × 16 in.   drawer section rails
     2 pcs. ¾ in. × 1 in. × 34 in.   sink section rails
     2 pcs. ¾ in. × 1 in. × 8 in.   towel bar section rails
     2 pcs. ¾ in. × 1 in. × 25¼ in   right cupboard rails

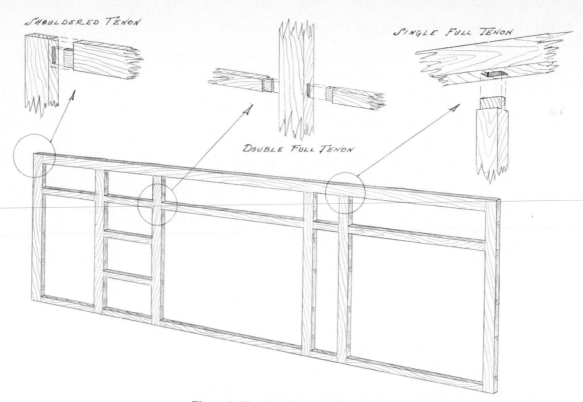

Figure 5-48 Face frame with mortise-and-tenon joints.

The length of each member of the face frame must be calculated carefully. One inch is added for the length of each tenon. This means that 2 in. must be added to the length of the dimensioned cabinet opening in the case of pieces that have a tenon on each end. This applies to all members of the face frame with the exception of the four short stiles—these have tenons on just one end. Most of the tenons are full tenons (no shoulder cuts). However, the top rail and the bottom rails all must have shouldered tenons (Fig. 5-48).

The bottom rails are often not mortised-and-tenoned at all but are simply face-nailed to the cabinet bottom. This certainly saves making quite a number of small shouldered tenons. Another method used by some cabinet builders is to shorten all the vertical stiles by ¾ in. The bottom rail is made of one piece ¾ in. × ¾ in. × 102½ in. and it is then screwed to the bottom of the stiles (Fig. 5-49). This piece is barely

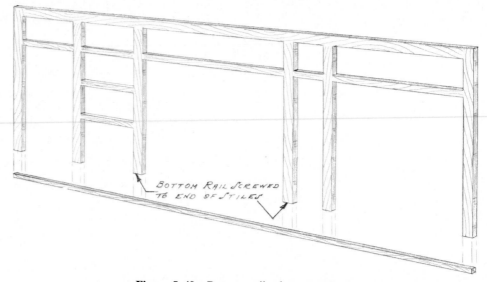

Figure 5-49 Bottom rail: alternate system.

146

visible in the finished cabinet, so appearance is not an item of great importance in the handling of this face frame member.

Great care must be taken when running out the material list insofar as accuracy is concerned. Equal care must be taken when machining the tenons on the end of the rails. All of the pieces must fit together very accurately; an error of even a small fraction of an inch can throw off the entire assembly.

Layout of the mortises

Working from the plan the mortises must be laid out with the try square correctly and, again, with great accuracy. Start by marking the required mortises on the vertical stiles. The two end stiles should be marked at the same time—each will have three mortises (Figs. 5–50A and 5–50B).

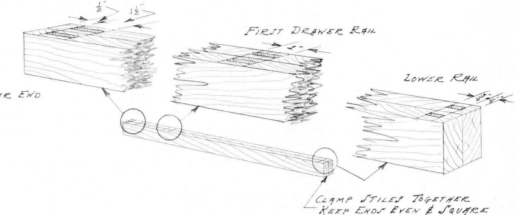

Figure 5–50A End stiles: mortise layout.

Figure 5–50B Clamp and square the stiles for accurate marking.

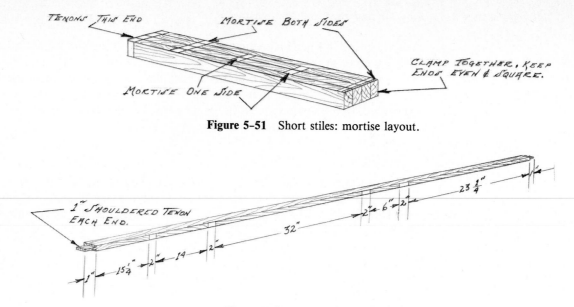

Figure 5-51 Short stiles: mortise layout.

Figure 5-52 Top rail: mortise layout.

Next, the four short stiles are marked. Two of these will have only two mortises marked, while the two forming the row of drawers will have four marked (Fig. 5-51). Either clamp the pieces together with the ends squared or, if a marking "box" is available, place the stiles in it for marking the mortises. Note also that most of the mortises on the short stiles are "double"—that is, mortised from both sides of the stile. The exception to this is the mortises to accommodate the rails for the two lower drawers.

The remaining member to be marked for mortising is the top rail. This was cut exactly 100½ in. long. First mark 1 in. off each end of the top rail to designate the 1-in. tenon that will be machined at those spots. Next, working carefully from the plan, mark each of the base cabinet sections, allowing 2 in. for each vertical stile (Fig. 5-52).

Mortising the face-frame members

Set the adjustments carefully on the mortiser for the width of stock being used. For ¾-in. face-frame stock, use the ¼-in. mortiser chisel, for ¹³⁄₁₆-in. material use the ⁵⁄₁₆-in. chisel. Center the chisel carefully and set the depth to a bit over 1 in. Proceed to make all the mortises as marked, working carefully and accurately between the pencil marks. More detailed instructions were presented in Chapter 4.

Cutting the tenons on the face-frame members

The detailed directions for a quick and easy means of cutting tenons was presented in Chapter 4 (Figures 4-14 to 4-16 illustrate these operations). Set the rip fence on the table saw for a length of tenon of 1 in. Using scrap of the same thickness as the face frame, make test cuts, adjusting the height of the dado head, until just the right thickness of tenon is the result. Be very careful in setting the rip fence for the length of tenon. Check a completed rail by holding it against the mortises made on the top rail. The rail, less the tenons on each end, should just match the distance between the mortises.

The shoulder cuts that are required on some of the tenons can be made by making two cuts on the table saw. Run the piece in a horizontal position with the blade set the exact height of the shoulder cut; second, run the piece in a vertical position with the blade set at a height equal to the length of the tenon and the rip fence set to the width of the tenon. Where it is impossible to stand the piece on end—the top rail, for example—raise the blade quite high and set the rip fence at the same width as the tenon. Run the piece in the horizontal position. Keep the face side *up* and the little bit of undercutting resulting from this operation will not be visible from the front side of the cabinet. Of course, the shoulder cuts can be made with a sharp, fine-toothed handsaw also; the bandsaw is another handy machine to use for cutting the shoulders of tenons.

Assembling the face-frame

Assembly begins with the rails and stiles that make up the row of drawers. Carefully make a trial assembly. Then for the final assembly, glue all tenons and clamp absolutely square with a couple of bar clamps. From the back side pin all tenons with a couple of ⅛-in. brads. This will allow removal of the clamps and continued assembly of the frame. Study Fig. 5–53 carefully.

Next add the rails and stiles, working to the left and right of the drawer section. Apply glue to each joint. Occasionally, a tenon might have to be trimmed if it is a bit long, especially the double tenons. Next place the top rail in position and slip all short stiles into their respective mortises. Finally, add the two end stiles (Fig. 5–54).

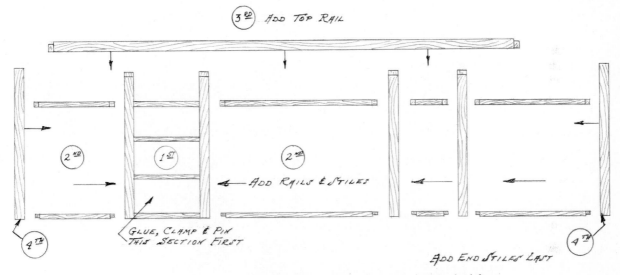

Figure 5–53 Assembly sequence: mortised frame.

Figure 5–54 Assembling the mortise-and-tenon frame.
(Courtesy Prieve Cabinets, Hutchinson, Minn.)

Figure 5-55 The face frame is clamped to a square work surface. (Courtesy Prieve Cabinets, Hutchinson, Minn.)

Figure 5-56 The tenons are pinned with the air stapler using ⅝-in. staples. (Courtesy Prieve Cabinets, Hutchinson, Minn.)

Using the bar clamp, clamp and pin all of the tenons with ⅝-in. brads. Work each section of the cabinet and each stile, pulling things together snuggly and squarely (Figs. 5-55 and 5-56).

If a continuous bottom rail is being used, screw that in position into the bottom of each stile using 1½-in. 8FH wood screws.

Doweled Face-Frame

Most small cabinet shops do not attempt doweling a cabinet face frame. With the proper production machinery—boring machines, frame clamps, and so on—doweling can be a fast and economical means of joinery. However, in the small shop where

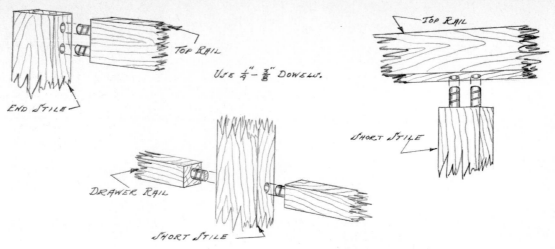

Figure 5-57 Typical face-frame dowel joints.

just a doweling jig and dowel centers would have to be used, doweling the joints would be very slow and costly (Fig. 5-57).

Bill of materials for a doweled face frame

A doweled joint is basically a butt joint, so the calculation of a bill of materials is a relatively simple matter, as no allowances need be made. A bill of materials for the face-frame for the model cabinet using doweled joints would have:

1. *Stiles*

   2 pcs. ¾ in. × 2 in. × 31¼ in.   end stiles
   4 pcs. ¾ in. × 2 in. × 29¼ in.   short stiles

2. *Rails*

   1 pc. ¾ in. × 2 in. × 98½ in.   top rail
   2 pcs. ¾ in. × 1 in. × 15¼ in.   left cupboard section rails
   4 pcs. ¾ in. × 1 in. × 14 in.   drawer section rails
   2 pcs. ¾ in. × 1 in. × 32 in.   sink section rails
   2 pcs. ¾ in. × 1 in. × 6 in.   towel bar section rails
   2 pcs. ¾ in. × 1 in. × 23¼ in.   right cupboard rails

These pieces must be machined to the exact dimensions. Again to ensure that several pieces of the same length dimension are identical, use of a length-cutting jig is a must. Even if only two pieces are to be cut the same length, a jig is worth using.

Very few other machining operations are required on these pieces for the doweled face-frame. The slot for the cutting board must be laid out with care so that it does not interfere with the joint at the end of the top rail. The bottom rail can be a continuous piece if desired, and can be screwed to the bottom of all stiles as was presented as an alternative for the mortised face frame.

Making the dowel joints

If a horizontal boring machine is available, making a dowel joint is a matter of accurate machine setup. The corresponding holes for the dowels are drilled accurately and at an exact centering (Figs. 5-58A and 5-58B). Lacking a horizontal boring machine, the craftsperson must rely on either the use of a doweling jig or dowel centers. In either case the measuring and marking of the center lines for the holes must be very accurate.

If a doweling jig is used, it is a simple matter to clamp the jig to either the side or end of the joining pieces and align the centering mark on the jig with the lines marked on the pieces (Figs. 5-59 and 5-60). The jig also holds the drill so that a square and true hole is drilled in the adjoining pieces.

Figure 5–58A Clever shop-built horizontal boring machine that drills both dowel holes quickly and accurately. (Courtesy Henderson Woodworking, Paynesville, Minn.)

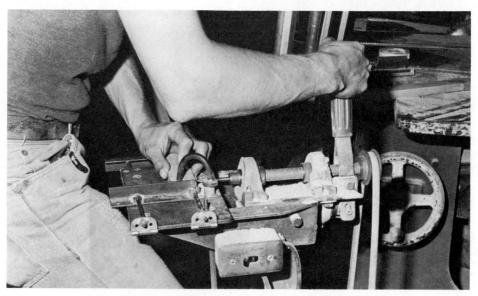

Figure 5–58B A foot-pedal/clamp holds the piece firmly while drilling. (Courtesy Henderson Woodworking, Paynesville, Minn.)

Figure 5–59 Dowling jig used on the stile.

Figure 5–60   Doweling jig used on the end of the rail.

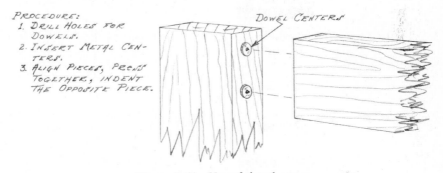

Figure 5–61   Use of dowel center.

The use of just dowel centers is a more difficult method of making a dowel joint. Here the first pair of holes is drilled in one of the members, the centers are then inserted in these holes, and the two pieces to be joined are pressed together so that the centers are transferred for one piece to the other. Extreme care must be taken to drill the holes square and true (Fig. 5–61).

Assembling the Doweled Face-Frame

A doweled face frame must be clamped until the glue is set, as there is no method of pinning the joints such as was accomplished with the mortise-and-tenon joints. Factories possess large face-frame clamping machines that clamp the entire face frame until the glue is set. Lacking such a clamp device, the best the small shop can do is glue and clamp in sections and, perhaps, use one of the hot glue guns on the market. These work well if the wood is warm. However, on cold material the glue sets so fast that assembly time is very minimal. The sequence of assembling the doweled face frame is identical to that presented for the mortised face-frame in Fig. 5–53.

Building the Basic Box-Type Base Cabinet

The choice of materials for building the box-type base cabinet has much to do with the size of the individual members that make up the cabinet. Many cabinetmakers use ½-in. particle board for wall ends, partitions, bottoms, and bottom support pieces. Particle board is relatively inexpensive and has little, if any, waste. For finish ends most builders still use ¾-in. plywood of their customer's choice, although ½-in. particle board with a hardwood veneer is becoming more popular.

The treatment of the toe space also varies considerably from cabinetmaker to cabinetmaker. These alternative treatments will be presented in drawings. The point to remember, however, is that different treatments and different materials vary the dimensions. The person will have to be aware of this and make whatever changes are necessary when building an actual cabinet with materials other than those used in the lessons presented herein.

Bill of materials for the model cabinet base section

The dimensions given are based on the base cabinet being built of ½-in. particle board for the wall end, divisions, bottom, and bottom supports. The finish end will be ¾-in. plywood to match the face frame. Of course, the bottom supports may be made of any type of material: ¾-in. plywood, inexpensive softwood, particle board, and so on, as these are not visible.

1 pc. ½ in. × 23¼ in. × 35¼ particle board	wall end
1 pc. ¾ in. × 23¼ in. × 35¼ in. hardwood plywood to match face frame	finish end
4 pcs. ½ in. × 23 in. × 30¼ in. particle board	interior divisions
1 pc. ½ in. × 23 in. × 101⅝ in. particle board	bottom
5 pcs. ½ in. × 4½ in. × 20¼ in. particle board or other	bottom supports
1 pc. ¾ in. × 3½ in. × 101 in. softwood	back brace
1 pc. ¼ in. × 30¾ in. × 100½ in. fir plywood (or other)	cabinet back
1 pc. ¾ in. × 4½ in. × 102½ in. hardwood to match face-frame	toe space board

Some explanations are required to explain how these dimensions were arrived at.

Wall and finish ends

The 23½-in. width is arrived at by subtracting the thickness of the face frame—¾ in.—from the total cabinet width of 24 in., leaving a net dimension of 23¼ in. for the panel width. The ¼-in. plywood back is rabbeted into the end panels so that it will not be visible from the end of the cabinet.

Interior partitions

The width of 23 in. is the same as the end panels *less* the thickness of the ¼-in. plywood back. The height of 30½ in. is measured from the upper surface of the cabinet bottom to the upper edge of the end panels.

Calculating the length pieces of the base cabinet

The actual length of the box making up the base cabinet will be 102¼ in. This is less than the total length of the face frame by ¼ in. The reason for this difference is that a ¼-in. lip is allowed for on the wall end of the cabinet. This is the scribing allowance that was explained earlier in the chapter in the section on the casework system.

Bottom: The bottom is dadoed into the end panels exactly half the thickness of each panel—¼ in. on the wall end panel and ⅜ in. on the finish end panel.

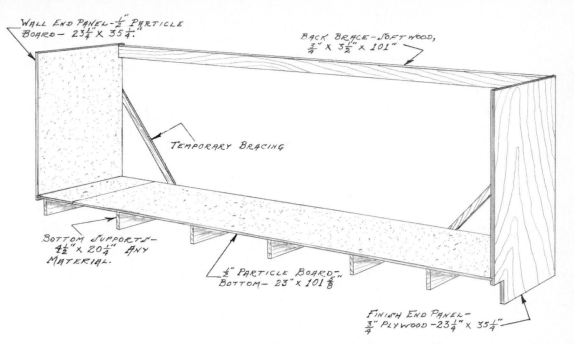

Figure 5-62 Basic box construction of base cabinet.

Thus the length of the cabinet bottom is arrived at by subtracting ¼ in. (one-half the thickness of the wall end panel) and ⅜ in. (one-half the thickness of the finish end panel), leaving a total of 101⅛ in. for the bottom panel. Note also that the bottom will have to be spliced to make this total distance if a standard 96-in. sheet of particle board is used (Fig. 5-62).

Back brace: This can be a piece of softwood or other ¾-in. material. The length is exactly the length of the interior of the cabinet. Simply measure the distance between the end panels once they are nailed and glued in position. This should be 101 in.

Cabinet back: The cabinet back will also have to be spliced to make up the total distance of 100½ in. Again this measurement will actually be taken from the partially assembled base cabinet. Simply measure the distance from the rabbet the wall end panel to the rabbet in the finish end panel. The height of the back is measured from the top edge of the end panel to the under side of the cabinet bottom—31 in. There is no need for the back to extend to the bottom edge of the end panels.

Toe space board: This is the same length as the face-frame, so it will extend ¼ in. beyond the "box" at the wall end, as does the face-frame. The width of 4½ in. matches the toe space cuts in the end panels. This should be of hardwood to match the face-frame. It is simply nailed to the ends of the bottom supports and to the toe spaces cut into the end panels. Some builders object to the end grain of the toe space board that is visible at the finish end when using this method. The alternative system presented in Fig. 5-63 still uses a solid piece of finish lumber for the toe space board, but the end grain is no longer visible. Both ends are mitered at 45 degrees to fit into corresponding miters on the end panels.

Another system that is by far the least expensive is presented in Fig. 5-64. This makes use of ½-in. particle board overlaid with ¼-in. plywood to match the face-frame. Although the end grain of the ¼-in. plywood is visible, it is very thin and should not be objectionable.

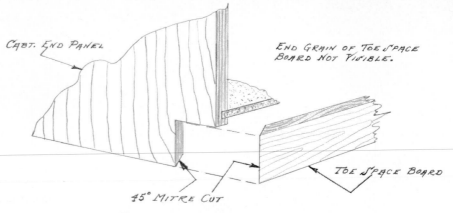

Figure 5-63   Toe space board alternative.

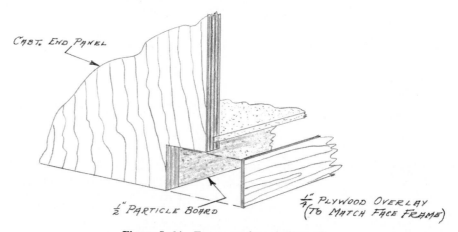

Figure 5-64   Toe space board alternative.

Note: In both alternatives the bottom support pieces must be shortened somewhat, as the toe space board is inset a bit. Verify this changed dimension on the cabinet itself.

Machining required on the base cabinet pieces

One of the advantages of the box-and-frame system is that a minimum of machining is required. The work that must be done is on the end panels and the interior partitions. These are simple operations that can be done efficiently using the table saw, shaper, and/or jointer.

Machining the end panels

A ½ in. × ¼ in. dado must be machined in the wall end panel for the cabinet bottom, and a ½ in. × ⅜ in. dado must be run in the finish end panel to receive the bottom (Fig. 5-65). A ¼ in. × ¼ in. rabbet is machined along the rear inside edge of each end panel to accept the ¼-in. plywood cabinet back.

The final cuts made are for the toe space in each panel. This will measure 3 in. deep by 4 in. high. These cuts can be made with a sharp handsaw, saber saw, or even freehand on the table saw. Note that the front frame extends below the cabinet bottom by ½ in. The bottom rail of the face frame is 1 in. wide while the bottom itself is only ½ in. thick. The bottom, however, must be flush with the upper edge of the bottom rail, hence the difference. Do not make the mistake of making the toe space cuts in the end panels even with the cabinet bottom—it must match the bottom of the face frame (Fig. 5-66).

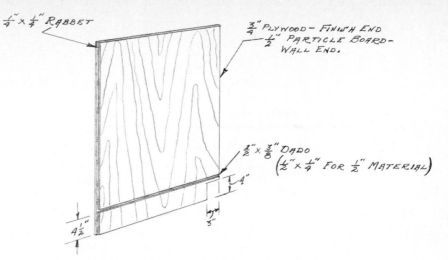

Figure 5-65 Required machining: wall end and finish end.

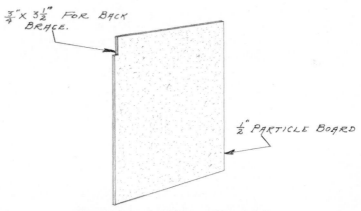

Figure 5-66 Detail of toe space cut.

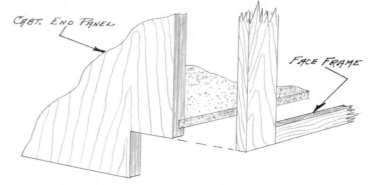

Figure 5-67 Partitions: cabinet interior.

Machining the interior partition panels

Once cut to size the only other machining required on the interior partition panels is to make the cut at the upper rear of the panel to receive the back brace. This can be done on the table saw, as a slight undercutting from the blade will not be visible in the finished cabinet (Fig. 5-67).

Assembly Procedures for the Base Cabinet

With the completion of the machining operations on the various pieces of the base cabinet, assembly of the base cabinet is the next step. Figure 5-62 illustrates the first steps in assembly.

Step 1: Position the bottom supports under the cabinet bottom about 18 in. apart and nail and glue in a square position with 4d finish nails. Note that the bottom piece of ½-in. particle board must be spliced to make up the total length of 101⅛ in. The simplest means of doing this is with a splicing piece about ½ in. × 4 in. of particle board. This is glued and nailed with 1-in. nails.

Step 2: Glue and nail with 4d finish nails each end panel in its respective dado. The builder may want to brace these with a piece of scrap in an exactly square position.

Step 3: Check the distance between the end panels and saw the back brace to this exact dimension. Nail the back brace in position with two 6d finish nails by nailing through the end panels.

Step 4: Mark the location of each interior partition on the cabinet bottom by locating the center of each short stile. Draw a light line ¼ in. either to the right or left of this center mark with a carpenter's square. Figure 5–68 illustrates the next few steps. Nail and glue each partition in its proper location through the back brace with 6d finish nails or a resin-coated box nail. Check each partition with the square! Tip the cabinet on its back and nail through the bottom into the partition with 4d finish nails. Be careful not to use too heavy a nail, as particle board will separate if nailed too close to the end of the panel.

Step 5: Lay the cabinet on its front and position the ¼-in plywood cabinet back in the rabbets of the end panels. Glue and nail along the rabbets in the end panels, the cabinet bottom, and the back brace, as well as into each partition. Use 1-in. nails along the back brace so that the nails do not show on the inside of the cabinet.

Fastening the Face Frame to the Cabinet Proper

Lay the cabinet on its back and run a bead of glue along all edges of the end panels, bottom, and interior partitions. Position the front frame carefully on the cabinet, checking the following:

1. The end stile is flush with the edge of the finish end panel.
2. The upper surface of the bottom is flush with the upper edge of the bottom rail.
3. The end stile on the wall end extends beyond the wall end panel ¼ in.
4. Each interior partition is centered on its respective short stile.

If everything lines up, proceed to nail the face frame with 4d finish nails. Nail the stiles to the end panels and partitions about every 8 in. Nail along the bottom rail into the particle board bottom with nails with the same distance apart. Remember to use the "nail in the drill" tip when nailing near the end of the rail or stile to prevent splitting the face-frame member.

The ¾ in. × 2 in. × 21¼ in. (verify on the cabinet itself) upper runners must be added over each drawer opening to prevent the drawer from tipping when opened. These can be omitted if metal drawer runners are to be used. Install the runners by nailing with 6d finish nails through the front and back (Fig. 5–69).

Side shelves may be installed under the sink opening as illustrated in the section on the casework system. Proceed, also, to install the type of shelf desired in each cupboard opening in the base cabinet.

Sanding the Cabinet

Set all nails about ¹⁄₁₆ in. deep, fill with a matching wood filler, and give the face-frame an initial belt sanding using the method described earlier in the chapter. Careful-

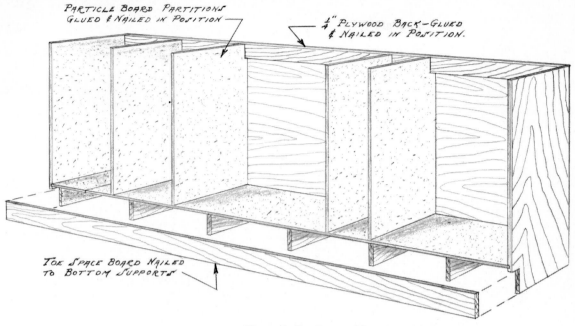

Figure 5–68 Base cabinet assembly.

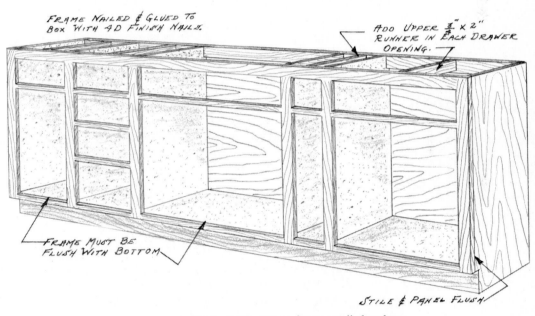

Figure 5–69 Front frame applied to box.

ly scrape any excess glue from the joints. Give the entire cabinet a careful sanding with the finish sander. Always use extreme care when sanding the veneer on the finish end panel to prevent "sanding through" the veneer.

REVIEW QUESTIONS

5.1. Name the two best known cabinet-building systems.

5.2. List three ways in which these cabinet systems differ.

5.3. What do you believe is the most important advantage of the casework system? Of the box-and-frame system?

5.4. Which disadvantage do you consider to be the most important for the casework system? For the box-and-frame system?

5.5. The actual construction of a base cabinet starts with the construction of which feature?

Questions Regarding the Casework System

5.6. What is the length of the toe space boards for a base cabinet measuring 120 in. with two wall ends?

5.7. What is the standard length of the end stiles for a cabinet with a 3-in. toe space?

5.8. In this system, how are the drawer rails fastened to the stiles?

5.9. What are the dimensions of the rabbet in a finish end stile?

5.10. What is the purpose of temporarily nailing all of the drawer rails on the top of the upper toe space board?

5.11. What size shank and pilot holes are drilled for the screw joint at the end stile to top rail? What size screw is recommended for this joint?

5.12. What material is best for lubricating screw threads for easy driving into hardwood?

5.13. Three "gauge" sticks are required for assembling the drawer rails to the stiles. What are their lengths in a normal assembly?

5.14. Why are the reinforcing pieces of softwood that are fastened to the edges of the ¼-in. plywood back nailed from the rear side? What size nail should be used for this?

5.15. Why is a 5-degree bevel jointed along the front edge of the finish end panel?

5.16. Why is a "top runner" required above each drawer opening in the top row of drawers in a base cabinet?

Questions Regarding the Box-and-Frame System

5.17. What are the two common joint methods used in the box-and-frame system?

5.18. In the model cabinet used in this chapter, what is the number of face-frame pieces compared with the number of face-frame pieces in the casework system?

5.19. Where are "shouldered" tenons required in the face frame when a mortise-and-tenon face frame is built?

5.20. What two machines are commonly used to make mortises?

5.21. What is done to the mortise-and-tenon joints that permits removing the bar clamps quickly and proceeding with the face-frame assembly?

5.22. What machine is required for fast, economical production of dowel joints?

5.23. What is the length of the ½-in. particle-board bottom of a base cabinet that measures 120 in. long with two wall ends using ½-in. particle board for the end panels?

5.24. Why is the face frame ¼ in. longer than the basic box at the wall end? (Did you remember this in your answer to Review Question 5.23?)

5.25. What is the danger in using too-coarse-grit sandpaper in the orbital finish sander?

5.26. What care must be exercised when sanding on or next to a veneered panel?

SUGGESTED CLASS ACTIVITIES AND STUDENT ASSIGNMENTS

5.1. Using the cabinet plan each student drew for a Chapter 1 assignment, have one-half of the class prepare a face-frame cutting list for the casework method and the other one-half of the class do the same for the box-and-frame system using mortise-and-tenon joints.

5.2. Have the class discuss and debate the two cabinet-building systems. Try to arrive at some agreement as to which system is the best.

5.3. Have each student build a "top rail to end stile" screw joint working with short scrap pieces ¾ in. × 2 in. Have them machine the ¼ in. × ½ in. rabbet in the stile piece as well. Judge each joint for accuracy and craftmanship and the rabbet for depth of ¼-in. plywood fit.

5.4. Have the class discuss which toe space system is most appealing. Would any of these be adaptable to the casework system? How?

5.5. Which features of either system would be adaptable to the other? For example, can a screwed face frame be used with a ½-in. particle-board cabinet bottom? Have the class attempt to arrive at a consensus as to which combination of features is the most efficient and least expensive.

6

Constructing Lipped Drawers

There is probably no greater test of the quality of cabinetwork than the fit of the drawers and the ease with which they slide. Experts tell us that one should be able to move a drawer back and forth in its opening by grasping a lower corner only. The construction of such a drawer is not difficult, but like all skills it is in the "tricks of the trade." The drawer construction method that follows is one good method—certainly not the only good method. It has withstood the test of time and consumer acceptance. It requires no special machinery such as would be required if dovetailed drawer joints were made.

Watch the next time someone examines a cabinet. Invariably they make a quick test of the product by sliding the drawers in and out. If the drawers glide smoothly and effortlessly, the cabinet is judged as being of good quality. Perhaps this is one reason why commercial roller-runners are so popular. However, following the procedures given and using the "tips" presented will produce drawers that will rival those installed with commercial runners and at less outlay of cash. So let's proceed to learn to make a good, practical, smooth-running drawer.

The drawer measurement formula that follows is critical to the building of these drawers. The measurements allow for the correct tolerance (or "play" as they say in the trade) so that the drawer will neither bind in the summer when the humidity swells the wood, nor rattle around in the opening during the heating season when the material dries out.

MAKING THE DRAWER FRONTS FOR A CASEWORK BASE CABINET

The construction of drawers starts with the machining of the drawer front itself. The dimensions involved are *critical*, so proceed carefully and follow the sketches exactly.

Determining the Overall Size of the Drawer Fronts

The handy chart shown in Fig. 6–1 is designed to make it easy to follow the formula and also to provide a cutting list for the fronts. Some decisions to make concerning these drawer fronts are contained in the answers to the following questions:

Will solid ¾-in. lumber or ¾-in plywood be used for the fronts? A nice design touch in a cabinet is to have vertical grained matching drawer fronts that are cut from the same piece of plywood.

Do you want horizontal- or vertical-grained fronts?

Will you be using overlaid molding, routed fronts, and so on, that will determine the direction of the grain?

Once the answers to these questions have been determined, cutting of the drawer fronts can proceed. The exact formula for determining the overall size of the drawer fronts is:

To the length of the cabinet drawer opening add $\frac{9}{16}$ in.

To the height of the cabinet drawer opening add $\frac{3}{8}$ in.

The resulting total is the overall length and height of the actual drawer front.

Dr. #	Opening width	+ $\frac{9}{16}'$	Width of dr. front	Opening height	+ $\frac{3}{8}''$	Height of dr. front

Figure 6–1 Drawer front machining chart.

Figure 6-2   First cut to form the rabbet at the end of the drawer front.

Figure 6-3   Second cut forming the rabbet on the end of the drawer front.

Drawer Front Rabbets

Perhaps the next most critical operation on the drawer fronts are the rabbets machined on all four edges. The end rabbets are usually machined on the table saw by making both a horizontal cut and a vertical cut (Figs. 6-2 and 6-3). The rabbets along the top and bottom edges can be made efficiently with a straight knife in the spindle shaper; however, if no shaper is available, a table saw and jointer will do the job satisfactorily. If done on the table saw, however, some sanding will be necessary to clean up the rabbets (Fig. 6-4).

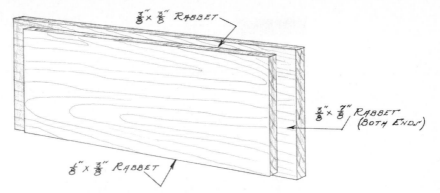

Figure 6-4   Drawer front rabbets (casework system).

End rabbets: The end rabbet is machined ⅜ in × ⅞ in.
Top rabbet: ⅜ in. × ⅜ in.
Bottom rabbet: ⅜ in. × ⅛ in.

Note: The sink front panel does not receive the same ⅜ in. × ⅞ in. end rabbets as the drawer fronts. The sink front is rabbeted ⅜ in. × ⅜ in. on the top and both ends. The bottom rabbet is ⅛ in. × ⅜ in.

The groove for the drawer bottom will be postponed until the drawer sides and backs are ready so that all can be done in one operation.

Shaping Edges of the Drawer Fronts

Put two or more cabinet makers together and a debate will soon be under way over the edge treatment for drawers and cabinet doors. Some prefer to leave the edges practically square, with only the sharp corners eased a bit with the sander. Others swear that to look presentable a bit of rounding must be done—and this can vary from a full quarter-round to much less. With the popularity of paneled doors in various period styles, the door edges are often shaped with fancy patterned knives. The decision is personal and also depends to some extent on the machines one has available. If a spindler shaper is available, the knife pattern that is appealing can be selected or one can be ground to the desired shape. If only the router is available to shape door and drawer edges, the number of available knife patterns is limited. In any event, once the decision has been made, proceed to shape the drawer front edges with the pattern selected.

Good machining technique calls for doing the ends first—especially on solid wood fronts—because some breakout is bound to occur in crossing the end grain. Machining the sides last will remove the chipped grain from the ends as the pass is made. On plywood and flakeboard this is not such a serious problem. However, it is always well to have nicely sharpened cutters and approach the corners slowly to prevent as much breakout as possible.

Machining the Sink Front Panel

The patterns that are cut in sink front panels are as varied as the imaginations of cabinetmakers. Often, no pattern for ventilation is cut in the front panel. With the modern use of plastic-laminate material for countertops and the more efficient rims used to install sinks, moisture is not a problem around and under the sink as it once was. However, if a pattern is desired in the sink front, the accompanying sketch and dimensions presents an attractive pattern (Fig. 6-5).

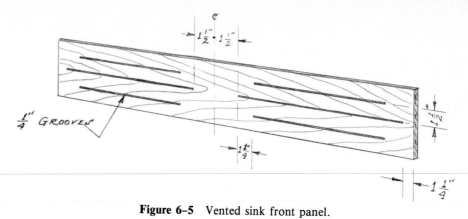

Figure 6-5 Vented sink front panel.

MAKING THE DRAWER FRONTS FOR A BOX-AND-FRAME BASE CABINET

The only difference in making drawer fronts for the two different cabinet systems is in the dimension of the bottom lip. Because of the narrow ¾-in. drawer rail used in the casework system, this bottom lip was reduced to ⅛ in. This drawer rail would be nearly completely covered by the drawer lip and the door lip if a full-size ⅜-in. lip were used on both the drawer and the cabinet door.

However, the wider 1-in. rails used in the box-and-frame system make it possible to use a ⅜-in. lip on both the top and bottom of the drawer front. This makes the machining a bit faster as only one setting is required instead of two as in the casework drawer fronts.

The drawer-front size formula is thus changed from that presented for the casework system. The formula for the box-and-frame drawer front and sink front is:

To the length of the cabinet drawer opening add ⁹⁄₁₆ in.

To the height of the cabinet drawer opening add ⅝ in.

Only the height dimension is changed—the length dimensions remain the same as for fronts made for the casework cabinet.

All other machining and building operations are the same for the two systems of cabinet building.

MAKING THE DRAWER SIDES AND BACK

For use as drawer sides and backs, ¾-in. stock is not acceptable to most cabinetmakers, as the resultant drawer has a very bulky look and is greatly increased in weight.

Materials and Machining Required on the Drawer Sides and Backs

Assume that the drawer sides are to be made from ½-in plywood or particle board and that a solid wood cap strip is to be applied (Fig. 6-6).

Pieces and sizes required for the drawers in the model cabinet:

8 pcs. ½ in. × 4⅛ in. × 23	top row	
2 pcs. ½ in. × 5⅛ in. × 23 in.	second drawer	
2 pcs. ½ in. × 6⅛ in. × 23 in.	third drawer	
2 pcs. ½ in. × 9 in. × 23 in.	bottom drawer	

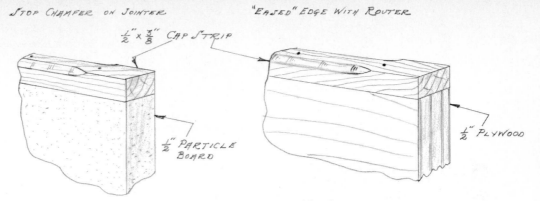

½" × ⅜" CAP STRIP

½" PARTICLE BOARD

½" PLYWOOD

Figure 6–6   Drawer side edge treatment.

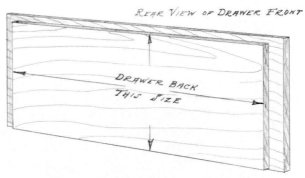

REAR VIEW OF DRAWER FRONT

DRAWER BACK THIS SIZE

Figure 6–7   Determining size of drawer back.

Sizes of drawer backs

While the drawer sides are being cut is a good time to run out the drawer backs, as they are made from the same material. Rather than give approximate dimensions, it is best to measure the back of the drawer front to obtain the exact size of the backs. The drawer back and the back of the drawer front should exactly match in size (Fig. 6–7). No cap strip is applied to the drawer back.

The measurements given for the sides result in pieces that are a bit oversize in height. They will be cut to exact height after the capstrip is applied. One edge of the drawer sides should be jointed to give a smooth surface for the application of the capstrips.

Machining and Application of Cap Strips

Of course, if solid lumber is being used for the drawer sides, this step on cap strips should be ignored. Cap strips are usually made of the same material as the face material of the cabinet. Pieces required are:

14 pcs. ⅜ in. × ½ in. × 23 in.

Rip and joint these pieces to the exact dimensions. If a surfacer is available, this machine will greatly facilitate the making of the cap strips, as the stock can be quickly planed to ½ in.

Applying strips to the drawer sides (Fig. 6–8)

1.   Glue and nail the cap strips to the jointed edge of each drawer side using 1-in. brads. (Use a 1-in. brad in the electric drill to predrill the nail holes and prevent splitting the cap strip.)
2.   Set the 1-in. brad rather deep with your nail set so that no possible interference with the machining process to follow will occur.

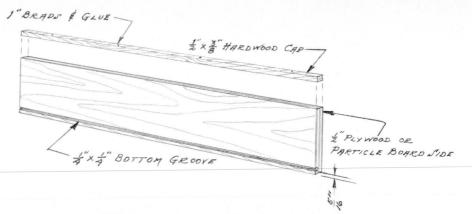

Figure 6–8 Cap strip and bottom groove detail.

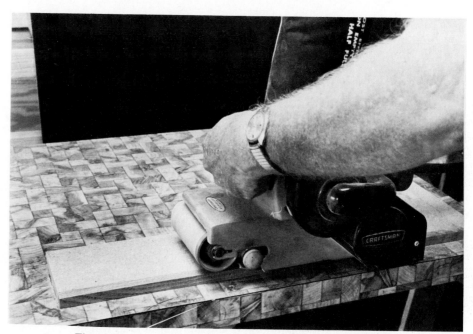

Figure 6–9 Belt-sand the drawer sides and the cap strips flush
and smooth.

3. Fill all holes with matching filler, let dry. Scrape and sand flush.
4. Belt-sand drawer sides with the 120-grit belt (Fig. 6–9).

Easing edges of cap strip

The drawer sides present a nice professional appearance if the cap strips have
the edges rounded or "eased." Easing the edges of the drawer sides can be done quickly and efficiently with a small-radius knife in the router. If a spindle shaper is available, this operation can easily be accomplished with a small ⅛-in radius knife. It is
also best to use a start-and-stop mark on the shaper fence rather than run the eased
edge the entire length of the drawer side. This leaves the ends of the drawer sides
square for about an inch on either end while the remainder of the cap strip is eased
(Figs. 6–10A and 6–10B).

If the jointer is used for this operation, both the front and rear tables of the
jointer are lowered a bit until the desired depth of cut is arrived at. This prevents
a tapered cut. Make a mark on the fence where your piece will be dropped on the
knives to start the cut and another mark on the fence where the piece is stopped and

Figure 6–10A Mark the shaper table where the easing cut is to start.

Figure 6–10B Mark the shaper table where the easing cut is to stop.

lifted off the jointer. Both ends are, again, left square by using this procedure (see Figs. 4–30 and 4–31).

Give the sides and cap strips a sanding with 100-grit paper on the finishing sander. A final sanding with 220-grit paper can be done at this time as well.

Saw and Joint the Drawer Sides to Exact Height

The sides are now ready to be machined to their exact height dimension. Check the exact size of the back of the drawer where the sides will be attached and saw and joint the side pieces to these exact sizes (Fig. 6–7 shows this clearly).

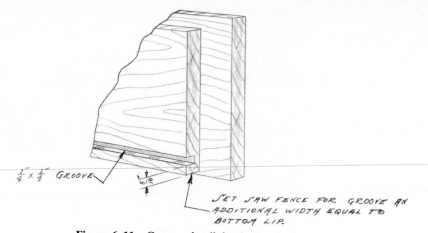

Figure 6–11 Groove detail for back of drawer front.

Running the Groove for the Drawer Bottoms

Grooving the sides and backs

Using just the two outside blades from the dado set with, possibly, one cardboard shim between, set the table saw fence so that the groove is $\frac{5}{16}$ in. from the bottom edge (Fig. 6–8). The groove should have enough width to it so the $\frac{1}{4}$-in. plywood drawer bottom will slip nicely into the groove. The blades should be set so the groove is $\frac{1}{4}$ in. deep.

At this setting, run the groove for the drawer bottoms in the sides and backs. *Do not do the drawer fronts at this setting*!

Grooving the Drawer Fronts

The saw fence must be adjusted to run the groove in the back of the drawer fronts because of the $\frac{1}{8}$-in. lip on the bottom edge. Make a test cut or two in the back of one of the drawer fronts by just barely marking the wood with the dado set. Check to see how this cut matches the groove on a drawer side. When the two grooves match perfectly, run the grooves in the back of the drawer fronts. The groove will still be $\frac{1}{4}$ in. deep (Fig. 6–11).

ASSEMBLING THE DRAWERS

Although the drawer bottoms still remain to be machined, good procedure calls for the sides to be attached to the drawer fronts prior to measuring and cutting the bottoms.

Nailing Sides to Drawer Fronts

1. Fasten a "stop" block to the top of the workbench against which the drawer front can be butted while the sides are being nailed in position. Cover the bench with cloth to prevent scratching the faces of the drawer fronts.
2. Using a 3d resin-coated box nail or other coated nail with good holding power, start the nails in the plywood sides about $1\frac{1}{2}$ in. apart and about $\frac{5}{16}$ in. from the end.
3. Run a bead of glue along the edge of the drawer front where the sides will be attached.

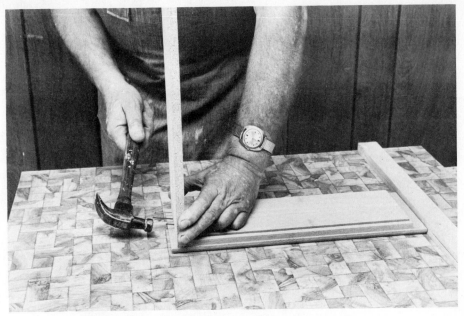

Figure 6-12 After aligning the side and front carefully,
nail the sides to the front.

4. Place the drawer side in position, *line up the grooves exactly*, and drive
    the nails into the drawer front. Proceed in the same manner for the op-
    posite side. Attach all sides to their respective fronts at this time (Fig. 6-12).

**Tip: When the nails are started in the sides, slant them a bit so that the nail
will be going *down* into the drawer front. This makes it easier to nail, eliminating
the risk of hitting the lip of the drawer. This also eliminates the possibility that
the nail might come "popping up" through the back of the drawer front. If
difficulty is encountered driving the nails home without hitting the drawer lip,
finish off the driving of these nails by using a good-sized drift punch or similar
device (Fig. 6-13).**

Figure 6-13 Use the nail set to drive the nails home. If
box nails are used, a drift punch works well.

Figure 6-14   After the sides are nailed, the bottoms are cut to size and slipped into the grooves.

Should the sides be nailed with box nails or finish nails? Again the debate rages. Finish nails no doubt present a neater appearance, but the coated box nail has greater holding power. In checking with many cabinet shops, practically all used box nails, and none reported receiving complaints from their customers. This to them was the practical test of a method—the reaction from their customers.

Many small shops are using airdriven staples as a means of fastening the drawer sides to the fronts. If the shop has a small compressor, here is another opportunity to use the air stapler in cabinet building.

Measuring and Cutting Drawer Bottoms

Once the drawer sides are nailed to the fronts, the bottoms can be measured accurately, cut, and installed. Because the grooves in the drawer sides were machined ¼ in. deep, the bottoms will be ½ in. wider than the width of the drawer back less ¹⁄₁₆ in. for clearance so that the bottom can slide into place.

Several of the drawer bottoms will be the same size—all of those in the vertical row of drawers, for example. The length of the drawer bottoms should be 22½ in. Give the A side of the ¼-in. plywood drawer bottoms a sanding with 100-grit paper in the finish sander. Slip the drawer bottoms into their respective grooves, glue, and nail the drawer backs in position with 4d resin- or cement-coated box nails (Figs. 6-14, 6-15A, and 6-15B).

MACHINING THE DRAWER RUNNERS

The drawer runners in this system are center runners that guide the drawer by a notch cut in the drawer back. They are easily made and installed and the end product is a smooth-gliding drawer (Fig. 6-16). Occasionally, on a large drawer two runners will be installed to support the drawer. (Note that if manufactured roller-runners are desired, the drawer formula presented in this chapter will not work. The manufacturer's directions for drawer tolerances and allowances will have to be followed.) Wood

Figure 6–15A Position the drawer back and nail through the sides.

Figure 6–15B Completely assembled drawer.

GLUED & NAILED

Figure 6–16 Center runner: casework system.

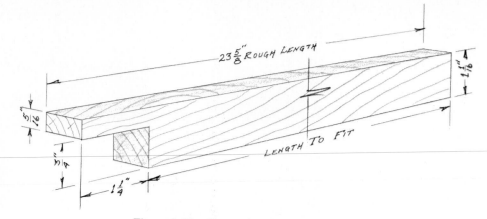

Figure 6–17   Center-type drawer runner.

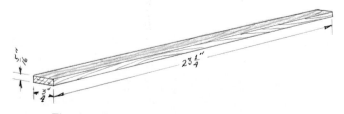

Figure 6–18   Strip runner for bottom drawer.

used for the runners is usually pine, basswood, or similar, but if a real high-quality runner is desired, hardwood can be used (Fig. 6–17).

Note that the drawer runner serves a dual purpose: (1) to guide the drawer into its opening straight and level; and (2) to act as an upper runner for the drawer just below to prevent its tipping downward when pulled from its opening. The runner for the bottom drawer, of course, cannot be the same as the others—all that is needed is a $\frac{5}{16}$ in. × $\frac{3}{4}$ in. strip to nail to the cabinet bottom for a guide (Fig. 6–18). Machine one runner for each drawer that is not a bottom drawer and one strip for each bottom drawer. Notice that the $\frac{5}{16}$-in. lip on the runner is the same amount that the groove was run from the bottom edge of the drawer side.

Tip: The length of the runners may be left a bit long and cut to exact fit when installing the drawer. In this way one is certain that the fit will be snug, and installing the drawer is somewhat easier.

MAKING THE DRAWER RUNNERS FOR THE MORTISED FACE FRAME

Both the center runner and the side runner can be used with the mortised face frame. Side runners have been the most popular in the past, but center runners are being used more frequently. Very popular, too, are manufactured rollers, which adapt nicely to the mortised face frame.

Side Runners

One disadvantage of the side runner is that two must be made, thus doubling the amount of material required for runners. Study Figs. 6–19 and 6–20 carefully. Note that the side runner is basically an L-shaped piece that guides the drawer and also acts as an upper runner to prevent the drawer below from tipping as it is pulled from the cabinet. The bottom portion of the side runner must be as wide as the drawer

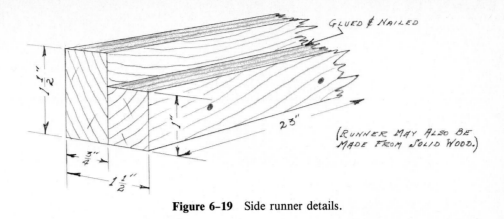

Figure 6–19 Side runner details.

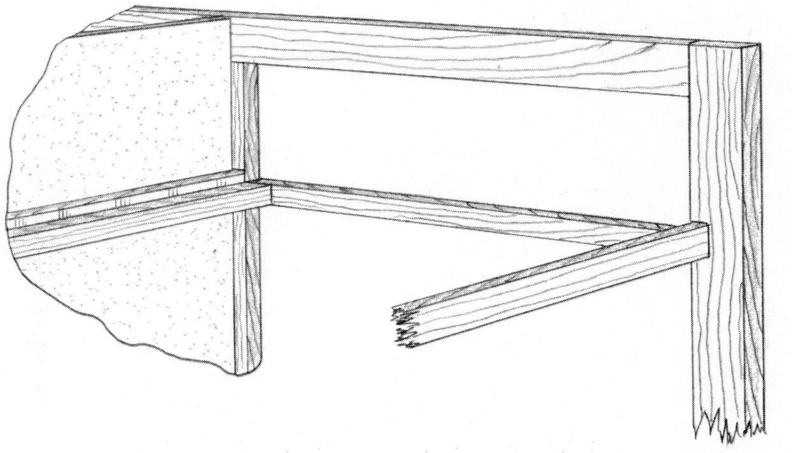

Figure 6–20 Side runners: box-and-frame system.

rail—1 in. in the case of the examples presented. The side portion of this type of runner can only be as wide as the distance from the edge of the drawer opening to the cabinet partition—usually about ¾ in. if ½-in. particle board is used for partitions. These runners can, of course, be made from a solid piece of lumber, but in terms of cost it might be more advantageous to make them from two pieces, as illustrated, as short scrap pieces may be utilized.

Center Runner Used in the Mortised Frame

With a bit of adaptation the center runner will work equally well in the mortised frame as in the casework system with the screwed frame. The main problem is the ¾-in. thickness of the drawer rail. The lipped drawer front will extend into the frame by ⅜ in., leaving only ⅜ in. as a bearing surface for the center runner (Fig. 6-21). This small lip on the runner is very difficult to fasten to the rail without splitting. Many cabinetmakers simply glue a small block of ¾-in. wood behind the drawer rail, thus increasing its thickness and providing the bearing necessary to do a good job of fastening.

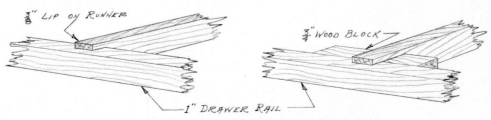

Figure 6-21 Center runners: mortised frame.

One other change must also be made. While the ⁵⁄₁₆-in. upper portion of the center runner will work fine, the lower portion must be enlarged to match the width of the drawer rail, which is 1 in. This is necessary so that the lower portion of the runner will do an efficient job as the "tip-out" runner for the drawer below.

Runners for the Bottom Drawer

In the case of side runners the bottom drawer requires only two pieces about ¾ in. × ¾ in. × 23¼ in. nailed to the cabinet bottom. These must be even with the drawer opening and positioned square and true to the face frame. The bottom drawer with a center runner can use the same ⁵⁄₁₆ in. × ¾ in. × 23¼ in. strip described previously in the casework discussion.

MANUFACTURED METAL DRAWER RUNNERS

Because of the wide variety of styles and designs of metal runners that are on the market today, no effort will be made to include information about these. Because of this wide variety, a cabinetmaker desiring to use metal runners will have to adapt the dimensions and allowances used in the making of the standard drawers to the directions that are included with the metal rollers.

The question might well be asked: Why use metal runners? Certainly their popularity must be due to the smooth action and ease of operation that metal runners have compared to the average shop-made drawer. Then, too, if your competitors are using metal runners, it often becomes necessary to follow suit. Ultimately, if the customer demands their use, the cabinet builder will have to use them.

Although it might be necessary for the commercial cabinet builder to use manufactured runners, a drawer built and installed using the directions and tips presented in this chapter and the next will be highly competitive with the commercial runner.

REVIEW QUESTIONS

6.1. What test is often used to determine if a drawer works smoothly and easily?

6.2. Which part of the drawer is made first? What is the formula for determining the overall size of the drawer front using the casework system?

6.3. Why is the bottom rabbet only ⅛ in. on a drawer front in the casework system?

6.4. What change is made on the drawer front rabbets on the sink front panel compared to the regular drawer front rabbets?

6.5. Why are the ends of drawer fronts machined first when using the shaper?

6.6. What changes are made on the drawer front rabbet cuts when using the mortised-and-tenoned frame?

6.7. What determines the height dimension of the drawer sides and backs?

6.8. What is the size of the groove that is run in the drawer sides and backs that will receive the ¼-in. plywood drawer bottom? What distance above the bottom edge of the drawer side should this groove be run?

6.9. Why is it not possible to run the groove in the drawer fronts at the same saw setting used for the sides and backs?

6.10. How much clearance should be allowed when cutting ¼-in. plywood for the drawer bottoms?

6.11. What difficulty needs correcting when using center runners with a mortised-and-tenoned frame?

6.12. How can the difficulty in Review Question 6.11 be overcome?

SUGGESTED CLASS ACTIVITIES
AND STUDENT ASSIGNMENTS

6.1. Using the kitchen cabinet plans drawn for previous assignments, calculate the overall size of the drawer fronts. Use the sizing chart presented in this chapter to organize your information.

6.2. Have the students bring to class sketches of sink front panels they have observed. How many of these are still cut with vent patterns?

6.3. Have the class discuss the use of cap strips on drawer sides. Is the extra cost in labor and material worth the result? Would extra sales result from their being used?

6.4. What other observations have the students made when visiting cabinet shops as to the joint used to fasten drawer sides to the drawer fronts? How often are dove-tailed joints used in the smaller shops?

6.5. Discuss box nails versus finishing nails for fastening drawer sides to the fronts. What observations have the students to report from their visits to cabinet shops? How many shops are using air-driven staples?

6.6. Have the students collect as many examples of commercial drawer runner systems as they can locate, using catalogs, magazines, and other materials. Be sure they bring the cost information as well. Analyze the cost plus labor of these commercial runners as opposed to shop-made runners.

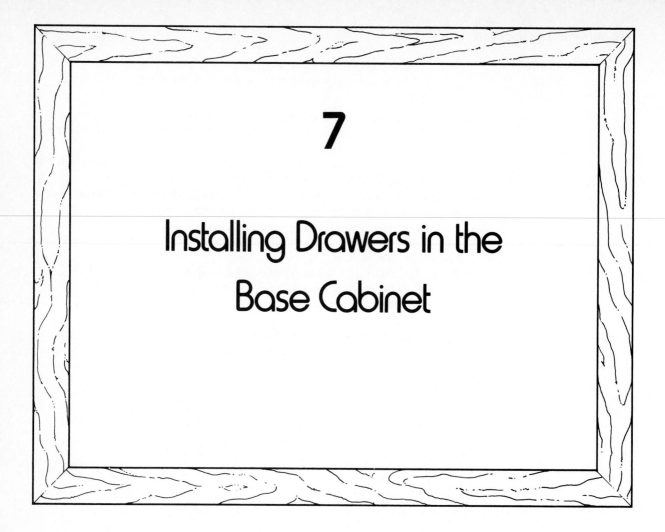

7

Installing Drawers in the Base Cabinet

One of the advantages of using the center runner system is that each drawer can be fit in its opening individually. This means that the front lip of the drawer fits against the front frame of the cabinet straight and even all around. Of course, the center runners could simply be nailed into position by squaring with the framing square both from the top and from the side. However, one would be taking the risk that the drawers might not meet the "fit" requirement. A drawer could touch along the top edge of the drawer front and be open somewhat along the bottom edge, or one end of the front could touch the frame and the other end have a gap. The only sure way to have neat-fitting drawers is to follow the installation methods as described. It takes only a few moments and, once mastered, assures nearly perfect fitting and aligned drawers. The installation is built one drawer on another working from the bottom up. So start by installing the bottom drawer of a row of drawers.

INSTALLING CENTER RUNNER DRAWERS

Installing the Bottom Drawer

1. The $\frac{5}{16}$-in. strip is the runner for the bottom drawer. Cut the strip to length by measuring from the back of the cabinet to within $\frac{1}{2}$ in. of the cabinet front, about $23\frac{1}{4}$ in.

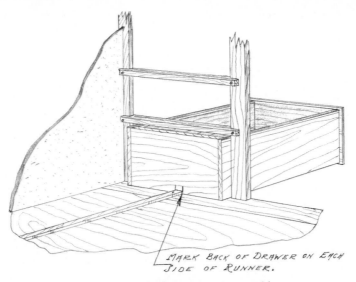

Figure 7–1 Marking drawer for notching.

2. Position this strip about in the middle of the drawer opening and nail near the front end with one ¾-in. brad (Fig. 7–1).

3. Place the drawer in the opening—see that the space is about even on both sides—and bump the drawer up against the end of the ⁵⁄₁₆-in. strip.

4. Reach in behind the drawer and mark with a pencil on the back of the drawer on each side of the ⁵⁄₁₆-in. strip (Fig. 7–1).

5. Remove the drawer, turn it upside down on the bench, and with a hand-saw cut *on the marked lines* down to the ¼-in. plywood drawer bottom. Make one or two more cuts if necessary and wiggle the saw blade enough to break out the material remaining between the outside cuts. Clean up the notch down to the plywood bottom. By making the first two cuts on the mark, enough play is allowed to have the drawer slide freely along the runner (Fig. 7–2).

Figure 7–2 Saw the notches in the back of the drawer on the lines to allow a bit of freedom.

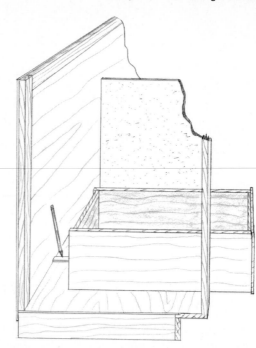

Figure 7-3 Runner marked for bottom drawer.

6. Place the drawer back into its opening and slide it all the way in. Make certain that the drawer fits firmly against the front frame. The $\frac{5}{16}$-in. runner will be moved to its correct position by this action.

7. Carefully pull the drawer out of the cabinet about 4 or 5 in. Be careful not to move the drawer runner when doing this.

8. Reach in behind the drawer and carefully make a pencil mark on each side of the runner on the cabinet bottom (Fig. 7-3).

9. Remove the drawer from the opening and move the runner aside by pivoting it on the nail at the front of the strip. Run a bead of glue on the cabinet bottom where the runner will be placed, move the runner back to its correct position, and nail the runner permanently to the cabinet bottom with $\frac{3}{4}$-in. brads.

Installing the Third Drawer (Drawer Just Above the Bottom Drawer)

1. The bottom drawer must be left in its position in the base cabinet while installing the drawer above it. Saw the runner for the third drawer to a snug-fit length and place the runner in position near the middle of the drawer opening (Fig. 7-4).

   a. Place a drop or two of glue under the lip of the runner and nail in place with one $\frac{3}{4}$-in. brad. (Remember to paraffin the brads to ease them into hardwood.)

   Tip: A peavey should be used under the drawer rail to make nailing easier and solid (Fig. 7-5).

   b. The rear of the third drawer runner is supported in approximate position by the back of the bottom drawer.

2. Mark and notch the back of the third drawer as instructed previously.

3. Make several shims from scrap plastic laminate about $\frac{3}{4}$ in. wide and 3 in.

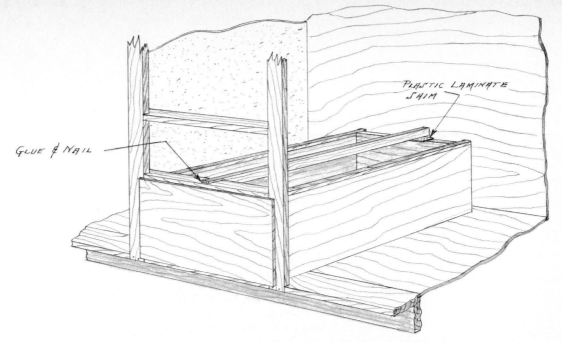

GLUE & NAIL

PLASTIC LAMINATE SHIM

Figure 7-4 Placement of shim under third drawer runner.

Figure 7-5 Use a peavey under the cross-rail when nailing the runner in place.

long or $\frac{1}{16}$-in. strips of wood about the same size. Place one of these shims under the third drawer runner so that the shim and runner are resting on the back of the bottom drawer (Fig. 7-4).

4. Check the fit of the third drawer against the front frame.
   a. The drawer runner may be moved right or left to bring the ends of the drawer front into alignment.
   b. Extra shims can be placed under the runner to bring the bottom edge of the drawer front into alignment.

Caution: No more than two or three shims can be placed under the rear of the runner. Too many will allow the drawer below to jump its own runner. This is seldom a problem, however.

5. Once all is in alignment, move to the rear of the cabinet, sight down the inside of the cabinet, and drive a 4d box nail through the plywood cabinet back into the end of the runner. The first nail may miss, but the second try usually is successful. Drive two nails into the end of each runner.

6. Return to the front of the cabinet and drive one more ¾-in. brad into the lip of the runner.

Installing the Remaining Two Drawers

Proceed to install the remaining two drawers of the row in the same manner.

Installing Single Drawers in the Top Row

The installation of these drawers is basically the same as for the drawers in the vertical row. The only problem is that there is nothing below the drawer to hold the runner in position while the drawer is being fitted into the opening. This difficulty can be overcome by making certain that the runner is cut to a snug fit so that friction holds it in position while being adjusted. Of course, a helper can hold the drawer while the cabinetmaker is nailing the runner from the rear.

THE SECRET OF SUPER-SMOOTH-RUNNING DRAWERS

The secret of a super-smooth-running drawer is contained in two items: thumbtacks and paraffin. Push a No. 4 thumbtack in the left and right corner of each drawer opening—two in each corner as illustrated—and one thumbtack in the notch at the back of the drawer (Fig. 7–6).

With a cake of paraffin, rub wax on the bottom edge of the drawer sides, along the center of the drawer bottom, and along the top and bottom edges of the center drawer runners. This combination of thumbtacks and paraffin will make the drawers run effortlessly in their openings!

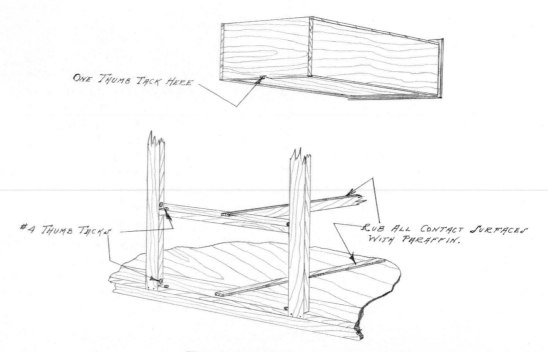

Figure 7–6 Placement of thumbtack glides.

Figure 7–7   Rear view of sink front panel.

INSTALLING THE SINK FRONT PANEL IN THE BASE CABINET

The sink front panel is held in place with a simple cleat. Two will usually do the job. Old-fashioned metal tabletop fasteners are also handy for this but are often difficult to find. Occasionally, woodworking specialty catalogs carry this item. However, the cleats are fast and easy to make (Fig. 7–7).

INSTALLING SIDE RUNNER DRAWERS

The installation of side runners is a bit simpler than is that of center runners, as no attempt is usually made to fit each drawer in its opening. The runners are usually fastened to the interior partitions and the end panels. Each runner must be squared with the face frame. This is why it was important to install the interior partitions square and true. If the partitions are off, trouble will be encountered with the drawer runners.

Installing the Bottom Drawer

The side runners for the bottom drawer were simply ¾ in. × ¾ in. × 23¼ in. strips. Glue and nail these to the bottom of the cabinet in a position squared with the front-frame (Fig. 7–8).

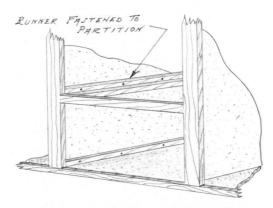

Figure 7–8   Installation of side runners.

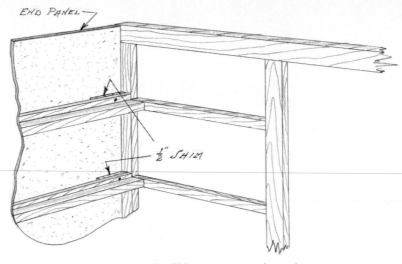

Figure 7-9   Side runner at end panel.

Installing the Other Drawers in the Cabinet

Each of the runners for the remaining drawers is nailed and glued to the interior partition panel or the end panel. Occasionally, when the runner must be fastened to an end panel, a shim will have to be installed first so that the runner will be even with the drawer opening (Fig. 7-9). Of course, the runner can be made to fit this extra space that is encountered when installing against the end panel. Be careful to install all runners square and true.

Use of Thumbtacks and Paraffin

Drawers with side runners can be made to work super-smoothly by using the thumbtacks and paraffin as described previously. Although two runners will probably have a bit more friction than just a center runner, by using these two items the results will be quite pleasing.

REVIEW QUESTIONS

7.1. Describe a well-fitting drawer.

7.2. How is the notch cut in the back of the drawer for the center runner?

7.3. Why and where is a plastic-laminate shim or shims used when installing center runner drawers?

7.4. Other than the bottom drawer, how are the other drawers adjusted to bring them into a good fit against the front frame?

7.5. How are center runners fastened at the rear of the runner?

7.6. What is the secret of super-smooth-running drawers?

7.7. How are side runners usually installed?

7.8. Explain the need for a shim when installing side runners against the end panels of a cabinet.

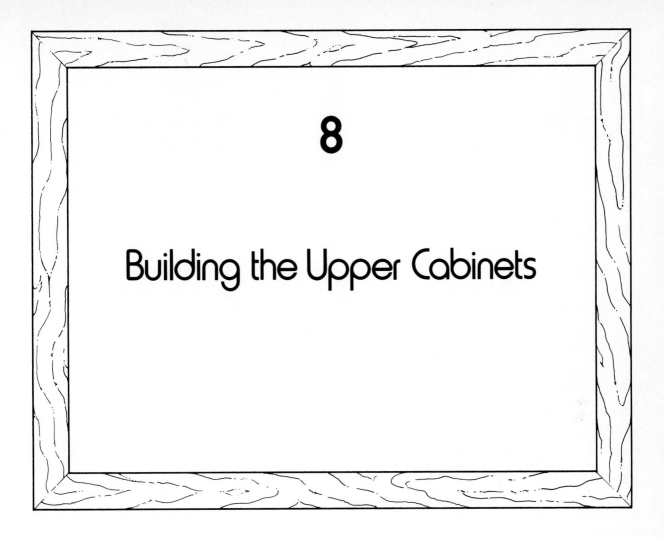

8

Building the Upper Cabinets

Once the base cabinets have been completed to the point that the drawers are installed, standard cabinet-building procedure calls for construction of the upper units next. The reason for leaving the base cabinet and moving along to the upper units is that the doors for both the base and upper cabinets will be made at the same time. This way only one setting of machines will be required to run out all the doors. As was done with the base cabinets, both the casework system and the box-and-frame system will be presented as techniques for the building of upper units.

Also as was done with the base cabinet, the model cabinets will be used as a basis for instruction. The novice cabinet builder should have no problem in adapting the lessons to a custom project of an individual nature.

BUILDING UPPER CABINETS USING THE CASEWORK SYSTEM

The model cabinets presented in this text call for two units. These will be referred to as the left-hand unit and the right-hand unit (Figs. 8–1 and 8–2). The building sequence is practically identical to that followed for base cabinets. Construction always starts with the front frames. Next, the backs are fabricated. The bottom is machined and attached to the back, the front frame is attached to the bottom, the side panels are positioned, and finally the top is added—in that sequence.

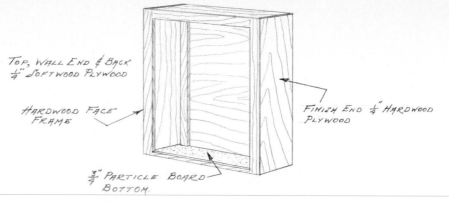

Figure 8-1 The casework system upper unit.

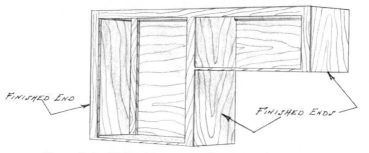

Figure 8-2 Right-side upper unit: casework system.

Although the upper cabinets will be built separately, the pieces for both units will be machined at the same time. Refer to the detailed plan for the model cabinets presented in Chapter 1.

Face-Frame Pieces Needed for Both Upper Units

The front frame for the upper left unit will require the following pieces run out of the builder's or owner's choice of material (Fig. 8-3):

2 pcs. ¾ in. × 2 in. × 32 in.	end stiles
1 pc. ¾ in. × 2 in. × 26¾ in.	top rail
1 pc. ¾ in. × ¾ in. × 26¾ in.	bottom facing piece

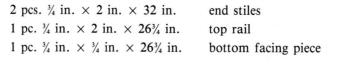

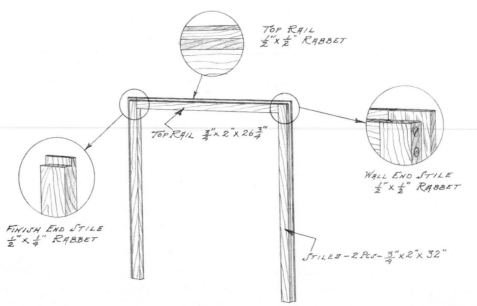

Figure 8-3 Upper left unit front frame details: rear view.

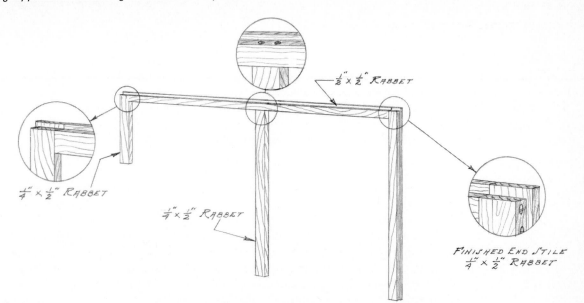

Figure 8-4 Upper right unit: front-frame rear view.

The upper right unit will have the following face-frame pieces (Fig. 8–4):

1 pc. ¾ in. × 2 in. × 32 in.	finish end stile
1 pc. ¾ in. × 2 in. × 30 in.	center stile
1 pc. ¾ in. × 2 in. × 14 in.	finish end stile
1 pc. ¾ in. × 2 in. × 59 in.	top rail
1 pc. ¾ in. × ¾ in. × 27 in.	bottom facing piece
1 pc. ¾ in. × ¾ in. × 30 in.	bottom facing piece

(*Note:* Do not cut the bottom facing pieces to exact length. Cut them to fit the actual cabinet later.)

Machining Required on the Face-Frame Pieces

The machining required on these face-frame pieces is basically the same as that used for the base cabinet face-frame.

Wall end stiles: Only the left upper unit has a wall end that requires a ½ in. × ½ in. rabbet (Fig. 8–3).

Finish end stiles: All of the other stiles for both units will need a finish end rabbet ¼ in. × ½ in.

Top rails: If the cabinets are to be installed under a soffet or ceiling, the top rails will need a ½ in. × ½ in. rabbet similar to the wall end rabbet (Figs. 8–3 and 8–4). If the cabinets are simply left open above them, a ¼ in. × ½ in. rabbet is machined on these members.

Special Machining on the Upper Cabinet End Stiles

The four end stiles of these upper units will require a special rabbet at their upper ends. (The center stile on the upper right unit does not receive this!) The special rabbet must match the rabbet run on the top rails, as explained above. Figure 8–3 clearly illustrates this special rabbet at the upper end of all the end stiles.

ASSEMBLING THE FACE FRAMES

Using the screw joints as instructed in Chapter 5, proceed to assemble the face frames by fastening the end stiles to the top rails. Be certain to align the rabbets at the upper ends of the stiles with the rabbet in the top rail. Finally, position the center stile and fasten it to the top rail of the right-hand cabinet.

Special Operation for Peg-Type Shelf Supports

If peg-type shelf supports (Fig. 8–5) are to be used, the holes for them should be drilled prior to assembly of the face frames. Inasmuch as all the end panels of the upper units are of ¼-in. plywood, it will not be possible to drill holes in the end panels for these supports. The holes must be drilled in the back side of the face-frame stiles and, later, in the pine reinforcing strips that are nailed and glued to the ¼-in. plywood cabinet back. These holes may be drilled using the drill press or the portable electric drill. A simple spacing jig should be made from hardboard or sheet metal which will assure that all holes are in alignment (Fig. 8–6). One jig will be needed for the holes to be drilled in the stiles and another for the holes to be drilled in the pine reinforcing pieces. The reason for the use of two jigs is that the pine reinforcing pieces will be ¾ in. shorter than the stiles.

Spacing of the holes for the shelf supports is up to the individual cabinetmakers, but a space between holes of anywhere from 1 to 2 in. would seem adequate. Note, too, that holes are not drilled within 4 to 6 in. of the top and bottom of the cabinet, as rarely are shelves ever placed in those positions.

This special operation is not required if metal shelf track and clips are to be used to support the shelves. These can be installed after the upper cabinet is assembled.

Building the Upper Cabinet Backs

When building cabinets the casework way, remember that the back of the cabinet must be the same size as the rabbets are deep on the face frame. For upper cabinets this is true for both width and height dimensions, as there is a rabbet along the top rail that must be considered. The same holds true for the upper right unit. This back must be the same size as the rabbets and special attention must be paid to the rabbet in the center stile. Check all dimensions carefully by measuring the distance between the rabbets and lay out the plywood back carefully to these dimensions.

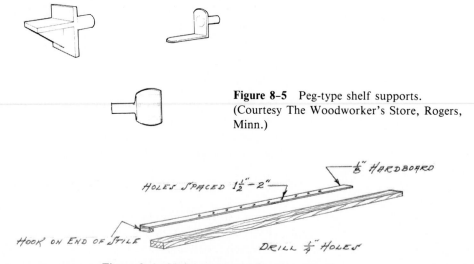

Figure 8–5 Peg-type shelf supports. (Courtesy The Woodworker's Store, Rogers, Minn.)

Figure 8–6 Hole spacing jig for peg supports.

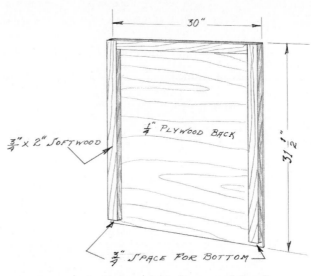

Figure 8-7 Plywood back for upper left unit.

Upper left unit

For purposes of instruction the assumption will be made that the upper cabinets will fit under a soffet as indicated in the plan. Thus a ½ in. × ½ in. rabbet has been machined along the top rails. The plywood back for this upper left unit will measure 30 in. × 31½ in. (Always verify the measurements on the frame itself!)

As was done for the base cabinet backs, the plywood will be reinforced with ¾ in. × 2 in. softwood strips. These will be glued and nailed to the plywood with 1-in. nails from the rear so that the interior of the cabinet will show no nail heads. Note that the lower ends of the reinforcing stiles are cut ¾ in. shorter than the height of the plywood back. This space is needed for the ¾-in. particle-board bottom that will be installed later. Of course, the A side or good side of the plywood is seen on the inside of the cabinet. Knot-free lumber should be used for appearance (Fig. 8-7).

Upper right cabinet back

The shape and dimensions of the upper right cupboard back are shown in Fig. 8-8. Study this illustration carefully for a full understanding of the dimensions.

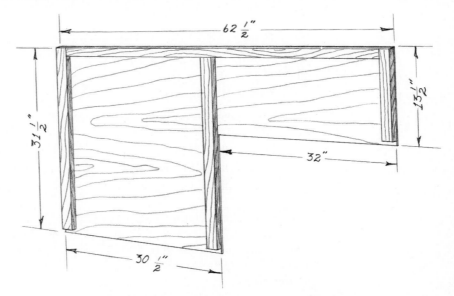

Figure 8-8 Plywood back for upper right unit.

Machining the Bottoms for the Upper Units

The bottoms of upper units may be made from any ¾-in. material—particle board, plywood, or even ¾-in. lumber. Particle board is by far the most commonly used.

The bottom of the cupboard over the refrigerator is made of ¾-in. hardwood plywood to match the remainder of the cabinet. An alternative to using ¾-in. plywood would be to laminate a panel for this bottom of ½-in. particle board and ¼-in. hardwood plywood. In any event, the bottom of sections over the refrigerator, range, and in some cases the sink, should be of matching hardwood plywood, because they are visible.

Upper left bottom

This bottom measures ¾ in. × 11 in. × 30 in. As usual, the length dimension must be verified by checking the length against the back of the cabinet.

Upper right bottoms

Two bottoms are required. The left section will need a piece ¾ in. × 11 in. × 30½ in., and the right section over the refrigerator will take a bottom piece of hardwood plywood that measures ¾ in. × 11 in. × 31¾ in.

End Panels for the Upper Cabinets

All end panels and tops for the upper units are from ¼-in. plywood. Softwood plywood will be used for the wall end and tops, and matching hardwood will be used for the finished ends. A distinct savings in the cost of materials is realized here over other cabinet systems.

Left unit end panels

The upper left unit has one wall end and one finished end. The size of these panels is identical and should measure:

1 pc. ¼ in. × 11¾ in. × 32 in.   softwood plywood
1 pc. ¼ in. × 11¾ in. × 32 in.   hardwood plywood

Run one edge of the hardwood panel over the jointer at 5 degrees to obtain a nice fit in the rabbet of the end stile. This was done for the base cabinets also.

Right unit end panels

Three plywood panels will be required for this section of cabinets.

1 pc. ½ in. × 11¾ in. × 32 in.   hardwood plywood
1 pc. ¼ in. × 11¾ in. × 14 in.   hardwood plywood
1 pc. ¼ in. × 11¾ in. × 31½ in.   hardwood plywood

All three panels will have one edge dressed at 5 degrees for a neat fit into the end stile.

However, the ¼ in. × 11¾ in. × 31½ in. panel requires careful and exacting machining. This is the end panel at the approximate center of this upper right unit. Figure 8–12 illustrates the cuts that need to be made for a proper fit at this section of the cabinet.

Tops for the Upper Cabinets

The tops are simply rectangular pieces of ¼-in. softwood plywood or other suitable ¼-in. material. Two pieces are required:

1 pc. ¼ in. × 11¾ in. × 30 in.   left cabinet top
1 pc. ¼ in. × 11¾ in. × 62½ in.   right cabinet top

Assembling the Upper Units

With all of the major pieces of both upper units now made, assembly can begin. A few pieces will have to be machined as assembly proceeds, but these are very minor and are made from softwood.

Step 1: Attach the cabinet bottoms to the plywood backs. A fairly large work surface is handy for this cabinet assembly. Three or four 2 in. × 8 in. planks about 10 ft long laid across two sawhorses works very well. Figures 8–9 and 8–10 illustrate the position of the bottoms and backs for joining. Glue and nail with 2d or 3d resin-coated box nails through the back into the bottom. Do not install the bottom over the refrigerator at this time. It is easier to machine and install the center finish end panel first. The bottom over the refrigerator then can be butted to the plywood panel after the panel is installed.

Step 2: Attach the front frame to the cabinet bottom. Two scrap pieces of ½-in. plywood will be needed to support the front frame at the top while it is being fastened to the cabinet bottom (Figs. 8–11 and 8–12). These should be cut 11¾ in. long and tack-nailed in the rabbet of the top rail. Glue and nail the front frame to the particle board bottom using 6d finish nails predrilled to prevent splitting the stile. Be certain that the end of the bottom lines up perfectly with the bottom of the rabbets in the end stile (Fig. 8–11).

Step 3: Attach the wall end panel to the front frame, back, and bottom. This panel should be glued and nailed using 1-in. wire nails. Nail along the rabbet of the stile, the particle board bottom, and along the edge of the cabinet back about every 4 in.

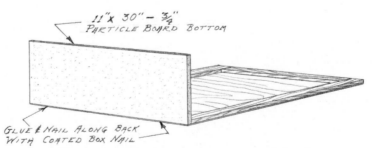

Figure 8–9   Fasten back to bottom: upper left unit.

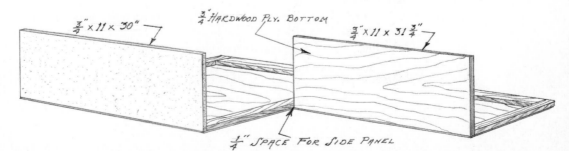

Figure 8–10   Fasten back to bottom: upper right unit.

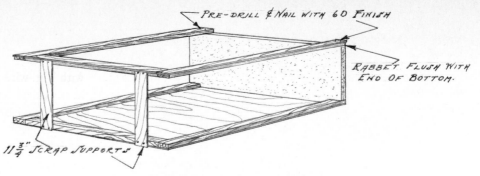

Figure 8-11 Attaching face frame.

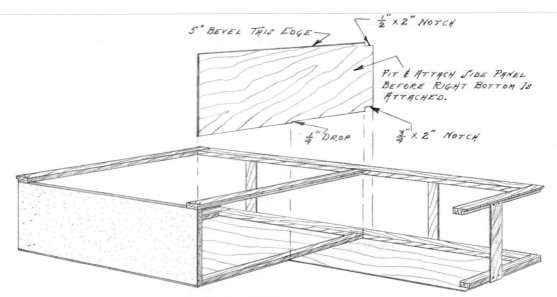

Figure 8-12 Machining and attaching center panel.

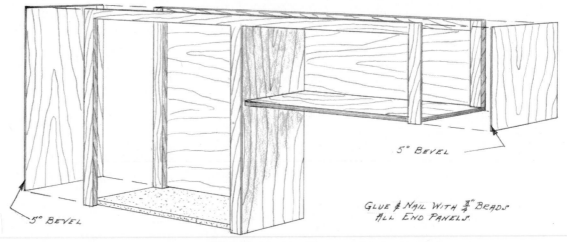

Figure 8-13 Installation of finish end panels.

Step 4: Attach the finish end panels. Carefully position these panels in the rabbet of the stile, pull into the rabbet tight, and nail and glue with ¾-in. brads. 4d finish nails may be used along the back edge and along the bottom (Fig. 8-13).

Step 5: Run out two pieces of softwood ¾ in. × 1½ in. × 11¼ in. Glue and clamp these pieces at the top of all panels (Fig. 8-14). These must be positioned so that they are even with the rabbet in the top rail and even with the upper edge of the cabinet back (Fig. 8-15).

Step 6: Install the cabinet top. Check to see that the plywood top fits nicely all around. Glue and nail it in position with 1-in. wire nails along all four edges (Fig. 8–16).

Step 7: Install the facing strips along the front edge of the cabinet bottom. Cut these ¾ in. × ¾ in. pieces to exact length and glue and nail with 4d finish nails. Predrill near the ends to prevent splitting.

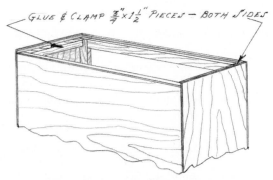

Figure 8–14　Nailers for cabinet top.

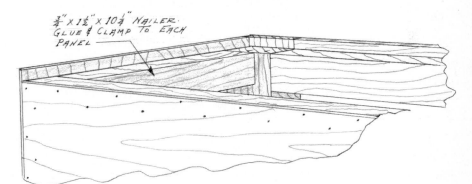

Figure 8–15　Top nailer detail.

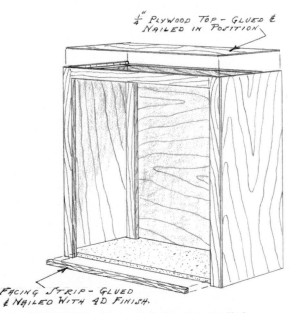

Figure 8–16　Top and facing strip applied.

Finishing Operations

As with the base cabinets, fill all the nail holes, open spots along the rabbets, and any imperfect joints with a matching wood filler. Belt-sand the entire face frame and follow by a finished sanding. Using the finish sander, dull off all sharp corners throughout the entire cabinet.

BUILDING UPPER CABINETS USING THE BOX-AND-FRAME METHOD

The basic construction methods learned in building the base cabinets using the box-and-frame method are applied to the upper units. The face frame may be either mortised-and-tenoned or doweled. The machinery available will determine the method used (Figs. 8–17 and 8–18).

Bill of Materials for the Face Frame

Mortised face frame

The bill of materials for the model cabinet upper units using the mortised face frame is:

1. *Left Unit* (Fig. 8–19)

> 2 pcs. ¾ in. × 2 in. × 32 in.   right and left stiles
> 1 pc. ¾ in. × 2 in. × 28¾ in.   top rail
> 1 pc. ¾ in. × 1 in. × 28¾ in.   bottom rail

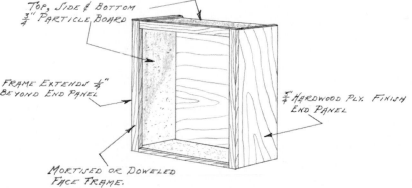

Figure 8–17   Upper left unit: box-and-frame system.

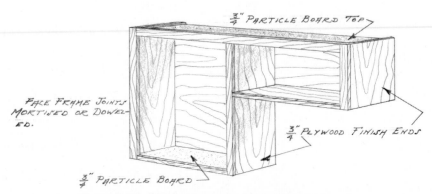

Figure 8–18   Right side upper: box-and-frame system.

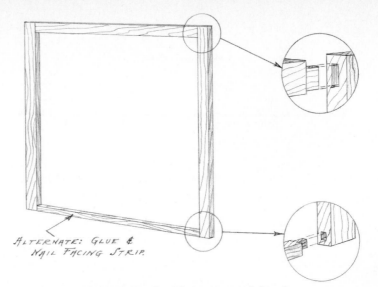

Figure 8–19 Face frame: upper left unit.

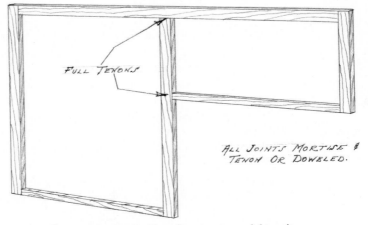

Figure 8–20 Face frame: upper right unit.

2. *Right Unit* (Fig. 8–20)

1 pc. ¾ in. × 2 in. × 32 in.	left stile
1 pc. ¾ in. × 2 in. × 31 in.	center stile
1 pc. ¾ in. × 2 in. × 14 in.	right stile
1 pc. ¾ in. × 2 in. × 61 in.	top rail
1 pc. ¾ in. × 1 in. × 28¾ in.	left bottom rail
1 pc. ¾ in. × 1 in. × 32 in.	right bottom rail (over refrigerator)

All of the front-frame pieces must be carefully and accurately machined to the net size listed.

The mortises must be carefully laid out on all the stiles as well as on the top rail where the center stile joins it. All of the tenons will be shouldered, with the exception of the tenon on the end of the center stile and at its midpoint. Use the methods as described in Chapter 5 for duplicate layout of mortises by using the layout box or clamping the pieces together. The tenons actually need no marking, as all are exactly 1 in. long and the machine setting will make these accurately.

Proceed to machine the mortises and cut the tenons followed by the shouldering of the tenons. Test fit all joints then glue, clamp, and pin all tenons with ⅝-in. brads as was done on the base cabinet front frame. Be certain to check for exact squareness as the frames are clamped.

Doweled face frame

The face-frame pieces for the doweled system are almost exactly the same as they were for the casework system. The exceptions are the bottom rails, which measure ¾ in. × 1 in. The complete bill of materials for a doweled face frame is:

1. *Left Unit*

    2 pcs. ¾ in. × 2 in. × 32 in.   right and left stiles
    1 pc. ¾ in. × 2 in. × 26¾ in.   top rail
    1 pc. ¾ in. × 2 in. × 26¾ in.   bottom rail

2. *Right Unit*

    1 pc. ¾ in. × 2 in. × 32 in.   left stile
    1 pc. ¾ in. × 2 in. × 30 in.   center stile
    1 pc. ¾ in. × 2 in. × 14 in.   right stile
    1 pc. ¾ in. × 1 in. × 27 in.   bottom rail (left)
    1 pc. ¾ in. × 2 in. × 30 in.   bottom rail (over refrigerator)

Drill all dowel holes using the doweling jig and centers or the horizontal boring machine as described in Chapter 5. Square and clamp the face frame with bar clamps and set aside until the glue has set.

Building the Basic Box for the Upper Units

For ease of calculating and demonstrating the building techniques for the upper units, all material will be ¾-in. plywood or particle board. The finish end panels will be ¾-in. hardwood plywood, while the bottoms, tops, and wall end panels will all be ¾-in. particle board. Needless to say, other thicknesses of material could be used. By now the learner should be able to adjust the measurements to adapt to the material being used.

As was done when building using the casework method, the face frame for the upper left unit will be ¼ in. larger along the wall and along the top edge than the basic box. The same will be true along the top edge only of the upper right unit. This method makes it easier to fit the cabinets tightly to the wall and to the soffet if some fitting needs to be done when the cabinets are installed.

Basic box bill of materials for the upper left unit

Remember that the left end of the frame for the left upper unit will extend beyond the basic box just ¼ in. to form the scribe extension at the wall end. The overall dimensions of the basic box are 30½ in. wide by 32 in. high. However, the top and the bottom will be inset ¼ in. each because the dado joints are placed ¼ in. from the ends of the side panels (Figs. 8–21 and 8–22).

The material required to build the left upper unit is:

    1 pc. ¾ in. × 11¼ in. × 32 in. hardwood plywood   finish end
    1 pc. ¾ in. × 11¼ in. × 32 in. particle board   wall end
    2 pcs. ¾ in. × 11 in. × 29¾ in. particle board   top and bottom
    1 pc. ¾ in. × 3 in. × 29 in. wood   hanging strip
                                                         (verify on cabinet)
    1 pc. ¼ in. × 29¾ in. × 31¾ in. plywood   cabinet back (verify
                                                         on cabinet)

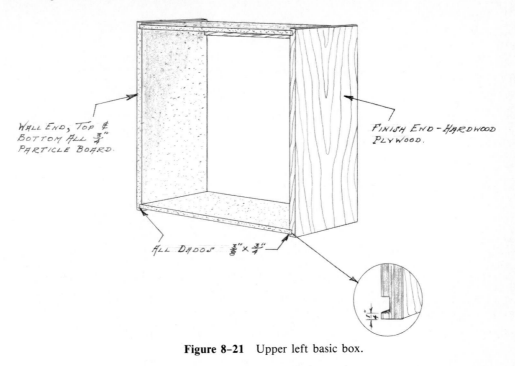

Figure 8–21 Upper left basic box.

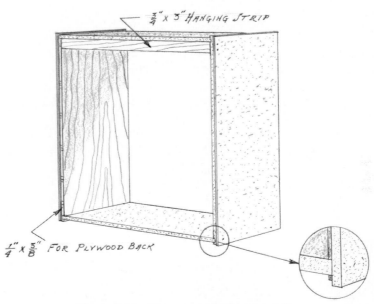

Figure 8–22 Rear view of left upper unit.

Basic box bill of materials for the upper right unit

It is efficient production practice to cut all the basic pieces for both cabinets at the same time. A machine setting for a special operation can efficiently handle many pieces and all panels should be run at the same time. It is a great waste of time and effort to have to reset a machine to do a piece forgotten or for another cabinet of the same kitchen layout.

The material required to build the right upper unit is:

1 pc. ¾ in. × 11¼ in. × 32 in. hardwood plywood   finish end

1 pc. ¾ in. × 11¼ in. × 14 in. hardwood plywood   finish end (refrigerator)

1 pc. ¾ in. × 11 in. × 31 in. hardwood plywood	finish end (center panel)
1 pc. ¾ in. × 11 in. × 62¼ in. particle board	top
1 pc. ¾ in. × 11 in. × 30¼ in. particle board	left section bottom
1 pc. ¾ in. × 11 in. × 32 in. hardwood plywood	bottom (refrigerator section)
1 pc. ¾ in. × 3 in. × 61½ in. softwood	hanging strip (verify length)
1 pc. ½ in. × 62¼ in. × 31¾ in. plywood	back cut to fit both sections

Note: The back can be two pieces of ¼-in. plywood spliced on the back edge of the center panel.

Saw and joint all pieces carefully and accurately to the net size listed.

Study Figs. 8–21 and 8–23 and the bills of materials for both upper sections so that it is clear how the dimensions of the various pieces are arrived at.

Machining operations required on the basic box pieces

Several dado cuts and rabbets will have to be made on the various members of the upper units.

Dado cuts

All the dado cuts are ¾ in. wide by ⅜ in. deep. A well-sharpened dado set should be used so that a minimum of tear-out will result when running the dado cuts in the plywood panels. Note that all dado cuts are run ¼ in. from the end of the panels. Ten dado cuts must be made on the pieces for both upper units of the model cabinets. Check the location of these carefully.

Of course, if the alternative bottom rail is used and a facing strip is nailed to the cabinet bottom, the dado cuts at the lower ends of the side panels will be cut flush with the ends.

The dado cut in the right side of the center panel must be located with great care. Butt the center panel and the refrigerator section end panel together and mark the exact location of the dado in the center panel (Fig. 8–24).

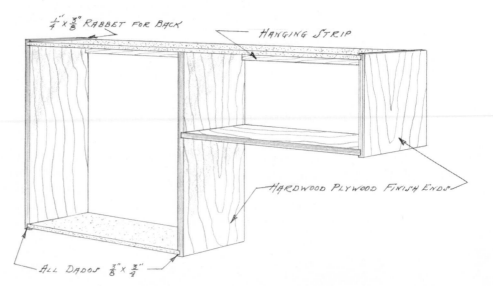

Figure 8–23 Upper right of basic box.

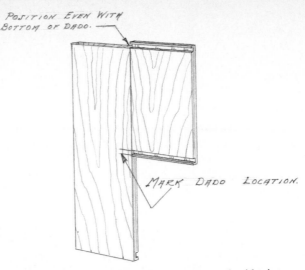

Figure 8-24 Locating dado at side panel midpoint.

Rabbet cuts

Rabbet cuts ⅜ in. wide and ¼ in. deep are run in all end panels to receive the ¼-in. plywood backs (Fig. 8–22). Note that this rabbet is not run in the top and bottom panels, as the plywood back simply overlaps these pieces. This is the reason these pieces are machined at 11 in. rather than 11¼ in. as are the side panels.

Assembly of the upper units

The assembly of these upper units is quite straightforward, but particular care must be paid to squaring the units and keeping them in square until the backs are positioned and installed. Glue and nail all dado joints with 6d finish nails.

Left unit

After assembling the basic box, position the ¼-in. plywood back and glue and nail in position wth 1-in. wire nails or similar. Pull everything into perfect square as the back is installed. Finally, the face frame is positioned carefully and glued and nailed to the basic box with 6d finish nails. Remember, the frame must extend beyond the box ¼ in. on the left side to form the wall end scribing allowance.

Right unit

The only minor problem connected with the assembly of the right unit is positioning the center panel accurately. Assemble the right unit in this sequence:

1. Attach top and bottom to the left panel.
2. Attach center panel to the bottom.
3. Measure accurately and mark on the top panel where the center panel is to be attached. Nail through the top into the end of the center panel.
4. Attach bottom of refrigerator section to center panel.
5. Install the end panel of the refrigerator section.
6. Check the assembly for squareness and install the ¼-in. plywood back.
7. Position and fasten the face frame to the cabinet box.

Sanding Operations

Set all nails; fill nail holes, imperfections, and so on, with matching wood filler; and give the face frames their initial belt sanding. Follow with a sanding using the finish sander and 150 grit and a final sanding using 220-grit paper. Sand all finish end panels with the finish sander, and sand off all sharp corners.

INSTALLING SHELVES FOR THE UPPER CABINETS

Both of the cabinet systems have been built to receive adjustable shelves. Although permanent shelves certainly can be installed in either system, adjustable shelves are used almost universally by today's cabinetmakers. However, if permanent shelves are desired, they can simply be cut to fit and nailed in position through the side panels, or the shelves could rest on cleats attached to the side panels.

Adjustable Shelves for the Casework Uppers

A disadvantage of the casework method of cabinet building is that the shelves must be notched to fit around the softwood reinforcing pieces in the back corners of the cabinets. Although this operation takes only a few minutes to do on the table saw, it is another machining operation.

As mentioned earlier, two common methods of adjusting shelves are used by most cabinet builders: adjustable shelf standard and metal clips or plastic or metal pegs fitted into predrilled holes. Drilling the holes for shelf pegs was discussed earlier in the chapter.

Installing metal shelf standard

The metal shelf track cannot be installed on the side panels, obviously, as the nails would pop through the ¼-in. plywood side panels. Therefore, the track must be installed on the back of the face-frame stiles and on the corner softwood reinforcing pieces (Fig. 8–25). The metal track may be purchased in lengths of 24 in., 36 in., 48 in., and so on. For the upper units that are built 32 in. high, the 24-in. track works very well. The track is installed about 4 in. from the bottom of the cabinet using a simple height jig, a 4-in. block of wood. Be certain to use a metal peavey to back up the face-frame stile when installing the track. This will prevent any damage to the face-frame due to hammering on the inside of the stiles.

Tip: The use of needle-nosed pliers to hold the nails while getting them started, especially in hardwood, is worth trying. Sometimes one's fingers are just too big to hold the nails in this awkward position inside the cabinet.

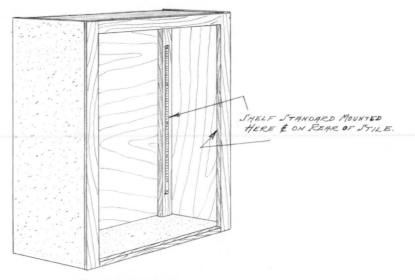

SHELF STANDARD MOUNTED HERE & ON REAR OF STILE.

Figure 8–25   Shelf standard: casework system.

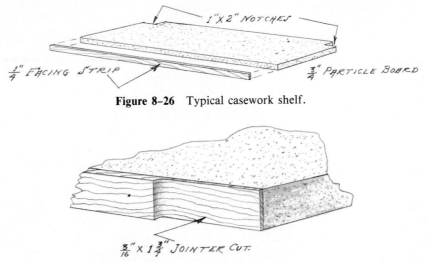

Figure 8-26 Typical casework shelf.

Figure 8-27 Detail of shelf edge jointer cut.

Making the casework shelves

Most shelving is made from ¾-in. cabinet-grade particle board with a ¼-in. facing strip applied to the front edge to conceal the rather unsightly inner core of the particle board (Fig. 8–26). This facing strip looks nice if it is made from the same material as the face frame. Another nice feature is to ease the edges of the facing strip using either a router or a spindle shaper.

Measuring for the size of shelves

Measure the inside of the cabinets and allow about ⅛ in. or so for "play" when cutting the shelves to actual length. The actual inside depth of the cabinet is 11 in. The shelves should be cut at 10⅝ in., which allows for the ¼-in. facing strip plus another ⅛ in. for play. These shelves will have to be angled to get them inside the cabinet, so there is no sense in having them so tight they are difficult to install. The shelf standard that is installed on the inside of the face-frame stile also must be taken into account when making the shelves. The standards are about 3/16 in. thick. Either the shelves will have to be made that much narrower or a jointer cut can be made at each end of the shelf to allow enough space for the shelf standard. Many prefer the jointer cut, as this does not narrow the useful space of the shelf (Fig. 8–27).

Shelf facing strips

Run out enough ¼-in. facing strip to face all the shelves. Joint one edge first, then rip using a smooth-cutting blade in the table saw. Cut the strips to rough length and glue and nail with 1-in. brads to the edge of the shelves. Do not nail closer than 2 in. to the end of the shelf! Be sure to have the jointed edge against the edge of the shelf. The rough side will thus be exposed. Set all brads quite deep, fill the holes with matching filler, and then trim the strip to exact length. Finally, set the jointer for a shallow cut and joint the exposed rough edge of the facing strip. By setting the brads quite deep, the possibility of the jointer hitting a nail is prevented.

With the facing strips applied, belt-sand the edges of the strips flush with the particle-board surfaces. Belt-sand the face of the strips also to remove any knife marks left by the jointer (Fig. 8–28).

The front edges of the shelves look nice if given a slight easing with the router or shaper. Use a knife with a small radius and run both the top and bottom edges of the facing strip.

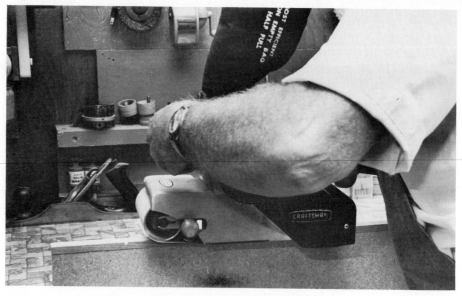

Figure 8–28   Belt-sand the shelf facing strips.

Cutting the notches in the shelves

The softwood reinforcing piece plus the thickness of the shelf standard will require a notch 2 in. wide by 1 in. deep. These can be quickly and easily cut on the
table saw. Set the blade quite high so that little if any undercutting is done. With
the fence set first at 2 in. and then at 1 in., make the two cuts necessary to remove
the corner notch. A slight undercutting is not objectionable, and even this can be
held to a minimum by holding the back edge of the shelf up while sawing the notch
(Fig. 8–29). The notches can also be cut on a bandsaw or by using a saber saw. However, in each of those operations the notches would have to be pencil-marked prior
to cutting.

Finally, set the jointer for a $\frac{3}{16}$ in. depth of cut and run the front edge of the
shelf into the cutter head a distance of about 1½ in. to 1¾ in. Do this on both ends
if required. Test-fit the shelf to see if it installs easily and with no binding.

Figure 8–29   Shelf notches can be cut carefully on the
table saw freehand.

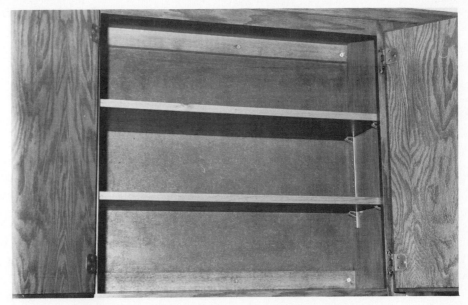

Figure 8–30 Adjustable shelves in a casework upper unit.

Shelves for the Box-and-Frame Uppers

Very little more need be written about the shelves for a box-and-frame cabinet. Of course, corner notches need not be cut. Allowance will have to be made for the shelf standard, which is placed against the end panels and the interior partitions. Measure carefully between the shelf standards and allow about ⅛-in. "play" for the length of the shelves (Fig. 8–30). The treatment of the facing strips is the same as for the shelves used in casework cabinets.

REVIEW QUESTIONS

8.1. Construction of the upper units begins with building which component of the cabinet?

8.2. List three differences in upper units built the casework way compared to building them using the box-and-frame method.

8.3. What is the purpose in rabbeting the top end of the stile in the casework upper cabinet?

8.4. What determines the size of the cabinet back in the casework upper unit?

8.5. Why are the softwood reinforcing stiles on the cabinet back cut ¾ in. shorter than the plywood in a casework cabinet upper unit?

8.6. Why is the bottom of the cabinet over the refrigerator and stove made of ¾-in. hardwood plywood while all other cabinet bottoms of ¾-in. particle board or other softwood material?

8.7. Explain how the upper cabinet bottoms measurement of 11 in. for the width is arrived at.

8.8. The upper left casework model cabinet is 30¾ in. long, yet the cabinet bottom is cut only 30 in. long. Explain.

8.9. In the casework unit the cabinet top is made from material of what thickness?

8.10. What is a facing strip? Name two places where a facing strip is used in the casework system of building uppers.

8.11. What size mortise-and-tenons should be used when building the face-frame for a box-and-frame cabinet?

8.12. If a facing strip is used along the cabinet bottom instead of a mortised piece at that point, what other dimensional and construction changes will have to be made in the upper cabinet?

8.13. What is the purpose of building the face frame ¼ in. longer and higher than the basic box?

8.14. The upper left unit is 30¾ in. long. The bottom and top panels of the basic box, however are cut only 29¾ in. long. Explain how this dimension is arrived at.

8.15. What is the purpose of the ¾ in. × 3 in. hanging strip?

8.16. Name two devices that are commonly used for cutting the dados in the end panels.

8.17. Where is shelf standard installed in the casework upper cabinet? Where in the box-and-frame cabinet?

8.18. When installing shelf standard, how can the builder be certain that the standard is exactly the same distance from the bottom of the cabinet?

8.19. Why is shelving usually made from ¾-in. material?

8.20. When attaching facing strips to casework shelf edges, the builder must not place the brads closer than about 2½ in. to the end of the shelf. Explain.

SUGGESTED CLASS ACTIVITIES
AND STUDENT ASSIGNMENTS

8.1. From the cabinet plans prepared as an assignment in Chapter 1, prepare a list of materials for your upper cabinets using the casework method.

8.2. Prepare a list of materials for the other components of your upper cabinets—backs, bottoms, side panels, tops, and facing strips—using the casework method.

8.3. Working from the same cabinet plans, prepare a list of materials for a box-and-frame mortised face-frame.

8.4. Prepare a list of materials for the remaining components for box-and-frame uppers from your plans. Calculate the net size of bottoms, tops, sides, backs, interior partitions, and hanging strips. (*Note:* If other interior partitions are required, figure using ½-in. particle board.)

8.5. Using the model cabinet left upper unit, calculate the dimensional difference that takes place when using ½-in. material for side panels.

8.6. Have the class members investigate and report on as many different adjustable shelf systems as they can discover. They should report on the following: (a) the physical description of the system, (b) where obtainable, (c) the cost per foot and lengths available, and (d) installation methods.

9

Designing and Making the Cabinet Doors

"The style of the cabinet is in the doors." Perhaps nothing determines the style of cabinetry more than the type of door that is installed on the basic face frame. After all, the basic construction of the cabinets is quite similar, as has been discovered in the preceding chapters. Only the doors and drawer fronts add the touches of individual style and design that create the differences among kitchens and other built-ins. In this chapter we examine the various types and styles of doors as well as present construction techniques for each.

There are many types of cabinet doors in common use: ¼-in. plywood doors, plain paneled doors, raised panel doors, overlay doors, glass doors, and sliding doors to name a few (Fig. 9–1). Doors differ, too, in the manner in which they are mounted or "hung" on the face frame of the cabinet. The most common method is to machine a ⅜-in. rabbet around the edge of the door and use a ⅜-in. inset hinge for hanging. A popular door in early-American-style kitchens is the flush door that is mounted inset and flush with the face frame and hung with butt hinges. Popular today, especially in the mass-manufactured cabinet, is the overlay door that is mounted over the face-frame using a special wraparound overlay hinge. Some doors are made with glass panels and some cabinets have plate glass sliding doors. Some kitchen cupboards have doors that slide horizontally back and forth on a special track. In this chapter we provide information and instruction for all these types of cabinet doors.

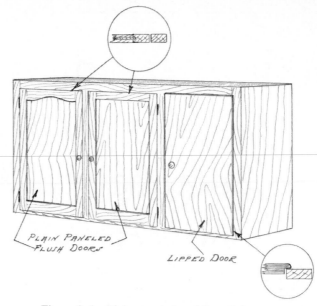

Figure 9-1   Plain paneled and lipped doors.

MAKING CABINET DOORS OF ¾-INCH PLYWOOD OR PARTICLE BOARD

It is safe to say that most cabinet doors are still made of ¾-in. hardwood plywood and/or particle board. The highest-quality plywood doors are made from lumber-core plywood. Plywood core is just a bit lower in quality but is often used. Particle core has become more popular as the cost of plywood has risen dramatically over the last decade.

One reason for the popularity of the ¾-in. plywood door is its versatility. It can be left plain with just the ⅜-in. rabbet; it can be decorated or stylized by routing a decorative groove on the surface to give a period look to the door (this can be also accomplished by applying a decorative molding to the surface of the door); it can be cut oversized and hung in the overlay position on the face frame for a modern look; and it can be used with a new special hinge to create the European style that is becoming quite popular—a type of cabinet construction in which no face-frame is used (see Fig. 16–3A).

⅜-Inch Lipped Door

Because it is by far the most popular type of cabinet door, the techniques for making lipped doors will be discussed first. Why is this style so popular? There are three basic reasons for its popularity. This type of door is fairly easy to make, as it requires a minimum of machinery; it is easy to install; and it provides a reasonably tight cabinet that is dust-free on the interior.

Calculating the size of lipped doors

How much larger than the cabinet opening are lipped doors made? An easy-to-remember rule for cutting lipped doors to the correct overall size that applies to either single doors or a pair of doors for a face-frame opening is (Fig. 9–2):

Measure the face frame opening carefully, and to the width of the opening add ½ in. To the height of the opening also add ½ in.

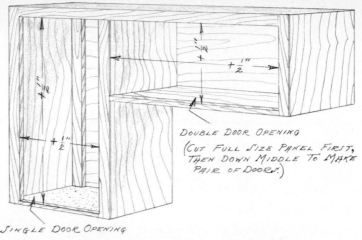

DOUBLE DOOR OPENING

(CUT FULL SIZE PANEL FIRST, THEN DOWN MIDDLE TO MAKE PAIR OF DOORS.)

SINGLE DOOR OPENING

Figure 9–2 Lipped door-cutting formula.

This formula provides the proper allowance or "play" to take care of the thickness of the inset hinges plus the proper space allowance so that the door or doors do not touch the face-frame after it is mounted.

The rule applies equally well when cutting a pair of doors to fit an opening. The plywood should be cut to overall size first, and then the panel should be cut down the middle to make the pair. The saw cut provides the necessary extra play for the other pair of hinges plus the space needed at the middle so that the doors do not touch. The matching grain of a pair of doors should be marked carefully with unobtrusive pencil marks.

Machining the lipped door

The operations and sequence of machining the ⅜-in. lip on the doors will depend on the machinery available.

Table saw and router

If these are the only two machines available, it is best to shape the door edge first. If the rabbet is cut first, there is not much surface remaining against which the router depth bead can be run. The shape of the curve on lipped door is pretty much an individual thing. Many cabinetmakers shape a full quarter-round on the lip, whereas others run less of a curve on the edge, and still others allow the lip to remain square with no edge shape whatsoever. The point to remember is that the more curve that is routed or shaped on the lip, the more inner core will be exposed. In the case of lumber-core plywood, this is not so objectionable. However, with plywood core or particle core the inner material can be quite unsightly. In any event, it is up to the builder to select the cutter and then adjust the cut to the amount of arc desired (Fig. 9–3).

Figure 9–3 Router cutters used to lip and rabbet cabinet door edges.

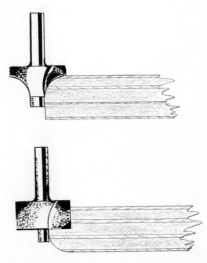

Figure 9-4 Cabinet doors can be rabbeted on the table saw with the dado head.

The rabbets can be cut handily on the table saw by making two passes over the blade. Select a smooth-cutting blade so that a lot of sanding is not necessary to clean up the rabbets. Remember to set the blade and fence carefully so that the final rabbet cut is exactly ⅜ in. × ⅜ in. The rabbet can also be cut with the dado set. An auxiliary wood fence must be attached to the regular saw fence so that the dado head can undercut without hitting the metal fence. The dado set should be well sharpened and the blades should cut evenly to produce a smooth rabbet on the edge of the door (Fig. 9-4).

Spindle shaper

The shaper is much to be desired for machining the lip and rabbet on cabinet doors, as it is fast and smooth cutting. A straight knife is used to machine the ⅜ in. × ⅜ in. rabbet, and a ⅜-in. quarter-round knife is used for rounding the lip. Again, this knife can be adjusted to produce as much of an arc on the lip as the builder desires (Figs. 9-5 and 9-6).

Available, too, are shaper knives that will machine the rabbet and curve the lip in one operation. These are available in either tool steel or carbide. Although they do an excellent job, the cabinetmaker has no control over the amount of curve desired on the lip and must accept the shape that is built into the cutter (Fig. 9-7).

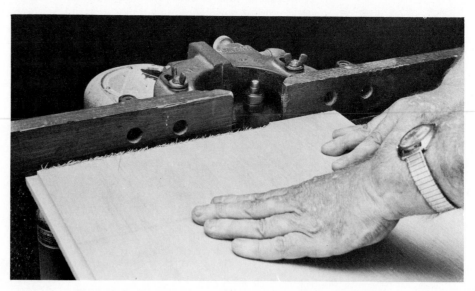

Figure 9-5 Door rabbet machined on the spindle shaper with a straight knife.

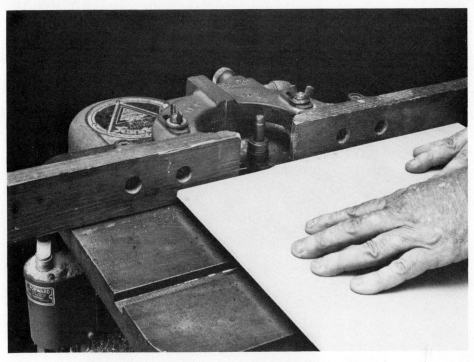

Figure 9–6 The lip of the cabinet door is rounded with a ⅜-in. quarter-round cutter.

Figure 9–7 Cabinet door lip three-wing cutter.

Single doors will be rabbeted on all four edges, while a pair of doors will receive the machining on just three edges. Care must be exercised so that the edges at the middle of a pair of doors are not rabbeted.

Finally, the edges should be sanded with the finish sander with 120-grit paper followed by a sanding with 220-grit paper. Both surfaces should also be sanded with 220-grit paper.

Decorating the lipped door

Two types of adornment are seen often on ¾-in. plywood doors. A routing jig is available on the market that provides several patterns for routing a stylized groove on the front of the door and drawer fronts (Fig. 9–8). These jigs are available at some mail-order houses, woodworking tool suppliers, and building material centers (Fig. 9–9).

An overlaid molding is often used, too, to give the plywood door and drawer front a provincial or period styling. The molding is available at cabinet supply houses and specialty woodworker's stores in both straight lengths and curved sections already mitered at the correct angle. Application is a matter of gluing and using brads to fasten the molding to the surface of the door and drawer front in the pattern desired (Fig. 9–10).

Figure 9-8 Doors are given a provincial look by routing a stylized groove.

Figure 9-9 A routing jig is used to style cabinet doors.

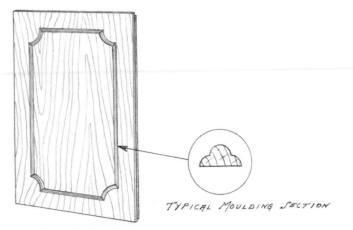

TYPICAL MOULDING SECTION

Figure 9-10 Plywood door with overlay molding.

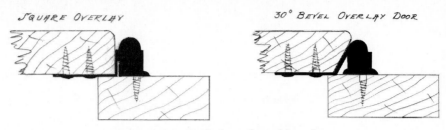

Figure 9–11   Typical overlay cabinet doors.

Overlay Door

For the modern look in cabinetry, doors and drawer fronts of plain ¾-in. plywood that overlay the cabinet frame are very attractive. Often, plastic laminate is applied to particle board to make a modern-type overlay door. In either case, the inner core of the panel must be edge-banded with solid wood or veneer.

The size of the door will depend on the type of overlay hinge chosen, as there are several on the market. Most of the standard hinges for overlay doors that have traditionally been used have the barrel of the hinge visible. One such hinge that is very popular calls for the overlay door to be made ⅜ in. larger than the opening all around. The builder interested in overlay doors would be well advised to examine the types of hinges available before designing and cutting the plywood (Fig. 9–11). Hinges are available that allow for a wider overlay, and some hinges are manufactured that are to be used with a cabinet face frame and some that mount directly on side panels with no face frame. The newer European completely invisible hinge is discussed in Chapter 16.

Of course, the paneled doors can be made with a ⅜-in. lip or they can be of the overlay type as well. Again the choice is up to the builder or the customer.

MAKING THE PLAIN PANELED DOOR

The plain paneled door is really a frame with a plywood insert. The design and construction of panel doors will depend to a great extent on the machines the builder has available. Lacking a shaper, the panel doors will have to be quite plain, as the fancy molded edges and coped joints that the shaper can produce will not be possible. However, nice-looking paneled doors can be made with just the table saw and router. With the addition of a decorative panel glued over the plain panel, both made of ¼-in. plywood, a very attractive door can be constructed.

Frame for the Paneled Door

Good design for the frame of a simple panel door with a ¼-in. plywood insert calls for the stiles and top rail to be of the same width, while the bottom rail should be somewhat wider. The decision must be made as to the type of door: Will it be a door with a ⅜-in. lip or a door that is flush with the face frame? The width of the stiles and top rail will have to be approximately 2 in. for a cabinet door with a ⅜-in. lip. The inside leaf of the inset hinge requires 1¹⁄₁₆ in. of the stile and lip another ⅜ in. Add to that the depth of the groove for the panel and the total width is approaching 2 in. With 2-in. stiles the bottom rail should be 2½ to 3 in. wide (Fig. 9–12).

If any type of curve is designed into the door, the width of the top and bottom rails will have to be adjusted. The narrowest width of the curved portion should be kept equal to the width of the stiles, if possible. The wider part of the curved rail should be about the same width as the bottom rail. Although these proportions are not "carved in stone," generally followed they will result in a well-proportioned and pleasing door.

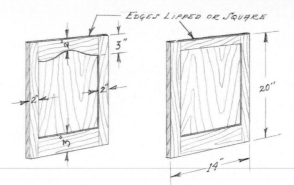

Figure 9-12   Plain or plywood paneled doors.

Determining the size of the paneled door

For a lipped door the formula presented in the section of this chapter on plywood lipped doors should be used: Measure the opening and add ½ in. to each dimension. It might be well to allow an additional $\frac{1}{16}$ in. to both the length and width and then machine the door to exact size after assembly. A bit too large is easily remedied—a bit too small is a disaster!

Length of the stiles: Height of the opening plus ½ in. ($\frac{9}{16}$ in. if the extra margin is decided on).

Length of the rails: Here some careful calculations must be done.

The net length of the rail is figured by subtracting the width of the stiles, but then the stub tenon on each end must be added to that net length. So if the width of the door is 14½ in., 4 in. must be subtracted for the width of the two stiles, leaving 10½ in. The groove for the ¼-in. plywood panel should be machined ⅜ in. deep so that much will have to be added back on to the 10½ in. for a total length for the rails of 11¼ in. (Fig. 9-13). (Note that the extra $\frac{1}{16}$ in. was not used for this example.)

Example bill of materials when face-frame opening measures 14 in. × 20 in.:

2 pcs. ¾ in. × 2 in. × 20½ in.   stiles
1 pc. ¾ in. × 2 in. × 11¼ in.   top rail
1 pc. ¾ in. × 3 in. × 11¼ in.   bottom rail
1 pc. ¼ in. × 11$\frac{3}{16}$ in. × 16$\frac{3}{16}$ in.   plywood panel ($\frac{1}{16}$ in. allowed for "play")

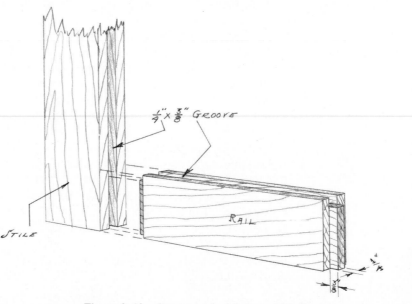

Figure 9-13   Groove and stub tenon details.

The size of the plywood panel can be verified after a trial assembly is made of the door.

Be sure to select straight stock for the rails and stiles. Pieces with even a slight warp or twist can result in panel doors that fit the cabinet very poorly.

Machining the stiles and rails

As long as the style of the door calls for no curves, all of the machining (except the curve of the lip) can be done on the table saw.

Groove for the plywood panel

The grooving can be done with the dado head set to cut ¼ in. wide. Usually, shims are not necessary when grooving for ¼-in. hardwood plywood, as the plywood runs a bit under ¼ in. thickness. Be sure to test-fit the plywood by running the groove in a piece of scrap first.

Set the saw fence so that the groove is in the middle of the edges of the stiles and rails. Run the groove ⁵⁄₁₆ to ⅜ in. deep. The groove can be run the full length of all the pieces. This is the simplest type of frame construction for panel doors. If the builder wants the joints doweled or mortised, the grooving will have to be stopped short of the ends of the stiles. However, this is not necessary, as a perfectly satisfactory joint is made by using the stub tenon provided at the end of the rails that matches the groove in the stiles.

Stub tenon on the rails

Machining the stub tenon requires the same setup as tenoning the joints for the face-frame (Chapter 5). Using the dado head and the saw fence as a length jig, carefully run the short tenons on the rails to match exactly the groove in the stiles.

Plywood panel

Make a trial assembly of the door and determine the exact size of the panel for the door. Allow about ¹⁄₁₆ in. for "play" when cutting the panel to size.

Assembly of the door

Using bar clamps, glue and clamp the door together checking for squareness. The panel is not glued in the groove. This allows the panel to expand and contract independently from the frame. The clamps should be cushioned so as not to mar the door stiles with clamp marks.

Sanding

The panel should be given a finish sanding before assembling in the frame. The frame should be belt-sanded using the same technique as for the face-frame.

Edge-shaping the door

If the door is to be lipped, use the router or shaper, as described earlier in the chapter. Be certain that the overall dimensions of the door are correct before doing the final edge shaping. Finally, give the routed edge a finish sanding with 120-grit paper followed by 220-grit paper.

Plain Paneled Door with a Curved Design

Once the design of the door has been accomplished, the procedure for building the curved door is very similar to that described for the rectangular paneled door. The only change will be in the techniques for machining the curved portions of the door frame (Fig. 9–12).

ROUTER 3-WING SLOTTING
CUTTER.

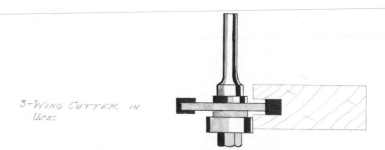

3-WING CUTTER IN
USE.

Figure 9-14   Slotting cutter used on curved stiles and rails.

Machining the stiles and rails

Cut all pieces to their proper dimensions and machine the grooves and stub tenons on the rails before cutting the curves that are required. It is difficult to machine the stub tenons on the rails if one edge of the rail is curved, as this edge cannot be placed against the miter gauge. Once the tenon is cut, the edges can be cut to shape on the bandsaw or with the saber saw, sanded, and then grooved with either a router or on a shaper. It is difficult to find a router cutter that will cut a ¼-in. groove. A slotting cutter for the router is available that will cut a ¼-in. kerf, however, and with the bearing guide will cut a slot ½ in. deep. This is a bit deeper than necessary but will cause no problems (Fig. 9-14). Most rabbet cutters for the router are not made in the ¼-in. size, only ⅜ or ½ in. A rabbet cutter would not work too well anyway, for this cutter is sharpened only on the bottom and edge. The top has no relief grinding to it and this could result in considerable tear-out when machining a groove.

The shaper is by far the most satisfactory machine to use when running curves along the edges of stiles and rails. This is done freehand using the starting pin and depth collars to control the depth of cut. This will be discussed in more detail in the section on raised panel doors.

Cutting the curved panel

Once the trial assembly has been made, the ¼-in. panel must be cut to fit. Using the rail as a pattern, carefully transfer the curves to the plywood panel, remembering to allow for the amount that goes into the groove.

Assembling and sanding

The final operations are the same as described previously for the rectangular paneled door.

Plywood Paneled Door with an Overlay Panel

The plain paneled door with the plywood insert can be given a simulated raised panel effect by overlaying a ¼-in. plywood panel on top of the panel inserted in the groove. A margin of 1½ to 2 in. is allowed all around from the frame of the door. The over-

Figure 9-15A Good example of an overlay panel door.

Figure 9-15B High-styled paneled doors. (Courtesy Kitchen Re-Stylers, Hutchinson, Minn.)

lay panel is then cut in the same design as the insert panel. A small cove routed around the edge of the overlay panel adds a nice touch. The overlay panel is then glued to the regular panel by placing weights on top of the assembled panels (Figs. 9-15A and 9-15B).

MAKING RAISED PANEL DOORS

Probably nothing can surpass the period-styled cabinet with solid raised paneled doors for beauty and styling. These have become increasingly popular over the last decade and even the small shop has been forced to include the raised panel door. Many small operators find a source of supply for these doors rather than go to the expense of purchasing expensive carbide knives in the required sets. Many of the larger shops are very willing to make to order the custom requirements of the one-person shop or the home workshop builder. For those builders who want to get into raised panel doors, however, in this section we provide the basic information and know-how.

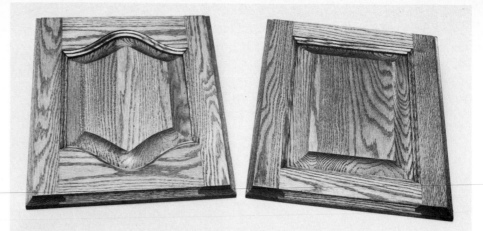

Figure 9–16A Raised panel doors are available in various styles. (Courtesy Kitchen Re-Stylers, Hutchinson, Minn.)

Figure 9-16B Other examples of raised panel doors. (Courtesy Kitchen Re-Stylers, Hutchinson, Minn.)

Designing the Raised Panel Door

The information regarding plain paneled doors is, for the most part, also applicable to raised paneled doors. The general size information for rails and stiles and design rules of thumb should be followed. Patterns for these doors are virtually unlimited, as a visit to any builder's supply center will attest (Figs. 9–16A and 9–16B). Because the doors are of high design, the edges of the rails and stiles are shaped and the joints coped. Thus use of a spindle shaper is absolutely mandatory for producing these doors. Unfortunately, most of the knives manufactured to do panel raising require a spindle shaper with a ¾-in. spindle or larger. These cutters are quite large and are usually not made for the smaller shapers with just a ½-in. spindle, although some cutters can be shimmed to fit a ½-in. spindle. This means that an investment should be made in a larger shaper if curved raised panels are desired in quantity.

Required Shaper Cutters

As is the case with most shaper cutters, they are available in both tool steel and carbide. The cost ranges from just a few dollars to several hundred dollars for sophisticated matched carbide production sets.

Sticker and coping knives

A matched set of sticker and coping cutters is available from Rockwell in the ½-in. bore to fit small shapers. These are available in tool steel or carbide (Fig. 9–17A). These are the numbers:

09–125 and 09–126: left- and right-hand female
09–123 and 09–124: left- and right-hand male

Cutters 125 and 126 are sticker cutters that will do the fancy edge molding on the rails and stiles. Cutters 123 and 124 are coping cutters that do the matching undercutting so that the rails fit nicely against and into the molded edge on the stile. Used with a standard ¼-in. straight knife, the molded edge and the ¼-in. groove can be run on one pass on straight pieces. These knives are also available in carbide and bear the number 43–921 for the complete set.

Figure 9–17B illustrates other patterns of sticker and coping knives that are available in carbide and for use with larger machines with the ¾-in. spindle or bigger. These are high-production cutters and cost well into the hundreds of dollars. As always, the choice is up to the cabinetmaker, and the decision as to which to purchase will depend on the volume of production and what capital expenditure can be afforded.

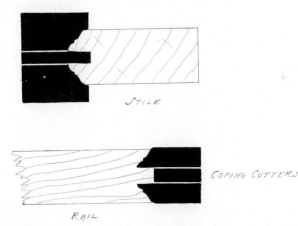

Figure 9–17A Three-wing stile and rail shaper cutters: ½-in bore.

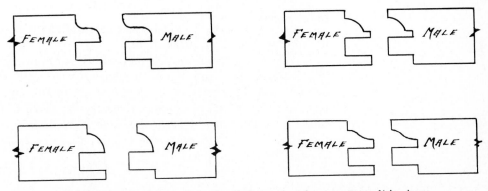

Figure 9–17B Other stile and rail three-wing shaper cutters: ¾-in. bore.

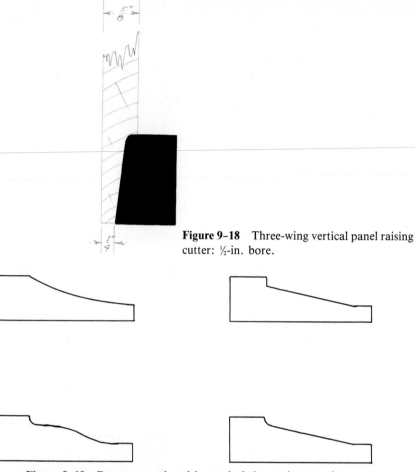

Figure 9-18   Three-wing vertical panel raising cutter: ½-in. bore.

Figure 9-19   Patterns produced by typical three-wing panel raising shaper cutters: ¾-in bore.

Panel-raising cutters

As mentioned previously, few horizontal panel-raising cutters are made for the shaper with a ½-in. spindle. Rockwell does make a vertical cutter for the small shaper, but it is not possible to do raised panels with a curved design with this cutter. This limits the small operator with the ½-in. spindle machine to rectangular panels. Rockwell carries this cutter under the number 09–214 in steel and 43–902 in carbide (Fig. 9–18).

Many cutters are available from numerous manufacturers to do panel raising on a production basis using the larger shapers. The profiles produced by a few of these cutters are illustrated in Fig. 9–19.

Making a Raised Panel without a Shaper

The same router techniques can be used for edging the door frame as was described in the section on plain paneled doors.

There are quite a few different means of producing a raised panel for these doors using the table saw or other machines. Home craftspersons have devised many unique means of accomplishing this, but very few, if any, lend themselves to economical production. For example, a rectangular raised panel can be beveled on the tilting arbor table saw by tilting the blade to the desired angle with the fence set at the proper setting. This technique requires a lot of cleanup sanding to have a presentable finished product.

Doing curved work on a raised panel is virtually impossible without a large shaper, at least on any sort of commercial basis. No doubt, ingenious home woodworkers have come up with clever jigs to allow them to produce a curved raised panel, but these would probably not be adaptable to a commercial setting.

The small shop owner would be much better off—and in the end make more profit—by locating a good source of commercially manufactured raised panel doors.

Bill of Materials for the Raised Panel Door

Once the design of the door has been decided on and the necessary shaper cutters secured, the next step is to figure the exact pieces and their sizes. For instructional purposes, the door being made is to fit a face-frame opening measuring 19½ in. wide by 22½ in. high. Figure 9–20 illustrates the door being made which will also be a lipped door. The material required is:

2 pcs. ¾ in. × 2 in. × 23 in.	stiles
2 pcs. ¾ in. × 3 in. × 16¾ in.	rails
1 pc. ⅝ in. × 16¾ in.× approx. 19 in.	panel

The length of the rails is determined by subtracting the width of the stiles—4 in.— from the overall width of 20 in. , leaving 16 in. But to that must be added the amount required to make the coped joint and tongue. An examination of the shaper knives reveals that this amount is very close to ⅜ in. Therefore, ¾ in. must be added to the 16 in. for a total rail length of 16¾ in. (Fig. 9–21)

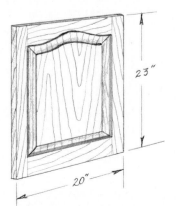

Figure 9–20 Raised panel door.

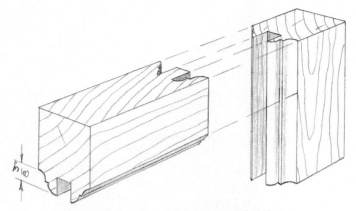

Figure 9–21 Coped joint for paneled door.

The standard thickness for a raised panel of solid wood is ⅝ in. The panel will be as wide as the rail is long—16¾ in.—and will have to be cut to a rough length of about 19 in. The exact length is difficult to determine until the frame is assembled and the amount of panel required for the curved end is established. No doubt the panel will have to be glued up to meet the width requirement of 16¾ in. There are on the market special plywoods that are used for door panels. These are available in extra-thick face veneers so that the inner plies are not visible when the raised panel is cut on the shaper. These plywoods are sold in both ⅜- and ⅝-in. thicknesses.

Machining the Pieces for the Raised Panel Door

The bill of materials is machined to the net sizes shown. The stiles and the bottom rail must next have one edge run on the shaper. This operation is performed with the full female cutter set, including the ¼-in. grooving cutter (Fig. 9–22). Adjust the knives and the shaper fence carefully so that the knives shape the edge evenly and the slot is exactly centered on the edge. Always run a test on scrap pieces of the same thickness.

The top rail, which has had the curved pattern cut and the edge sanded, is next edge-shaped. This must be done freehand on the shaper by running the material against a depth collar and the starting pin. The shaping cannot be done with the three-knife setup as the edges were because there would be nothing to bear against the depth collar. The best technique is to do the curved edges in two setups: the molding cutter to do the two edges of the piece, followed by another setup with the ¼-in. grooving cutter.

Setup 1 (Figs. 9–23A and 9–23B): Adjust the cutter vertically so that it matches the pattern run in the stiles. Start the cut by bracing the piece against the starting pin, gradually and carefully moving the piece into the cutters. The danger of kickback is greatest at the starting point. Once the cut has been started, move the piece forward evenly, keeping the wood in contact with the depth collar at all times. Flip the piece over and do the other edge.

Setup 2 (Fig. 9–24): Two depth collars and the ¼-in. slotter are used in this setup. Adjust the cutter vertically so that it matches the groove run in the stiles. The depth of the groove is controlled by the size of the collars. Run the groove using the technique described previously.

Figure 9–22 Running the pattern and groove on the door stiles.

Figure 9–23A This shaping cut must be started with the work against the pin, then held against the depth collar.

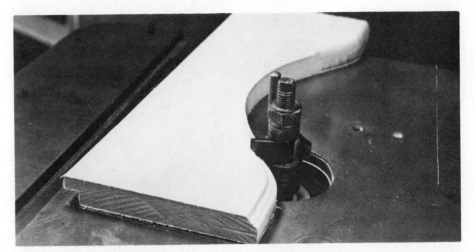

Figure 9–23B Each side must be run separately.

Figure 9–24 The ¼-in. groove is run with just the depth collars.

Freehand shaping is not quite as dangerous as it appears. Sharp knives are a must. The trick of starting the cut is soon mastered. Feeding the piece evenly and steadily will hold the slight burning of the edge to a minimum. The charring results from the friction of the wood against the depth collar. There are ball-bearing collars available that will prevent this. However, some quick sanding soon removes the burn from the edges. Be alert to grain reversals and small knots that could kick or jerk the material while being run.

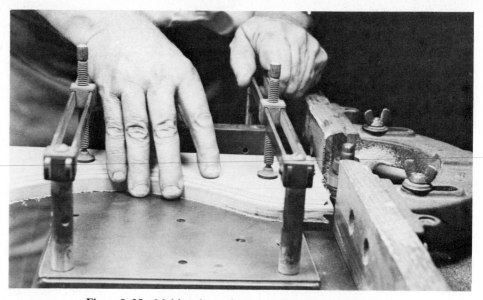

Figure 9-25   Making the coping cut at the end of the rails. The clamp-type miter gauge is a necessity for this operation.

Figure 9-26   Reverse the clamp-type miter gauge for running the opposite end of the rail.

Making the coped cuts on the rails

The male knives of the cabinet set are used for this machining on the rails (Fig. 9-25). A ¼-in. spacer must be used between the knives to provide for the matching stub tenon on the rail. The fence on the shaper must be adjusted to control the depth of cut while the clamping attachment for the miter gauge holds the rail firmly. Once the setup has been made, make a trial run with a scrap piece of the same thickness as the rails. Adjust the cutters and the fence until the result is an excellent fit against and into the stile pattern.

Run the coping on both ends of the rails. The top rail will have to be run by reversing the position of the holding jig when making the second cut (Fig. 9-26). Some breakout will probably occur as the coping cut nears completion. This can be held to a minimum by finishing the cut very slowly.

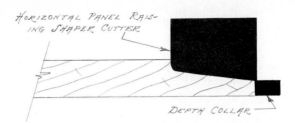

Figure 9-27   Shaper cutter setup for raised panels.

Cutting the panel to size and shape

After the shaping of the stiles and rails is completed, the panel can be cut to the correct size and the curve on the end can be also cut. Make a trial assembly of the frame and determine the exact width and length of the panel. Transfer the shape of the curve to the panel from the top rail. Allow about ¹⁄₁₆ in. of "play" as was done with the plywood paneled door. Sand the curved edge so that this edge will run smoothly against the collar of the shaper.

Raised panel shaping

With the door design used for this instruction, three edges of the panel are shaped against the fence while the curved portion must be run with the starting pin and collars. The panel raising cutter is adjusted vertically so that the thin edge of the panel is ¼ in. thick to fit the slot in the rails and stiles (Fig. 9–18). The curved end of the panel should be shaped first. Thus, if there is any breakout at the edge, it will be removed when doing the side cuts. Use a depth collar with this cutter that allows the cutter to machine 1½ in. into the panel surface (Fig. 9–27).

Because of the large knife and the depth of the cut, this seems like a dangerous operation. However, the operator is usually running good-sized pieces, so his or her hands are not close to the cutter head.

The second run will be the other end of the panel. Again, if breakout should result from doing the cross grain, it will be removed by the machining of sides. Set the fence accurately and use a clamping jig to run the narrower panels. If the panels are 10 to 12 in. wide or wider, a holding jig will probably not be required.

Assembling the Door

All the edges should be checked to see that any shaper collar burns have been removed. Sand the surface area of the raised panel with the finish sander and touch up the shaped border if required. Good sharp cutters will result in cuts that need no sanding, however.

After a trial assembly, apply glue to all joints and clamp with bar clamps cushioning the jaws of the clamps so that the stiles are not marred. Do not glue the panel in the groove. It is allowed to expand and contract free of the frame, as was the plywood paneled door. Frame sanding and lipping operations are then completed as described previously.

MAKING CABINET DOORS WITH GLASS PANES

A glass-paned cabinet door is very similar to a plain paneled door. The difference is that the glass pane must be replaceable if it breaks. It is therefore necessary to change the construction technique so that the glass is replaceable from the rear of the door.

Building the Frame without a Shaper

Building a frame for a door to hold a glass pane presents some special problems if a spindle shaper is not available. The joint will probably have to be doweled or mortised, as there will be no stub tenon to provide the necessary gluing surfaces (Fig. 9–28). To make this joint fit properly, the glass bead must be carefully chiseled and sawed away so that the rail fits evenly against the stile. Another alternative (as long as all edges are left square) is to rabbet the end of the rail to accept the glass bead on the stile, making a lap joint (Fig. 9–29). Many builders use the method of cutting away the glass bead on the stile when they have run a molded edge on the frame members. In this way a presentable door is made even though a coped joint is not fabricated.

Some cabinetmakers miter the corners of doors framed for glass. Mitering the joints makes it possible to ignore coped or chiseled joints. The major drawback to this is twofold: First, a miter joint is weak compared to a mortised or doweled joint; and second, if the stiles and rails are of unequal width, the miter joint is more difficult to make and not as nice looking.

Shaping curved door frame members with a router

It is quite a simple operation to run a ⅜ in. × ⅜ in. glass bead on curved members of the frame for a glass door. It is often easiest to mount the router in a

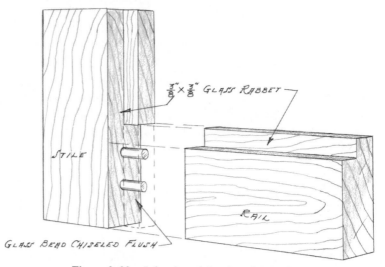

Figure 9–28   Joint for plain glass frame door.

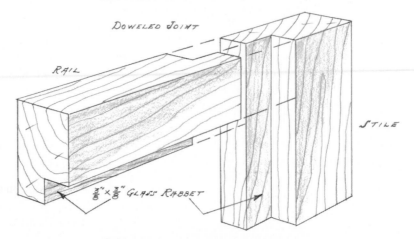

Figure 9–29   Lap-type door frame joint.

Figure 9-30 A router table is often used to hold the router for shaping operations.

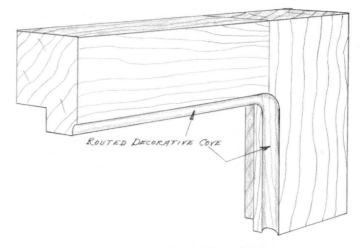

ROUTED DECORATIVE COVE

Figure 9-31 Routed door frame.

worktable for running pieces of various kinds. There are many plans for router tables in trade magazines. The router is mounted underneath the table with the cutter extending through the table. Using the router table leaves both hands free to feed and guide the work against the guide pin (Fig. 9-30).

Another trick is to assemble the door and then run a decorative bead around the inside edge of the glass retaining edge (Fig. 9-31). This is usually done with a small router cutter so that the rounding left at the corners is not too objectionable.

Building the Frame with a Shaper

Beautiful glass-paned doors can be built by using the sticker and coping knives on the spindle shaper. The knives described in the section on raised panel doors are used for the frame for a glass door as well. The change, of course, is that a ⅜ in. × ⅜ in. glass rabbet must be run with a straight knife using a depth collar on curved pieces and the fence for straight pieces.

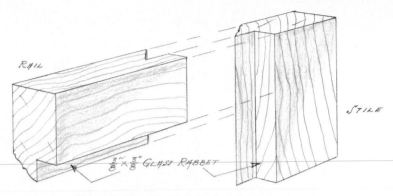

Figure 9-32   Coped joint for glass-paned door.

Coped joint on the frame

After the desired pattern is run on the glass bead of the door frame members, the rabbet for the glass is run. This is done on all frame members, both straight or curved. The coping on the door joints is the next operation (Fig. 9–32). Just one of the male coping knives is used. Again, when running across the grain on the ends of the door rails, a hold-down miter gauge is a necessity to keep the work from drifting. Carefully run test cuts in scrap and make test fits on the stile.

> **Tip: Keep a piece of wood with the correct pattern machined on it as a setup piece for the next time the same operation is to be done. This saves a lot of setup time and test runs!**

Should the joints be doweled or mortised?

Here is another controversial point in cabinetmaking! Many cabinet builders no longer dowel or mortise coped joints. They simply glue them together, depending on the fit of the coped pattern to hold the joint securely. Others still dowel and/or mortise, fearing that the coping alone will not stand up. From personal experience, the author has used both methods and can report no difficulties using coping alone. This saves several time-consuming operations. With modern glues and a well-fitted joint, no poor door joints have been experienced.

Routed Plywood Frame for Glass Doors

Some cabinet builders make frames for glass cabinet doors from plywood or veneered particle board. This is done by first cutting a plywood cabinet door to correct size, rabbeting the lip on the door around the outside edge, and then using a saber saw or goodsized jigsaw, make a glass cutout on the inside of the panel (Fig. 9–33). The cutout carefully preserves the normal width of the stiles and rails. After the cutout is completed, a glass retaining rabbet is routed around the inside edge of the opening. The corners are squared off by hand chiseling.

A curved pattern on the door can be accomplished using this method as well. Often, too, the builder, using the router, cuts away much of the curved pattern on the inside surface of the door, allowing a square pane of glass to be used.

Glass Retaining Methods

There are several methods of retaining the glass pane in the door frame. These are a few of the most common methods.

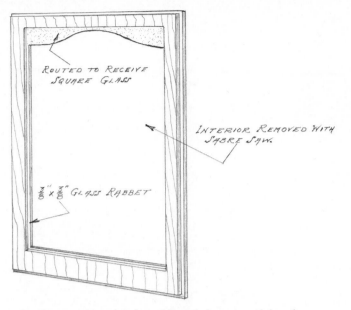

ROUTED TO RECEIVE
SQUARE GLASS

INTERIOR REMOVED WITH
SABRE SAW.

$\frac{3}{8}"\times\frac{3}{8}"$ GLASS RABBET

Figure 9-33 Particle-board lipped door routed for glass.

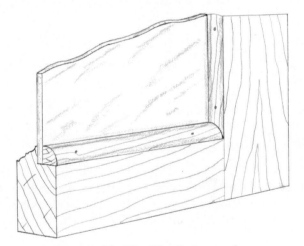

Figure 9-34 Wood bead glass retainer.

Wood retaining bead

This is the most common and oldest method and works well on doors with no curves. A simple wood beading is machined to the correct size (approximately ⅜ in. × ¼ in.). (This will depend on whether single-strength or double-strength glass is used.) This bead is often machined with a small rounding for a nicer appearance. The beading is mitered at the corners and fastened in place using small, thin brads (Fig. 9-34).

Retaining buttons

These are available in several sizes and shapes (Fig. 9-35).

1. *Plastic offset button.* No machining or recessing is required, as the button has a lip that fits into the glass rabbet, holding the pane firmly in place.
2. *Disc type retaining button.* The disc must be recessed into the frame so that it is flush with the glass surface. The button has a flat spot on the edge which, when rotated, allows for easy removal of the glass.

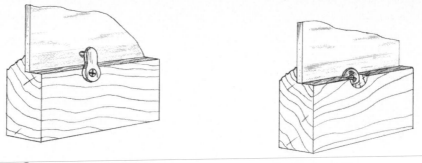

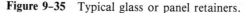

PLASTIC OFFSET RETAINER   DISC TYPE RETAINER

Figure 9–35 Typical glass or panel retainers.

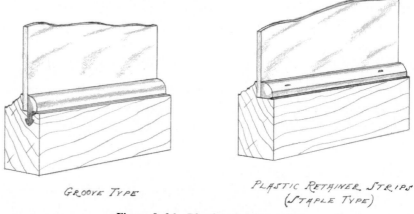

GROOVE TYPE   PLASTIC RETAINER STRIPS
                             (STAPLE TYPE)

Figure 9–36 Plastic retaining strips.

Plastic retaining strips

Plastic stripping is sold in two styles. One style is designed to slip into a groove machined into the door frame. The other is stapled or tacked in position. Both work well on straight frames and on gentle curves. They do not work well on sharp curves. The strips are usually available in a walnut and a fruitwood color (Fig. 9–36)

Glazier points

Although these are ordinarily used to retain glass in a window sash, they can also be used in a cabinet door. They are rather unsightly, however, compared to the other methods described. Probably the best use of these would be in a wood-framed, sliding-glass showcase door where the inside would not be seen.

Other Materials Used as Door Panels

Occasionally, other materials are used in connection with framed doors. Often, a wire grille insert is used that is made of polished brass. Or the homeowner may decorate the panel with fabric of his or her choice. In any event, one of the retaining methods described above should apply to these other materials.

MAKING SLIDING DOORS FOR CABINETS

Although most modern kitchen cabinets do not make use of sliding doors, other built-ins for the home often will be designed with this type of door. Too, the cabinetmaker often is called on to build showcases for retail stores, and these fixtures very often have sliding doors. China cabinets are designed with plate glass sliding doors, so these will be covered in this chapter as well.

Building Bypass Sliding Doors

Bypass sliding doors can be built as simply as using two ¼-in. plywood panels with a plastic track. They also can be designed in any of the patterns for paneled or glass-framed doors and to roll on mortised "sheaves" on a metal track. The construction of these doors will often depend on the type of track system to be used. In all cases, however, the installation of the door is the same. The door is designed to lift up into a rabbet in the top rail far enough to clear the track, and then to drop down onto the track with still enough lip remaining in the top track to hold the door. This sounds much more complicated than it really is, as the drawings will illustrate.

Designing bypass sliding doors

The width of sliding doors is the first consideration. The doors should overlap ½ to 1 in. at the middle of the cabinet. A cabinet with an opening of 48 in. would therefore have two bypassing doors each 24½ to 25 in. wide. The height of the doors requires some careful planning and measuring, which will depend to a large extent on the type of track system being used.

Aluminum or plastic track

This type of sliding door track is available in three widths to accommodate ⅛-, ¼- and ¾-in. sliding doors. (The ⅛-in. track will nicely handle sliding doors of double-strength window glass.) The track is sold in lengths of 4, 5, and 6 ft. It can be secured to the cabinet with brads, small nails, or adhesive. The wider track must always be used as the top runner, as Fig. 9–37 illustrates. Colors available are tan and walnut.

This track system is designed for sliding doors that have no wheels or other friction-reducing mechanisms. Although they do not roll back and forth quite as easily as the track-and-sheave system described in the next section, they do work well enough for the average installation. They are less expensive to make and install than other systems.

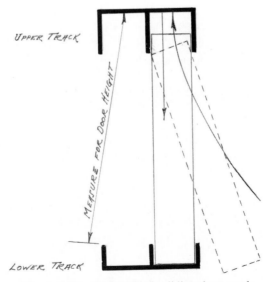

Figure 9–37 Metal/plastic sliding door track.

Track-and-sheave system

This type of sliding door hardware is customarily used on showcase fixtures. The track is of metal, as are the sheaves, although the sheaves often will have a nylon wheel, which makes for a nice, quiet-running door. The sheaves are available in two basic styles: enclosed and round groove (Fig. 9–38). They are designed to be mortised into the bottom of doors of ¾ in. or more width.

The track is made in both single-runner and double-runner styles. The single runner is most commonly used, with two tracks installed side by side at the proper spacing to accommodate the width of door being used (Fig. 9–38).

There is no commercial upper guide for this system, which means that the cabinet builder must plan and groove the upper rail. The top of the sliding door must be lipped to run easily in this grooved rail. Figure 9–39 illustrates the necessary designing for a pair of ¾-in. sliding doors using the track-and-groove method. Notice that the bottom of the sliding doors has a ⅛-in. groove. This is required because the nylon roller is recessed that amount into the sheave.

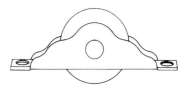

TYPICAL SLIDING DOOR SHEAVES

FLUSH FINGER PULL

SINGLE TRACK   *DOUBLE TRACK*

Figure 9–38 Sliding door hardware. (Courtesy Knape and Vogt.)

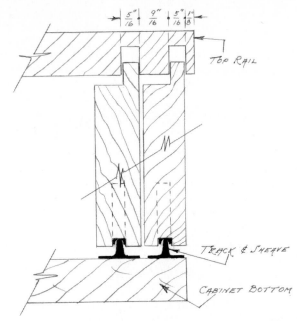

Figure 9–39 Sliding door details.

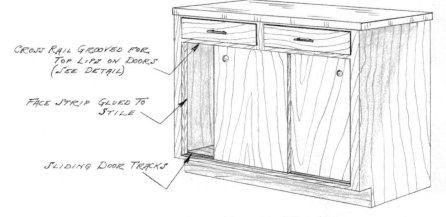

Figure 9–40 Base cabinet with sliding doors.

Stiles for sliding door cabinets

For practically all sliding doors wider than ¼ in. the cabinet stile must be widened so that the door does not slip behind the stile. This is usually a simple matter of gluing a ¾ in. × ¾ in. stile extension piece to the inside of the stile (Fig. 9–40).

Pulls for the sliding doors

Flush finger pulls are manufactured for bypassing doors that are easy to install. They are available in two normal stock offerings of ¾ in. diameter × ¼ in. deep and 1¾ in. diameter × ¹³⁄₃₂ in. deep. The correct-size hole is simply drilled in the door and the finger pull is tapped in position using the flat end of a dowel of the correct size.

Installation of the sheave

The mortise for the sheave can be a rough mortise done with the electric drill and a ¼-in. drill bit. Rough-out the mortise with a series of holes to the approximate size of the body of the sheave. Test the mortise for depth and width, making certain

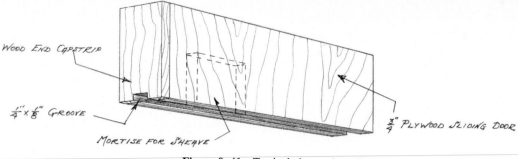

WOOD END CAPSTRIP

¼″ × ⅝″ GROOVE

MORTISE FOR SHEAVE

¾″ PLYWOOD SLIDING DOOR

Figure 9-41   Typical sheave installation.

that enough wood remains to catch the prongs at the end of the sheave. When the fit is correct, simply drive the prongs into the adjacent wood using the nail set (Fig. 9-41).

Plate Glass Sliding Doors

China cabinets and other built-ins that are designed to display fine glassware and china often are equipped with plate glass sliding doors. Store fixtures often require these doors for the display of merchandise.

Designing the cabinet for plate glass doors

No drastic change in cabinet design is necessary to accommodate plate glass sliding doors. The same design features for wood doors are applicable for glass doors. The stiles must often be widened so that the doors do not slide behind the stile, and the top rail might have to have the same treatment to take care of the upper track (Fig. 9-42). Cabinets with plate glass sliding doors will have their interiors visible. This means that the interior construction must be of the same materials as the exterior of the cabinet. Chapter 14 presents the techniques for building interior visible cabinets.

One other item must be watched closely and that is the weight of plate glass sliding doors. If an upper cabinet unit, for example, is equipped with these doors, the weight of the doors could, in time, cause the bottom of the upper unit to sag. The span or width of opening must be kept to a minimum to forestall this. If the

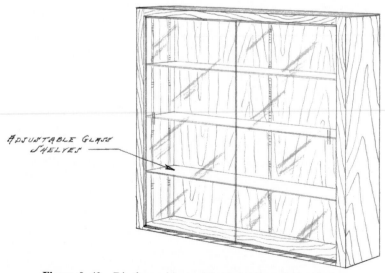

ADJUSTABLE GLASS SHELVES

Figure 9-42   Display cabinet with plate glass sliding doors.

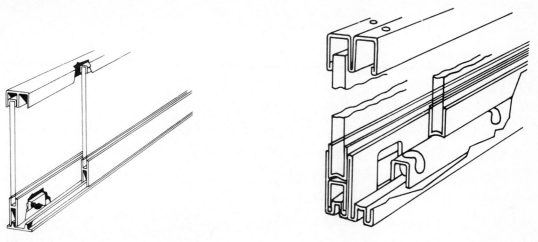

Figure 9-43 Roller hardware for plate glass sliding doors. (Courtesy Knape and Vogt.)

upper unit rests directly on the base cabinet, this is no problem, as the bottom of the upper unit is supported adequately. Fortunately, this is very often the way china cabinets are designed.

Ordering plate glass sliding doors

Most cabinet builders order these doors from specialty glass dealers in their area. They simply give the glass dealer the size of the opening—width first, then height—and the dealer fabricates the doors. If finger slots are desired, these, too, must be ordered, as there is usually an extra charge for grinding finger slots. The doors come complete with the track; the cabinet builder simply installs the doors in the completed cabinet.

Track and hardware for plate glass doors

Cabinet supply houses and specialty woodworking concerns usually carry plate glass sliding track and hardware items such as locks.

The same plastic track that is used for ¼-in. wooden sliding doors can be used for plate glass doors. However, better-quality installations use a ball-bearing track assembly that allows the doors to slide with minimum effort (Fig. 9-43).

Installation in the cabinet

The track is screwed to the top rail and the bottom of the cabinet. The cabinet must be exactly square for the sliding glass doors to meet the stiles properly when closed. There is practically no adjustment possible other than shimming the lower track a bit to compensate for out-of-squareness.

APPLYING HINGES TO THE DOORS

Most cabinetmakers do not hang the doors on the cabinet until the units are installed in the home. This is not always true, as some of the larger shops have installation crews who specialize in this work and the cabinets have the doors already hung when they leave the shop. The danger is that the cabinets will be twisted when fastened to the wall and the doors thrown out of alignment. The installers know just how

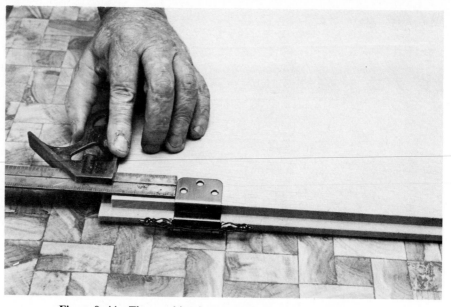

Figure 9-44   The combination square makes a convenient jig for hinges.

to shim the cabinet to bring the doors back into proper alignment. For the average cabinet builder, however, hanging the doors after the cabinet is screwed to the wall is a better procedure. The units are not as heavy to handle and the doors are in perfect alignment when hung on the job.

The hinges are applied to the doors prior to installation, however. It is much easier to apply the hinges using the shop tools in an efficient atmosphere. Care must be taken that the doors are not scratched while transporting them to the installation site.

A simple gauge is used to assure that the hinges are installed at the same distance from the top and bottom. The combination square works fine as a gauge for setting hinges (Fig. 9-44).

REVIEW QUESTIONS

9.1. What edge treatment is considered to be the most popular for custom cabinet doors?

9.2. Explain what a ⅜-in. inset hinge is and where it is used.

9.3. Name two treatments that lend style to a plywood cabinet door.

9.4. How much is added to the width and height of the cabinet opening to determine the overall dimensions of a ⅜-in. lipped door?

9.5. What is the dimensional difference for calculating the size of a pair of doors as compared with a single door?

9.6. To what size will the plywood be cut to make a pair of ⅜-in. lipped doors to fit an opening that measures 30¼ in. wide by 28⅛ in. high?

9.7. List three ways that a ⅜ in. × ⅜ in. rabbet can be machined on a plywood cabinet door.

9.8. In the plain paneled door, what is most often used for the panel?

9.9. What is the standard width of the stiles, top rail, and bottom rail for a plain paneled door?

9.10. Calculate the correct size of the stiles and rails for a plywood paneled door to fit a cabinet opening that measures 16½ in. × 22¾ in.

9.11. What is an overlay panel, and where is it used?

9.12. What machine is practically a necessity in the manufacture of raised panel doors?

9.13. What is the standard thickness of a panel of solid lumber in a raised panel door?

9.14. What are coping knives and sticker knives? Where are each used?

9.15. What is a starting pin? What is its purpose?

9.16. When making coping cuts at the end of door rails, what shaper accessory is required?

9.17. Describe the procedure required to make a glass-paned door from a plywood panel.

9.18. List three ways that the glass pane is held in the cabinet door frame.

9.19. What is a sheave, and where is it used in cabinetry?

9.20. How and from whom are plate glass sliding doors ordered?

SUGGESTED CLASS ACTIVITIES AND STUDENT ASSIGNMENTS

9.1. These are the door openings from the model cabinet plan in this text:

15½ in. × 22¾ in.   Single door
32 in. × 22¾ in   Pair of doors
6 in. × 22¾ in.   Single
23½ in. × 22¾ in   Pair
26¾ in. × 29¼ in.   Pair
27 in. × 29¼ in.   Pair
30 in. × 11¼ in.   Pair

(a) Calculate the overall dimensions for cutting ⅜-in. lipped doors from ¾-in. plywood for all the openings.

(b) Determine the number of square feet of plywood that will be required for these doors.

(c) Convert the number of square feet into an actual order to be placed for this plywood. Plan the sizes to be ordered and the cutting to be done so as to be as economical as possible.

9.2. Have the members of the class bring pictures of various styles of plain paneled and raised paneled doors.

9.3. Have the class members determine sources of applied decorative molding for cabinet doors. What is the cost of the various pieces and styles? How is this sold—lengths, etc.?

9.4. Determine local sources for router and shaper cutters. Secure catalogs from these sources so that each class member has them. What national sources are there? Determine actual costs for shaper cutters in steel and carbide to accomplish the shaping required for raised panel doors.

9.5. Determine local sources for sliding glass doors and hardware.

9.6. Arrange a visit to a manufacturer of raised panel doors. Determine if they sell to small shops on a custom basis. Investigate costs. While touring the establishment attempt to observe (a) the types of joints used in the doors; (b) shaper cutters used for sticking and coping; (c) which machines are used for sticking and coping (are high-production auto-feed tenoners and multiple-head molding machines being used?); and (d) how the raised panels are being machined and from what material they are being made.

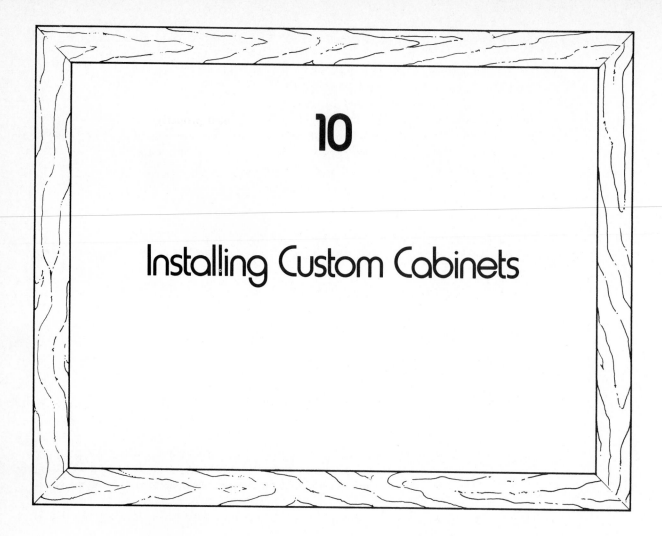

10

Installing Custom Cabinets

Next to the building of the cabinets themselves, the installation is of almost equal importance: "Quality cabinets require quality installation." Two items are of prime concern when placing the cabinets in the home. First, the process must give the cabinets a finished appearance so that they become an integral part of the residence; and second, the cabinets must be installed so as to carry the load for which they were designed. Both of these items will be discussed in this chapter.

PREPARING FOR CABINET INSTALLATION

Because the installation takes place on-site away from the builder's shop, adequate planning and preparation should be done. Often, the cabinets will be installed some distance from the shop, which means that the installer cannot return handily for a forgotten item. Many shops have a checklist that is followed prior to the loading of cabinets, tools, and other equipment that will be required on the job.

Quality Check of Completed Cabinets

These are some of the quality control checks that should be made before the cabinets leave the shop:

1. Cabinets are given their final sanding; fingerprints, smudges, blemishes, and so on, are all removed.
2. All drawers are checked for fit and ease of operation.
3. Shelves are all completed, track installed properly.
4. The shop plan is double-checked to see that all features desired by the customer are included.

All Shop Processes Completed

Every effort should be made to do as much of the work in the shop as possible. Many jobs become quite difficult on-site when the installer must rely on portable and hand tools. Such things as prefabricating as much of the countertop and backsplash as possible should be accomplished prior to leaving the shop. The sink cutout, rough sizing the plastic laminate, preparing laminate joints, ripping laminate self-edging, preparing cabinet casing strips, and so on, are a few of the procedures that should be done, if possible, in the cabinet shop.

Loading the Cabinet

Nothing is more disheartening than to arrive at the installation site only to find that the cabinets have been scratched and damaged due to poor moving preparations. It is well worth the time to take adequate precautions to prevent damage in transit. An adequate supply of moving quilts should be used to cushion all cabinet fronts and finished ends. Cabinets should be packed in such a way that drawers do not vibrate out of the cabinet. The doors should be carefully cushioned so that no damage is done in the moving. Finally, the load itself should be carefully lashed so that no unit could possibly fall or be blown from the truck.

Tools and Equipment

Most cabinet builders or installing crews have a well-organized set of tools and equipment they regularly transport to the job. Their portable electric tools are protected in cases, and their hand tools are cased in toolboxes of various sizes and descriptions. Nails, screws, brads, and so on, are well organized in portable "bins" with an adequate supply kept on hand. Installation jigs, step ladders, required hardware items, edge molding for plastic laminate, contact cement, and all laminate installing equipment is included on the tool list.

Everything that will be required to complete the installation job should be included so that there are no unnecessary delays or running back and forth.

Arrival at the Installation Site

The cabinets are one of the last items to go into the home after most of the carpenter work has been completed. The installers will probably be working under the watchful eyes of the interested homeowner. The installation crew should be attentive to such things as protecting any carpeting or other floor covering that must be walked across. Care should be exercised when bringing the units into the home that newly plastered or sheetrocked walls are not marred in any way. The crew should be pleasant, courteous, and workmanlike as they go about their business. After all, future jobs could very well depend on the recommendation of the homeowner who is observing the installers at work.

INSTALLING THE BASE CABINETS

Which should be installed first—the upper units or the base cabinets? This, again, is one of those personal preferences among cabinetmakers. Many prefer to install the upper cupboards first. They dislike the base cabinets in their way while placing the upper units. Other builders prefer to set the base cabinets first and they even install the particle-board countertop. They then have a built-in "workbench" and a "halfway" support for the upper cupboards when they position these. The sequence recommended in this text is to set the base cabinets prior to the upper cupboards.

Fastening the Cabinets to the Wall

The first job when installing cabinets is to locate the wall studs. This can range from a simple matter of following the covered nails in the drywall to a frustrating "no-logical" location of seemingly anything in the wall. Studs are most often located 16 in. on center—meaning that from the center of one 2 × 4 to the center of the next should be exactly 16 in. (Fig. 10–1). The frustrating part of all this is knowing just where the framer started the 16-in. spacing. Thankfully, once one stud is located, the adjacent ones are properly spaced—unless, that is, the carpenter happened to space the studs 24 in. apart as is sometimes done in less expensive construction such as cabins and lake cottages!

There are many hints and devices for locating studs. There are patented devices on the market that are supposed to locate interior wall studs. Many installers simply find where they think a stud is located and pound a small nail into the wall in the area they suspect. Once they have hit a stud, they then measure and mark each one in the wall. (They drive the nail below the countertop level of the base cabinet so that the holes do not show after the unit is positioned.) On older homes that may have had substantial remodeling, the outside siding might reveal the stud location

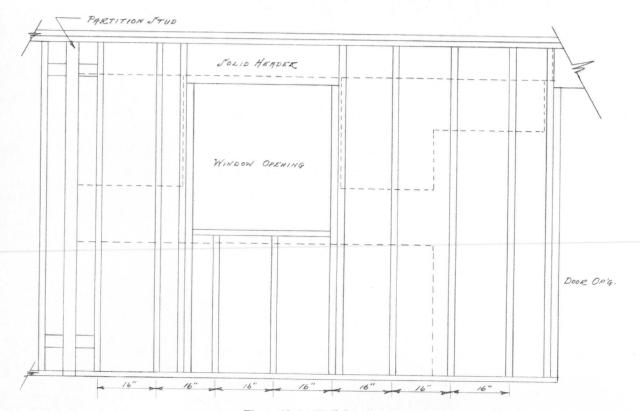

Figure 10–1 Wall framing for model cabinet wall.

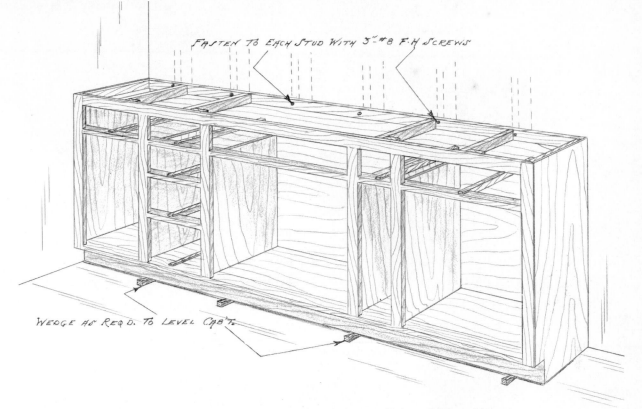

FASTEN TO EACH STUD WITH 3"-#8 F.H SCREWS

WEDGE AS REQ'D. TO LEVEL CAB'T.

Figure 10-2 Installation of base cabinet.

by looking where the siding is nailed. In any event, locate and mark each stud in the space between the upper and lower units. These marks will have to be referred to when working on the inside of the upper cabinets.

Leveling the base cabinet

The base cabinets should be set in position and leveled both front to back and horizontally. In new construction this is not much of a problem. In an older home substantial shimming might have to be done. A number of shims should be made of softwood 3 to 4 in. long and about ¾ in. high. These will be driven under the toe space until the back of the cabinet is tight against the wall. Later after the cabinet is permanently fastened, the shim is cut to the right length, replaced, and then covered with a base shoe or a linoleum base (Fig. 10-2).

Fastening to the wall

The base cabinets are fastened to the wall using 3-in. flathead wood screws of size 8 or 10. Fasten by drilling through the pine bracing strip and driving a screw into each stud.

INSTALLING THE PARTICLE BOARD FOR THE COUNTERTOP

If the cabinetmaker is to fabricate the countertop and lay the plastic laminate, the particle board should be installed next (Fig. 10-3). This will close up the base cabinet and offer a convenient "workbench." Naturally, if a post-formed countertop is to be used, it will not be installed until the very last, as the chance for scratching the laminate would be very great.

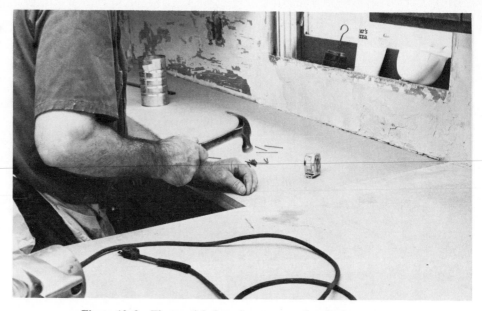

Figure 10-3   The particle-board countertop is nailed onto the base cabinet.

Fabricating the Countertop

Much of the work on the countertop, it was suggested, should be done in the cabinet shop where all machines were available. The top is made from ¾-in. high-density particle board. The counter is ripped to a width of 24 in. and a facing strip of ½-in. plywood is glued and nailed to the edges where required (Figs. 10-4A and 10-4B). Some builders rip the particle board to a width of 25 in. and glue and nail a ¾ in. × ¾ in. strip to the underside of the counter to form the edging. The edging should be 1⅜ to 1½ in. wide. The dimension should be carefully checked to see that the edging does not interfere with the pull-out cutting board.

The top edge of the banding must be carefully sanded flush with the particle board using the belt sander. Care must be exercized that the countertop is not rounded while performing this operation. If even a slight rounding of the front few inches

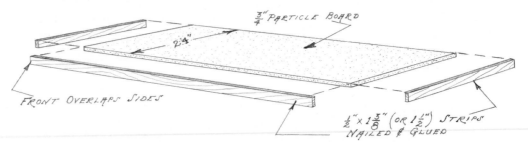

Figure 10-4A   Basic countertop construction: type 1.

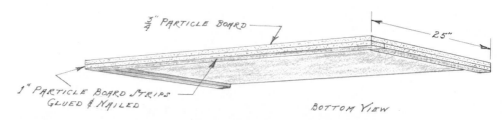

Figure 10-4B   Countertop construction: type 2.

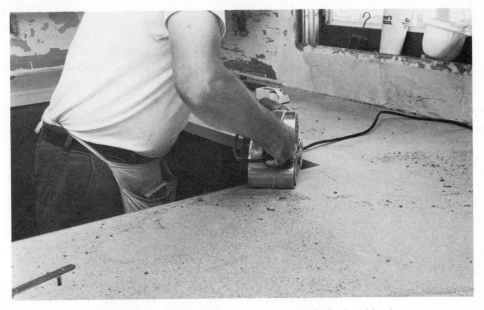

Figure 10-5 The edging must be sanded flush with the countertop.

of the counter occurs, the laminate might not adhere well because it is quite stiff and will not bend (Fig. 10-5).

Sink cutout

The location of the sink in the countertop must be laid out carefully. Most often the sink is centered under a kitchen window, so the measurements must be carefully made to locate it exactly center. The directions of the sink manufacturer must be followed and are usually on the box—together with a template—for stainless steel sinks. If a separate mounting rim is to be used, the rim itself can be used as a template. Self-rimmed sinks have the mounting directions on or in the container in which the sink is packed.

Locate the front edge of the sink cutout approximately 2 in. from the front edge of the countertop (Figs. 10-6A and 10-6B). After the pattern lines are drawn, drill a starting hole near the front edge (Figs. 10-7 and 10-8) and with a saber saw proceed to saw the sink cutout. Test-fit the rim or the rimless sink and do whatever touch-up is required so that the unit does not bind at any spot.

Countertop for a corner base unit

Preparing the top for a base corner unit is quite similar to a straight section of cabinet. The main difference is fabricating the corner joint where the two countertops meet. This joint must be supported with either a cleat screwed to the under-

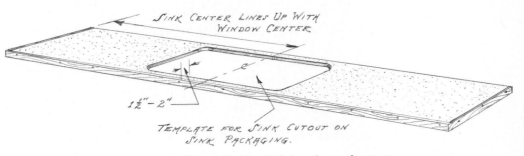

Figure 10-6A Sink location and cutout.

Figure 10–6B The sink template is positioned carefully on the countertop.

Figure 10–7 A pilot hole is drilled for the saber saw blade. (Courtesy O&M Cabinets, Hutchinson, Minn.)

Figure 10–8 The sink cutout is made with the saber saw. (Courtesy O&M Cabinets, Hutchinson, Minn.)

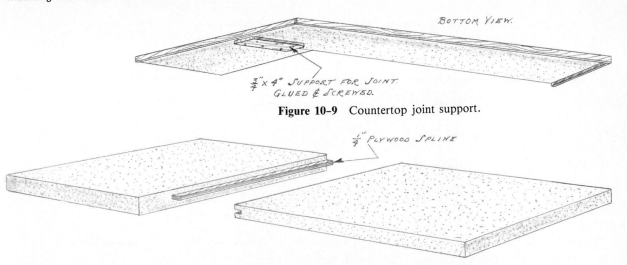

Figure 10-9 Countertop joint support.

Figure 10-10 Spline-joint countertop support.

neath surfaces of the two meeting tops, or a spline joint (Figs. 10–9 and 10–10).

The top can be given the final assembly on the job. That way if some fitting to the walls is required, it can be done prior to completing the joint reinforcing.

Nailing the particle board to the cabinet

If most of the fabricating of the top was done in the shop, it is then fastened to the base cabinet by nailing with 6d finish nails or coated box nails. If the top is actually made on the job, the top would be nailed to the base cabinet before the edging strips are applied.

Backsplash

There are three alternatives to consider when planning the backsplash.

1. *Ledge type:* This backsplash is made from ¾-in. particle board and covered with laminate. It is usually made 5½ to 6 in. high. Metal molding is not used with this type and it is customary to caulk the joint between the backsplash and the counter with a good grade of caulking to prevent moisture from getting into the joint (Fig. 10–11). This type can be made up in the shop and transported to the job for installation. It is installed with a good panel adhesive.
2. *Metal-trimmed type:* This backsplash is the same height as the ledge type but ¾-in. particle board is not used. The laminate is simply trimmed with

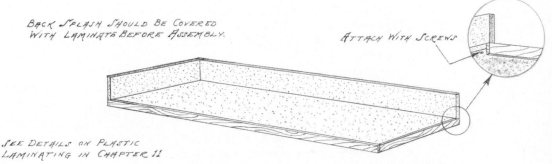

Figure 10-11 Fabrication of ledge-type backsplash.

Figure 10–12   Counter with metal-trimmed backsplash.

metal cap molding and a small cove or a small quarter-round molding is used at the countertop joint. Once fabricated, the entire backsplash is fastened to the wall with contact cement (Fig. 10–12).

3. *Full backsplash:* Although this type is still used, it is not as popular as it was a few years ago. The full backsplash is simply laminate applied to the wall the full distance between the upper and lower cabinets. Metal end cap is used to cover exposed edges, while a cove or ¼-in. round molding is used at the countertop joint. Because the laminate must be cut and fit around all switches and outlets, the full backsplash becomes quite time consuming and costly to install.

With both the ledge type and the metal-trimmed type a lot of the fabrication can be done in the shop before moving to the installation site. With the full type, most of the work will have to be done on the job.

For complete information and fabricating instructions, refer to Chapter 11. Installation of the post-formed top is also discussed in Chapter 11.

INSTALLING THE UPPER CABINETS

Once the base cabinets are installed and the rough counter tops fastened to the lower unit, the base cabinet becomes a convenient workbench for the remainder of the installing to be done. No laminate is applied to the particle-board tops until the very last to prevent damage to the laminate. If a post-formed countertop is to be installed, the shelves from the upper units can be used as a temporary counter-top to support the wedge boards or "horses."

Preparations for Installing Upper Cabinets

Upper cabinets fall into two categories. Some upper units are made to fit under a dropped ceiling or soffet such as has been presented in the model cabinets in this text. Others have the space above the cabinets left open. Often, the top of the cabinet is decorated with a plate rail. Occasionally, the homeowner wants the upper cabinets built to the ceiling, but that is quite rare in today's cabinet market.

Figure 10-13 Installation of upper cabinets using wedge boards.

For those cabinets that will be installed under a soffet or to the ceiling, the installer will have prepared several "wedge" boards. These are pieces of plywood ½-in. thick or thicker that measure about 10 in. × 16½ in. They are used to wedge the upper unit in place once they have been raised to the soffet or ceiling. These are made up ahead of time and used on a regular basis (Fig. 10-13).

For installing cabinets that do not go to a soffet or ceiling, the builder will prepare several miniature sawhorses on which the upper unit can safely rest prior to being permanently screwed to the wall. These, too, are made up by the installation crew and taken from job to job. Individual cabinetmakers have their own ingenious method of supporting the cabinets while installing (Fig. 10-14).

For those builders who prefer to install the upper cabinets first, a "resting" strip is often tack-nailed to the wall at the proper height. This strip is leveled and tack-nailed to the studs. The cabinets are then lifted into position and are held to the wall by a helper while resting on this strip.

Installing the Upper Units

If the upper cabinets are of any length, a helper should be on hand to assist with the lifting. The cabinets are then first lifted onto the base cabinets. They are then raised to the correct position and the wedge boards or "horses" quickly slipped into position to hold the cabinet in place. The units are carefully positioned and butted accurately to the window or door trim. Once in final position they are then screwed to the studs using 3-in. size 8 or 10 flathead wood screws through the pine mounting strip.

Some scribing may have to be done if the wall is slightly out of plumb or if the plaster or drywall job is quite wavy. The amount of scribing will depend on whether

Figure 10–14 Installation of uppers with no soffet.

or not the cabinet is to be "cased." If a small trim molding or cabinet casing is to be applied around the cabinet, very little scribing or fitting of any kind is necessary. The scribe molding will cover most gaps between the cabinet and the wall or soffet.

A nice touch that looks good is to use stop washers under the heads of the flat-head wood screws when installing the upper cabinets. It is also a good idea to secure the bottom part of the wall cabinet by driving 1½-in. wood screws through the plywood back into the wall studs. Use stop washers under the heads of these screws for a nice appearance.

CASING IN THE CABINETS

Although casing the cabinet with a scribe molding is not as necessary as it once was due to the nice straight walls that usually result from excellent sheetrock installations, many cabinetmakers still prefer to trim their installation. However, if the cabinet has a nice tight fit all around, trimming the cabinet is probably not necessary.

Preparing the Casing Strips

These narrow moldings are ripped from ¾-in. lumber using the same species as that used for the frame of the cabinet. The edge of the board is jointed smooth, then one corner is either chamfered slightly or rounded on the shaper. The strip is then ripped from the board with the fence set at about ³⁄₁₆ in. or a bit wider. A 10- or 12-ft board should be used so that the molding is available in lengths that will require very little splicing. The strips are then given a light sanding with the belt sander to remove any machine marks.

Applying the Casing Strips

To trim the upper cabinets the strips are applied all around the upper edge at the soffet, along the face frame at a wall end, and along finish ends at the wall. All joints

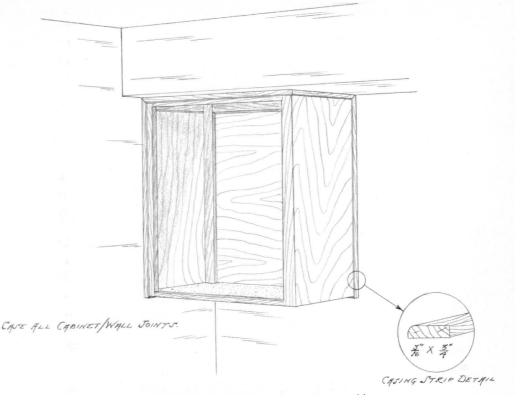

CASE ALL CABINET/WALL JOINTS.

CASING STRIP DETAIL

$\frac{3}{16}" \times \frac{3}{4}"$

Figure 10-15   Applying casing strips to cabinet.

are carefully mitered. The strips are thin enough so that they can be pushed to fit tightly against the wall. If a rather deep curve in the wall is encountered or a plaster buildup in the corner, the molding might require some hand-planing to make it conform to the wall. The strips are applied with ¾-in. brads and all nail heads are set, filled, and sanded clean (Fig. 10-15).

The base cabinets are trimmed at the face-frame and finished ends where they butt against the wall.

Any base shoe along the toe space is usually applied by the carpenter, or the linoleum base, if used, is installed by the floor-covering mechanic.

INSTALLING OR HANGING THE CABINET DOORS

If the hinges for the cabinet doors were applied back in the cabinet shop, the doors are next hung on the cabinets. With the proper jigs and "know-how," installing cabinet doors is no great challenge.

Hanging the Single Cabinet Door

A number of door spacing strips of scrap plastic laminate should be ripped about ¾ in. wide. Pieces of this laminate will be used as spacers to position the door correctly in the cabinet opening. A piece of this stripping is snapped off at a length to fit the door opening. The strip is positioned along the front edge of the cabinet bottom so that the lip of the door, when placed in its opening, will rest on the strip of laminate (Fig. 10-16). Sometimes, two strips need to be used.

The cabinet door is shifted slightly in the opening so that it is not touching either side stile. If self-closing hinges are being used, push the door firmly against the cabinet frame so that the hinges lay perfectly flat. Now mark the hinge holes with a pen-

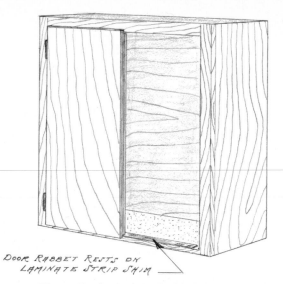

DOOR RABBET RESTS ON LAMINATE STRIP SHIM

Figure 10–16 Hanging cabinet doors.

Figure 10–17 Hanging a single cabinet door.

cil. Remove the door and center-punch the marked holes; predrill for the screws with a $\frac{3}{32}$-in. bit. Replace the door in the opening, beeswax the screw threads, and install all hinge screws (Fig. 10–17).

Hanging a Pair of Doors

The difficulty in installing a pair of doors is in trying to hold the two doors in position while marking and drilling holes. A simple holding jig that can be made of wood or metal comes in very handy for holding a pair of doors in position while installing (Fig. 10–18). The jig has a built-in spacer to separate the doors correctly. A piece of laminate is used along the bottom of the doors as was done with the single door. A single piece of laminate is inserted between the doors at the bottom to provide the correct spacing (Fig. 10–19).

The pair of doors is placed in the opening so that the lower rabbet rests on the laminate strip. The lower spacer is inserted and the holding jig is placed in position at the top of the doors. The spacer strip, which is the part of the jig with the hook on its end, is pushed into the cabinet and is positioned so as to catch the inside of the upper rail. The wing nut on the jig is tightened so that the hook strip will not slip and the doors will now stay in position while being installed.

Adjust the pair of doors in the opening so that some space is evident on both sides. Push the doors tightly against the frame (if self-closing hinges are being used) and proceed to mark, drill, and screw the hinges to the frame. Remove the jig and spacers and carefully check the doors to see that they swing freely and that no rubbing is evident. Double-check to see that the doors do not touch at the midpoint.

Figure 10–18 Holding jig for installing a pair of cabinet doors.

Figure 10–19 Installation jig holding a pair of doors for installing.

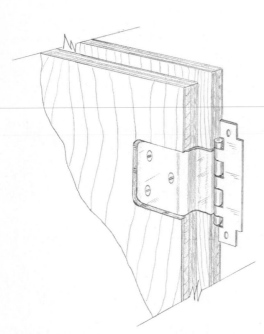

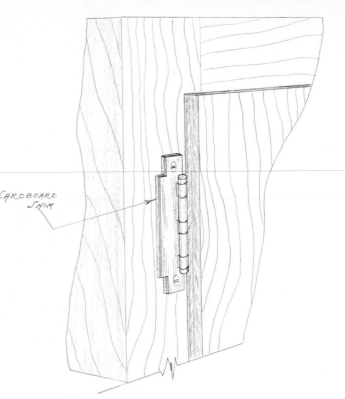

CARDBOARD SHIM

Figure 10–20   Hinge set into door surface to correct slight warp.

Figure 10–21   Slight warp corrected with shim.

Quality checks after hanging doors

After completing the installation, the doors should be checked to see that they swing freely and close tightly against the cabinet frame. The bottom edge of the lips should be exactly aligned. If they are just slightly off, one edge can be given a few strokes with the block plane until it matches the other.

Hinges of adjoining doors should be aligned as well. This is usually no problem if the hinges have been installed using a jig and if the laminate spacer was used correctly while hanging the doors.

Techniques for handling a slightly warped door

If a door is badly warped, it should be replaced immediately. However, a door that is just a bit twisted can often be corrected satisfactorily. If, for example, the door sticks out a bit at the bottom left, the upper right hinge can be adjusted somewhat to compensate for this. The upper right hinge can have a cardboard shim or two inserted under the butt of the hinge. This shim should be cut to the shape of the hinge butt. This will raise the hinge slightly and lower the bottom corner of the door. Another alternative is to set the lower hinge into the wood slightly by carefully mortising the leaf of the hinge into the door surface. Either of these tricks will often bring doors into alignment so that a slight warp is not noticeable (Figs. 10–20 and 10–21).

INSTALLING KNOBS, PULLS, AND CATCHES

After the doors are all hung, the job still remains to attach the knobs or pulls of the owner's choice. There are literally hundreds of styles available from several major manufacturers. Lumberyards, discount stores, and building centers all carry cabinet hardware. The professional builder will want to locate a wholesale supplier who has an adequate stock on hand to meet the volume needs of the cabinet shop.

Attaching Door Hardware

The location of the door pulls or knobs is largely a matter of taste. As a practical matter, however, the pulls or knobs on the upper units usually are installed about 6 in. or so from the bottom of the door and about 2 in. in from the edge of the door. Often the type of door and its decoration will determine where the hardware must go. A paneled door, for example, must usually have the pull located in the center of the stile.

Because measuring the holes for each door is a time-consuming chore, an installation jig is a handy item to have available. These are simple to build and most cabinetmakers have several on hand to take care of pulls with a variety of mounting dimensions between the screw centers. Figure 10–22 illustrates a simple jig made of ¼-in. plywood and ¾ in. × ¾ in. strips of wood. The jig can be flipped over so that either left- or right-hand doors can be drilled. Several different installing centers can be on one jig. To prevent confusion the holes may be colored so that the 3-in. on-center holes are one color, the 3½-in. on-center holes another, and so on.

A ³⁄₁₆-in. drill bit is used to drill the holes for the ⅛-in. hardware bolts that are furnished with the pulls. This slightly larger hole makes installation easy if the holes should be just a bit off center.

Installing drawer pulls

Drawer pulls, too, must usually be measured individually and a drilling jig will save much time for the installer. A jig for installing two-bolt drawer pulls is illustrated in Fig. 10–23. To use the jig, simply locate and lightly mark the center of the drawer, place the centering thread or wire on the mark, and drill the holes that are correct for the height of the drawer. Most builders standardize the height of their drawers that are in a vertical row of drawers so the jig can be used from job to job. The jig can easily be adapted to single-bolt knobs by keeping the centering thread or wire near the top of the jig. The holes for the knobs can then be drilled at the center of the jig.

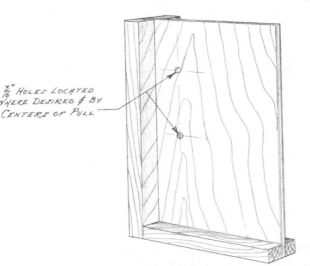

Figure 10–22 Flip-over door pull installation jig.

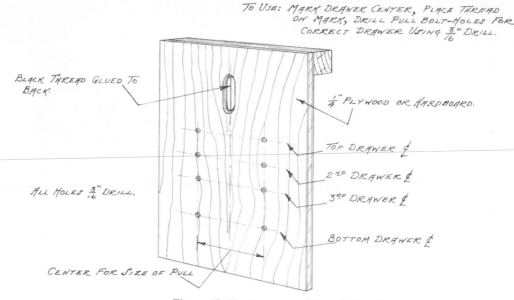

Figure 10-23   Drawer pull installation jig.

Quality checks for hardware installation

Knobs or pulls should line up perfectly. The hardware on cabinet doors should be in perfect horizontal alignment and on drawers, the pulls on a row of drawers should line up vertically. Sloppy installation of hardware can ruin the looks of an otherwise high-quality cabinet job.

Installing Door Catches

If self-closing hinges are not being used, the friction or magnetic catches will be installed as the last job. With the popularity of the self-closing hinge, the cabinet door catch has decreased in use dramatically. However, there are owners who still prefer the door catch, and some information regarding their installation is included.

Mounting and locating the catch

The catches should be located at the top of the door so as to lessen the chance of interference. For doors on the upper cabinets the catches can be mounted on the top rail, while for lower cabinet doors the lower edge of the first rail is a handy spot (Fig. 10-24). Usually, a ¾ in. × ¾ in. block of softwood must be glued to the back edge of the rail to give enough mounting surface for the catch.

If a cabinet door is slightly warped, often the catch is all that is needed to hold it in position. The catch can then be located in the best position to disguise the warp of the door.

Installing catches is a simple job that becomes easier with a bit of experience. Start by mounting the body or magnet of the catch about ⅜ in. from the front edge of the face frame and drill the screw holes about in the middle of the slotted area. Fasten the body of the catch to the frame. The trick, of course, is to attach the plate or bayonet of the catch so that it lines up correctly with the body. This is mainly a matter of eye-balling and judging the location correctly. Once the complete catch has been installed, it should be adjusted to hold the door positively in position. If a bayonet-type catch becomes difficult to operate, a little Vaseline on the bayonet will allow it to work smoothly.

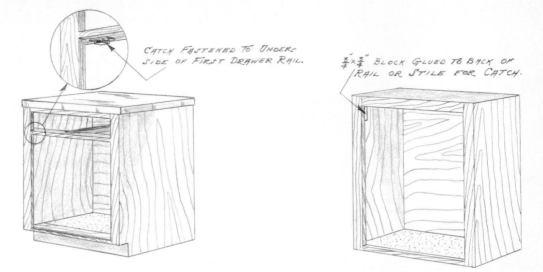

CATCH FASTENED TO UNDER-SIDE OF FIRST DRAWER RAIL.

¾"×¾" BLOCK GLUED TO BACK OF RAIL OR STILE FOR CATCH.

Figure 10-24 Techniques for fastening catches.

COMPLETING THE INSTALLATION

The professional cabinet builder is careful to complete the job by doing a final checking of the entire installation. All cabinets are cleaned of sawdust and shavings, laminate scraps, and so on. The entire cabinet is looked over for smudges, fingerprints, and other flaws, which are then sanded clean. The shelves are set in the cabinets even though the homeowner might later readjust them. Doing this gives the impression of a completed job. Finally, the entire kitchen area is swept free of all litter and debris and disposed of so that the room is left neat and clean.

REVIEW QUESTIONS

10.1. List four quality checks that should be made before the cabinets leave the shop.

10.2. Why should as much work as possible be done on the cabinets in the shop?

10.3. Describe how cabinets should be loaded and protected for transporting to the installation site.

10.4. List three ways of locating wall studs. What is their "normal" spacing?

10.5. What size wood screws should be used to fasten cabinets to the wall?

10.6. Describe the process for making the sink cutout in the particle-board countertop. Why is this cutout made before the top is nailed to the base cabinet?

10.7. If the complete countertop is made in the shop and the laminate even applied there, how would this countertop be fastened to the base cabinet?

10.8. Why does a joint in the countertop require support underneath?

10.9. List three types of commonly used backsplashes.

10.10. What is cabinet casing? Describe where it is applied.

10.11. What material makes a convenient "spacer" for installing cabinet doors?

10.12. List three quality checks for inspecting the hanging of cabinet doors.

10.13. What should be done with a badly warped cabinet door?

10.14. Why does a ¾ in. × ¾ in. × 3 in. block of softwood have to be glued to the inside of the face frame for the installation of catches?

10.15. What can be done to bayonet-type metal catches to make them operate smoothly and easily?

SUGGESTED CLASS ACTIVITIES
AND STUDENT ASSIGNMENTS

10.1. Borrow or purchase one or two of the "stud locators" on the market and evaluate their performance.

10.2. Visit several homes where recent cabinets have been installed and check the countertop installations. Are they post-formed or fabricated by the cabinet builder? What is their front-to-rear measurement? What is the dimension of the self-edging? How has the builder fabricated the self-edge?

10.3. Try to visit several homes where custom cabinets are being installed to observe the methods and tricks used by the installers. What clever jigs are being used? Are the doors hung on the job or were they installed at the shop?

10.4. Design a door installing jig for use with overlay-type cabinet doors.

10.5. How can the drawer pull installing jig presented in this chapter be adapted for use with single-bolt knobs?

11

The Plastic–Laminate Countertop and Backsplash

Nothing has contributed more to the beauty of the modern kitchen than plastic laminates developed for the countertop. This product, available in a wide variety of colors, patterns, and textures, is not only beautiful but is extremely durable. Once on the market it quickly replaced linoleum as the chief material used for kitchen countertops. The clamp-type sink rim used for installing the sink with this material provides a tight, waterproof seal around the sink that does not rot and discolor in a few years as did linoleum.

Plastic laminates appeared on the market shortly after World War II, having been developed as a hard, durable, inexpensive product for small machine gears. Westinghouse Micarta and General Electric Textolite were among the first countertop laminates to be marketed. At first these were available to cabinetmakers only after being bonded to plywood. The cabinet builders fabricated countertops from 4 ft. × 8 ft. sheets (or larger) of this prebonded product and finished the edges with metal moldings of various styles and shapes. This was short-lived, however, as contact cement was soon developed that allowed cabinet shops to bond the laminates to the plywood backing and use the same material for edging the countertop.

Today an almost unlimited variety of patterns is available under various trade names, such as Formica, Wilson Art, Consoweld, and Nevarmar, just to name a few. The cabinetmaker must be equipped with the skills and tools necessary to fabricate countertops of this modern, decorative laminate.

GENERAL INFORMATION ABOUT PLASTIC LAMINATES

Size Information

Laminate sheets are available in widths of 24, 30, 36, 48, and 60 in., although this will vary somewhat from company to company. Most laminate sheets are furnished ½ to 1 in. oversize, which makes for economical cutting, as most countertops are a minimum 24½ in. front to rear.

Lengths available (again, depending on the company) are most commonly 60, 72, 84, 96, and 144 in. The fabricator should plan a counter installation carefully so that the most economical use of the laminate is made. Laminate is expensive and the cabinetmaker does not want a lot of money tied up in excess stock that may remain unused for many months.

The laminate is available in two thicknesses. The standard thickness is $\frac{1}{16}$ in. and is used for most installations of countertop and backsplash. Most fabricators also use the $\frac{1}{16}$-in. material for edging the countertop, especially if there are no particularly sharp bends to make. Also available is a laminate $\frac{1}{32}$ in. thick. This is used primarily for edging, where bending is required with sharp radii. For fabricating postformed countertops commercially where sophisticated heating devices are available, a $\frac{1}{20}$-in. thickness is used.

Bending Plastic Laminate

The $\frac{1}{16}$-in. thickness is quite springy and difficult to bend. Unheated, this thickness can be bent to a radius of approximately 9 in. Carefully heated, it can be bent successfully to a radius of about 2½ in.

The $\frac{1}{32}$-in. edge banding thickness can be bent to a 3-in. radius at room temperature; heated to 325°F it can be bent to a ¾-in. radius.

Heating the plastic laminate for bending

One of the best means of heating laminate for bending is to use an ordinary heat lamp. A good trick is to mark the area being heated with a wax crayon (special crayons are available for this). Heat the area carefully until the wax melts—about 300°F—then bend the strip carefully around the corner to which it will be applied. Gloves must be worn while doing this operation. Roll the strip after it is positioned so that good contact is made.

MACHINING PLASTIC LAMINATES

Because plastic laminate is a very hard material, ordinary woodworking tools soon dull when used to cut and trim laminate. Carbide tools are much more successful and stay sharper much, much longer. However, standard saw blades and router cutters can be used if just a small job is being done and they are resharpened after use.

Machines Needed to Cut Plastic Laminate

Table saw

Equipped with a carbide fine-toothed blade the table saw is used to cut the sheets of laminate to the approximate size the job requires. Standard procedure calls for the countertop pieces to be cut about ¼ in. oversize and then trimmed to exact size with a router or laminate trimmer. Because the laminate is so thin, it will slip under the rip fence. Of great help to correct this is to fasten a wood strip to the fence that

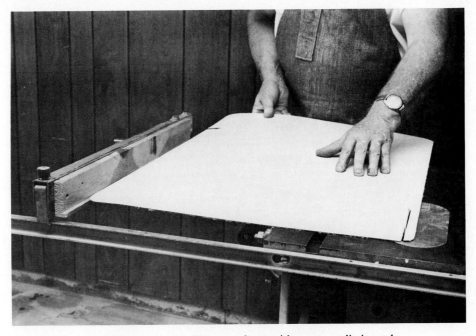

Figure 11–1 An auxiliary saw fence with a support lip is used to saw laminate.

fits snugly against the top of the table saw. If the saw fence is extended beyond the top of the table saw, an auxiliary fence is screwed to the rip fence that has a lip on it that will support the plastic while it is being ripped (Fig. 11-1).

The laminate is very brittle and the chips are thrown toward the operator when it is being ripped. It is good practice to wear safety glasses or goggles while cutting laminate on the table saw.

Cutting a 12-ft. sheet of laminate on the table saw is a two-person job. Some cabinetmakers will lay the sheet on the floor, mark the necessary cuts, and with a piece of lumber carefully positioned under the laminate sheet, make the rough cuts with a portable circle saw.

Jointer

While a jointer is not used too often in working with laminate, there are times when it is indispensable. Occasionally, the laminate top must be spliced. To secure a nice tight fit, a jointer is needed. Again a helper is required to assist in holding the often awkward pieces while running the edge on the jointer.

Some fabricators make clever holding jigs that hold both pieces of the laminate to be joined and trim the edges to a perfect match by running the router along both edges at the same time (Fig. 11-2).

Router

If there is any one machine that is indispensable in working with plastic laminate, it is the router. Most beginning cabinetmakers start out by using a router for trimming laminate and then invest in a special machine called a laminate trimmer as their business warrants this purchase (Fig. 11-3). The main advantage of the laminate trimmer is that it will allow trimming flush to a wall or adjacent surface. The router, of course, cannot do this, as the size of the base of the router permits coming within only about 3 in. of a wall. This is not a serious handicap, however, for the occasional laminate fabricator, as the router will perform most machining required with the proper accessories.

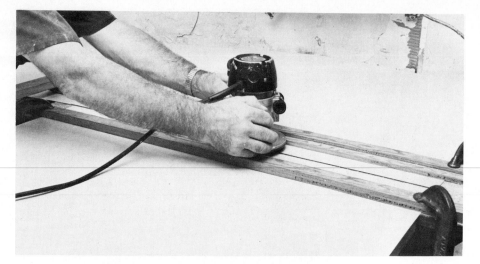

Figure 11-2 Shop-built jig that makes nearly perfect splices in laminate. (Courtesy O&M Cabinets, Hutchinson, Minn.)

Figure 11-3 A special laminate trimmer is available for working with laminates. (Courtesy Prieve Cabinets, Hutchinson, Minn.)

Available for most routers is a laminate trimming accessory. This consists of a special base plate and adjusting mechanism together with a special carbide cutter. This attachment is fastened to the bottom of the router and after being carefully adjusted will trim the laminate exactly even with the edge of the countertop. (Fig. 11-4). Although this mechanism works well for trimming the edge of the countertop, it does not work very efficiently for routing the laminate where the sink cutout has been made.

Many laminate fabricators find it less costly to purchase special carbide cutter bits that do the trimming jobs very efficiently. Only two cutters are required to handle practically all trimming operations. These are available from Stanley in the bevel trimmer bit that produces a 7½-degree bevel on the trim and the hole and flush-cut trimmer. The hole and flush-cut trimmer drills through the surface laminate into a precut opening such as a sink cutout and trims the edge flush (Fig. 11-5). Also available is a flush trimmer that will trim vertically with no bevel.

Figure 11-4 Special laminate trimmer attachment for the router.

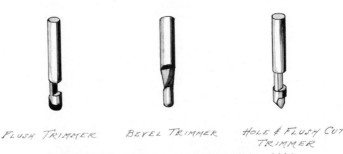

FLUSH TRIMMER   BEVEL TRIMMER   HOLE & FLUSH CUT TRIMMER

Figure 11-5 Laminate trim bits (solid carbide).

The one precaution that must be taken when using these Stanley trimmer bits is to lubricate the laminate edging with Vaseline to prevent the cutter from burning the laminate self-edging. If this is not done, the friction caused by the high-speed cutter would quickly burn the laminate.

Special Plastic-Laminate Hand Tools

There are a few special tools on the market that have been developed especially for use on plastic laminates. These can be used in lieu of a router or in places where the router cannot be used. All are carbide and will do the job for which they were designed, although much slower than a router or laminate trimming machine (Fig. 11-6).

Carbide scribing knife

This tool, similar to a linoleum knife but made with a carbide point, can be used to cut plastic laminate (Fig. 11-7). The plastic laminate is scored on its surface by making several passes with the knife held against a straight edge. The laminate is then broken off at the scored line by breaking the laminate upward. The breaking pressure must be up toward the surface of the laminate. If the pressure is down, the backing of the laminate will not break evenly along the scored line (Fig. 11-8).

Hand trimming tool

This tool was designed to trim the laminate flush with a countertop edging. It has two carbide points that score the laminate as the tool is held against the edge of the counter (Fig. 11-9). The tool will cut when moved in either direction. After scoring the laminate deeply, the waste edge is broken clean by breaking in the same

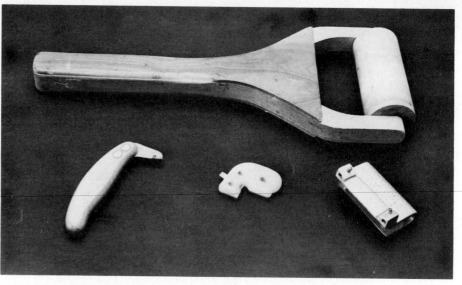

Figure 11-6 Special hand tools for cutting and trimming laminate: *(top)* shop-built laminate roller; *(bottom: left to right)* carbide scribe knife, beveling tool, trimming and cutting tool.

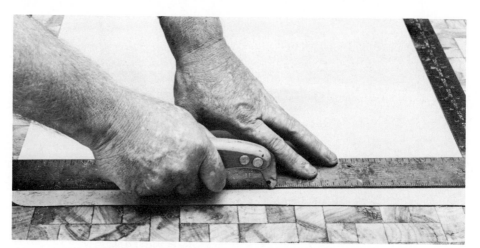

Figure 11-7 To use the carbide scribe, make several cuts on the surface of the laminate until the backing is reached.

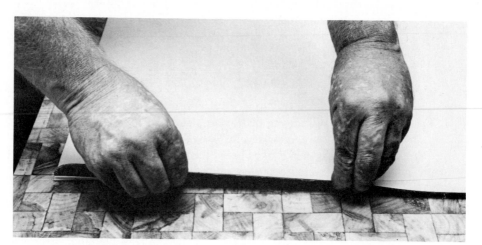

Figure 11-8 Complete the cut by breaking the laminate with upward pressure.

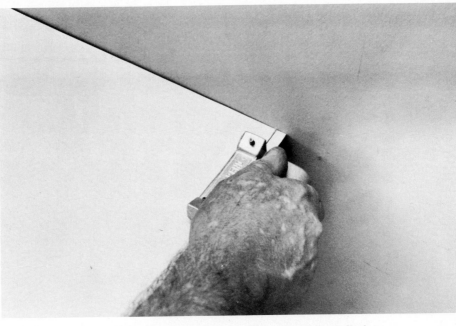

Figure 11-9 The hand trimmer will cut the laminate flush to the wall where a router will not reach.

upward motion as was performed when using the scribing knife. The hand trimming tool is especially handy for completing the edging up to the wall when the router has been stopped because of the diameter of its base plate. The edge is then hand filed to a smooth finish to complete the edging job.

Hand beveling tool

This simple little cutter contains a carbide knife that will produce a beveled edge on the laminate countertop. It saves a lot of hand filing and in certain situations is a lifesaver (Fig. 11-10).

Figure 11-10 Hand beveling tool in use.

Figure 11-11   Laminate snip makes easy work of cutting the plastic.

Laminate snip

Built like a small tin shears, this tool does an excellent job of cutting laminate quickly and cleanly (Fig. 11-11).

Laminate roller

A roller is used to pressure the laminate into making an excellent bond with the particle-board countertop. These are available from specialty woodworking concerns, or the cabinetmaker can easily make a roller if a lathe is available. The roller must be rugged enough to take quite a bit of weight so that sufficient pressure is exerted to bring the laminate and countertop together firmly.

Common Hand Tools Used with Plastic Laminate

Most of the ordinary hand tools commonly carried in the cabinetmaker's toolkit will probably be used in plastic-laminate countertop fabrication. Squares, hacksaw, metal files, rubber mallet, hammer, straightedge, and so on, will all be put to use at some stage of the installation.

Portable Electric Tools Needed

Mention has already been made of the use of the portable circular saw in rough-cutting the laminate to size. The portable belt sander will be used to sand the self-edging exactly even with the particle-board countertop. A saber saw may be needed to make cutouts for electrical outlets in the backsplash.

METAL MOLDINGS USED WITH PLASTIC LAMINATES

Many installations of laminate require the use of metal cove moldings, cap moldings, and tee moldings. Generally, these moldings are used when the countertop is fabricated on-the-job (Fig. 11-12). Most patterns are available at lumberyards and building supply dealers and come in 12-ft. lengths.

COVE MOLDING

QUARTER ROUND MOLDING

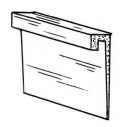

CAP MOLDING

SPLICING MOLDING

Figure 11-12 Plastic-laminate moldings.

Tools required for working with metal moldings are a metal cutting miter box (or hacksaw with a wooden miter box) and assorted metal files.

More will be discussed in the section on actual laminate installation.

ADHESIVES FOR USE WITH PLASTIC LAMINATES

The development of special adhesives for use with plastic laminates has made it practical and easy for the cabinetmaker to fabricate countertops. These adhesives, called contact cement, are available at lumberyards and building supply dealers.

Contact Cements

Contact cement is just what the name implies—the surfaces coated with the adhesive adhere on contact. The adhesive is applied to both surfaces to be bonded, allowed to dry, and the surfaces are then brought into contact and pressed or rolled to make a good firm bonding. Once brought into contact the surfaces cannot be adjusted, so extreme care must be taken to see that the material is in the correct position prior to making contact.

Types of contact cement

There are several types of contact cement on the market. These are available from suppliers of plastic laminate in 1-gallon, 5-gallon, and drum sizes. The types suitable for use by the average installer or home craftsperson can be purchased at lumber dealers or building supply outlets.

Industrial contact cement: This grade is extremely volatile and is not ordinarily used by the cabinetmaker. It is available in a grade suitable for spraying or by application by automatic glue-spreading devices. This type is used primarily by manufacturers who fabricate hundreds of square feet.

Craftsman grade: Although this is still a volatile product, it is not nearly as fast as the industrial grade. This is the contact cement that is available at most building supply dealers. Although adequate ventilation should be provided when being used, it is not as dangerous as the industrial grade.

Water-based contact cement: This type of contact cement, developed in recent years, is not dangerous to use, as it is a water-based product and contains nothing that can explode. However, its main disadvantage is that it is very slow to dry compared with the volatile types.

Applying contact cement

Contact cement of the type most commonly used by laminate fabricators is applied mainly with a brush or roller. The average countertop fabricator will use inexpensive, throwaway rollers to apply the cement. For coating narrow surfaces such as the counter self-edging, small bristle brushes should be used. Be certain that the brushes are bristle, as nylon bristles will deteriorate because of the solvents in the contact cement. Solvents are available for contact adhesive, although lacquer thinner is very suitable for cleanup.

The contact cement is applied to the back of the plastic laminate and to the particle-board countertop or other backing material to be used. A good, heavy, even coating is required. On porous material or end grain, more than one coat may be needed. The cement is allowed to dry until no stickiness is noticeable. A good test is to touch the cement with a piece of brown wrapping paper. If the paper does not stick, the surfaces are ready for joining. Open time for the coated surfaces is an hour or more, but recoating might be required if the surfaces are left unassembled for much longer.

Joining the Cemented Plastic Laminate and Backing

As mentioned previously, the material to be bonded must be carefully positioned, as once contact is made, no adjustment is possible.

Many installers prepare strips of ¼-in. plywood about 1½ in. wide by 36 in. long that are used to support the laminate above the countertop. These strips are carefully cleaned and sanded so that no stray chip or piece of sawdust can accidently get between the surfaces to be bonded. The installer positions these strips about 12 to 16 in. apart the length of the countertop, which has already been cement-coated and allowed to dry (Fig. 11–13). The cemented plastic laminate is laid atop the strips and the laminate is then carefully adjusted to its correct position. When the installer is satisfied that the laminate is correctly positioned, the strips are simply pulled out from under the laminate—one by one—allowing the surfaces to make contact. The surface of the laminate is then rolled to assure good contact between the surfaces. Lacking a roller, a block of wood and a hammer or a rubber mallet can be used. The strips of wood are saved to be used over again on later installations.

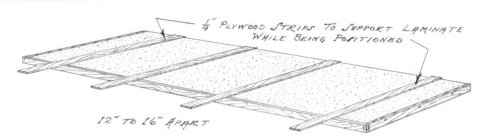

Figure 11–13 Supporting strips for laminate.

Unjoining a Misplaced Piece of Plastic Laminate

If the laminate has not been rolled, it is sometimes possible to carefully separate the laminate by pulling it up from the backing material. This might take some of the backing material with it, however. If the surface is not too damaged, the surfaces can be recoated and reassembled.

Some installers carry with them a squirt-type oil can filled with solvent or lacquer thinner. If removal of a piece of laminate is necessary, a corner is carefully pried up and solvent squirted underneath. By careful pulling and squirting the solvent as the separation proceeds, the two surfaces can often successfully be delaminated. However, if the bonded surfaces have been allowed to set for any length of time—a day or longer—separation is practically impossible without destroying the laminate.

FABRICATING A PLASTIC-LAMINATE COUNTERTOP AND BACKSPLASH

Once the particle-board underlayment for the countertop has been installed on the base cabinet (see Chapter 10), the next step is to install the plastic laminate. This can be done in the shop, but the entire countertop will then have to be fastened to the base cabinet from underneath by using screws. This procedure is used to fasten post-formed tops to the base cabinets. This section will address the techniques for applying laminate to the particle-board countertop that has been nailed to the base cabinet.

Installing Plastic-Laminate Self-Edging

Strips of laminate will have to be ripped about $\frac{1}{16}$ in. wider than the counter edging. This is usually done on the table saw with the aid of a helper using the techniques discussed previously in this chapter. If the sawn edge is unusually rough, one edge will have to be jointed smooth. The strips should be of adequate length so that no splicing is required on the self-edging.

Applying the self-edging

The short ends of the countertop are applied first. Cut the laminate just a bit longer than the end dimension. Apply contact cement to the back of the laminate and the counter edge with a small brush and allow to dry (Fig. 11–14). Recoating

Figure 11–14 At least two coats of contact cement are applied to the edges.

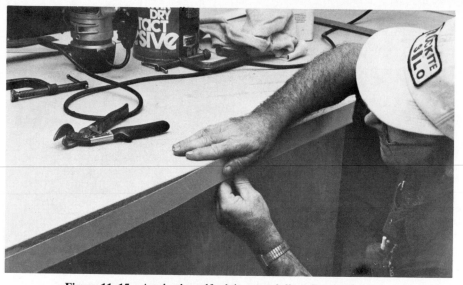

Figure 11-15 Apply the self-edging carefully, allowing it to extend both above and below the countertop. (Courtesy O&M Cabinets, Hutchinson, Minn.)

at least once is a good technique. Apply the laminate strips carefully allowing the top edge of the laminate to extend a bit above the surface of the particle-board countertop (Fig. 11-15). Tap with a rubber mallet or the flat face of a claw hammer being extremely careful not to mar the laminate. The edging can also be rolled. Trim the extra length at the front corner with the router, or lacking a router, use a hacksaw and then file the laminate flush with the corner.

The front strip is applied in the same manner. The corners are trimmed flush with the router and then filed smooth and with a slight rounding to take the sharpness off the corner.

That portion of the self-edging that extends above the surface of the counter must next be removed. This can be done with the belt sander or the router or laminate trimmer. If the belt sander is used, extreme care must be taken so that the surface of the countertop is not rounded (Fig. 11-16). A flat file is used to be certain that the edging is exactly flush with the countertop.

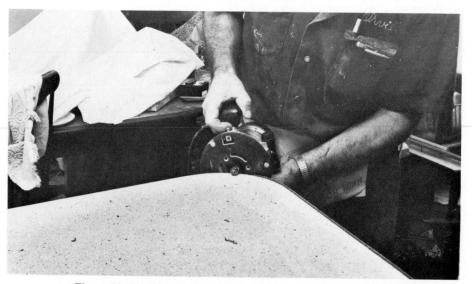

Figure 11-16 The router makes quick work of trimming the self-edging even with the countertop. (Courtesy O&M Cabinets, Hutchinson, Minn.)

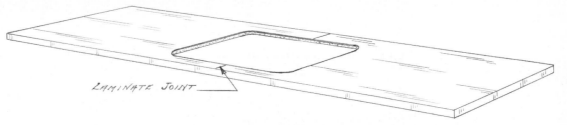

LAMINATE JOINT

Figure 11–17 Laminate spliced at sink opening.

Applying the plastic laminate to the countertop

Carefully plan the cutting of the sheets of laminate so that the most economical use is made of the material and also so that the least number of joints is required. Many installers find that if a joint is required, planning that joint at the sink is a fairly simple means of making a respectable seam (Fig. 11–17). Only a couple of inches of seam will show at the front and rear of the sink, and distances that short are quite easy to match successfully.

Cut the sheets of laminate to fit the measurements of the countertop, leaving a ¼- to ½-in. margin all around. If a joint in the laminate is required, this will call for jointing the edges, testing the joint repeatedly before assembly, and even some hand-filing to secure a tight-fitting seam.

Apply the contact adhesive with a roller or brush to both surfaces and allow it to dry. (Fig. 11–18A and 11–18B). Position the supporting wood strips and lay the laminate on top of the strips, moving the laminate to its correct position (Fig. 11–19). Remove the strips, allowing the laminate to make contact with the particle-board surface (Fig. 11–20). Roll the entire surface to make good contact between the two surfaces. (Fig. 11–21).

Trimming the excess plastic laminate

If a carbide trimming bit is used in the router for trimming, apply Vaseline to the edge of the countertop so that the cutter will not burn the self-edging. If a laminate trimming attachment is used with the router, be certain to check the depth of the cut carefully so that it is exactly flush with the self-edging. Proceed to trim the entire countertop (Fig. 11–22).

Figure 11–18A The countertop receives two coats of contact cement. (Courtesy O&M Cabinets, Hutchinson, Minn.)

Figure 11–18B Usually, two coats of contact cement are applied to the back of the laminate. (Courtesy O&M Cabinets, Hutchinson, Minn.)

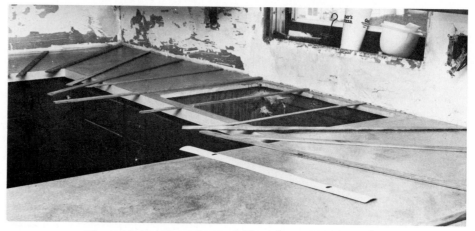

Figure 11–19 The strips are laid on the countertop ready to receive the laminate.

Figure 11–20 The strips are removed, allowing the laminate to bond to the countertop. (Courtesy O&M Cabinets, Hutchinson, Minn.)

Figure 11–21 Pressure for good bonding is applied with the laminate roller. (Courtesy O&M Cabinets, Huchinson, Minn.)

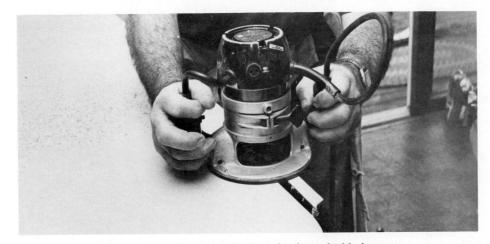

Figure 11–22 The excess laminate is trimmed with the router using the trimmer bit. (Courtesy O&M Cabinets, Hutchinson, Minn.)

Because the router cannot trim all the way to the wall, about 3 in. will remain that will have to be trimmed with a hacksaw blade or special cutter as described under "Special Plastic-Laminate Hand Tools" earlier in the chapter. File smooth all sharp edges of the countertop.

Special note: Interior corners on an L-shaped countertop should be left with a slight rounding. Do not file the corner to a sharp square corner. The laminate has a tendency to crack in a sharp corner, but this can be prevented if the rounding that remains after the trimmer cutter is used is allowed to remain (Fig. 11–23).

Figure 11–23 Do not square laminate at corner.

Figure 11–24A   A pilot hole is drilled for the router if required.
(Courtesy O&M Cabinets, Hutchinson, Minn.)

Figure 11–24B   The sink hole is quick routed.

Routing the sink cutout area

The carbide trimming cutter with the drill point works very well for trimming the laminate even with the edge of the sink cutout. Simply drop the router on the laminate (the hole for the sink has been already cut in the particle-board top) well within the area of the sink cutout and move the router to the edge of the cutout and rout the laminate even with the edge of the particle board (Figs. 11-24A and 11-24B). The one difficulty encountered is at the back edge—the router base will not allow the cutter to rout the laminate even with the rear edge of the sink cutout. The 2 in. or so remaining can be removed by using a saber saw with a fine-toothed metal cutting blade. Many installers use just a hacksaw blade fitted with a handle to work into tight spots. The blade is shortened so that only about 3 in. of the blade is exposed. Wood pieces are fitted to each side of the blade and wrapped with electrician's tape to make the handle.

When using the saber saw on plastic laminate, the bearing plate of the saw should be cushioned with green felt or other material. The vibration of the saw seems to cause scratches on the surface of the laminate if this is not done.

The sink cutout should be cleaned up nicely with a rasp or file, and if a separate sink rim is being used, it should be test-fit. The rim should fit snugly but easily into the sink cutout hole.

Fabricating and Installing the Backsplash

There are three types of backsplashes in common use: the "ledge" type, the short backsplash fitted with metal trim, and the full backsplash (extends from the countertop to the upper cabinets), which is also fitted with metal trim at the ends and corners. This section deals with all three types as well as techniques for installing the metal trim molding.

Ledge-type backsplash

This type of backsplash is fabricated from ¾-in. particle board and covered with laminate on one surface as well as the ends and top edge. The height will vary from 4 to 6 in. or more and is often determined by the distance from the countertop to the bottom edge of the kitchen window trim. The ledge-type backsplash simply rests on the rear of the countertop and is set in caulking compound to make a water-resistant joint along that area. The backsplash itself is fastened to the wall by using a good grade of panel adhesive or PL 200, another good type of adhesive in a tube that is applied with a caulking gun (Fig. 11–25).

If the countertop is fabricated in the shop, the ledge-type backsplash can be screwed to the top from below, as discussed in Chapter 10.

Short backsplash with metal trim

This backsplash is nothing more than a piece of laminate of the desired height that is fit with metal trim and glued to the wall with contact cement. The top edge and ends receive cap molding, while the bottom edge receives a cove molding. These pieces must be cut and fit very carefully (Fig. 11–26).

Metal-cutting miter boxes are available for cutting the metal trim, although a simple wooden miter box can be made that utilizes an ordinary hacksaw. Some installers use their regular wood-cutting miter box, as the trim is aluminum and cuts easily. The saw will, however, require more frequent sharpening if put to this use. All the required metal moldings to fit ⅟₁₆-in.-thick plastic laminate are available at most building supply dealers in standard 12-ft. lengths.

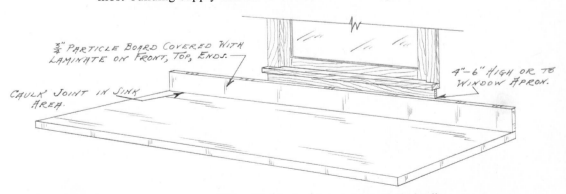

Figure 11–25 Ledge-type backsplash details.

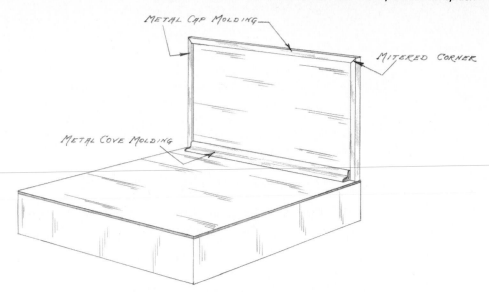

Figure 11–26 Short backsplash with metal trim.

The cap molding is cut and fitted to the ends and top edge of the laminate back-splash. The corners are carefully mitered using the miter box. Professionals who do a lot of laminate work have a special mitering tool that will cut a perfect 45-degree joint. This tool operates by squeeze pressure with a special cutting die to form the miter joint. Any real sharp edges on the miter should be smoothed with the file. One problem that is encountered with the cove molding is where the cove and the cap molding meet. The backing of the cove molding must be cut away with the hacksaw to allow room for the backing of the cap molding (Fig. 11–27). This is a problem also when the cap molding is bent to form a curve instead of a square corner. The backing must be cut away to allow the cap portion of the molding to be gently bent around the curve. This is easily done with a metal-cutting blade in the saber saw.

The molding to be used in the corner can be either a cove or quarter-round and is available in several sizes. The corner molding should fit between the end caps

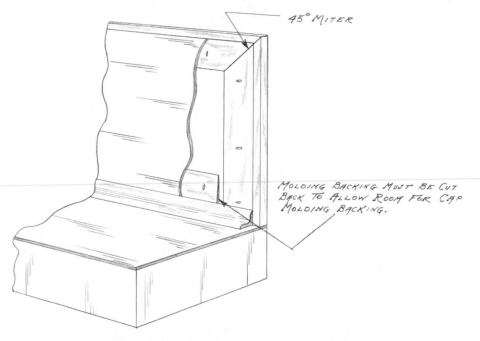

Figure 11–27 Detail of metal molding installation.

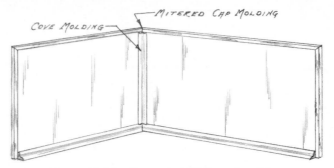

Figure 11-28 Corner installation of molding.

(Fig. 11-26). The ends of the corner molding should be given a slight rounding with the file.

Once all the metal trim pieces are cut and fit, the entire piece of laminate as well as the back edge of the moldings should be given a coat of contact cement. Note that the metal moldings are applied to the laminate before it is positioned on the wall. The wall is also coated with contact cement and allowed to dry. After drying, the entire backsplash with moldings in place is carefully positioned and pressed into place.

If the countertop is L-shaped, the moldings must be mitered at the corner as well. It is also good practice to use a short piece of corner molding in the corner of the backsplash itself. (Fig. 11-28). The corner molding should fit snugly against the countertop. If some slight gaps should be noticeable, the molding can be tapped down using a block of wood and hammer.

It is sometimes awkward to handle the laminate backsplash, as the fitted molding pieces want to fall off the laminate. Some installers find that a hot glue gun is handy to tack the moldings in position. A drop or two of hot glue in the crack of the molding will hold the metal in place and handling of the backsplash becomes much easier.

Installing the full backsplash

The full backsplash (laminate from countertop to bottom of the upper units) is not nearly as popular as it was several years ago. The popularity of the post-formed countertop with its short ledge-type backsplash has, no doubt, influenced the thinking of housewives and laminate installers. Also, the extra cost of both materials and labor has made the full backsplash less popular. Extra labor can run into several hours, as the laminate must be fit around the window as well as each electrical outlet on the wall between cabinets. If the customer demands a full backsplash, however, the cabinetmaker must be prepared to satisfy the demand.

The first step is to remove the window trim, including the stool and the apron if a window is present. This will be reinstalled after the laminate has been applied to the wall. Note that the laminate is going to be covered by the window trim pieces after they are replaced.

The laminate must be cut to fit the space between cabinets allowing about $\frac{3}{16}$ in. for the thickness of the cove molding. Some installers cut the laminate a bit less and apply a wood molding to the bottom of the upper units to cover any gap that might be visible at that point (Fig. 11-29).

To locate the electrical outlet cutouts, the laminate is laid face up on the countertop and the location of the outlets is transferred to the laminate by the use of a framing or carpenter's square. This technique locates the width of the outlet boxes. The height of the box from the countertop must be measured carefully and accurately. Once the limits of the box openings are located, a pilot hole is drilled about $\frac{3}{8}$ in. in diameter and the opening in the laminate is cut with a saber saw. The laminate

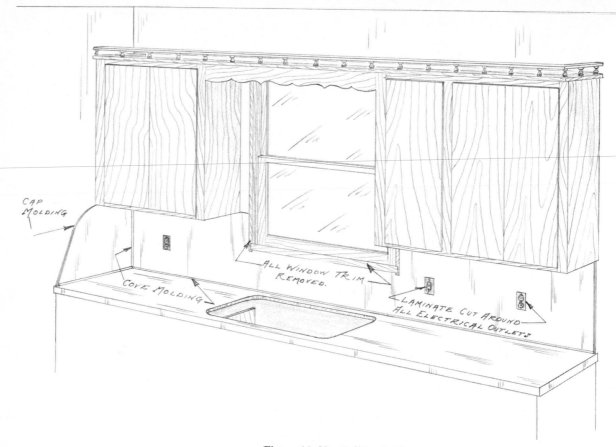

CAP MOLDING

COVE MOLDING

ALL WINDOW TRIM REMOVED.

LAMINATE CUT AROUND ALL ELECTRICAL OUTLETS

Figure 11–29   Full backsplash details.

is cut to fit around the window opening being certain that the laminate will extend under the trim when it is reapplied.

Next cut and fit all metal moldings to the laminate as was done with the short backsplash, tacking them in place with the hot-glue gun. Test-fit the entire assembly prior to applying contact adhesive.

When an L-shaped counter requires a corner backsplash, always fit and apply the longer piece first. The shorter piece is then applied and pushed carefully into the corner to make a nice-fitting joint, then carefully pressed to the wall.

Finishing touches in plastic-laminate installation

Check to see that the cove or corner molding is tight against the countertop laminate. Tap with a block of wood and hammer to move the molding tightly into position. All outlet boxes should have the screw holes free of obstructing laminate, and all plates should be screwed in place if they are available. Remove any contact cement residue with solvent; simply rubbing with a dry rag works almost equally as well. File smooth any sharp edges or corners of the laminate (Fig. 11–30). Finally, sweep up the kitchen area, removing all debris and laminate shavings or dust.

INSTALLING NEW PLASTIC LAMINATE ON AN OLD COUNTER

Often the cabinetmaker is called upon to replace a worn plastic laminate countertop or even to replace linoleum. The best procedure for this seems to be to replace the entire countertop—particle board and laminate. Although some installers have suc-

Figure 11-30 File all sharp edges of the laminate countertop. (Courtesy O&M Cabinets, Hutchinson, Minn.)

cessfully laid new laminate over old, there is considerable risk of delamination. Rather than accept this risk, they remove the entire countertop and backsplash and replace with new materials.

Problems Encountered in Replacing Countertops

Several unique problems are often involved in replacing an old countertop. The cabinetmaker should be aware of these and plan carefully so that serious difficulty is avoided.

Coordinating the job with the plumber

The old sink must be removed, the pipes disconnected, and the electric garbage disposal disconnected prior to removal of the old countertop. To hold the "downtime" for the kitchen to a minimum, the services of a plumber is all-important. The plumber will have to be on the job to accomplish these tasks prior to the laminate installer arriving to remove the old countertop. The plumber's services will be needed again to reconnect and reinstall the sink and its fittings. A reliable plumber will make the replacement of a countertop a much less aggravating chore for all.

Undersized base cabinets

Even today—particularly in a very old house—undersized base cabinets are encountered. Many early base cabinets were built 23 in. deep and 32 in. high. A 23-in.-deep base cabinet will probably have only 21¼ in. as an inside dimension. Installing a 32 in. × 21 in. two-bowl sink in that space can be extremely challenging. The use of a separate clamp-type sink rim can be especially aggravating to install. Because of the limited space, the inside of the front frame and the pine bracing piece at the rear will have to be notched to accept the sink frame clamps (Fig. 11-31). Installing these clamps can be a real "pleasure" as well because the space is so limited.

Removing old laminate or linoleum from the wall

Particular care must be taken when removing old laminate from the wall—especially if the wall is plaster board. Considerable damage can result to the plaster

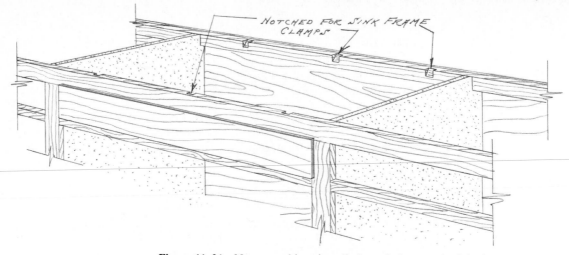

Figure 11–31 Narrow cabinet installation of clamp-type sink rim.

board if the job is done carelessly, and some damage is sure to result in spite of how carefully the job is done. Usually, considerable scraping of old glue or adhesive must be done to prepare the surface for the new laminate. In some cases the wall will require repair with new patching plaster or troweled on sheetrock cement.

Installing the new countertop

If at all possible, the new countertop should be fabricated in the shop. The housewife is spared much of the mess if this can be done. The smell of the contact cement and the chips and residue of routing the laminate on the job are just two of the ''messy'' items avoided by doing most of the work in the shop.

The shop-fabricated countertop must be fastened to the base cabinet by screws driven into the bottom surface of the countertop. Screws 2½ in. long can be driven through the upper drawer runners, front frame, or the back supporting pieces (Fig. 11–32). If this is too awkward, special ¾ in. × ¾ in. cleats can be installed along side of these members and 1¼-in. screws used to fasten the top (Fig. 11–33). In any case, care must be exercised so that the laminate is not damaged by a screw driven in too deep.

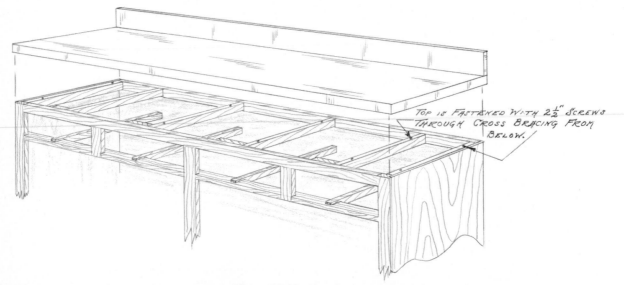

Figure 11–32 Detail of fastening top to base cabinet.

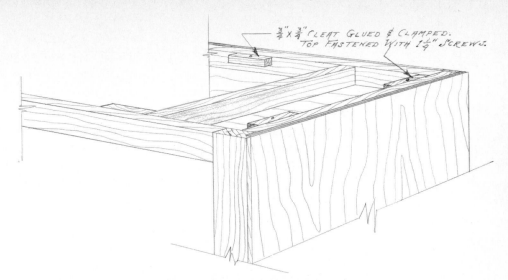

Figure 11–33 Cleat method of fastening top.

INSTALLING THE POST-FORMED COUNTERTOP

The post-formed plastic-laminate countertop is readily available from building supply dealers, lumberyards, and even mail-order houses. Patterns are limited in comparison to the number of patterns manufactured by the laminate makers. The countertops are priced by the foot. There are, too, specialists who deal in the fabrication and installation of post-formed countertops.

The post-formed countertop has no sharp corners but has a rolled or gently curved profile from front to rear. Also at the rear is a scribing strip that allows the installer to fit the backsplash very close to the wall. This is sometimes necessary if the wall has irregularities that would leave quite a gap at the top of the backsplash.

Straight lengths of countertop can be handled and installed by the average cabinetmaker. End caps can be purchased in matching laminate patterns that are applied to the end section of the countertop and trimmed flush with the router or laminate trimmer. Installation is no more difficult than with a shop-made countertop (Figs. 11–32 and 11–33). The sink cutout is carefully located and cut out with a saber saw and the top is then fastened to the base cabinet from below as described earlier in the chapter.

L-Shaped or U-Shaped Countertops

Fabricating an L-shaped or U-shaped countertop is usually not attempted by the cabinetmaker, as the miter joint at the corner is very difficult to cut without special equipment. Specialty countertop manufacturers have large radial arm saws that will cut these miters. Using these machines, they fabricate mitered countertops that have beautifully tight, exact joints at the corners.

The purchaser must furnish exact measurements to the manufacturer when placing an order for an L-shaped or U-shaped countertop. The exact location for the sink cutout must be furnished as well. The manufacturer will fabricate the top and ship it to the customer ready for assembly. Special bolts are used along the mitered sections to pull and hold the sections together. Upon installation the cabinetmaker will do any wall scribing necessary. The top is fastened to the base cabinets with screws from below.

REVIEW QUESTIONS

11.1 What is the standard thickness of plastic laminate used for countertops?

11.2. True or false: Ordinary wood-cutting machines, tools, and blades cannot be used to cut and work plastic laminates.

11.3. What are the problems encountered when ripping plastic laminate on the table saw? What attachments can be made to help solve these problems?

11.4. What one machine is needed over any other when working with laminates?

11.5. What is the main advantage of the laminate trimmer over the router?

11.6. What two types of carbide router cutter trimming bits are used extensively by laminate workers?

11.7. Why is Vaseline applied to the laminate edging of a countertop when trimming the laminate countertop?

11.8. Describe how a laminate scribe knife is used and the breaking technique.

11.9. Why is water-based contact cement not preferred by many laminate installers?

11.10. How is contact cement applied by most cabinetmakers?

11.11. Why is the surface of the laminate rolled after being applied?

11.12. If a laminate countertop is fabricated in the shop, how is it then fastened to the base cabinet?

11.13. Where is the easiest spot to splice laminate in a countertop installation?

11.14. What are the three most common types of backsplashes?

11.15. Why are "full" backsplashes seldom installed today?

11.16. Describe a post-formed countertop.

11.17. If the countertop is to be fabricated and installed on-the-job, how is the ¾-in. particle board underlay then fastened to the base cabinet?

11.18. How is a ledge-type backsplash installed?

SUGGESTED CLASS ACTIVITIES AND STUDENT ASSIGNMENTS

11.1. What are the retail and wholesale sources for plastic laminate in your area? Obtain information from these sources as to sizes available, cost per square foot, and patterns in stock.

11.2. What are the retail and wholesale sources for contact cement in your area? What types are stocked, what is the cost, and what size containers are normally stocked?

11.3. Where are metal moldings for laminates available in your area? Locate both wholesale and retail sources and secure price, lengths available, and patterns and finishes normally stocked.

11.4. Practice heating and bending ¹⁄₁₆- and ¹⁄₃₂-in. plastic laminate using a heat lamp and temperature crayon.

11.5. Design a device for making a spliced joint using the router. Both ends of the laminate should be held firmly and both ends cut by the same pass of the router.

11.6. What are the sources and prices of laminate trimming machines, carbide trimmer cutters, a trimming attachment for the router, and a commercial laminate roller?

11.7. Write the Formica Company, 114 Mayfield Avenue, Edison, New Jersey 08837, for their technical bulletins and other information on the handling and installing of plastic laminate.

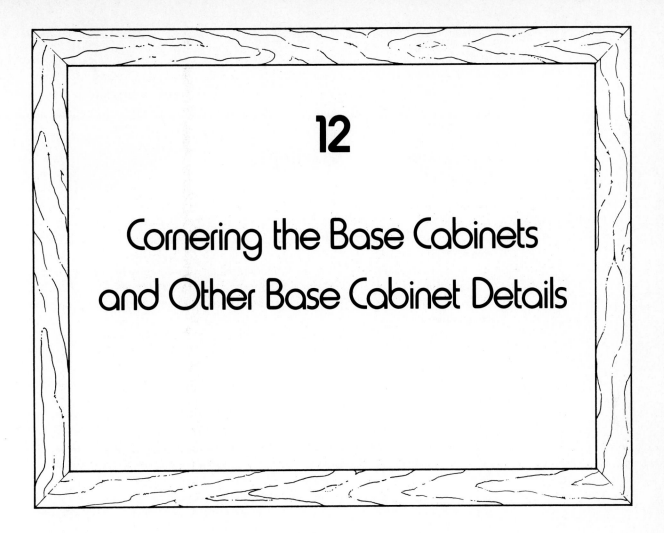

12

Cornering the Base Cabinets and Other Base Cabinet Details

Up to this point only straight cabinets have been dealt with. However, many kitchens are L-shaped or U-shaped, which calls for building the cabinets "around the corner." Chapter 1 dealt with the design features of the corner cabinet as well as the problems of making efficient use of the "dead" space in the corners. This chapter deals with the construction details of the various types of corner units as well as the interior features of base cabinets.

VARIOUS STYLES OF CABINET RETURNS

When a base or upper cabinet makes a 90-degree corner from the main section of the cabinet, the part that goes around the corner is termed a *return*. This problem in cabinet construction is mainly one of butting two straight cabinets together at a 90-degree angle. This should be accomplished, however, so that the interior of the corner area is free from obstructions. Thus this space can make efficient use of a number of means of utilizing the corner space such as shelves, lazy Susans, or swing-out units.

Basically there are just two styles of base cabinet returns: (1) the L-shaped or U-shaped base cabinet that goes against the wall its entire length, and (2) the base cabinet that serves as a peninsula-type divider between the kitchen and the dining area, for example. The peninsula type can be further categorized as having a face frame with cabinet drawers and doors on either one or both sides of the peninsula. Construction details are presented for all of these and for both the box-and-frame method of cabinet building and the casework system. The drawings throughout this chapter illustrate many of the options for building peninsula returns.

Wall-Type Base Cabinet Return

Although the complete L-shaped or U-shaped cabinets are built in the shop, they are only "tacked" together, for they must be disassembled for moving to the installation site.

Careful preliminary measurements must be taken at the owner's site, scaled plans drawn, and even in some cases a full-scale drawing of the corner assembly should be made. As the builder becomes thoroughly familiar with the construction techniques of cornering the cabinets, building will proceed much faster. However, the first few times one attempts a corner cabinet, extreme care must be taken to hold mistakes to a minimum.

The basic techniques learned in the previous chapters for building base cabinets are used in corner cabinets. The only new skills will be those involved in actually making the corner section.

The type of corner access the builder chooses will affect the design of the cornered face frame. These are (1) corner doors that open directly to the corner space, or (2) "side" door access which opens next to the corner space. Both of these were discussed and illustrated in Chapter 1. A third type of access (which is used only with the peninsula return) is access to the corner space from the dining side of the peninsula rather than from the kitchen side. The 45-degree angle front will not be discussed, as it is seldom used.

If a lazy Susan is a desired feature of the corner area, corner doors will be required. If only a shelf is required, either corner doors or a "side" door can be used. For swing-out units a side door is needed.

Peninsula-Type Base Cabinet Return

The main difference in the two types of returns is that the peninsula type does not butt up to a wall and must be finished on three of its four sides (Fig. 12–1). The builder has several options as to how the three sides will be finished: (1) The penin-

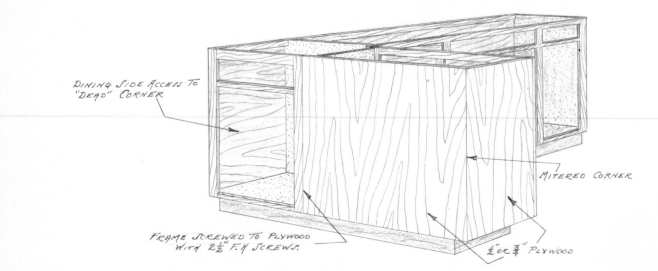

Figure 12–1 Peninsula-type return with corner access.

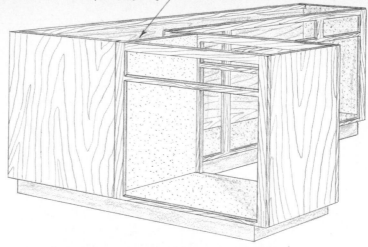

Figure 12–2 Double-face-framed peninsula return.

sula can have a face frame on just the kitchen side with the other two sides of the peninsula paneled, (2) the cabinet can have a face frame on both sides of the peninsula (Fig. 12–2), or (3) the cabinet can have part face frame and part paneling on the dining side depending on which corner space treatment is desired. If a lazy Susan or other corner access feature is desired, the dining side of this space must then be paneled.

CONSTRUCTING THE BASE CABINET RETURN

Once the design of the L-shaped or U-shaped kitchen has been decided upon and the working plans drawn, construction of the units can proceed. Construction details for both the wall-type return and the peninsula return will be presented in this section. The box-and-frame method of building these corner units will be shown, as will the casework system.

Building the Wall and Peninsula Return Using the Box-and-Frame Method

Study Figs. 12–3 to 12–5 carefully, as these drawings are pretty much self-explanatory. Many of the details have been omitted from the illustrations, such as interior partitions, top drawer runners, and so on, so the construction of the interlocking bottoms and toe spaces is clear.

Usually, the bottom of the main wall cabinet runs through the corner area with the bottom of the return cabinet butted to it. Note that the toe space board of the return cabinet is extended to meet the toe space board of the main cabinet.

Figure 12–6 illustrates the corner framing for a side access to the corner area. The two stiles that meet at the corner are fastened with 1½-in. 8FH screws. Of course, one stile must measure 2¾ in. wide, while the other is just 2 in.

Figures 12–1 and 12–2 show the construction of box-and-frame peninsula cabinets.

Building the Wall-Type Return Using the Casework Method

The face-frame options using the casework system are similar to those in the box-and-frame system of building cabinets. The use of corner doors for access to the "dead" corner and a side access door to this space are the two choices basically available. The main differences between the two systems are the use of ¼-in. plywood for end panels and cabinet bottoms and the unique interlocking toe space. Figure 12–7 illustrates a typical wall-type return built the case work way that has been framed for corner door access to the "dead" corner.

NOTE: PARTITIONS OMITTED FOR CLARITY.

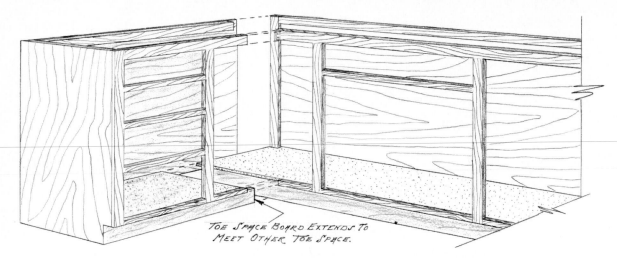

TOE SPACE BOARD EXTENDS TO
MEET OTHER TOE SPACE.

Figure 12-3   Assembly of main section and return.

TOP RAILS FASTENED HERE WITH
1½" F.H SCREWS

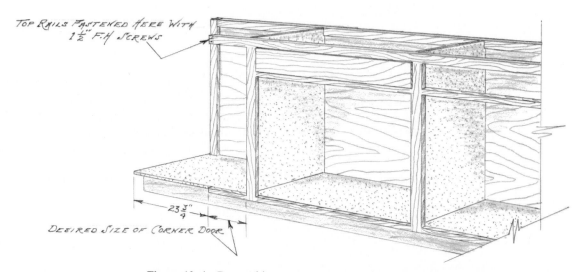

23¾"

DESIRED SIZE OF CORNER DOOR

Figure 12-4   Base cabinet: corner construction details (box and frame).

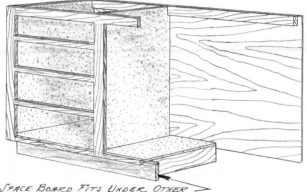

TOE SPACE BOARD FITS UNDER OTHER
CABINET.

Figure 12-5   Base cabinet "return" details.

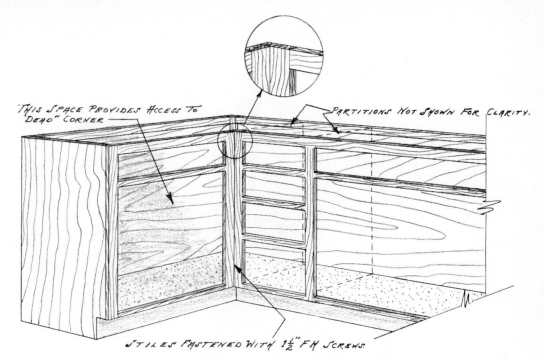

Figure 12-6 Framing for side access to "dead" corner.

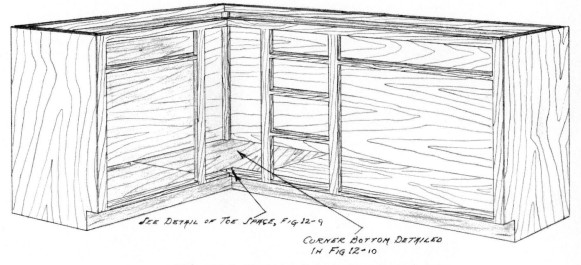

Figure 12-7 Typical wall-type return-casework system.

Cabinet base

Study Fig. 12-8 carefully as well as the detail drawings in Figs. 12-9 and 12-10. The toe space intersection is held together by 1½-in. flathead screws. This allows the base cabinets to be easily taken apart for moving to the installation site. The ¼-in. plywood bottom panel actually fits around the corner. This panel, too, is just tacked into place while the cabinets are being built, as it will have to be removed to take the cabinets apart. Note that the rabbet for the plywood bottom must extend around the corner also. This means that the end of the one upper toe space board must be rabbeted ¼ in. × ½ in. This is easily done with the dado head on the table saw.

The builder may want to support the plywood corner panel with a bottom support piece similar to the others used in base construction. If a lazy Susan is to be installed in the corner, a supporting piece is absolutely necessary to carry the weight of the turntable.

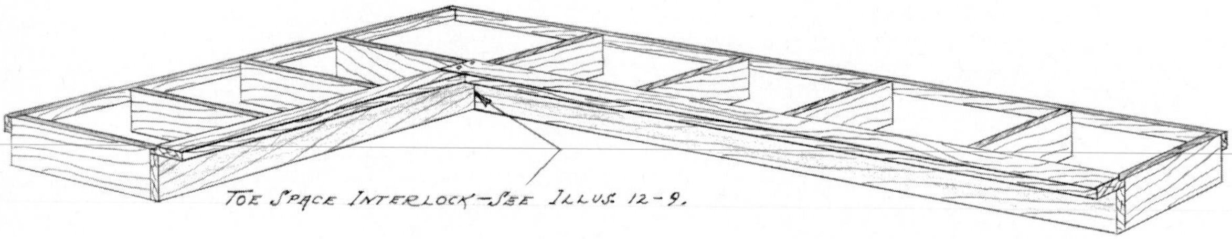

TOE SPACE INTERLOCK—SEE ILLUS. 12-9.

Figure 12–8   Base construction: wall-type return (casework system).

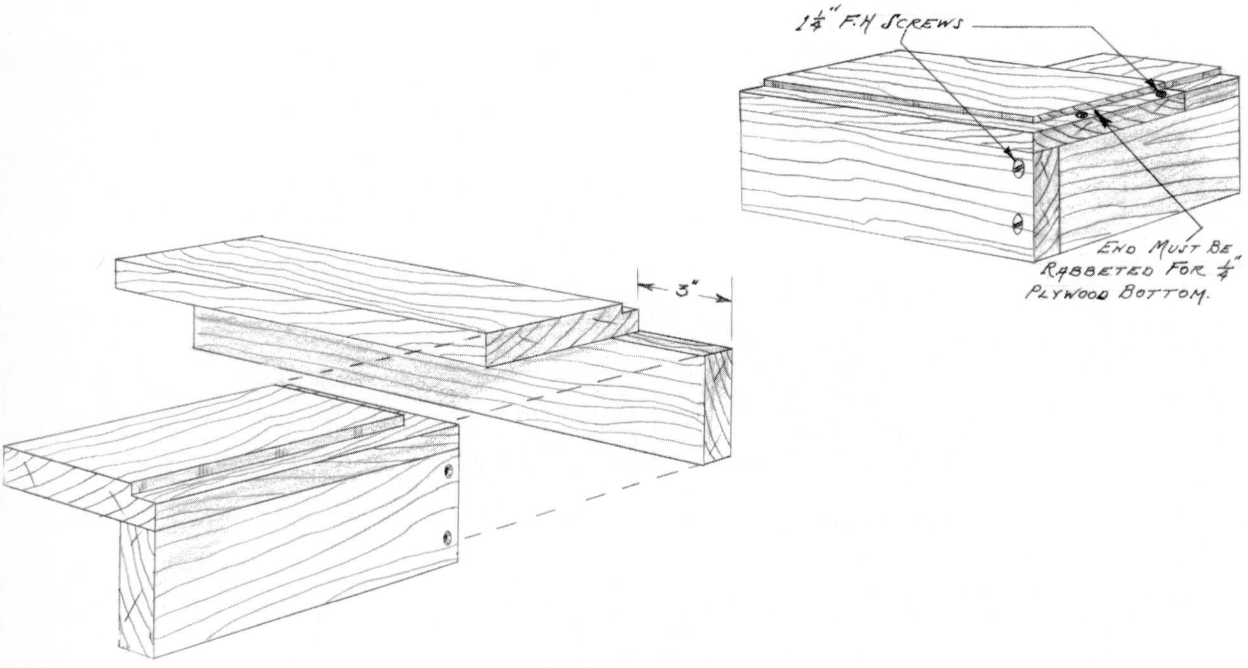

1¼" F.H SCREWS

END MUST BE RABBETED FOR ¼" PLYWOOD BOTTOM.

3"

Figure 12–9   Toe space interlock details.

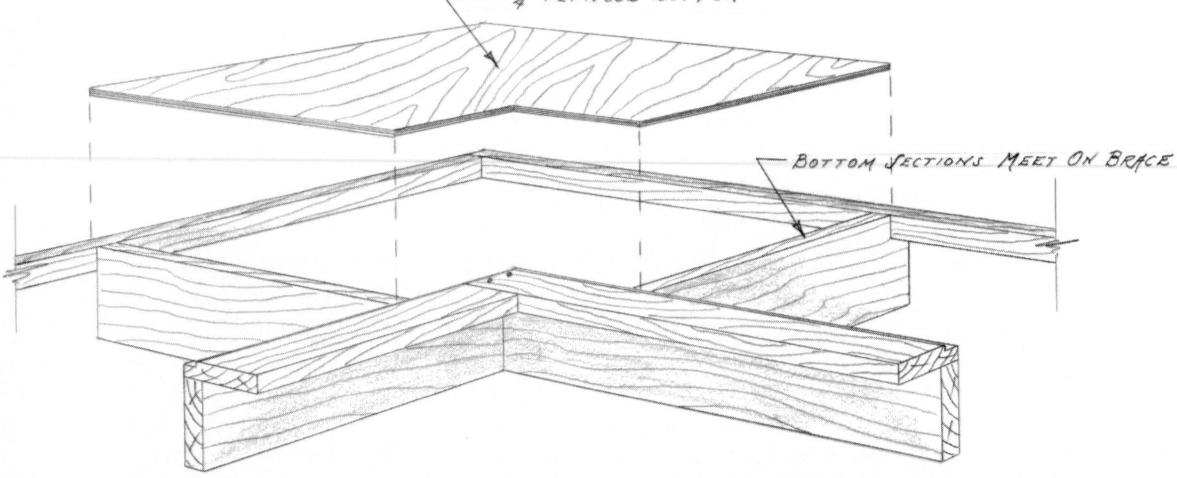

¼" PLYWOOD BOTTOM

BOTTOM SECTIONS MEET ON BRACE

Figure 12–10   Installation of corner bottom panel.

Rear corner

The ¼-in. plywood cabinet backs must overlap at the rear corner. The vertical reinforcing piece in the corner is glued and nailed to either one or the other of the plywood backs. The other plywood back is then just tacked because it, too, will have to be taken apart later. When final assembly is made in the home, the backs can be assembled with glue and nails.

Assembling the corner cabinet

Once the cabinet base has been completed, it will probably be easier to proceed with the base section taken apart. The fastening of the face frames can be done using the same "moves" that were described in Chapter 5. After the face frames, partitions, and cabinet backs have been installed, the sections can then be put together again. The face frames can then be screwed together where required using 1½-in. flathead screws. The sections can remain fastened together while the interior cabinet items are built.

Building the Peninsula Return Using the Casework System

Construction of the peninsula base cabinet using the casework system presents some interesting problems in cabinetwork. The use of ¼-in. plywood paneling for the exposed surfaces of the peninsula calls for careful and skilled workmanship. Figure 12–11 illustrates a peninsula return with dining room access to the "dead" corner. As this is one of the more difficult cabinets to build, it will be used for instruction purposes.

Double toe space

The peninsula cabinet must have a toe space on each side of the cabinet. The intersecting toe space on the kitchen side is identical to that described for the wall-type return. The dining side, however, must have a toe space as well that extends the full length of the peninsula. Figure 12–11 shows this dining side toe space. The bottom support pieces are simply shortened and nailed in position through both vertical toe space boards (Fig. 12–12).

Face frame on both sides

The face frames are built exactly as instructed for straight cabinets in Chapter 5. The end stiles are rabbeted to receive the ¼-in. paneling on the finished end. The

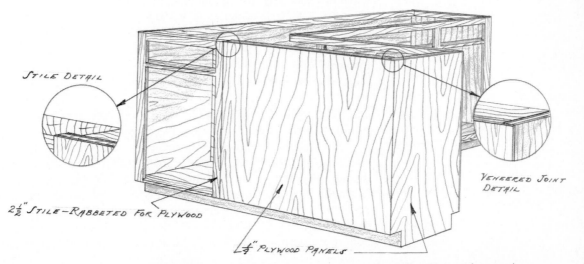

Figure 12–11   Peninsula return with plywood paneling (casework system).

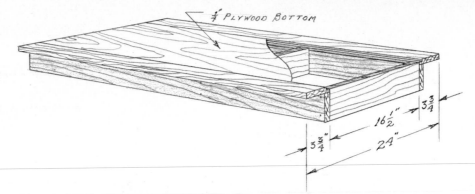

Figure 12-12   Double toe space for peninsula return.

end stile that butts to the wall on the dining side face frame is also rabbeted and the cabinet back fits into the rabbet. However, the back can only be nailed temporarily into position, as it will have to be taken apart at this point for moving to the installation site.

Attach first one face frame to the toe space, lay the cabinet face down, and attach the other side using support strips as instructed previously.

Installing the paneling

If the peninsula cabinet is to be paneled as shown in Fig. 12-13, the paneling will have to be cornered where the end panel meets the panel on the dining side.

Making a corner joint with ¼-in. plywood may be done one of several ways. Figure 12-14 illustrates three types of corner plywood joints.

1. *Miter joint:* The edges of the panels are sawed at 45 degrees. for ⅝- or ¾-in. plywood, no reinforcing strip is required. For thinner plywood, however, a ¾ in. × 1½ in. softwood reinforcing strip is required. Glue and clamp this strip to either of the two panels before attempting to assemble the joint. After the strip has been glued in position, install that panel on the cabinet. With the first panel glued and nailed in position with ¾-in. brads, it is a simple matter to apply the second section of paneling.

2. *Edging of solid wood:* This is probably the easiest means of covering the edge grain of the plywood and to make a presentable corner joint. The technique is the same as for the miter joint. After the panels are in position, a ½ in. × ¼ in. strip of matching wood is glued and bradded in place. The strip is sanded flush with the plywood panels and, if desired, given a slight rounding with a block plane.

3. *Veneered corner joint:* Although perhaps the most difficult to make, the veneered joint makes a splendid-looking corner for ¼-in. panels. The backing of the plywood is cut away on the table saw, leaving just the veneer plus a bit of the backing. This cut is the tricky part. It is best to make this cut on the smaller panel, as a big piece becomes quite unwieldy.

   Carefully set the blade on the table saw so that the thin strip of veneer is to the left of the blade—not next to the fence. This way, if the panel should have some errant movement while sawing, the veneer will not be destroyed. Practice the cut on a scrap of ¼-in. plywood and do the test cutting also on scrap before attempting the final sawing. The veneer should be just a bit over ¼ in. long and will be sanded or planed to the exact dimension after assembly. The veneer should be no thicker than about ¹⁄₃₂ in.

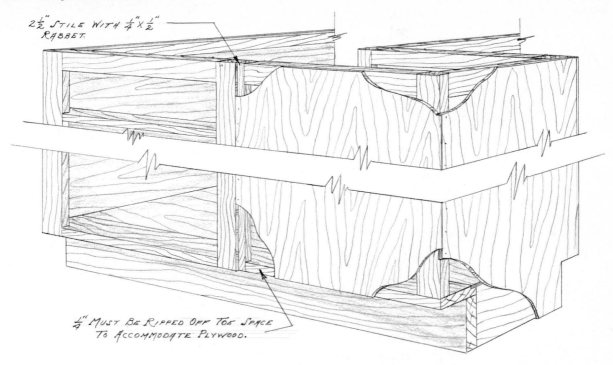

2½" STILE WITH ¼"X ½" RABBET.

¼" MUST BE RIPPED OFF TOE SPACE TO ACCOMMODATE PLYWOOD.

Figure 12–13 Details of paneling on peninsula return.

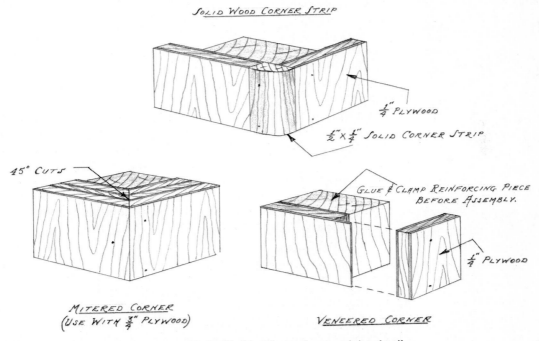

SOLID WOOD CORNER STRIP

¼" PLYWOOD

½"X ¼" SOLID CORNER STRIP

45° CUTS

MITERED CORNER (USE WITH ¾" PLYWOOD)

GLUE & CLAMP REINFORCING PIECE BEFORE ASSEMBLY.

¼" PLYWOOD

VENEERED CORNER

Figure 12–14 Plywood corner joint details.

Once the first cut has been completed, set the saw blade just high enough to cut away the plywood backing, leaving a nice square shoulder cut. Handle the panel with care, for a slight bump can break the flimsy veneer.

The secret of assembling the veneer joint is the same as for the other two. Glue and clamp the reinforcing strip in position before assembling. The strip should be glued to the panel with the edge-covering veneer on it. This panel is also installed on the cabinet first. The second panel is then installed with glue and brads and the veneer is glued to the edge of the second panel, holding it in place with many short strips of masking tape placed tightly around the corner.

When any of the joints have been completed and are completely dry, the brads should be set and filled with matching wood filler. Any slight imperfections along the edge of the joint should also be filled. After allowing the filler to set, the entire edge should be carefully scraped and sanded.

Reinforcing strips at the top of the panels

Each of the ¼-in. panels must have a ¾ in. × 2 in. softwood reinforcing strip glued and clamped to its top edge. This will have to be done before the cross-braces and the upper drawer runners can be installed.

INTERIOR BASE CABINET FEATURES

Kitchen designers and kitchen specialty companies have many unique products on the market to be used on the interior of base cabinets. These range from metal drawers for bread and vegetables to specialty hardware for making lazy Susans. Most cabinet hardware wholesalers carry at least a few of these lines and have catalogs available. The cabinet builder may choose to make use of some of these items especially if the customer demands their installation.

Building the Lazy Susan

One of the most desired base cabinet features is the lazy Susan. It makes fairly efficient use of the "dead" corner space in the L- or U-shaped base cabinet. The builder has a choice when asked to include a lazy Susan in the kitchen design. Hardware components can be purchased for the turntable that include the main shaft and the individual shelf supporting brackets. Also available are manufactured metal lazy Susans that are complete and ready to install in the cabinet. Finally, of course, the builder can make the lazy Susan in the shop, completely of wood. The cabinetmaker will want to study carefully the options and decide which method to use based on which will be the most profitable and still be satisfying to the customer. Only the shop-built lazy Susan will be dealt with in this text.

Designing the lazy susan

The general rule for the size of the lazy Susan is to make it as big as will fit into the "dead" corner space (Fig. 12–15). The shelves of the carousel can be almost 32 to 36 in. in diameter, depending on the size of the corner doors. Plywood or particle board ½ in. thick will do nicely for the shelves. These shelves should have an edging around them about 1½ in. high of either plywood or metal. The edging helps prevent items from falling off the turntable. If metal is used, all edges should be filed smooth to prevent the homeowner from receiving a nasty cut. Some builders use an edging of plastic laminate around the turntable shelves.

The shelves must be cut out to allow space for the corner doors. The shelves must also be supported adequately—½-in. dowels will provide the needed support. The main shaft can be a straight 1-in. dowel. Study Figs. 12–16 and 12–17 carefully for details of building the lazy Susan.

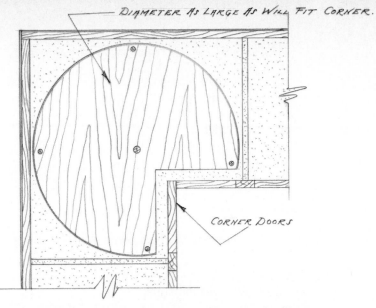

DIAMETER AS LARGE AS WILL FIT CORNER.

CORNER DOORS

Figure 12-15 Plan view of lazy Susan in "dead" corner.

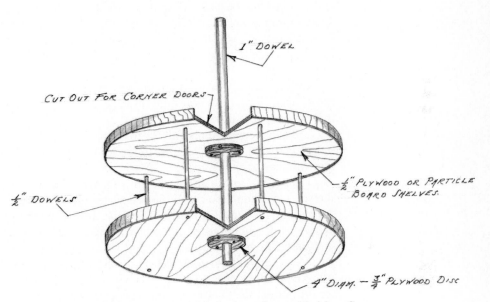

1" DOWEL

CUT OUT FOR CORNER DOORS

½" DOWELS

½" PLYWOOD OR PARTICLE BOARD SHELVES.

4" DIAM. — ¾" PLYWOOD DISC.

Figure 12-16 Bottom view of assembled lazy Susan.

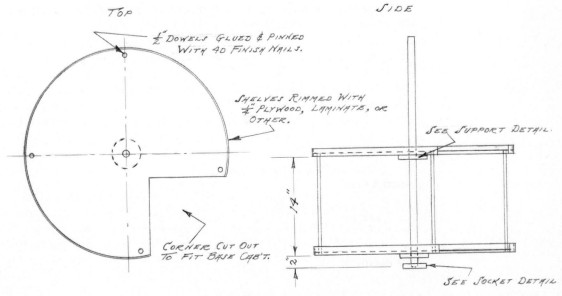

TOP

SIDE

½" DOWELS GLUED & PINNED WITH 4D FINISH NAILS.

SHELVES RIMMED WITH ¼" PLYWOOD, LAMINATE, OR OTHER.

SEE SUPPORT DETAIL.

CORNER CUT OUT TO FIT BASE CAB'T.

14"

½"

SEE SOCKET DETAIL.

Figure 12-17 Plan views of lazy Susan.

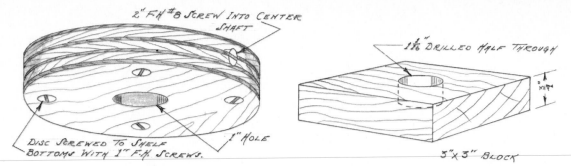

Figure 12-18   *(Left side)* shelf support detail; *(right side)* shaft socket detail.

Construction steps

Construction starts by tack-nailing the plywood or particle-board blanks together, marking the circles as well as the corner cut-out, and bandsawing the shelves. If a bandsaw is not available, a saber saw will do the job. Once the circular shelves have been sawed, some sanding will probably be required to true up and smooth the edges. The shelf-support disks of ¾-in. plywood should also be made at this time (Fig. 12–18).

With the shelves still tack-nailed together, drill the 1-in. center hole and the holes for the ½-in. dowels around the edge of the shelves. Drill the 1-in. hole through the shelf-support disks also.

Fasten the shelf-support disks to the bottom of each shelf using 1-in. flat-headed screws and glue. Be certain to drill a pilot hole and countersink for the 2-in. screw that fastens the shelf-support disk to the 1-in. center dowel.

The ½-in. dowels should be cut to length. As these dowels will space the two shelves, they should be cut to the proper length for the desired spacing—about half the base cabinet opening height. The ½-in. dowels are then placed in their predrilled holes, glued, and pinned in place by driving a 4d finish nail through the edge of the shelf and through the dowel.

Next, drive the 1-in. dowel center shaft through the center hole in the shelves. Allow the shaft to extend 2 in. or so below the bottom shelf—whatever height is wanted for the bottom shelf above the base cabinet bottom. Drive the 2-in. flat-headed screw into the shaft through the shelf-support disk. This anchors the shelves firmly to the center shaft.

Finally, bend and fasten the edging around each shelf. Be certain that all edges are sanded or filed smooth on the edging material.

Installing the Lazy Susan in the Base Cabinet

The lazy Susan will be completely installed while the base cabinets are still in the shop. However, disassembly must be possible for moving to the installation site. Thus screws should be used for fasteners as was done on the base cabinet itself.

Installation members required

Two additional pieces are required for installing the turntable: (1) a socket block to take the lower end of the center shaft, and (2) a ¾ in. × 4 in. piece of softwood of a length to extend from corner to corner of the base cabinet.

The socket block is simply a piece of wood or plywood about 3 or 4 in. square with a 1¹⁄₁₆-in. hole drilled about halfway through at the center point (Fig. 12–18).

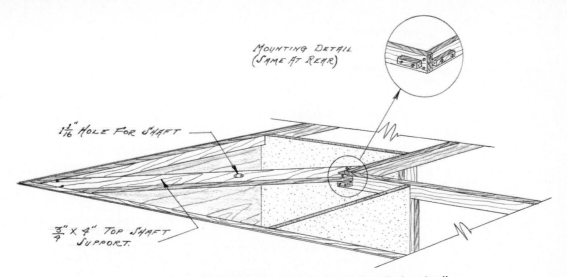

Figure 12–19 Lazy Susan top installation details.

The upper piece must be carefully cut and fit as illustrated in Fig. 12–19. To support this piece in position, ¾ in. × ¾ in. softwood blocks are glued and nailed to the frame, as shown in the detail drawing of Fig. 12–19.

The spot to drill the hole in this upper piece must be carefully calculated. After this is located, drill a 1¹⁄₁₆-in. hole through the upper shaft support.

Installation in the corner cabinet

As mentioned earlier, the ¼-in. plywood cabinet bottom must have a support piece installed to carry the weight of the lazy Susan. With this installed, nail and glue the socket block in place on the cabinet bottom. This, too, must be located carefully so that it lines up exactly with the hole in the upper shaft support piece.

Place the assembled lazy Susan in the corner cabinet and fit the lower end of the shaft in the socket block. A large-diameter thumbtack driven into the end of the shaft and a little paraffin rubbed around the end of the shaft will do wonders for having an easy-rotating carousel.

The upper shaft support piece is then positioned and the length of the shaft is marked. Remove the carousel and saw the shaft just a bit shorter than the upper surface of the support piece. By sawing the shaft a bit short, there will be no danger of the shaft rubbing against the lower surface of the countertop when it is installed.

Finally, paraffin the upper end of the shaft, reassemble all components, and fasten the upper shaft support piece in position with 1-in. flat-headed screws. Give the carousel a trial spin to see that it rotates freely with no binding or excessive friction.

PENINSULA CABINET AS A SNACK BAR

In many homes the peninsula cabinet serves not only as a divider between the kitchen and dining areas but also doubles as a snack bar. Two things must be taken into consideration when designing this cabinet: the amount of overhang that is built into the countertop, and the height of this eating level.

The countertop must extend beyond the structure of the base cabinet a minimum of 8 to 10 in. and 12 in. is preferable. This overhang will provide a proper amount of space to accommodate the knees of the persons sitting at the counter.

Figure 12–20   Snack counter on standard base return.

Figure 12–21   Snack bar at "sit-down" height.

The height of the counter must also be planned carefully. If the regulation 36-in. countertop is to double as a snack bar, stools will have to be used because 36 in. is much too high for a regulation chair (Fig. 12–20). Standard dining table height is 30 in., while regulation card table height is 28 in. Often an 8- to 10-in. snack bar countertop is fastened just 28 or 30 in. high to the side and end of a peninsula cabinet. At that height regular chairs can be used for snacking at the counter (Fig. 12–21).

KITCHEN PLANNING CENTER

Often the homemaker wants a portion of the kitchen set aside for a planning center. Such activities as menu planning, home accounts and record keeping, letter writing, and so on, are efficiently accomplished in this area. Provision is usually made for the storage of cookbooks, and a telephone outlet should be provided as well.

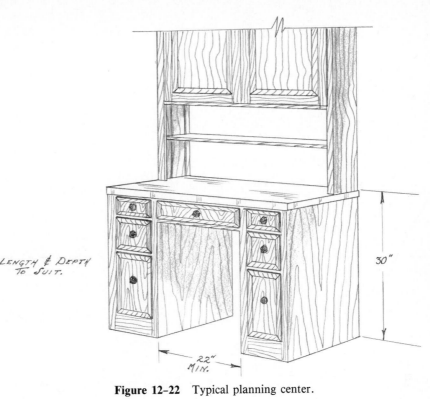

Length & Depth To Suit.

30"

22" Min.

Figure 12-22 Typical planning center.

Planning Center Specifications

As the planning center will be a place where the homemaker will sit down to do the chores related to running the home, the standard desk height of 30 in. should be observed when building this unit. Another important dimension is the width of the knee-hold space, which should be no less than 22 in. This width of the knee opening and height of the work surface will allow the use of a standard chair at this station (Fig. 12-22). Provision should be made for a center desk-type drawer as well as drawers that will accommodate standard file folders.

OTHER BASE CABINET DETAILS

Although it will be impossible to present details of all the varied interior cabinet ideas, some of the more common will be offered. Many times the homeowner simply presents the cabinet builder with a picture of a cabinet detail that has been snipped from a magazine. It is then up to the builder to adapt the homeowner's idea into a practical cabinet application. Many of the commercially manufacturered accessories for base cabinets come with installation instructions, so it is a relatively simple matter for the cabinetmaker to adapt the fixture to the style of the cabinet being built.

Cupboards with Vertical Divisions

A section of the base cabinet is often used for the storage of large pan covers, cookie sheets, and so on. Vertical dividers spaced 2 to 3 in. apart allow efficient use of this type of storage. Quarter-inch plywood or particle board is used for the dividers, which are placed into grooved strips fastened to the bottom of the base cabinet. The upper edge of the dividers can be set into either grooved strips or a plywood piece grooved to take the dividers. Here a bit of imagination and ingenuity will serve the cabinet-

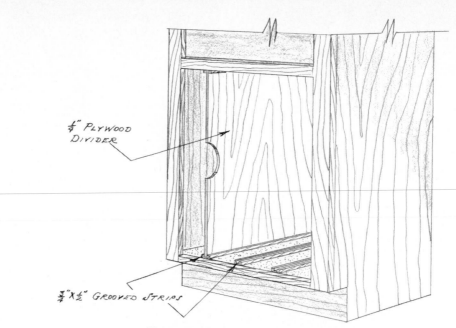

Figure 12-23 Detail of storage dividers.

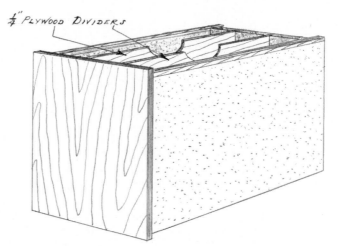

Figure 12-24 Storage drawer with dividers.

builder well as a scheme is devised to hold the dividers in place. Figure 12-23 is one suggested method. Often, too, a large drawer is adapted for this type of storage by placing ¼-in. dividers on the inside of the drawer as illustrated in Fig. 12-24.

Building and Installing Sliding Shelves

Although there are on the market any number of metal roller-runners that can be used for sliding shelves, many cabinetmakers still prefer to make their own runners from hardwood. The shelves, of course, must still be made by the builder, even though manufactured slides are to be used.

Most base cabinets will have two sliding shelves installed—one near the bottom of the opening and the other near the midpoint of the opening (Fig. 12-25).

Making the grooved runners

Most builders will select hardwood from which to make their runners, as they will hold up much longer under the friction of the sliding shelf. Two pieces are required for each shelf, ¾ in. × 1¾ in. × 23 in. (check this length dimension on the

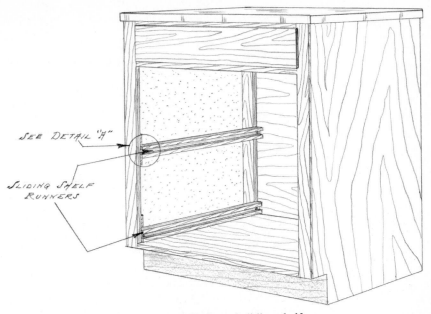

Figure 12-25 Installation of sliding shelf runners.

base cabinet itself). As most sliding shelves are made from either ½-in. plywood or particle board, the groove in the runner must be about ⁹⁄₁₆ in. wide × ⅜ in. deep. The dado set on the table saw will run the grooves quickly and smoothly. Sand a slight curve on the front end.

Installing the runners

The runners must be installed so that the bottom of the groove is just even with the edge of the face frame. A supporting block is glued to the back edge of the face frame just ⅜ in. in from the edge. The runner can then be screwed to this block using 1-in. flathead screws and glue. Figure 12-26 (detail A) shows this quite clearly.

The rear of the runner must have installation blocks as well. These can be fastened to the cabinet divider or end panels or even the back of the base cabinet. Just be certain that the block lines up exactly with the front so that the runners are parallel.

Sliding shelf

Measure from the bottom of one groove to the bottom of the opposite groove and cut the bottom of the sliding shelf about ¹⁄₁₆ in. less. This will allow the proper

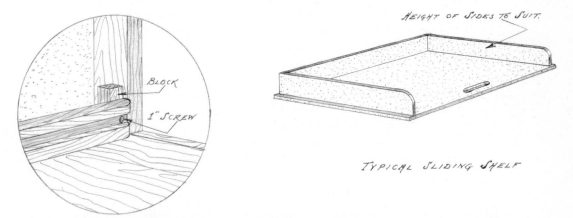

Figure 12-26 *(Left)* detail A runner installation; *(right)* typical sliding shelf.

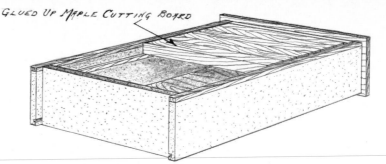

GLUED UP MAPLE CUTTING BOARD

Figure 12-27   Drawer with sliding cutting board.

amount for easy sliding of the shelf in the groove. The height of the sides is a matter of personal or customer preference, but in any event the sides must be set in about ½ in. so that the runners can clear easily. Assemble the sides to the shelf bottom by nailing through the bottom into the sides. The front can be shorter than the sides or omitted altogether (Fig. 12-26). A finger grip cut into the shelf front or the bottom is a nice touch. After the assembly is completed, test-fit the shelf in the runners and for easy operation apply paraffin to the friction edges.

Specialty Drawers for the Base Cabinet

Often the cabinet builder is called upon to provide drawers in the base cabinet that serve a special purpose. These can range from silverware drawers to a drawer lined with plastic laminate and a sliding cover to store bread. These were presented in detail in Chapter 1.

Occasionally, a drawer is fitted with a sliding cutting board (Fig. 12-27). There are available to the builder manufactured accessories of many types that can be placed in the cabinets and the cabinet drawers.

Building and Installing the Cutting Board

In Chapter 1 the design of a pull-out cutting board was discussed and the face-frame layout presented. In Chapter 5 the making and installation of the cutting board runners were detailed. Finally, the cutting board itself must be considered.

Building the Cutting Board

Old standard board

Before the advent of plywood, the cabinet builder was required to fabricate the cutting board from solid wood. This was done by gluing up a panel of softwood—usually basswood or white pine—and cross-banding this panel with a hardwood facing strip to match the face frame of the cabinet. The facing strips were placed both at the front and rear of the cutting board so that it could be reversed and inverted in the opening when the surface became worn. The facing strips were usually mortised into the softwood panel with a tongue-and-groove joint. The cross-banding prevented the entire panel from warping and gave the cutting board an edge that matched the rest of the cabinet facing (Fig. 12-28). Finger pulls were cut into the board by using the dado head on the table saw for a short, shallow cut.

Plywood cutting board

Most builders today simply fabricate a cutting board from hardwood ¾-in. plywood and apply facing strips on the front and rear edges. Finger grips or finger holes

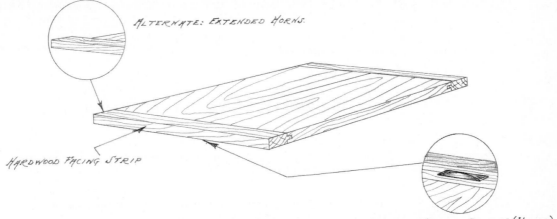

Figure 12–28 Glued-up softwood cutting board.

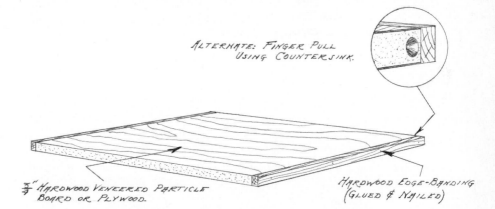

Figure 12–29 Edge-banded plywood cutting board.

are cut into the board in a variety of ways. Figure 12–29 illustrates a few of the options used on cutting boards. The finger holes or gripping area are cut both front and rear on alternate surfaces so that the board may be reversed in its opening and thus secure additional life of the working surfaces.

Plywood cutting boards will not last as long as the standard glued-up boards. However, many cabinet builders offer free replacement of the boards for "the life of the cabinet." This is used as a sales inducement, and several cabinet builders say that they have never replaced a cutting board.

REVIEW QUESTIONS

12.1. Describe the term "cabinet return."

12.2. What is the difference between a peninsula-type return and a wall type?

12.3. List three different options open to the cabinet builder for designing the peninsula-type return.

12.4. What type of door(s) are generally used when a lazy Susan is built into a "dead" corner?

12.5. List three types of corner joints when using plywood.

12.6. What is the general rule for designing the size of a lazy Susan?

12.7. A cabinet builder has three options when a customer desires a lazy Susan. What are they?

12.8. What is the minimum dimension acceptable for the overhang of the countertop serving as a snack bar on a peninsula return?

12.9. What is the correct height of a snack bar that is designed to be used with chairs?

12.10. What is the correct height of a kitchen-planning-center desk?

12.11. Why are grooved runners for sliding shelves made of hardwood?

SUGGESTED CLASS ACTIVITIES
AND STUDENT ASSIGNMENTS

12.1. On a large piece of brown wrapping paper or a 30 in. × 30 in. piece of plywood draw to full scale the details of the intersecting cabinet backs and face frames of a wall-type corner base cabinet with corner doors.

12.2. Examine several custom-built L-shaped or U-shaped kitchens and determine what cornering system the builder has used. How have the toe spaces been interlocked?

12.3. Secure manufacturer's catalogs and prices of base cabinet accessories and feature items such as lazy Susans, carousel hardware, and other manufactured items.

12.4. Examine plywood corner joints on various cabinet installations. Determine which type has been used and is most generally used in your area.

12.5. What method of handling the building of lazy Susans is most generally used by the cabinet builders in your area?

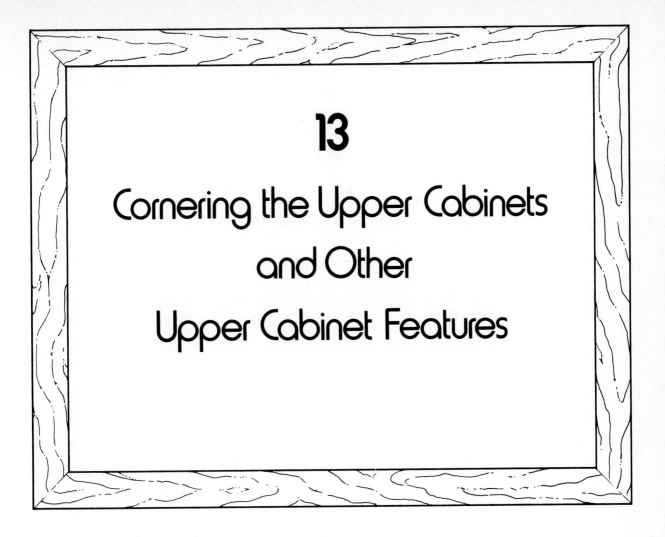

13

Cornering the Upper Cabinets and Other Upper Cabinet Features

Much of what has been presented concerning the cornering of base cabinets could be repeated in this chapter on cornering the upper units. Actually, the building of upper units "around the corner" is much simpler than base cabinets because the builder does not have to contend with the interlocking toe space. The design features of the base cabinet should be carried through the upper units. For example, if corner doors were used in the base cabinet, they should also be used in the upper cabinets.

The other designs option, too, are applicable to the upper cupboards. They may be built with a small lazy Susan in the corner or with corner shelves. The corner space may have side door access as the other option for gaining access to the "dead" corner.

DESIGNING THE UPPER CABINET RETURN

There are just two basic types of upper cabinet returns: the wall type and the open type. The wall type, of course, is built to fasten to the wall while the open type is a return unit that is installed above a base peninsula return.

The open type may be designed with a face frame on just one side and paneling on the other, or it may be built with a face frame on both sides, giving the homeowner access to the upper unit from both the kitchen and dining sides of the cabinet.

Upper cabinet returns placed above a peninsula base cabinet must have a continuation of the dropped ceiling or soffet also returning above the base cabinet return. The illustrations throughout the chapter show these various design options.

BUILDING THE UPPER CABINET RETURN

This section deals with the actual building of the upper returns. Both methods of cabinet construction—the box-and-frame and the casework—will be illustrated for both the wall-type return and the open type.

Building the Wall-Type Return Using the Casework Method

The first thing to determine when building an upper return is whether or not disassembly will be required. Often, if the return is not very long, the main upper unit and the return can be permanently assembled when built in the shop. The deciding factor will be the ability to get the cornered unit into the kitchen. Because the upper units are only 12 in. deep they can often be worked around corners and into doorways even though they are assembled.

A typical wall-type return is illustrated in Fig. 13–1. The details of the intersection of the cabinet bottoms and backs are shown in Fig. 13–2. The joining of the top rail of the intersecting cabinets is detailed in Fig. 13–3. Note that the rabbet for the cabinet top in Fig. 13–3 is just ¼ in. × ½ in., which would be correct for an upper unit with no dropped ceiling above. If the upper cabinet were to butt to a dropped ceiling, a rabbet of ½ in. × ½ in. would provide a scribing lip that is often desirable for such an installation. The unit illustrated is framed for corner doors. If side door access is desired, the framing is shown in Fig. 13–4.

Shelves for corner units may be glued up from ¾-in. particle board and faced on the exposed edges with hardwood facing strips. Note that a corner shelf must be supported in five spots with shelf standard and clips or other shelf-support method (Fig. 13–5).

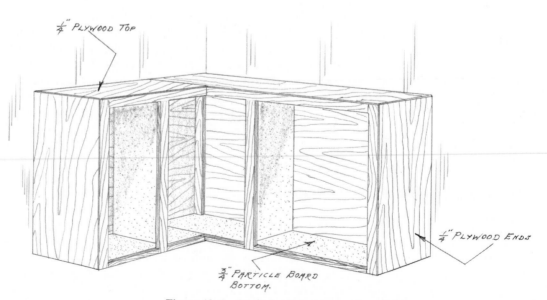

Figure 13–1 Typical return: casework wall type.

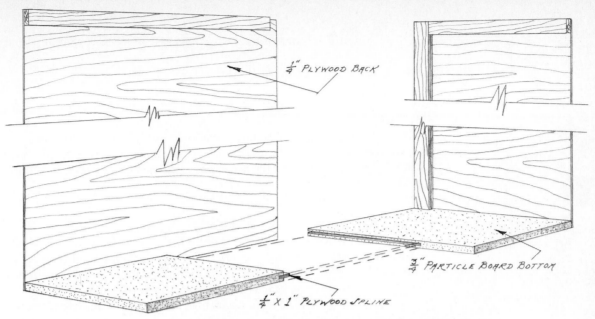

Figure 13-2 Wall-type return: corner intersecting details.

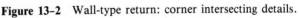
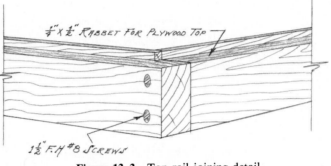

Figure 13-3 Top rail joining detail.

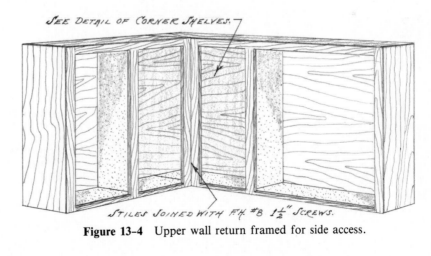

Figure 13-4 Upper wall return framed for side access.

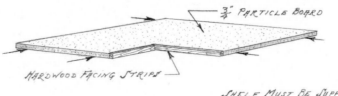

Figure 13-5 Typical adjustable corner shelf.

Building the Upper Peninsula Return

The same options are available in designing the upper peninsula return as were available for the base peninsula. The upper cabinet may be faced on one side and fully paneled on the opposite side. It may be faced on both sides for cupboard access from both the kitchen and dining sides of the peninsula. Finally, the upper unit may be faced part of the distance on the dining side and paneled partway. An upper return with a double face frame and corner access by side door is illustrated in Fig. 13–6.

Cabinet top

Usually, the top panel of a casework upper unit is made of ¼-in. plywood. In the case of the upper peninsula cabinet, however, a ¾-in. top must be used. This unit is installed by screwing the cabinet to the dropped ceiling using 2½-in. or 3-in. flat-headed screws. These screws must be driven through the cabinet top, thus the need for the extra strength of the ¾-in. cabinet top. Figure 13–7 illustrates this peninsula top construction.

Building the Upper Return Using the Box-and-Frame Method

Very little need be said about these upper returns built the box and frame way. Once the principles of construction for the box-and-frame method have been mastered, the techniques for building upper returns are almost self-explanatory. The reader will

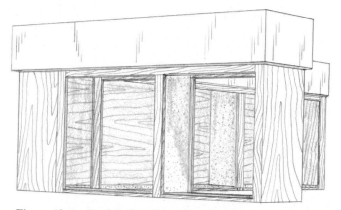

Figure 13–6   Double-face-framed peninsula upper cabinet.

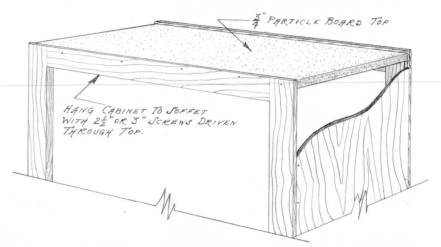

Figure 13–7   Peninsula-type upper return top detail.

note little difference, too, in the two methods of construction. The box-and-frame system makes use of ¾- or ½-in. material for the top, bottom, and ends, but the method of intersecting the main cabinet and the return is the same as for the casework cabinets. The single main difference is the use of ¼-in. plywood for the end panels in the casework system and the fact that the face frames are screwed together rather than mortised or doweled as in the case of the box-and-frame system.

BUILDING UPPER CABINETS TO THE CEILING

Modern homes make little use of the space above the kitchen window as was done years ago. Today the style is to drop the ceiling or to allow the space above the 32-in. upper units to remain open with just a plate rail or other decoration around the front edge and ends. Occasionally, however, the cabinetmaker may be called upon to build cabinets for a kitchen where the homeowner desires the cabinets to go to the ceiling. Because there are some special construction techniques for this type of cabinet, these details are contained in this chapter.

Designing the ''To the Ceiling'' Cabinet

The location and height of the window above the kitchen sink is in most cases the determining factor as to the usefulness of the space above the window. The use of a 32 in. × 16 in. two-light window was the standard window used in these older kitchens. When installed so that the top of the window lined up with the top of the doors in the room, about 13 or 14 in. remained above the window trim. With this amount of space to work with the cabinet builder could construct an upper cabinet with a row of small doors above the regular doors of the upper units. The rule of thumb was: The space above the window should be large enough so that at least 10-in. doors can be used for this space. If 10 in. was not available, the builder had two choices: (1) to drop the ceiling, or (2) to run the doors of the upper cabinet clear to the ceiling. The second option was not particularly desirable as the doors became quite large and unwieldy, with a tendency to warp.

Building the Full Upper Cabinet

To illustrate the construction techniques involved in building a cabinet to the ceiling, the model cabinet used for instructional purposes in the early chapters of the text will be adapted to this design. Figure 13–8 illustrates this cabinet with a row of upper doors above the window.

Figure 13–8 Model cabinet uppers built to the ceiling.

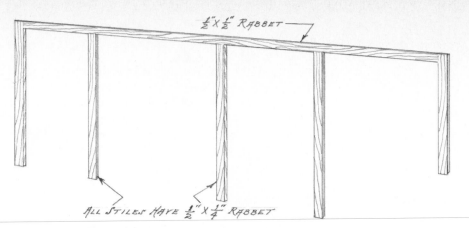

Figure 13–9 Casework face for model cabinet full uppers.

Construction starts as usual with the building of the face frame. These upper cabinets are built in one piece rather than sections. The cabinet will measure 134½ in. long by 44 in. high. The height may vary somewhat depending on the distance allowed between the base cabinet and the upper cupboards. If 16 in. is allowed for the space between cabinets, then with a 36-in. high base cabinet and a finished ceiling height of about 95 in., the upper units will figure out to be 43 in. high. The distance from the top of the window to the ceiling will usually be around 13 in. Again this may vary somewhat due to the placement of the window.

The height of the cabinet above the refrigerator will be around 30 in. Of course, this will depend to a great extent on the height of the refrigerator itself. With a refrigerator 64 in. high, a 30-in. cabinet will work out nicely. Some homeowners may prefer more space between the refrigerator and the bottom of this unit, in which case the height of the unit will have to be shortened.

Face frame

Other than its size, there is actually nothing particularly new in building a cabinet to the ceiling. A casework face frame is shown in Fig. 13–9. All stiles need to have ½ in. × ¼ in. rabbets and the top rail requires a ½ in. × ½ in. rabbet. The joints are assembled with 2½-in. 8FH screws. The frame will be too large to assemble using the vise, so the joints will have to be held with C-clamps and a backing block.

Back and bottom assembly

This layout requires careful measuring. Remember to take the actual dimensions from the notches in the face frame. The bottom of the cabinet above the window and the bottom of the cabinet over the refrigerator will be faced with ¼-in. hardwood plywood to match the face frame. Be certain to allow for this in calculating the layout.

Because the unit is well over 96 in. long, the plywood back will require a piece spliced on to make up the overall required length of 133¾ in. The shelf above the window will require this as well. A spline joint works well to make up the required length for this piece. The groove for the ¼-in. plywood spline can be run on the shaper or with a groove cutter in the router.

Apply the ¾ in. × 2 in. reinforcing strips and attach the bottoms as was done with the smaller cabinets, as instructed in previous chapters.

The back and bottom assembly is illustrated in Fig. 13–10.

Attaching the face frame

Once the back/bottom assembly is completed, the face frame is attached by gluing and nailing with 6d finish nails carefully predrilled to prevent splitting the stile (Fig. 13–11).

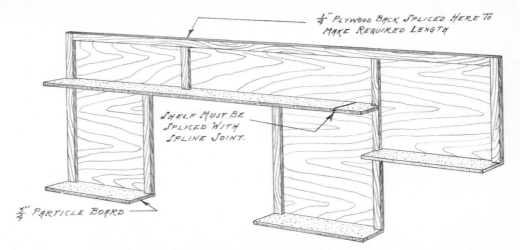

Figure 13–10 Assembly of back and bottom for upper model cabinet.

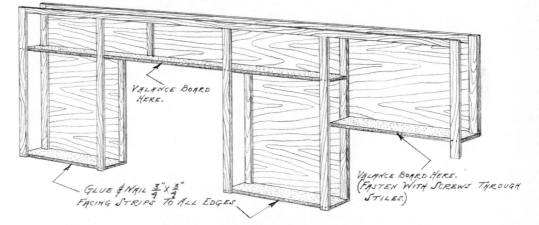

Figure 13–11 Face frame applied to back assembly.

The exposed edges of the particle-board shelf and bottoms are then faced with ¾ in. × ¾ in. hardwood strips. Again these are glued and nailed in position.

The valance boards are finally installed using 2½-in. screws driven through the stiles and nailed along the particle-board bottoms.

Completing the cabinet

The ¼-in. plywood panels are applied as well as the ¼-in. softwood plywood top. Reinforcing strips must be glued and clamped at the tops of all side panels. Note that reinforcing and nailing strips are needed as well for the panels on either side of the window opening. These need to be fastened to the bottom of the shelf above the window as well.

DESIGNING VALANCE BOARDS

Traditionally, valance boards of various designs have been installed in at least three places in kitchens. These places are above the sink and window, over the refrigerator, and over the range. With the popularity of the range hood, however, a decorative board is no longer used there. Modern designing of kitchens more often than not eliminates the valance board from the other two spots as well. The more tradi-

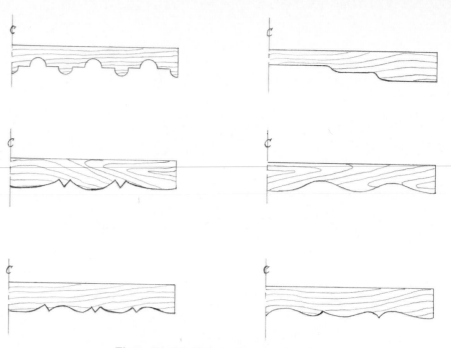

Figure 13-12 Valance board patterns.

tional-style kitchens may, however, still require this decorative touch, especially over the window above the sink.

Many, many patterns of valance boards have been used by cabinet builders over the years. Regardless of the pattern selected, they should be laid out carefully and proportionately and the curved areas should be pleasing to the eye. Care should be taken so that the valance is designed symmetrically—that is, the left half of the design should be identical to the right half. Figure 13-12 contains several suggested designs of valance boards that the builder might find helpful.

DESIGNING CABINETS WITH A PLATE RAIL

One of the nice decorative touches for upper cabinets that are open above to the ceiling is to install a plate rail. These are usually made from small turnings that are available from woodworking supply houses. Combined with moldings and attached to the top and sides of the upper units, the plate rail adds a touch of style to the kitchen decor.

Figure 10-13 illustrates a plate rail installed on the upper units. The spindles should be set on 6-in. centers and started about 2 in. from the corners. Figure 13-13 provides the details of this installation.

REVIEW QUESTIONS

13.1. On upper return units, what two ways are used to gain entry into the "dead" corner of return units?

13.2. Name the two basic types of upper return units.

13.3. The upper peninsula return must usually have a dropped ceiling over it. Why?

13.4. How many shelf supports are needed to support a corner-type shelf?

13.5. Why is a ¾-in. top used in an upper peninsula return?

13.6. What is the shortest acceptable door height for cabinet doors above the kitchen window on a "to the ceiling" cabinet?

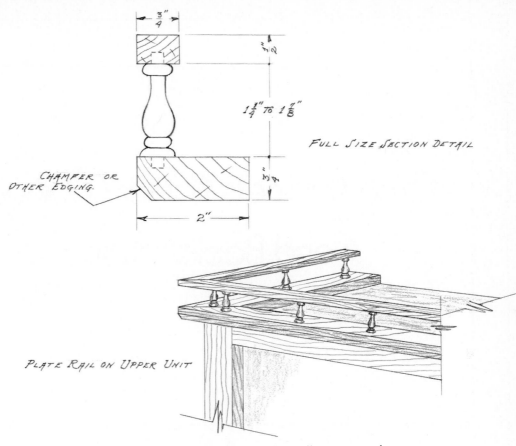

$\frac{3}{4}''$

$\frac{1}{2}''$

$1\frac{1}{4}''$ TO $1\frac{7}{8}''$

FULL SIZE SECTION DETAIL

CHAMFER OR OTHER EDGING.

$\frac{3}{4}''$

$2''$

PLATE RAIL ON UPPER UNIT

Figure 13–13   Plate rail on upper unit.

13.7. In Fig. 13–8, how long will the top rail of this cabinet be if the overall length is 134¼ in.?

13.8. In Fig. 13–10, the stated length of the cabinet back is 133¾ in. This is ¾ in. less than the overall length of 134¼ in. Explain.

13.9. If the overall height of the upper unit in Fig. 13–10 is 43 in., how high should the cabinet back be made?

13.10. In today's kitchen where would be the most common place for a valance board to be used?

SUGGESTED CLASS ACTIVITIES AND STUDENT ASSIGNMENTS

13.1. From class member's observations, what other methods do cabinetmakers use to corner upper cabinets?

13.2. Calculate the size of all face-frame members for the upper cabinet illustrated in Fig. 13–8. Use these dimensions: overall length, 134½ in.; main cabinet height, 43 in.; height over window, 13 in.; height over refrigerator: 30 in. For other dimensions, use those from Fig. 1–17.

13.3. Check with a building inspector to discover if there are any specific requirements for the installation of peninsula-type returns.

13.4. What other clever design factors have the class members observed that are built into upper return cabinets?

13.5. Locate sources, prices, and sizes of spindles used in the making of plate rails. In what species of wood are these available?

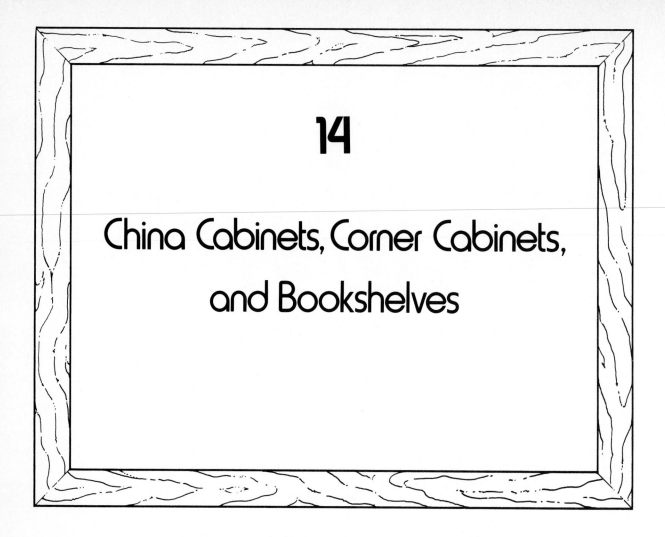

14

China Cabinets, Corner Cabinets, and Bookshelves

Very often the cabinetmaker is called upon to construct cabinets that are not a part of the kitchen. This chapter and the next deal with the design and fabrication of these cabinets.

INTERIOR-VISIBLE CABINETS

The cabinets being dealt with in this chapter are those that have their interiors visible because they have either glass doors or no doors. This raises some interesting problems in construction. Less expensive materials are commonly used on the interior of cabinets with solid doors. However, on cabinets with a visible interior, the same materials must be used inside and out. This raises the cost of these units substantially not only because of the extra cost of materials but because of the extra labor involved in having to finish the inside (Fig. 14-1).

Adapting the Casework System

When building visible interior cabinets, two problems confront the casework builder.

1. *The use of ¾-in. plywood sides:* Because the plywood sides will be visible from both the inside and outside of the cabinet, the ¼-in. plywood common-

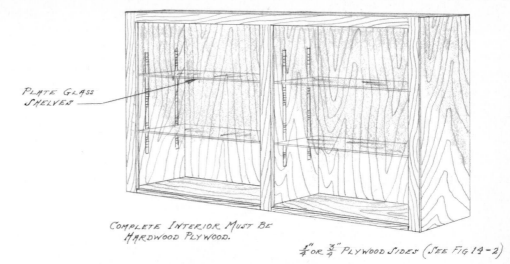

COMPLETE INTERIOR MUST BE
HARDWOOD PLYWOOD.

¼" OR ¾" PLYWOOD SIDES (SEE FIG 14-2)

Figure 14-1   Wall-type china cabinet.

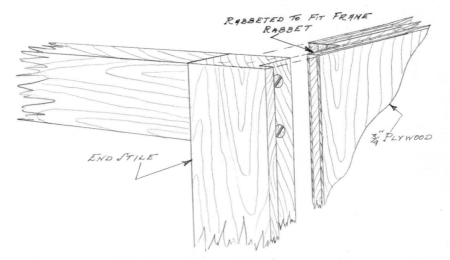

RABBETED TO FIT FRAME
RABBET

END STILE

¾" PLYWOOD

Figure 14-2   End panel made of ¾-in. plywood.

ly used for panels must be of the A-A grade. This is exceedingly difficult to purchase and expensive when it is located. The answer to this problem is to compromise with the box-and-frame method and use ¾-in. A-A plywood for sides and still use the screwed face frame. The ¾-in. plywood sides simply have a rabbet cut along the edge to fit the rabbet in the face-frame stile (Fig. 14-2).

When ¾-in. plywood sides are used, the cabinet back of ¼-in. plywood can be rabbeted into the sides in the traditional box-and-frame method. Remember, too, any reinforcing pieces that appear on the inside of the cabinet must be of matching hardwood and sanded nicely.

2. *Using ¼-in. plywood sides and back:* Plywood sides of ¼ in. thickness can be used if the panel is of good quality on both sides, or if the cabinet is to be built into the wall so that the outer sides are not visible.

The back of this cabinet must have the reinforcing strips applied to the back or D face of the plywood (Fig. 14-3). This will give the inside of the cabinet a clear, unbroken, finished plywood back, although the inside of the cabinet will lose 1 in. of interior space.

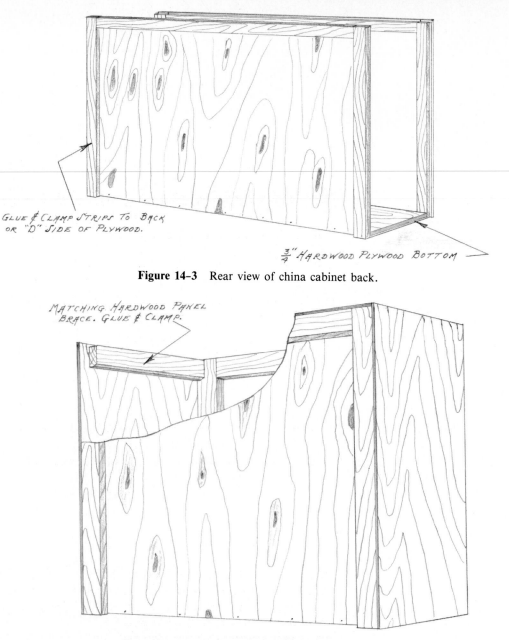

GLUE & CLAMP STRIPS TO BACK
OR "D" SIDE OF PLYWOOD.

¾" HARDWOOD PLYWOOD BOTTOM

Figure 14-3   Rear view of china cabinet back.

MATCHING HARDWOOD PANEL
BRACE. GLUE & CLAMP.

Figure 14-4   Rear view of china cabinet interior.

The sides and top of the cabinet will then be glued and nailed to the back as in regular upper cabinet construction. Matching hardwood corner pieces must be installed at the top of the ¼-in. plywood sides, as these will be seen in the inside of the cabinet (Fig. 14-4).

Using the Box-and-Frame Method

The building of china cabinets or other cabinets with their interiors visible using the box-and-frame method is about the same as building other cabinets with this system. The main difference is that materials must be used that are of good quality on both sides if both the inside of the cabinet and the outside will be seen. This includes all interior partitions as well.

If the cabinet is to be hung on the wall, of course, a hardwood hanging strip must be installed at the top rear of the cabinet. If the cabinet is free-standing, this hanging strip may be omitted and the plywood back rabbeted into the cabinet top as well as the sides.

Designing the Interior-Visible Cabinet

Figure 14-5 is a fairly typical open cabinet which can be adapted to a number of uses. This design could be used for a china cabinet, a library unit, or even a gun cabinet if the shelves were omitted and the bottom of the upper section routed to receive the gun butts. Certainly, other door styles could be used on this basic design—even plate glass sliding doors. The top unit could be entirely open; that is, have no doors at all. This design could easily be adapted to be either free standing (as illustrated) or a typical, built-in type cabinet which is screwed to the wall and cased in. The length is also easily adapted to the space available. The cabinet illustrated was drawn 72 in. long. As long as the length and height are kept in pleasing proportion and the shelves are not allowed to get so long that there is a danger of them sagging under a load, the length is no particular problem. If, however, a whole wall were to be filled with a cabinet of this style, it would be wise to consider building the installation in two or three sections.

The cabinet illustrated in Fig. 14-5 is designed to be built in two parts. The base unit is one separate construction, as is the upper unit. The two parts are fastened together with screws driven from below through the top of the lower unit into the bottom of the upper section.

Note that cabinets of this styling do not have a toe space as do typical kitchen cabinets. The bottom rail should be 3 or 4 in. high, with 4 in. probably preferred. If a carpet and pad are installed along the front of this cabinet, a 3-in. bottom rail would be quite skimpy.

Figure 14-5 Typical interior-visible cabinet.

The other dimensions can be changed to suit the desires of the customer. The depth dimensions of the lower unit could be 20 in. or even 24 in., while the depth of the upper cabinet could be 14 in. or more. The height of the lower unit should not be made higher than about 30 in. in any case. Drawers, too, could be built into the bottom section.

DESIGNING AND BUILDING CORNER CABINETS

Corner cabinets are still popular in today's homes even though they have been placed in American homes since colonial times. Often, a pair of corner cabinets are installed in the dining room and used to display fine china and silver pieces. The corner cabinet can be built with or without glass doors. It is not unusual to see corner cabinets with no doors on the upper part, although the bottom section always seems to have a pair of doors. The usual pattern is to have solid plywood or paneled doors on the lower section while the upper part is fitted with glass doors or has no doors (Fig. 14–6).

Designing the Corner Cupboard

The width of the corner cupboard is of extreme importance. As the width across the front becomes wider, the distance the cabinet must occupy along the walls increases. For example, a corner cabinet that measures 25½ in. across the front will use about 18 in. along each wall in the corner. However, a cabinet measuring 34 in. across the front will use 24 in. of corner wall space. The width-to-height proportion of the corner cabinet must be planned carefully. A 24-in. corner cabinet that is built 84 in. high can look quite spindly, while a 36-in.-wide cabinet built only 72 in. high will look very stubby. Ideally, the corner cabinet should be built 30 to 36 in. wide, while the height should be around 80 to 84 in. Often, the top of period-style corner cabinets have a decorative finial that adds to the height impression and must be taken into account (Fig. 14–7).

Many cabinet builders like to make a full-size pattern layout of the plan of the corner cabinet on a piece of plywood. From this they can calculate the exact size and shape of the shelves as well as the measurements of the face frame (Fig. 14–8).

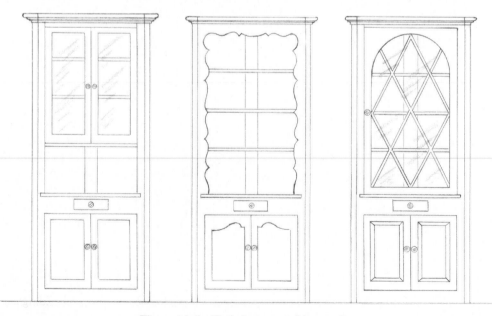

Figure 14–6 Varied corner cabinet styles.

Figure 14-7 Period-style corner cabinet.

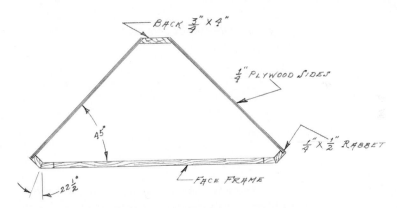

Figure 14-8 Typical plan view of corner cabinet.

Many corner cupboards have a small drawer in the midsection. This provides a nice design break between the upper and lower sections. The drawer must be made quite small because the depth is controlled by the slant of the sides of the cabinet. The wider the drawer, the shorter the drawer sides will be.

The angled face-frame stiles make for a nice fit to the walls, as the stiles meet the walls at right angles. If this is not done, the stiles must be cut at 45 degrees to fit to the wall. This not only does not look as good, but it is much more difficult to fit the back into that type of face frame.

Building the Corner Cabinet

Some special construction problems are met when building a corner cabinet. The steps are discussed in sequence in the following paragraphs.

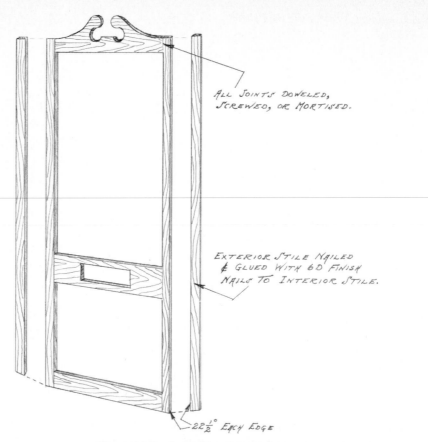

ALL JOINTS DOWELED, SCREWED, OR MORTISED.

EXTERIOR STILE NAILED & GLUED WITH 6D FINISH NAILS TO INTERIOR STILE.

22½° EACH EDGE

Figure 14-9 Assembly of front frame.

Building the face frame

The face-frame joints may be doweled, screwed, or mortised, as the builder prefers. Note that the face frame has four stiles: two interior and two exterior. These meet at 22½ degrees (Fig. 14–9). Build the face frame by joining the rails to the interior stiles first. After that is completed, add the exterior stiles by carefully gluing and nailing to the interior stiles. Predrill the nailing with a 6d nail in the drill. The exterior stiles must be rabbeted ¼ in. × ½ in. to receive the cabinet sides.

Shelves and back

From the full-size plan drawing, carefully make a pattern of the shelves from plywood, cardboard, or hardboard. The visible shelves as well as the top and the bottom of the open cabinet will have to be made from ¾-in. hardwood plywood or veneered particle board. It may be possible to get by with ½-in. hardwood plywood for the top and bottom of this space. The shelf in the enclosed space below and the bottom of this area can be of ¾- or ½-in. particle board.

The back is a piece of matching hardwood lumber 4 in. wide by the required height. Each edge must be sawed or jointed to a 45-degree angle. On the back board mark the location of each shelf, top and bottom. The shelves in a corner cabinet are usually permanent and not adjustable, although it would not be difficult to have the shelves adjustable. Carefully line up and nail each shelf, top and bottom, to the back piece. Figure 14–10 illustrates this assembly.

Assembling the units

Carefully lay the assembled back and shelves on the floor with the back board down. A couple of temporary supports will prevent the assembly from tipping while the face frame is being attached (Fig. 14–11). Carefully mark the location of each

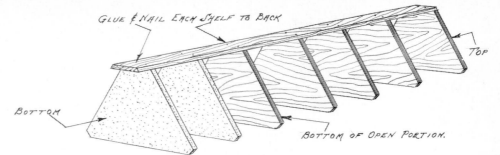

Figure 14-10 Assembly of shelves to back.

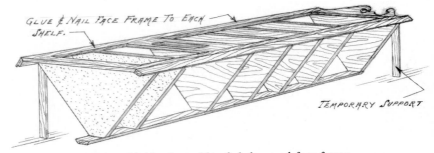

Figure 14-11 Assembly of shelves and face frame.

shelf on the back of the face frame so that each will be square. Fasten the face frame to each shelf with 6d finish nails and glue. Be sure to predrill for the nails.

Completing the corner cabinet

The sides of ¼-in. hardwood plywood are next installed being glued and nailed to each shelf and along the back board. Pull the entire cabinet into square as the backs are applied.

Apply facing strips to all exposed shelves. Complete the cabinet with the style of door desired.

DESIGNING AND BUILDING BOOK SHELVES

It is a rare home that does not have some wall area devoted to the storage of books. Often in the traditional-style home this will be on either side of a fireplace, or it is not unusual to see a whole wall lined with bookshelves. Although not difficult to build, the planning and designing must be done tastefully and carefully (Figs. 14-12 and 14-13).

Designing Bookshelf Areas

The first question that usually arises when dealing with bookshelf design is: How deep should the shelves be? Traditionally, bookshelves are built from 8-in. lumber, that is, lumber with an actual width of 7½ in. However, books come in many sizes and often the home decorator will make use of these shelves to display things other than books. For example, fine china, knick-knacks, trophies, sound components, clocks, and pictures are all frequently found on "bookshelves"!

When designing a bookshelf for a customer, it pays to spend some time with the homeowners in deciding just what depth will best serve their needs. Attention must also be paid to the length of the individual shelf units. Loaded with books a

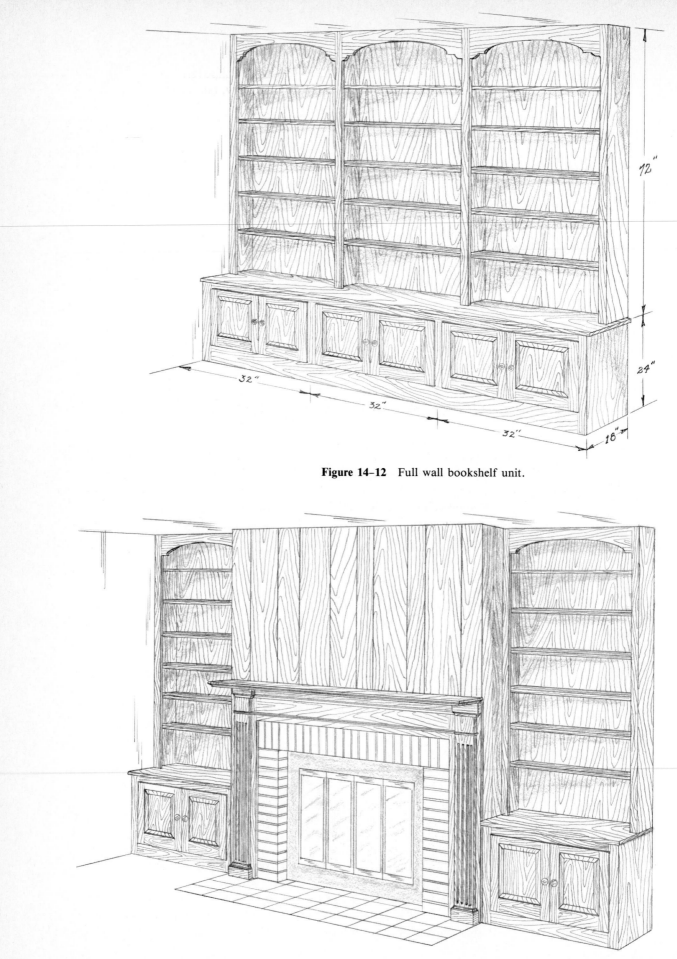

Figure 14–12 Full wall bookshelf unit.

Figure 14–13 Bookcase—on fireplace wall.

shelf has a tendency to develop an unsightly sag if built overly long. A sturdy shelf of solid oak 36 in. long will bear this load successully, but one of ¾-in. plywood or softwood is questionable. Rarely should bookshelves be longer than 36 in. with 32 to 34 in. preferable.

Because they must accommodate a variety of sizes and heights of books and other displayed items, the shelves should be made adjustable. A nice touch is to set the shelf standard flush with the surface of the sides by plowing a groove to take the shelf track. Using a shelf track that matches the color of the finished cabinet is another nice feature that makes the track much less noticeable.

Bookshelves are usually built without doors, but it is not too rare to see glass doors on some library units in homes. For example, Fig. 14–5 could readily be adapted to book storage.

Building Bookshelves

For the shelving systems themselves, solid lumber or plywood is most often used for the sides and shelves. Thus the casework system does not adapt itself well to bookshelves. Either the shelves are dadoed into the sides or the shelf track is placed in a groove in the sides, so ¼-in. plywood sides do not work well. However, a screwed face frame can readily be used as long as the edges of the frames are not visible and the screwheads seen.

Backs on bookshelf systems are a matter of decorative choice. It is not unusual for the decorator to want the wall to be visible and will paint or wallpaper this space to match the rest of the room decor. However, if a back is used, ¼-in. matching hardwood plywood is rabbeted into the side pieces as is commonly done with the box-and-frame method. The above applies, of course, to built-in book storage units. A free-standing bookshelf would be quite wobbly with no back to provide strength.

The units must be fastened securely to the wall. This can be accomplished by screwing through the sides into the wall or with a mounting strip at the top rear of the unit.

Supporting longer shelves

Adjustable shelves that must be made longer than what seems safe and practical can be supported by an extra shelf track located near the middle of the shelf. This will provide additional support for the back edge of the shelf and will help the shelf support its load.

Permanent shelves in a bookshelf with a plywood back can be provided with additional support strength by nailing through the back into the edge of the shelves. However, in both cases, it is best to keep the length of book-loaded shelves close to the lengths suggested.

REVIEW QUESTIONS

14.1. Why are china cabinets and other interior-visible cabinets more costly to build than regular kitchen cabinets?

14.2. How can ¾-in. plywood side panels be used with a screwed face frame?

14.3. In the casework system, how is the ¼-in. plywood back panel reinforced that is different than the back of a regular kitchen cabinet?

14.4. How high should the bottom rail be made on the face frame for china cabinets and other cabinets that have no toe space?

14.5. Why is a full-sized pattern layout of a proposed corner cabinet a good idea?

14.6. The interior and exterior stiles on the face frame of a corner cabinet must be jointed at what angle?

14.7. What is the traditional width of book shelves?

14.8. What is the recommended length for individual book shelves?

14.9. What is the preferred treatment for shelf standard that is to be installed in bookshelves?

14.10. How can adjustable bookshelves be provided with additional support?

SUGGESTED CLASS ACTIVITIES AND STUDENT ASSIGNMENTS

14.1. Design and draw a traditional-style china cabinet for the dining area of a home.

14.2. Locate, cut out, and save pictures of china cabinets, corner cabinets, and bookshelves taken from leading home magazines.

14.3. Visit building centers and lumber dealers and request copies of their mill work and cabinet catalogs that contain interior-visible cabinets.

14.4. Design and draw a china storage space that is part of a regular set of kitchen cabinets.

14.5. Discuss the comparative advantages and disadvantages of building interior-visible cabinets using the box-and-frame method versus the casework method.

15

Bathroom Vanities, Broom Closets, and Linen Closets

Another area of cabinetry that must be looked at are those cabinets for the bath, those used for storage of linens, and storage cabinets for the kitchen such as broom closets. Building these cabinets requires no special or new knowledge of cabinet building technique. Rather, building these units is a matter of knowing the standards and designing them properly.

DESIGNING AND BUILDING BATHROOM VANITIES

The display floors of building supply dealers are literally filled with many styles of bathroom vanities. These, however, are standard units and are not made to fit a particular space. The homemaker often calls on the custom cabinetmaker to build the bathroom vanity together with the other cabinets in the home (Fig. 15–1).

Designing the Vanity Cabinet

The generally accepted measurements for vanity cabinets are 30 to 32 in. for the height and 20 to 22 in. for the depth (Fig. 15–2). The design and style of the bathroom sink could affect these standards. If a precast, one-piece countertop and sink is to be installed, for example, the specifications must be obtained from the dealer and the cabi-

Figure 15-1 A beautiful vanity cabinet is also a cabinetmaker's job. (Courtesy Merillat Industries, Inc., Adrian, Mich.)

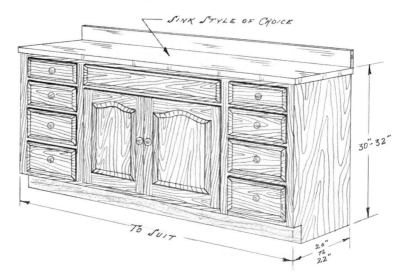

Figure 15-2 Vanity cabinet standards.

net built accordingly. It is always a good move to request from the customer the size and style of sink being used so that the cabinet depth can be correct for the type being used (Fig. 15-3). The length, of course, is designed to fit the available space. It is not unusual to see bathroom vanities built to accommodate two sinks in the same unit.

Very often, too, the cabinet builder is called on to install the plastic-laminate countertop and backsplash on the vanity cabinet.

The style of vanities can vary as much as the style of kitchen cabinets. Here, again, the homeowner/decorator will tell the builder the style desired and the cabinetmaker must then detail the face frame into drawer space and cupboard space to use the available length most pleasingly and efficiently (Fig. 15-4).

Figure 15-3 Vanity sinks come in a variety of styles and materials. (Courtesy Elkay Mfg. Co., Oak Brook, Ill.)

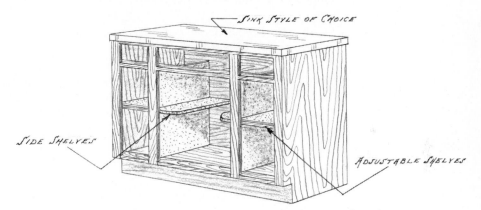

Figure 15-4 Suggested interior treatment of small vanity.

Building the Vanity Cabinet

The building of the vanity cabinet is nothing more than straightforward base cabinet construction with the height and depth adjusted to the standard dimensions given. Notice that a toe space is required on the vanity. Either method—the box-and-frame or the casework—adapt well to this construction.

Installation is also the same as for a standard kitchen base cabinet.

DESIGNING AND BUILDING BROOM CLOSETS

This unit, usually in or near the kitchen, adapts to a number of storage solutions. First, it definitely is used for the storage of brooms, mops, vacuum cleaners, and other long-handled items, as well as cleaning supplies. Second, the entire unit can be equipped with sliding shelves and used for the storage of canned goods. Third, the space can even be equipped with a tall multishelved lazy Susan and used to solve any of a number of storage problems. Perhaps the name "broom closet" is no longer appropriate for this unit; a better name might be "kitchen storage unit."

Designing the Kitchen Storage Unit

From the discussion above the cabinetmaker can quickly discern that this kitchen unit must be designed to meet the use the homemaker desires. The standard dimension of the usual "broom" closet is 24 in. wide by 24 in. deep by the height that usually extends to the ceiling. The face of this cabinet is designed in two sections: the lower section about 5 ft. high and the upper section using the remaining space (Fig. 15–5). The larger lower space is used for the storage of the long-handled items, while the upper section can be equipped with shelves or, on occasion, vertical dividers for the storage of cookie sheets, large covers, serving trays, and so on.

One serious problem encountered when building the floor-to-ceiling cabinet is the installation of the unit. It must be able to stand upright once the cabinet is placed in the room. The solution to this rests in designing and building a separate toe space for the unit. The main portion of the cabinet is built 3 or 4 in. less than the room height (whatever height the toe space is to be). This will allow the cabinet to be placed vertically in the room and then raised to the ceiling so that the separate toe space can be slipped under the cabinet. A 24 in. × 24 in. broom closet can stand upright with at least a 3-in. toe space allowance (Fig. 15–6).

Building the Kitchen Storage Unit

Building the broom closet or storage unit is very similar to building an upper cabinet. Because of the separate toe space that is required, the bottom of this unit must be ¾-in. particle board or plywood. This will provide the bottom with sufficient strength to carry the weight of the cabinet and its contents.

The casework method calls for building to begin with the front face frame as usual, followed by the cabinet back. The bottom and the main shelf are first nailed

To Ceiling or
Desired Height.

4"

SEPARATE TOE SPACE

24"   24"

Figure 15–5 Typical kitchen storage unit.

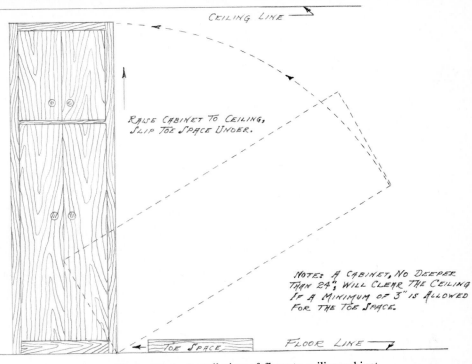

Figure 15-6 Installation of floor-to-ceiling cabinet.

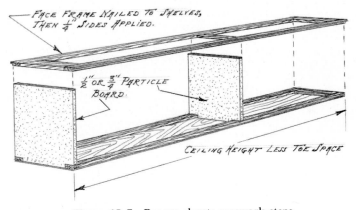

Figure 15-7 Broom closet: casework steps.

to the cabinet back, then the face frame is fastened to the front of the shelves. The ¼-in. plywood sides are then applied and, finally, the top is installed as is done for an upper unit (Fig. 15–7).

DESIGNING AND BUILDING LINEN CLOSETS

Occasionally, the cabinetmaker is called on to build a cabinet that is designed specifically for the storage of household linens. Often a hall closet is adapted for this purpose and the carpenter simply equips this space with shelves. However, if the homeowner desires a more elaborate treatment of this storage space, the cabinet builder will be called on to design and build this unit (Fig. 15–8).

The linen closet is usually designed so that both shelves and drawers are available for the efficient storage of linens. The drawers can be regular lipped drawers or they can be pull out shelves operating on wooden runners or metal guides (Fig. 15–9).

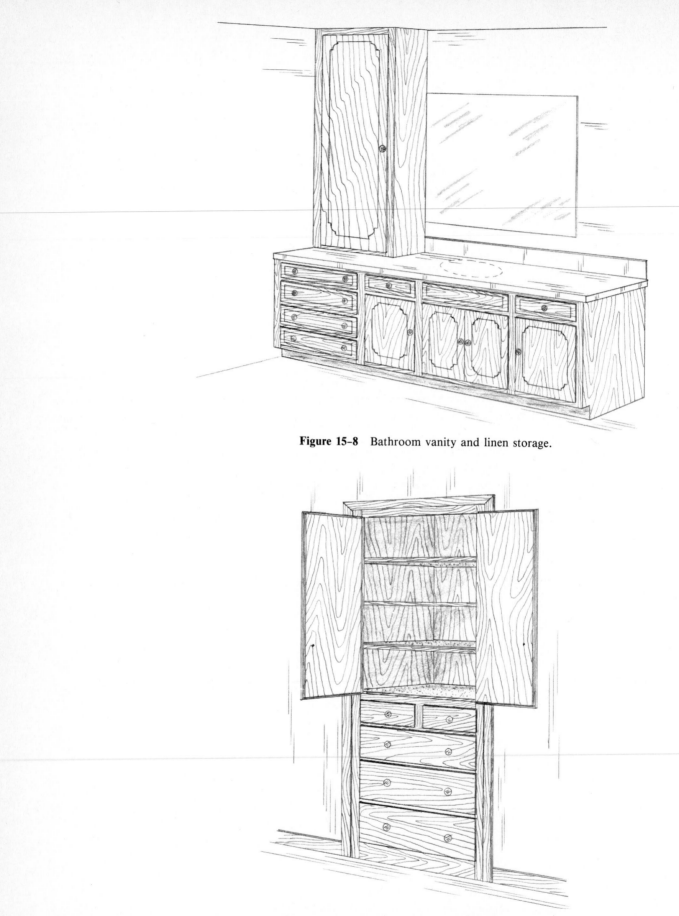

Figure 15-8 Bathroom vanity and linen storage.

Figure 15-9 "Case-in" linen closet (built into wall).

As linen closets are often large in size, the builder must be careful to see that the finished cabinet can be moved into the installation area. If this is a problem, the cabinetmaker may have to deliver the closet partially assembled or do some of the actual building at the site. This is especially true where the contractor has left a blank but plastered closet area that is to be equipped with shelves, drawers, and cabinet doors. Although cabinet sides and back are not required for this type of installation, some imagination will have to be exercised to figure a method of installing the drawers. The face frame can be built as usual and installed flush with the plastered walls and then cased like a doorway with regular casing.

Building the Linen Closet

As with the other cabinet units discussed in this chapter, no particular new problems of construction are encountered when building linen closets. The building of these units is adaptable to the instruction already presented using either the box-and-frame method or the casework system.

REVIEW QUESTIONS

15.1. What is the standard depth and height of vanity cabinets?

15.2. What other types of materials are used for vanity cabinet tops other than plastic laminate?

15.3. Why must one of the dimensions—either the width or depth—of a floor-to-ceiling cabinet be held very close to 24 in.?

15.4. What is the minimum height for a separate toe space so that a 24-in.-deep floor-to-ceiling cabinet can be stood upright in a room with a normal ceiling height of about 96 in.?

15.5. What is meant when a linen closet is termed a "cased" cabinet?

SUGGESTED CLASS ACTIVITIES AND STUDENT ASSIGNMENTS

15.1. Calculate the bill of material for the face frame of the vanity cabinet illustrated in Fig. 15–1. Cabinet front dimensions are 66 in. long by 30 in. high. Use either the casework or the box-and-frame method.

15.2. Visit several plumbing establishments and request material and specification sheets on vanity sinks and one-piece molded sinks and tops.

15.3. Collect illustrations from home magazines and builder's supply catalogs of storage ideas for linen closets and kitchen storage units.

16

Cabinet Hardware

The hardware used in and on custom cabinets is unique and varied. Generally, this hardware falls into two classifications: decorative and utilitarian. The decorative hardware is that which is visible on the finished cabinet and includes all styles of hinges, drawer and door pulls, and knobs. All of these are available in an abundance of styles and finishes. The utility hardware is described as that functional hardware which is used on the inside of the cabinet for a definite purpose. This category includes catches, shelf standard and clips, metal drawer runners, and many other useful and practical hardware items. Both categories will be presented and discussed in this chapter.

DECORATIVE HARDWARE

Several major manufacturers of cabinet hardware have produced beautiful cabinet decorative hardware in a wide variety of styles and finishes. These vary from antique brass early American to ceramic knobs. Hinges are made to match the finishes and styles of the pulls and handles. Most cabinet shops do not maintain much of an inventory of decorative hardware because of the wide variety available. They order from their wholesalers after the customer has selected the color and style.

Cabinet Hinges

There are several types of cabinet hinges available to the cabinet builder. The type used will depend on the kind of cabinet door being used as well as the style of the cabinet inself. For example, a ⅜-in. lipped door will call for a ⅜-in. inset hinge in the style desired, while a ¼-in. overlaid door will call for an entirely different type of hinge.

Inset hinges

The ⅜-in. inset cabinet hinge is by far the most used hinge by cabinetmakers. Available both as self-closing or non-self-closing, the butt or visible portion of the hinge is that which determines the style. Figure 16–1 illustrates just a sampling of the styles of ⅜-in. inset hinges available. These are made in a multitude of finishes. Satin black, old iron, zinc plated, bright brass, antique brass, brass with white accent, white gold, old copper, bright chrome, and dull chrome are all finishes and colors that are manufactured. Of course, all styles are not made in all colors.

Hinges for flush doors

A flush door is one that is mounted flush with the face frame of the cabinet. To hang this style of door, a common loose-pin butt hinge may be used that is pur-

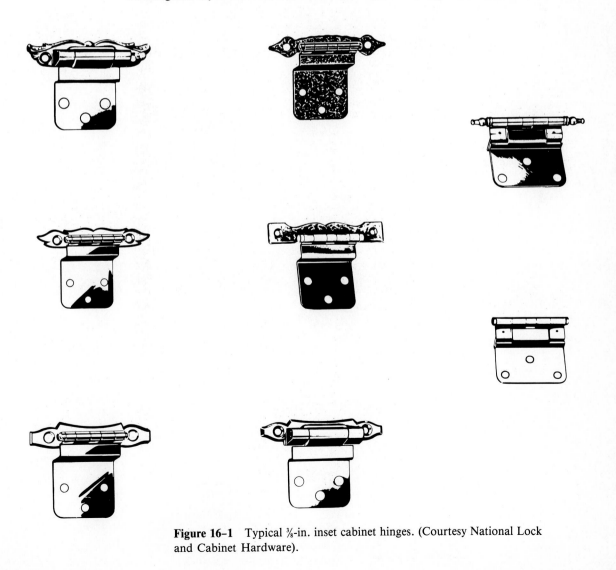

Figure 16–1 Typical ⅜-in. inset cabinet hinges. (Courtesy National Lock and Cabinet Hardware).

Figure 16–2 Sampling of hinges for flush doors. (Courtesy National Lock and Cabinet Hardware).

chased to fit the thickness of the cabinet door being used. The butt hinges are available in fixed pin as well. Another style of hinge available for flush doors is illustrated in Fig. 16–2. These are similar in style to the inset hinges but are straight hinges with no bend to fit a rabbet.

Gaining in popularity is the newer invisible hinge for flush or overlaid doors that gives a cabinet what is termed the European look. Figure 16–3A pictures this hinge, which must be installed with a special drill. Most of these hinges are adjustable in several directions, which makes them a delight to use, as the doors can be moved around to be a perfect fit (Fig. 16–3B). This hinge is used primarily where a modern unbroken front is desired with overlaid doors.

Figure 16–3A New type hinge for overlaid doors for the "European" look. (Courtesy Julius Blum, Inc.)

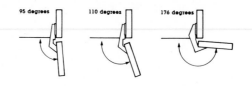

3 TYPES OF "EUROPEAN" STYLE HINGES

A SPECIAL BIT IS REQUIRED FOR INSTALLING

Figure 16–3B Data on the new-style hinge. (Courtesy The Woodworker's Store, Rogers, Minn.)

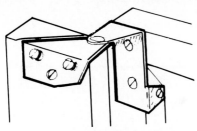
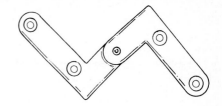

Figure 16–4 Knife hinges for overlaid doors. (Courtesy The Woodworker's Store, Rogers, Minn.)

Hinges for overlaid doors

There are many types of hinges on the market for overlaid doors, several of which are illustrated in Fig. 16–4. Some of these must have special saw cuts made on the edge of the door to receive the hinge butt. Knife hinges, too, are used on overlaid doors.

Specialty hinges

It simply is not possible to list all the different types of hinges available for cabinetwork. Some of the more popular specialty hinges are the continuous hinge (sometimes referred to as a piano hinge) and the invisible hinge, as well as the double-action hinge. All are illustrated in Fig. 16–5.

Gallery or Plate Rail

Although often made of small wood turnings and wooden rail, this decorative feature is sometimes made from brass gallery hardware, as pictured in Fig. 16–6. This makes a beautiful addition to the top of upper cabinets.

DOUBLE ACTION HINGE   INVISIBLE HINGE

CONTINUOUS OR "PIANO" HINGE

Figure 16–5 Examples of specialty hinges. (Courtesy The Woodworker's Store, Rogers, Minn.)

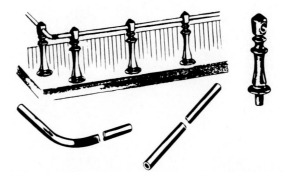

Figure 16–6 Gallery or plate rail hardware. (Courtesy National Lock and Cabinet Hardware)

Figure 16–7 Samples of door and drawer handles. (Courtesy National Lock and Cabinet Hardware)

Cabinet Door and Drawer Handles

Many, many styles, shapes, colors, and metal finishes are available in handles for drawers and doors. The styles and colors available in hinges are matched by the door handles and knobs. Several major manufacturers produce these beautiful pieces of hardware, so even the most discriminating homeowners can find a color and style to satisfy their needs. Some are made to be used with decorative back plates, while others are to be used without this added feature.

The styles vary from sleek modern to the highly decorative Mediterranean and Early American. Figures 16–7 and 16–8 illustrate just a sampling of the handles and knobs available.

Figure 16–8 Period-style door hardware. (Courtesy National Lock and Cabinet Hardware)

Many hardware stores, discount stores, building supply dealers, and lumber dealers carry cabinet hardware. Professional builders have a wholesale source for their needs, as they order in quantities usually larger than that which is carried in stock by the local dealers mentioned.

UTILITY HARDWARE

Utility hardware is that which is used on the inside of cabinets and is not ordinarily seen by the observer unless the doors or drawers are opened. Most of this hardware serves a definite purpose and includes all types, from door catches to shelf standard as well as storage aids.

Cabinet Door Catches

Although not used as much since self-closing hinges have become so popular, cabinet door catches are still preferred by some cabinet builders and homeowners.

Friction catch

There are several styles of friction catches available but all rely on friction to keep the door closed. Some have rubber rollers and others a bayonet, while some simply work with a spring action. Figure 16–9 pictures five different types of friction catches.

Magnetic catch

These catches rely on the power of small magnets to hold the door in place. They are available in several styles, as well as a more powerful double-magnet type for heavier doors. Prior to the advent of the self-closing hinge, most cabinetmakers used magnetic catches, as they were smoother working than the friction catch.

Specialty catches

The touch latch, the elbow catch, and the bullet catch are three specialty types in common use.

The touch latch is just that—a push on the door releases the catch and the door swings open. These are used where an unbroken surface is desired—that is, no door or drawer pulls are desired on the surface of the door.

The elbow catch is often used where a pair of doors is to be locked. The elbow catch is placed on one of the doors and the second door has the lock installed so that the bar of the lock slides into the first door or slips behind it. The elbow catch must be released manually by reaching behind the door and tripping the catch lever. Figure 16–9 illustrates these two types of catches also.

The bullet catch does resemble a bullet in appearance. The end of the catch is spring loaded and will slip over the receiving piece. These catches are used on small doors where there is no room for larger catches. Figure 16–10 shows two styles of bullet catches.

Drawer/door locks

Several types of drawer locks are illustrated in Fig. 16–9. Some of these require the drilling of a certain size hole, while others may need to be mortised into the door.

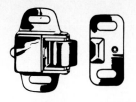

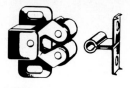

FRICTION CATCHES

MAGNETIC CATCHES

TOUCH LATCH

ELBOW CATCH

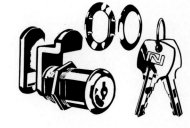

DRAWER LOCKS

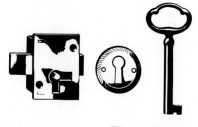

Figure 16–9

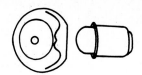

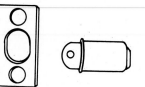

Figure 16-10 Bullet catches. (Courtesy Knape and Vogt)

In most cases the bolt is designed to slide into a slot in the face frame, which may or may not be covered with a metal strike plate. Some locks may be used on doors as well. When a pair of cabinet doors is desired to be locked, such as on a gun cabinet, the lock is mounted on one of the doors and the bolt slides behind or into the opposite door. The second door is locked by installing an elbow catch which must be released by reaching inside the cabinet after the first door is unlocked.

Shelf Supporting Hardware

Shelves are supported in several ways in a cabinet, as discussed earlier in the text. They may be fastened permanently so that no adjustment is possible. They may rest on cleats that are permanently fastened to the cabinet sides, which, again, allows no adjustment in the shelf. The shelf may be made adjustable, however, by using either metal shelf standard and clips or by the use of small metal or plastic pegs that fit into holes drilled in the cabinet sides.

Metal shelf standard

Two styles of metal shelf standard are generally used for cabinet shelves. Both are designed to be used with shelf supports that fit into the openings of the track (Fig. 16-11). The standard is fastened to the sides of the cabinet using the ⅝-in. nails that accompany the track. The track may also be fastened by using a staple gun adapted to exactly fit the pairs of holes in the track. In high-production shops the staple method is often used and the gun is powered by air. A cutter is also available for quickly and easily cutting the standard to required lengths (Fig. 16-11).

The shelf standard is usually available in lengths from 2 to 8 ft in 2-ft intervals. When the standard must be cut in the small shop, it is best to clamp all four pieces together in a vise and cut them all at the same time with a hacksaw. This way, the slots in the standard will be exactly in line.

Peg-type shelf supports

The three types illustrated in Fig. 16-12 are designed to fit into holes drilled in the sides of the cabinet. The holes must be drilled exactly the same distance apart

SHELF STANDARDS

SHELF SUPPORT

CUTTER

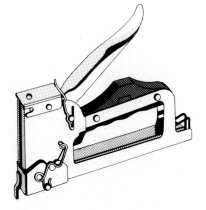

GUN ADAPTED FOR STANDARD
INSTALLATION

Figure 16–11

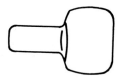

Figure 16-12 Shelf supports requiring no track. (Courtesy Knape and Vogt)

and a simple jig is usually designed for this (see Chapter 8). Four supports are commonly used on each shelf, although on long shelves another support might be used near the middle of the rear edge.

Lazy Susan Hardware

Many cabinetmakers have found it more profitable to purchase the hardware components for their lazy Susans rather than build the entire carousel in the shop. Many will buy just the shaft and upper and lower plates adding the shelves fabricated from plywood or particle board. They may, however, choose to purchase the entire assembly and fabricate none of the lazy Susan in the shop. Figure 16-13 pictures the manufactured lazy Susan components.

Another style of lazy Susan is pictured in Fig. 16-14. The corner door is an integral part of the carousel and revolves with the unit. A bullet catch is used to hold the carousel in position when closed.

Reversible Shelf Hardware

This popular unit is usually built into storage cabinets and upper units. Again the shelf unit itself may either be purchased or built in the shop and used with the required hardware (Fig. 16-15).

The hardware enables the shelf unit to be pulled slightly forward, and then the entire assembly can be reversed so that both sides are accessible.

Metal Drawer Slides

Manufactured drawer slides come in a wide variety of types. Only a couple of styles are illustrated in Fig. 16-16. Most cabinetmakers, it would seem, have adopted this

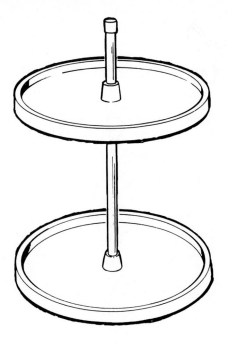

COMPLETE LAZY SUSAN

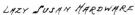

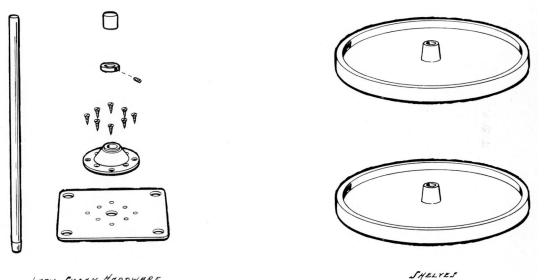

LAZY SUSAN HARDWARE   SHELVES

Figure 16–13 Manufactured carousel components. (Courtesy National Lock and Cabinet Hardware)

drawer slide over the wooden type. When purchased in quantity, they are economical to use and many homeowners demand these in their cabinets.

Builders must adapt their drawer building to the specifications of the type of runner being used. These specifications accompany the runners, and once mastered, almost any style of drawer can be used with metal runners.

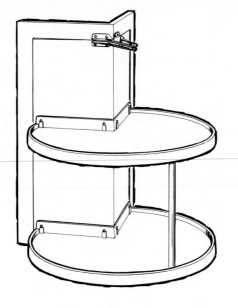

DOOR CAROUSEL

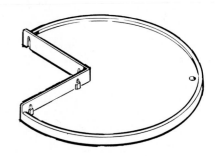

CAROUSEL HARWARE

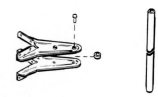

Figure 16–14 Manufactured door carousel components. (Courtesy National Lock and Cabinet Hardware)

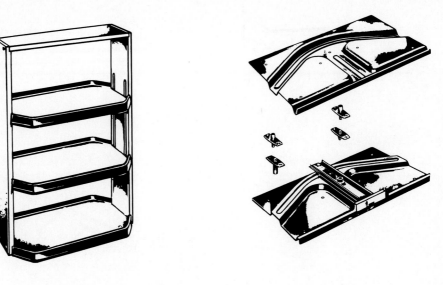

SHELF UNIT   SHELF HARDWARE

Figure 16–15 Reversible shelf hardware. (Courtesy National Lock and Cabinet Hardware)

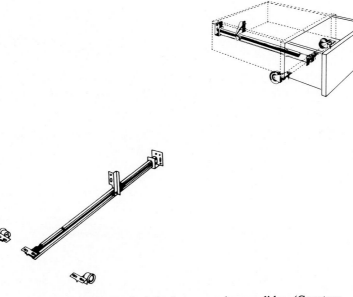

Figure 16–16 Typical single-runner drawer slides. (Courtesy Knape and Vogt)

Kitchen Storage Aids

Figure 16–17 pictures several storage aids that are available to cabinet builders and homeowners. These are just a few of the various devices on the market. Also on the market are metal drawers that are designed to be used with the builder's drawer fronts. These can be used for the storage of baked goods, flour, sugar, and so on. Wire storage racks are also marketed and are used for vegetable storage.

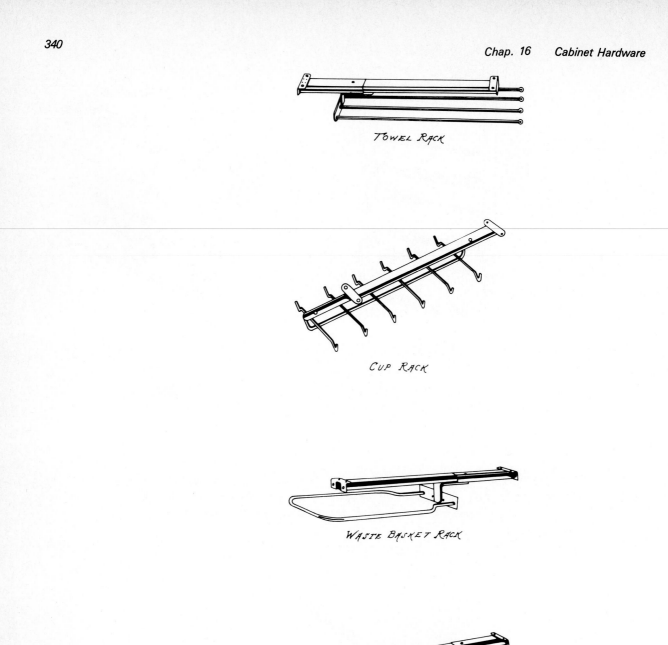

Figure 16–17   Kitchen storage aids. (Courtesy Knape and Vogt)

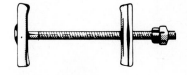

Figure 16-18   Joint fastener hardware. (Courtesy Knape and Vogt)

Joint Fasteners

Countertop fabricators will often use the joint fasteners illustrated in Fig. 16–18. These are used on countertop joints such as a 45-degree miter in the L-shaped and U-shaped countertops, as well as splices required in overly long counter tops.

Glossary

A

ACTUAL SIZE   The size of lumber after being dried and planed.

APRON   A piece of window trim installed beneath the stool on the interior of a window frame.

ARBOR   The assembly in a table saw that holds the saw blade and shaft and revolves and tilts.

B

BACKSPLASH   The plastic laminate that is applied vertically to the wall above and back of the countertop and between the base cabinet and the upper units.

BASE CABINETS   The lower cupboards in a set of kitchen cabinets that rest on the floor and usually measure 36 in. high by 24 in. deep.

BASEBOARD (Base)   Interior trim installed at the wall and floor corner.

BASE SHOE (Shoe)   Small trim molding nailed in the corner formed by the baseboard and the floor.

BOARD FEET   The standard unit of measure for solid lumber. A board foot measures 12 in. wide by 12 in. long by 1 in. thick, for a total of 144 cubic inches. Or 1 square foot of lumber that is 1 in. thick.

BOX NAIL   A common nail with a head.

BRAD   Small, almost headless, mild steel, sharp-pointed nails in length ½ to 1½ in. and in gauge sizes from 20 to 14.

C

CAP STRIPS   Solid wood strips applied to the upper edge of plywood or particle-board drawer sides to hide the unsightly interior core material.

CASING   The trim molding applied around a window or door jamb.

CENTER RUNNER   A type of drawer guide that is installed at the center of a drawer opening to guide the drawer straight and level into the cabinet.

CHAMFER   An angled cut (usually 45 degrees) along the edge or edges of a piece of lumber or plywood.

CLOSED COAT   Coated abrasives on which the grit is applied very close together and completely covers the adhesive. Closed coat abrasives are used primarily for semifinishing and finish sanding.

CONTACT CEMENT   A type of rubber- or butane-based adhesive that bonds on contact and requires no clamping. Widely used to apply plastic laminate to a core material.

COPED JOINT   A joint used on cabinet doors where the stiles and rails meet. The end of the rail is cut with a shaper cutter to fit the pattern machined along the edge of the stile.

COPING   The undercutting machined at the end of a door rail that fits the pattern machined along the edge of the stile.

COVE MOLDING   A trim molding with a face that is concave in shape. Used to finish corners of interiors and sometimes to trim or "case" cabinet installations.

CROSS-BANDS   Layers of veneers that are glued together at 90 degrees to make plywood.

CROSSCUT   A saw blade that is designed to efficiently cut across the grain of wood.

CUSTOM CABINET   A cabinet designed and built to a customer's specifications and to exactly fit a particular sized installation site.

CUTTING BOARD   *See* Pull-out board.

D

d   *See* Penny.

DADO   A groove cut across the grain by using a dado head or other type of dado cutter on the table saw or radial arm saw.

DADO HEAD   A set of saw blades consisting of two outside saw blades and several inner blades called "chippers" that are mounted between the saw blades and used to make dadoes and grooves in lumber and plywood.

DOVETAIL JOINT   A special interlocking finger joint widely used on high-quality furniture and cabinet drawers to attach the drawer sides to the drawer fronts.

DOWEL JOINT   A cabinet joint assembled with round, wooden pegs for reinforcement and strength.

DRYWALL   (Sheetrock) Gypsum-board panels of various thicknesses used to finish interior walls. The joints are usually taped and cemented.

F

FACE FRAME   The facing structure, usually of hardwood, of cabinets and furniture composed of horizontal and vertical pieces that form the openings for drawers and cabinet doors.

FACE-NAIL   Driving nails through the visible surface of a piece of wood or face frame of a cabinet.

FACING STRIPS   Lumber strips, usually of hardwood, that are glued to the edge of plywood or particle-board panels to cover the unsightly inner core.

FEATHERBOARD   A shop-made wooden hold-down cut from a ¾ in. × 2 in. (or wider) piece of softwood with several saw cuts made a portion of the length to provide a spring hold-down action. These are usually clamped to the machine with C-clamps and adjusted to hold the work firmly while being machined.

FIBER CORE   A hardwood veneered panel that has its inner core composed of wood particles (shavings, chips, sawdust) bonded with a special adhesive.

FINISH END   The visible end panel of a cabinet, usually made of hardwood plywood.

FINISH NAIL   Almost headless nails used on cabinetwork trim that are most often "set" below the surface of the wood and the resulting small hole filled with a matching filler. Sizes vary from 1¼ to 3 in. in length and the gauge from 15½ to 11½.

G

GALLERY   *See* Plate rail.

GREEN LUMBER   Lumber that has been through no drying process.

GROOVE   The cut made in a piece of lumber by using a dado head on the table saw and running the cut with the direction of the grain.

H

HOLD-DOWN   A spring steel, adjustable mechanism attached to a woodworking machine in pairs to hold the work firmly and safely while being passed through the machine.

I

IDENTIFICATION INDEX   The stamp placed on plywood panels that informs the purchaser as to its grade and use.

INTERIOR TRIM   (Trim) Those moldings used to finish the interior of a home. These wooden moldings are used around doors, windows, and cabinets at the floor line and sometimes at the ceiling line.

J

JAMB   The side members of door and window frames.

K

KERF   The path or cut made by a hand or power saw. The kerf is wider than the thickness of the saw blade because of the "set" in the teeth of the saw blade.

KILN-DRIED LUMBER   Lumber dried in an ovenlike device to reduce its moisture content to an acceptable level for furniture and cabinet work.

L

LAZY SUSAN   A revolving, tiered carousel used in kitchen cabinet corners to make efficient use of the problem corner space.

M

MILLWORK   That branch of woodworking that specializes in wood products used in home building. Cabinets, doors, door frames, window frames and sash, door and window trim, shutters, mantels, stairways, and so on.

MOLDING   Decorative or patterned wood strips used to decorate and trim the interior of a house. Also refers to decorative strips of metal used for the same purpose. (*See also* Casing and Interior trim.)

MORTISE   The squared hole machined in the stile to receive the tongue or "tenon" on the end of the rail. A part of the mortise-and-tenon joint commonly used on furniture, windows, and doors.

N

NOMINAL   The stated size of lumber, which is somewhat larger than the actual size. *Example:* The 2 in. × 4 in. board used in home construction is the nominal size; the actual size is 1½ in. × 3½ in.

O

OFFSET HINGE   A type of cabinet door hinge designed to fit a particular size of rabbet cut along the edge of the cabinet door. One of the most common sizes is that made to fit a ⅜ in. × ⅜ in. rabbet.

ON CENTER   A measurement term used to designate measuring from the center of one object to the center of an adjacent object. *Example:* Wall studs are commonly installed 16 in. on center.

OPEN COAT   Coated abrasive (sandpaper) on which the grit or abrasive grains are applied to 50 to 70% of the coated surface. These abrasives resist clogging and filling.

P

PARTICLE BOARD   A composition-type panel manufactured from chips, sawdust, shavings, and so on, combined with an adhesive. Widely used in the higher-quality, denser grades for interior work in cabinets and as a core material for plastic-laminate countertops.

PENINSULA CABINET   A kitchen base cabinet open on three sides which forms an L-shaped or U-shaped kitchen. Widely used as a divider between the kitchen and dining areas.

PENNY   The term used in reference to the size of nails. The symbol "d" refers to the penny size of nails.

PLAIN PANEL DOOR   A framed cabinet door that has a ¼-in. plywood panel inset within the rails and stiles.

PLASTIC LAMINATE   A highly durable and beautiful surfacing material widely used on kitchen countertops. Laminates are made by impregnating layers of kraft paper with special resins and adding a pattern sheet protected by more resins.

PLATE RAIL   A decorative railing made from small spindles and solid wood rails that is attached to the top of upper kitchen cupboards. Also referred to as a "gallery" and sometimes made of metal spindles and rails.

POINTS PER INCH   The designation of the coarseness or fineness of a handsaw by measuring the number of tooth points in 1 in. of saw blade length.

PULL-OUT BOARD   (Cutting Board) A cutting surface made for a kitchen base cabinet of solid wood or plywood that pulls out of the top rail of the base cabinet on special grooved hardwood runners.

PULL-OUT SHELF   A base cabinet shelf that is built to be pulled out of the cabinet on slides or rollers to provide easy access to the base cabinet's contents.

Q

QUARTER-ROUND   A small molding whose shape in section is exactly one-fourth of a circle.

R

RABBET   An L-shaped or 90-degree shoulder machined along the edge of a board.

RAIL   (Cross-rail) The horizontal members of a cabinet door, face frame, sash or house door, and so on.

RAISED PANEL DOOR   A style of door that has a solid wood or plywood panel inset within the rails and styles. The panel is given a raised effect by shaping a beveled pattern on its edges.

RE-SAWING   A sawing operation in which thinner boards are ripped from a larger, wider piece.

RETAINER BUTTON   (Disc) A small metal or plastic device used to keep glass in a cabinet door rabbet.

RETURN   On a L-shaped or U-shaped kitchen that shorter portion of the cabinet making a 90-degree corner with the main section.

RIP   To saw with the direction of the grain of a board.

S

SCALE   (Scale Drawing) The process of drawing large objects by using a proportional value of the true size, such as ¼ in. to represent 1 ft., 1 in. to represent 1 ft., and so on.

SCRIBING   The process of marking and fitting material, such as a board or cabinet to fit snuggly against an irregular or slanted surface.

SELF-EDGING   Plastic laminate of the same pattern as the countertop that is applied to the edges of the countertop.

SET   The amount of bend or slant given to alternate teeth of a saw blade—hand or power—to provide a path or "kerf" that is wider than the thickness of the blade.

SHELF TRACK   (Shelf Standard) A manufactured metal strip with regular perforations designed to accept "clips" or supports that allow cabinet shelves to be adjusted to desired heights within the cupboard.

SIDE RUNNER   (Side Guide) A type of drawer guide made to support and guide a drawer from the bottom outside edges of the drawer.

SILL   The bottom member of a door or window frame.

SINKER   The type of box nail usually coated with resin that has the lower surface of the nail head slanted or beveled.

SOCKET BLOCK   The piece of wood that is drilled to receive the lower end of the center shaft of a lazy Susan.

SOFFET   The undersurface of a dropped ceiling.

SOLID-LUMBER CORE   Plywood that has as its inner core pieces of solid lumber rather than cross-bands or layers of veneer.

SPINDLE   The shaft of a wood shaper upon which the pattern cutting knives are mounted.

SPLINE JOINT   A type of wood butt joint reinforced with a piece of $\frac{1}{4}$-in. plywood that is set in grooves along the edges to be joined.

STARTING PIN   A short steel rod that fits vertically into the table of a spindle shaper against which pieces are held when starting a freehand shaping cut on a curved wood edge.

STICKER CUTTERS   The spindle shaper cutters or knives that are used to run the desired pattern along the edges of door, window, and cabinet stiles and rails.

STILE   The vertical members of a cabinet face frame, cabinet door, sash, house door, and so on.

STOOL   An interior trim molding that is cut to fit between the jambs of a window frame, on top of the sill and against the sash.

STOP CHAMFERING   The operation of beveling the edge of a board for only a portion of its length by "stopping" the bevel at a desired position.

T

TENON   The tongue cut on the end of a rail that is made to fit into the mortise or squared hole in the stile.

THREE-WING CUTTER   A patterned spindle shaper cutter that has three cutting edges set at 120 degrees around its center.

TOE NAIL   To drive nails into lumber at a slant.

TOE SPACE   The 3- or 4-in. inset space built at the bottom of the kitchen base cabinets so that a person has foot room and may comfortably stand close to the cabinet.

U

UPPER CABINET   The 12- to 14-in.-deep kitchen cupboards that are mounted to the wall 14 to 16 in. above the base cabinets.

V

VALANCE BOARD   A decorative piece of wood usually cut with an interesting edge pattern and installed between upper cabinet units over the window, stove, refrigerator, and so on.

VENEER CORE   Plywood with interior cross-bands or plies of less expensive wood.

W

WALL END   The end of a cabinet that butts to a wall and is not visible when installed.

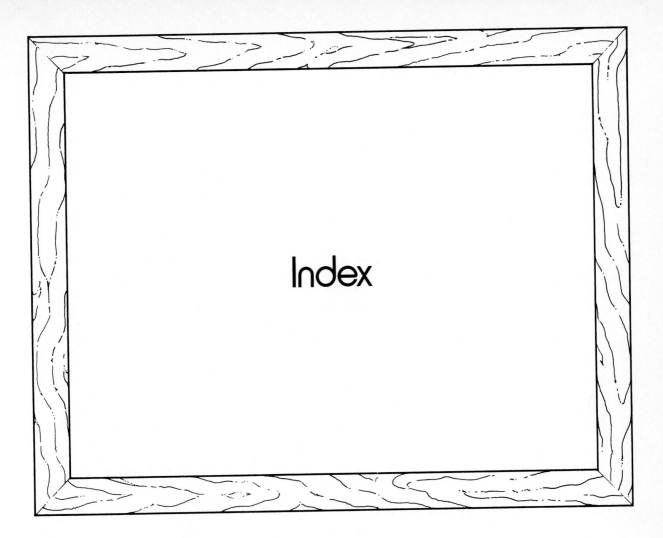

Index